SOMETHING ABOUT THE AUTHOR®

Something about
the Author *was named
an* "**Outstanding
Reference Source,**"
*the highest honor given
by the American
Library Association
Reference and Adult
Services Division.*

ISSN 0276-816X

sOmeTHInG ABOUT THe AUTHOR®

**Facts and Pictures about Authors
and Illustrators of Books for Young People**

volume 238

GALE
CENGAGE Learning·

Detroit • New York • San Francisco • New Haven, Conn • Waterville, Maine • London

Something about the Author, Volume 238

Project Editor: Lisa Kumar

Permissions: Christine Myaskovsky

Imaging and Multimedia: Christine Myaskovsky, John Watkins

Composition and Electronic Capture: Amy Darga

Manufacturing: Rhonda Dover

Product Manager: Mary Onorato

For product information and technology assistance, contact us at
Gale Customer Support, 1-800-877-4253.
For permission to use material from this text or product,
submit all requests online at **www.cengage.com/permissions.**
Further permissions questions can be emailed to
permissionrequest@cengage.com

Since this page cannot legibly accommodate all copyright notices, the acknowledgments constitute an extension of the copyright notice.

While every effort has been made to ensure the reliability of the information presented in this publication, Gale, a part of Cengage Learning, does not guarantee the accuracy of the data contained herein. Gale accepts no payment for listing; and inclusion in the publication of any organization, agency, institution, publication, service, or individual does not imply endorsement of the editors or publisher. Errors brought to the attention of the publisher and verified to the satisfaction of the publisher will be corrected in future editions.

EDITORIAL DATA PRIVACY POLICY: Does this publication contain information about you as an individual? If so, for more information about our editorial data privacy policies, please see our Privacy Statement at www.gale.cengage.com.

Gale, Cengage Learning
27500 Drake Rd.
Farmington Hills, MI, 48331-3535

LIBRARY OF CONGRESS CATALOG CARD NUMBER 62-52046

ISBN-13: 978-1-4144-8094-7
ISBN-10: 1-4144-8094-6

ISSN 0276-816X

This title is also available as an e-book.
ISBN-13: 978-1-4144-8240-8
ISBN-10: 1-4144-8240-X
Contact your Gale, Cengage Learning sales representative for ordering information.

Printed in Mexico
1 2 3 4 5 6 7 16 15 14 13 12

Contents

Authors in Forthcoming Volumes

Below are some of the authors and illustrators that will be featured in upcoming volumes of *SATA*. These include new entries on the swiftly rising stars of the field, as well as completely revised and updated entries (indicated with *) on some of the most notable and best-loved creators of books for children.

*Blue Balliett ▮ Balliett trained in art education, and her interest in the work of seventeenth-century Dutch painter Johannes Vermeer ultimately inspired her award-winning first novel, *Chasing Vermeer*. Published in 2003 and geared for readers in the upper elementary grades, *Chasing Vermeer* inspired Balliett to leave her work as a teacher and embark on a writing career that has won her further acclaim and produced the novel sequels *The Wright 3* and *The Calder Game*, as well as the tantalizingly titled mystery *The Danger Box*.

*Ross Collins ▮ Collins is an award-winning author and illustrator whose work has appeared in many books for young readers. In addition to creating artwork for stories by a legion of children's authors—Vivian French, Jamie Rix, Tony Bradman, Wendy Cope, Allan Durant, and Julia Donaldson among them—the Scottish-born Collins has also created engaging picture books such as *The Elephantom*, *Dear Vampa*, and *Doodleday*. Popular with young audiences, the energetic artist visits schools throughout the United Kingdom and is a welcome guest at literary festivals and workshops for both children and adults.

*Mini Grey ▮ British-born author and illustrator Mini Grey has a knack for reimagining nursery rhymes and other children's classics. She has relied on her English degree, training in both theatre arts and fine arts, experience as a puppet-maker, and six years' work as a teacher in South London schools to fashion a successful career creating children's picture books. In addition to producing illustrations for stories by other writers, Grey is also the author and illustrator of award-winning self-illustrated stories such as *The Pea and the Princess*—published in the United States as *The Very Smart Pea and the Princess-to-Be*— *Egg Drop* and *Traction Man Is Here!*

Jon Klassen ▮ Canadian-born artist Klassen moved to California, where his work as a concept artist included contributing to the film version of Neil Gaiman's novel *Coraline*. As an illustrator, he has become known for the creating graphically sophisticated artwork in Maryrose Wood's "Incorrigible Children of Ashton Place" novels and *House Held up by Trees*, a picture-book story by Pulitzer Prize-winning poet Ted Kooser. His self-illustrated story *I Want My Hat Back* earned him further acclaim, as well as Canada's 2010 Governor General's Award and a Theodor Seuss Geisel Award Honor Book selection.

*Gail Carson Levine ▮ While Levine writes fairy tales featuring princesses, dragons, elves, and fairies, hers are modern renditions of traditional themes. Although she sometimes bases her novels on such familiar stories as *Cinderella* or *Sleeping Beauty,* and adopts characters from J.M. Barrie's childhood classic *Peter Pan,* the heroes and heroines in her award-winning books such as *Ella Enchanted, The Princess Tales,* and *Fairy Dust and the Quest for the Egg* are decidedly modern in their outlook.

Joanna Nadin ▮ Nadin's background is not typical of many authors of teen fiction: with a master's degree in political communications, she eventually parlayed a journalism career into a stint as speechwriter and special adviser to U.K. Prime Minister Tony Blair during part of his term in office. While her work in politics kept her focused on current events, fiction-writing became an outlet for her imagination and led to her diary-style "My So-Called Life" novel series. Based on Nadin's typical suburban childhood, the "My So-Called Life" books follow Rachel Riley through her teenage years as she suffers dysfunctional parents, an annoying little brother, and the quandary of not having experience with boys.

Margaret Pokiak-Fenton ▮ A native Inuvialuit raised in the nomadic traditions of her Northern people, Pokiak-Fenton left tribal life at age eight to learn to read at a Catholic boarding school in the fur-trading town of Aklavik. Westernized by the experience, which was common to many native children during the 1940s, she ultimately found herself between two cultures. Helped by daughter-in-law Christy Jordan-Fenton, she chronicles her school experiences in the highly acclaimed middle-grade novels *Fatty Legs: A True Story* and *A Stranger at Home,* both illustrated with family photographs and artwork by Liz Amini-Holmes.

*Darren Shan ▮ Writing under a pen name, Shan is an Irish author who is best known for his "Saga of Darren Shan," a twelve-volume series that follows its young hero—also named Darren Shan—as he becomes a vampire's assistant, battles his own transformation, and fights against rival undead enemies. The real-world Shan has also written the "Demonata" books, which focus on three youngsters and their ongoing battle with demonic entities, as well as the adult-themed "City Trilogy" and the standalone novel *The Thin Executioner,* which finds a young teen undertaking a nightmarish quest in preparation for inheriting his father's job as an axe-wielding executioner.

Angela Farris Watkins ▮ The niece of noted civil-rights leader Dr. Martin Luther King, Jr., Watkins is an associate professor of psychology at Spelman College. Following in the tradition of her mother, Christine King Farris, who also taught at Spelman, Watkins reaches out to younger generations in her stories for children. She shares her family's legacy of compassion and tolerance in books that include *My Uncle Martin's Big Heart* and *My Uncle Martin's Words for America: Martin Luther King Jr.'s Niece Tells How He Made a Difference,* both which come to life in Eric Velasquez's dynamic art.

Daniel H. Wilson ▮ A line of research undertaken while completing his Ph.D. in robotics inspired Wilson's first book, *How to Survive a*

Robot Uprising: Tips on Defending Yourself against the Coming Rebellion. With its take-notice title and humorous approach, the book transformed its author into an expert on the dangers posed by robots and other creations of overambitious scientists. His writing career has progressed from instructional manuals such as *How to Build a Robot Army: Tips on Defending the Planet Earth against Alien Invaders, Ninjas, and Zombies* and *Bro-Jitsu: The Martial Art of Sibling Smackdown* to the equally whimsical middle-grade novel *A Boy and His Bot* and the sci-fi thriller *Robopocalypse.*

Introduction

Something about the Author (*SATA*) is an ongoing reference series that examines the lives and works of authors and illustrators of books for children. *SATA* includes not only well-known writers and artists but also less prominent individuals whose works are just coming to be recognized. This series is often the only readily available information source on emerging authors and illustrators. You'll find *SATA* informative and entertaining, whether you are a student, a librarian, an English teacher, a parent, or simply an adult who enjoys children's literature.

What's Inside *SATA*

SATA provides detailed information about authors and illustrators who span the full time range of children's literature, from early figures like John Newbery and L. Frank Baum to contemporary figures like Judy Blume and Richard Peck. Authors in the series represent primarily English-speaking countries, particularly the United States, Canada, and the United Kingdom. Also included, however, are authors from around the world whose works are available in English translation. The writings represented in *SATA* include those created intentionally for children and young adults as well as those written for a general audience and known to interest younger readers. These writings cover the entire spectrum of children's literature, including picture books, humor, folk and fairy tales, animal stories, mystery and adventure, science fiction and fantasy, historical fiction, poetry and nonsense verse, drama, biography, and nonfiction. Obituaries are also included in many volumes of *SATA* and are intended not only as death notices but also as concise overviews of people's lives and work. Additionally, each edition features newly revised and updated entries for a selection of *SATA* listees who remain of interest to today's readers and who have been active enough to require extensive revisions of their earlier biographies.

Autobiography Feature

Beginning with Volume 103, many volumes of *SATA* feature one or more specially commissioned autobiographical essays. These unique essays, averaging about ten thousand words in length and illustrated with an abundance of personal photos, present an entertaining and informative first-person perspective on the lives and careers of prominent authors and illustrators profiled in *SATA*.

Two Convenient Indexes

In response to suggestions from librarians, *SATA* indexes no longer appear in every volume but are included in alternate (odd-numbered) volumes of the series, beginning with Volume 57.

SATA continues to include two indexes that cumulate with each alternate volume: the Illustrations Index, arranged by the name of the illustrator, gives the number of the volume and page where the illustrator's work appears in the current volume as well as all preceding volumes in the series; the Author Index gives the number of the volume in which a person's biographical sketch, autobiographical essay, or obituary appears in the current volume as well as all preceding volumes in the series.

These indexes also include references to authors and illustrators who appear in *Gale's Yesterday's Authors of Books for Children, Children's Literature Review,* and *Something about the Author Autobiography Series.*

Easy-to-Use Entry Format

Whether you're already familiar with the *SATA* series or just getting acquainted, you will want to be aware of the kind of information that an entry provides. In every *SATA* entry the editors attempt to give as complete a picture of the person's life and work as possible. A typical entry in *SATA* includes the following clearly labeled information sections:

PERSONAL: date and place of birth and death, parents' names and occupations, name of spouse, date of marriage, names of children, educational institutions attended, degrees received, religious and political affiliations, hobbies and other interests.

ADDRESSES: complete home, office, electronic mail, and agent addresses, whenever available.

CAREER: name of employer, position, and dates for each career post; art exhibitions; military service; memberships and offices held in professional and civic organizations.

MEMBER: professional, civic, and other association memberships and any official posts held.

AWARDS, HONORS: literary and professional awards received.

WRITINGS: title-by-title chronological bibliography of books written and/or illustrated, listed by genre when known; lists of other notable publications, such as plays, screenplays, and periodical contributions.

ADAPTATIONS: a list of films, television programs, plays, CD-ROMs, recordings, and other media presentations that have been adapted from the author's work.

WORK IN PROGRESS: description of projects in progress.

SIDELIGHTS: a biographical portrait of the author or illustrator's development, either directly from the biographee—and often written specifically for the *SATA* entry—or gathered from diaries, letters, interviews, or other published sources.

BIOGRAPHICAL AND CRITICAL SOURCES: cites sources quoted in "Sidelights" along with references for further reading.

EXTENSIVE ILLUSTRATIONS: photographs, movie stills, book illustrations, and other interesting visual materials supplement the text.

How a *SATA* Entry Is Compiled

SATA editors examine a wide variety of published sources to gather information for an entry. Biographical and bibliographic sources are consulted, as are book reviews, feature articles, published interviews, and material sometimes obtained from the biographee's family, publishers, agent, or other associates. Whenever possible, the author or illustrator is sent a copy of the entry to check for accuracy and completeness.

Entries that have not been verified by the biographees or their representatives are marked with an asterisk (*).

Contact the Editor

We encourage our readers to examine the entire *SATA* series. Please write and tell us if we can make *SATA* even more helpful to you. Give your comments and suggestions to the editor:

Editor
Something about the Author
Gale, Cengage Learning
27500 Drake Rd.
Farmington Hills MI 48331-3535

Toll-free: 800-877-GALE
Fax: 248-699-8070

Something about the Author Product Advisory Board

The editors of *Something about the Author* are dedicated to maintaining a high standard of excellence by publishing comprehensive, accurate, and highly readable entries on a wide array of writers for children and young adults. In addition to the quality of the content, the editors take pride in the graphic design of the series, which is intended to be orderly yet inviting, allowing readers to utilize the pages of *SATA* easily and with efficiency. Despite the longevity of the *SATA* print series, and the success of its format, we are mindful that the vitality of a literary reference product is dependent on its ability to serve its users over time. As literature, and attitudes about literature, constantly evolve, so do the reference needs of students, teachers, scholars, journalists, researchers, and book club members. To be certain that we continue to keep pace with the expectations of our customers, the editors of *SATA* listen carefully to their comments regarding the value, utility, and quality of the series. Librarians, who have firsthand knowledge of the needs of library users, are a valuable resource for us. The *Something about the Author* Product Advisory Board, made up of school, public, and academic librarians, is a forum to promote focused feedback about *SATA* on a regular basis. The nine-member advisory board includes the following individuals, whom the editors wish to thank for sharing their expertise:

SOMETHING ABOUT THE AUTHOR

ALBARN, Jessica 1971-

Personal

Born 1971, in London, England; daughter of Keith (a designer and writer) and Hazel (a stage designer and artist) Albarn; children: Etta, Rudy, Lola. *Education:* Middlesex University, degree.

Addresses

Home—London, England. *E-mail*—jessica@jessicaalbarn.co.uk.

Career

Artist, designer, author/illustrator, and filmmaker. Lecturer and presenter at workshops. *Exhibitions:* Work included in numerous exhibitions, including at Notting Hill Arts Club, London, England; Hames Levack, London; The Union (Soho), Ltd., London; Fermoy Gallery, Norfolk, England; Marmalade Gallery, London; Visual Arts Centre, Essex, England; Nelly Duff Gallery, London; (with Helmut Lang) Tokyo, Japan; Liberty of London exhibition, London; Foyles Gallery, London; and Rochelle School, London.

Writings

SELF-ILLUSTRATED

Bee-headed, Cederteg (Stockholm, Sweden), 2008.

Jessica Albarn (Reproduced by permission.)

The Boy in the Oak, Simply Read Books (Vancouver, British Columbia, Canada), 2010.

Contributor to periodicals, including *BACU, Marmalade, Super,* and *Vogue.*

Biographical and Critical Sources

PERIODICALS

Booklist, December 1, 2010, Ian Chipman, review of *The Boy in the Oak,* p. 55.

Canadian Review of Materials, January 21, 2011, Linda Ludke, review of *The Boy in the Oak.*

Kirkus Reviews, November 1, 2010, review of *The Boy in the Oak.*

Times Magazine (London, England), July 10, 2011, interview with Albarn.

ONLINE

Independent Online http://www.independent.co.uk/ (June 4, 2010), "Faerie Queen Jessica Albarn Draws on Nature."

Jessica Albarn Home Page, http://www.jessicaalbarn.co.uk (January 9, 2012).

*   *   *

ASHLEY, Carol

Personal

Female. *Education:* Attended Art Center College of Design, 1981-84; California Institute of the Arts, B.F.A. (animation and motion graphics), 1986, M.F.A. (film/video and studio art), 1992.

Addresses

Home—Atlanta, GA. *Agent*—Caryn Wiseman, Andrea Brown Literary Agency, 2225 E. Bayshore Rd., Ste. 200, Palo Alto, CA 94303. *E-mail*—carol@carolashley.com.

Career

Animator, photographer, educator, and illustrator. Will Vinton Studios, animator, 1988-89, Cinesite, composite supervisor, 1993-97; Manex, composite supervisor, 1998-99; lighting artist for Centropolis Effects, 2001-02, DreamWorks Animation, 2003-06, and Hammerhead Productions, 2003-08; Crawford Communications, senior video special-effects designer, 2008-09; Devi Designs, Atlanta, GA, designer and animator. Creator of animated short films, including *The Tales of Perdita.* Art director for video games. Art Institute of Atlanta, Atlanta, GA, professor of media arts and animation, beginning 2010. *Exhibitions:* Work included in exhibits at Alcove Gallery, Atlanta, GA; and Deborah Martin Gallery, Los Angeles, CA.

Awards, Honors

Colorado Book Award finalist in children's category, 2011, for *Scarum Fair* by Jessica Swaim.

Illustrator

Jessica Swaim, *Scarum Fair,* Wordsong (Honesdale, PA), 2010.

Biographical and Critical Sources

PERIODICALS

Kirkus Reviews, September 15, 2010, review of *Scarum Fair.*

School Library Journal, November, 2010, Jessica Swaim, review of *Scarum Fair,* p. 94.

ONLINE

Carol Ashley Home Page, http://www.carolashley.com (January 10, 2012).*

*   *   *

BAEHR, Patricia 1952-
(Patricia Goehner Baehr)

Personal

Born May 14, 1952, in Long Island, NY; daughter of Herman and Doris Goehner; married Edward W. Baehr (a police detective), October 14, 1972; children: Peter, Gemma. *Education:* Hofstra University, B.S., 1974, M.A., 1977. *Hobbies and other interests:* Training dogs, reading.

Addresses

Home—Bayville, NY. *Agent*—Jean V. Naggar Literary Agency, 216 E. 75th St., New York, NY 10021.

Career

Author and educator. Archer Street and Leo F. Giblyn schools, Freeport, NY, teacher of instrumental music, 1974-80; freelance writer, beginning 1980. Clarinetist with Long Island Original Music Ensemble, 1984-88.

Member

Society of Children's Book Writers and Illustrators.

Awards, Honors

Jane Tinkham Broughton fellow, Bread Loaf Writers' Conference, 1980; Notable Children's Book in the Field of Social Studies citation, National Council for the Social Studies, 1989, for *School Isn't Fair!;* Pick of the Lists citation, *American Bookseller,* 1990, for *Summer of the Dodo;* Paul A. Witty Short Story Award, International Reading Association, 2003, for "Blizzard"; *Smithsonian* magazine Notable Children's Book selection, 2010, for *Boo Cow.*

Writings

(As Patricia Goehner Baehr) *The Way to Windra,* illustrated by Gail Owens, F. Warne, 1980.

(As Patricia Goehner Baehr) *The Dragon Prophecy,* F. Warne, 1980.

Always Faithful, New American Library (New York, NY), 1983.

Indian Summer, New American Library (New York, NY), 1984.

Faithfully, Tru, Macmillan (New York, NY), 1984.

Falling Scales, Morrow (New York, NY), 1987.

Louisa Eclipsed, Morrow (New York, NY), 1988.

School Isn't Fair!, illustrated by R.W. Alley, Four Winds Press (New York, NY), 1989.

Summer of the Dodo, Four Winds Press (New York, NY), 1990.

Mouse in the House, illustrated by Laura Lydecker, Holiday House (New York, NY), 1994.

The Search for Happily Ever After, BridgeWater Books (Mahwah, NJ), 1995.

Boo Cow, illustrated by Margot Apple, Charlesbridge (Watertown, MA), 2010.

Contributor of short fiction to periodicals, including *Cricket,* and to anthologies and educational materials.

Sidelights

With her training in music, Patricia Baehr taught instrumental music near her home on Long Island, New York, until 1980, when she acquired a publisher for her first book, the children's novel *The Way to Windra.* In the years since, Baehr has continued to write for children and has produce novels such as *Indian Summer, Summer of the Dodo,* and *The Search for Happily Ever After* as well as lighthearted picture-book stories that include *School Isn't Fair!, Mouse in the House,* and *Boo Cow.* "I don't think I've ever made a conscious decision

to writer for children and young adults," the author once told *SATA.* "I always set out to tell a story that interests me, hopefully that it will interest others as well."

"When I was growing up, I was fortunate to have an aunt who supplied me with wonderful books each birthday and Christmas," Baehr later recalled, "books that nurtured and influenced me tremendously. I came to identify strongly with Louisa May Alcott's character Jo March in *Little Women* since Jo was the second oldest of four girls in her family, and so was I. I identified with any family I read about that contained four children, assigning myself the role of the second eldest, whether that was male or female, but the Marches are the family I remember best. It helped that I saw Jo as the main character. I certainly considered myself the main character in my own family. Perhaps it's no wonder that since Jo put on plays and wanted to be a writer, so did I. The curious thing about it all is that I would up marrying a man of the last name of Baehr, a name uncannily similar to that of Jo's gentle professor Bhaer."

In her picture book *Boo Cow* Baehr teams up with artist Margot Apple to tell a tale designed for reading aloud. A silly husband and wife decide to go into the egg-selling business and purchase hundreds of laying hens. They become frustrated when the birds refuse to lay, and even more upset when strange moo-ing sounds echo from the chicken coop each night. Told that the coop is haunted by a ghostly Boo Cow, the couple brings several hens into their home, and fresh eggs are quickly produced. As Baehr's story plays out, the nervous hens are calmed when the mystery is solved, and the path to that solution is paved "with a text chock full of action and playful words," according to *Booklist* contributor

Margot Apple creates the funny-scary illustrations for Patricia Baehr's award-winning picture book **Boo Cow.** (Illustration copyright © 2010 by Margot Apple. Reproduced by permission of Charlesbridge Publishing, Inc.)

Randall Enos. The "soft, bucolic illustrations" in *Boo Cow* "gently milk the situation for all its available humor," observed a *Kirkus Reviews* writer, and in *Publishers Weekly* a critic dubbed Baehr's story "a mix of mystery and hilarity" that contains subtle "messages of protection and forgiveness."

In her novels for preteen readers, Baehr often focuses on characters who are beginning to hone the character they will take in adulthood. In *Summer of the Dodo*, for example, shy Dodo Penny is worried about starting sixth grade in a few months, knowing that her unusual height and gawkiness will make her stand out from the crowd in her new middle school. A summer experience helping injured animals helps the girl shed some of her adolescent self-consciousness and also gain social skills that will win her new friends. *The Search for Happily Ever After* mixes real life and fantasy as eleven-year-old Ketti Watson is transported to a fairy-tale world where she assists minor characters in attaining their own happy ending. Recommending the novel to fairy-tale fans, Frances Bradburn added in her *Booklist* review that *The Search for Happily Ever After* leaves its heroine knowing "how truly loved she is by her family."

Biographical and Critical Sources

PERIODICALS

Booklist, February 15, 1996, Frances Bradburn, review of *The Search for Happily Ever After*, p. 1019; July 1, 2010, Randall Enos, review of *Boo Cow*, p. 65.
Kirkus Reviews, July 1, 2010, review of *Boo Cow*.
Publishers Weekly, June 21, 2010, review of *Boo Cow*, p. 45.
School Library Journal, July, 2010, Ieva Bates, review of *Boo Cow*, p. 55.*

*   *   *

BAEHR, Patricia Goehner
See BAEHR, Patricia

*   *   *

BAETEN, Lieve 1954-2001

Personal

Born October 24, 1954, in Zonhoven, Belgium; died in an automobile accident, October 15, 2001; daughter of Albert (an electrician) and Emma (a homemaker) Baeten; married Koen Fossey (a high-school teacher and illustrator), November 19, 1976; children: Wietse, Kobie. *Education:* Koninklijke Academie voor Schone Kunsten (Andwerp, Belgium), certificate of graphic design.

Career

Illustrator and author of books for children.

Member

International Board of Books for Young Children.

Awards, Honors

Special Mention, Critici in Erba (Bologna, Italy) 1993, for *Nieuwsgierige Lotje;* Kinderboekwinkelprijs (Netherlands), 1996, for *Lotje is Jarig.*

Writings

SELF-ILLUSTRATED

Aapje doet mee, Clavis (Hasselt, Netherlands), 1997.
Bibberbang, Clavis (Hasselt, Netherlands), 1997.
Blauwe handjes, Clavis (Hasselt, Netherlands), 1997.
Snoep op stokjes, Clavis (Hasselt, Netherlands), 1997.
Kleine draak, Clavis (Hasselt, Netherlands), 2000.

"LOTJE/NICKY"/"LITTLE WITCH" SERIES; SELF-ILLUSTRATED

Nieuwsgierige Lotje, Clavis (Hasselt, Netherlands), 1992, reprinted, 2005, translated as *Nicky at the Magic House,* Annick Press (Toronto, Ontario, Canada), 1992, published as *The Curious Little Witch,* North-South (New York, NY), 2010.
Lotje is jarig, Clavis (Hasselt, Netherlands), 1994, translated as *Nicky's Birthday,* Annick Press (Toronto, Ontario, Canada), 1994, translated as *Happy Birthday, Little Witch!,* NorthSouth (New York, NY), 2011.
De kerstboom van Lotje, Clavis (Hasselt, Netherlands), 1996.
Lotje en de heksenprinses, Clavis (Hasselt, Netherlands), 1998, translated as *Up and away with the Little Witch,* NorthSouth (New York, NY), 2011.
Slimme Lotje, Clavis (Hasselt, Netherlands), 2003.

BOARD BOOKS

Tom and His Pot, Clavis (Hasselt, Netherlands), 1993.
Tom and His Pyjamas, Clavis (Hasselt, Netherlands), 1993.
Tom gaat naar bed, Clavis (Hasselt, Netherlands), 1995, translated as *Is Tom Ready for Bed?,* Barron's Educational Series (Hauppauge, NY), 1997.
Waar is Tom?, Clavis (Hasselt, Netherlands), 1995, translated as *Where Is Tom?,* Barron's Educational Series (Hauppauge, NY), 1997.
Kleertjes voor Nina, Clavis (Hasselt, Netherlands), 1995, translated as *What Is Maggie Wearing?,* Barron's Educational Series (Hauppauge, NY), 1997.
Een hapje voor Nina, Clavis (Hasselt, Netherlands), 1995, translated as *What Is Maggie Eating?,* Barron's Educational Series (Hauppauge, NY), 1997.

ILLUSTRATOR

Paul Jacobs, *Een zondag in de middeleeuwen,* De kleine Uitgeverij (Sint-Niklaas, Belgium), 1982.

Gudrun Mebs, *Jan Klaassen speelt niet meer,* Omniboek (The Hague, Netherlands), 1985.

Anke de Vries, *Wat een mop,* Infoboek (Meerhout, Belgium), 1986.

Jaak Dreesen, *Het jongensbed,* Altiora (Averbode, Belgium), 1986.

Marita de Sterck, *Sander en de kippen,* Omniboek (The Hague, Netherlands), 1986.

Corrie Hafkamp, *Het raadsel van de hond,* Infoboek (Meerhout, Belgium), 1987.

Bettie Elias, *Papa is een grote lummel!,* Infodok (Leuven, Belgium), 1987.

Lidy Peters, *Je hebt me verraden!,* Infoboek (Meerhout, Belgium), 1987.

Mieke Vanpol, *Het etiket van juffrouw Jet,* Clavis (Hasselt, Netherlands), 1987.

Jaak Dreesen, *Ik weet zeker dat ik ooit beroemd wordt!,* Altiora (Averbode, Belgium), 1987.

Mieke Vanpol, *Ben je betoeterd opa?,* Clavis (Hasselt, Netherlands), 1988.

Lian de Kat, *Mijn baas liegt,* Infoboek (Meerhout, Belgium), 1988.

Mieke Vanpol, *Zes onder zeil,* Clavis (Hasselt, Netherlands), 1988.

Geertje Gort, *De man met de flaphoed,* Infoboek (Meerhout, Belgium), 1988.

Bettie Elias, *Blubberpudding,* Infodok (Leuven, Belgium), 1988.

Nancy Luenn, *Eenhoorns bestaan niet* (translation of *Unicorn Crossing*), Lannoo (Tielt, Belgium), 1988.

Jaak Dreesen, *Bas gaat naar school,* Altiora (Averbode, Belgium), 1989.

Geertje Gort, *Weg met dat beest!,* Infoboek (Meerhout, Belgium), 1990.

Sine van Mol, *Geluk in een papiertje,* Clavis (Hasselt, Netherlands), 1991.

Geert de Kockere, editor, *Eefje Donkerblauw,* De Eenhoorn (Amsterdam, Netherlands), 1992, reprinted, 2008.

Dian Curtis Regan, *The Thirteen Hours of Halloween,* Albert Whitman (Morton Grove, IL), 1993.

Rosemarie Künzler-Behncke, *Wer kommt mit in den Kindergarten?* 1997.

Riet Wille, *Toverling* Nationaal Centrum voor Jeugdliteratuur (Antwerp, Belgium), 1998.

Stefan Boonen, *Halloween,* Clavis (Hasselt, Netherlands), 2002.

Siska Goeminne, *Springversjes en tuimelgedichten,* De Eenhorn (Amsterdam, Netherlands), 2011.

Contributor to periodicals in Europe, as well as to *Ladybug* and *Cricket.*

Books featuring Baeten's work have been translated into fourteen languages, including French, German, Japanese, Norwegian, and Swedish.

Sidelights

Flemish artist and author Lieve Baeten studied at Antwerp's Koninklijke Academie voor Schone Kunsten and trained for over ten years before beginning her career in children's literature. Her stories about a young witch named Lotje have been translated into more than a dozen languages and earned her several European awards for children's books. Baeten's career ended tragically in 2001, when she was killed in an automobile accident. Reviewing *The Curious Little Witch,* a

First published in Belgium, **The Curious Little Witch** *is among Lieve Baeton's most-popular illustrated stories for children.* (Illustration copyright © 2010 by Lieve Baeten. Reproduced by permission of North-South Books.)

translation of Baeten's award-winning *Nieuwsgierige Lotje* in which a young witch explores an unusual house, Carolyn Phelan noted in *Booklist* that the text "features simple conversations, and the detailed pencil-and-watercolor illustrations are full of intriguing details." "A sweet import," according to a *Kirkus Reviews* writer, Baeten's picture book is also "ideal for budding architects."

"In the books I make I do not want to put in a moral," Baeten once told *SATA*, "or an explicit actual problem; I just want it to be a book full of affection and humor, with, of course, a strong story. . . . The book should add something extra to the children's (or parents') life. This is what you can see also in the books of Steven Kellogg, an illustrator I admire a lot." "It is perfectly possible to do a book in your very own way," she added. "This is a great feeling!"

Biographical and Critical Sources

PERIODICALS

Booklist, September 15, 2010, Carolyn Phelan, review of *The Curious Little Witch,* p. 69.
Children's Bookwatch, June, 2011, review of *Up and away with the Little Witch.*
Kirkus Reviews, July 1, 2010, review of *The Curious Little Witch*; August 1, 2011, review of *Up and away with the Little Witch.*
Publishers Weekly, September 20, 1993, review of *The Thirteen Hours of Halloween,* p. 29.
Resource Links, October, 1996, review of *Nicky's Birthday,* p. 12.
School Library Journal, November, 2010, Linda Ludke, review of *The Curious Little Witch,* p. 65; June, 2011, Catherine Callegari, review of *Up and away with the Little Witch,* p. 76.*

* * *

BARNER, Bob 1947-

Personal

Born November 11, 1947, in Tuckerman, AR; son of Jewel and Jean Barner; married; wife's name, Catherine. *Education:* Columbus College of Art and Design, B.F.A., 1970; studied with Milton Glaser at School of Visual Arts.

Addresses

Home—San Francisco, CA. *E-mail*—bobbarner@aol.com.

Career

Illustrator and author. Riverside Hospital, Columbus, OH, art therapist, 1970-78; Art Institute of Boston, Boston, MA, instructor in art, 1978-79; freelance writer and artist, beginning 1979. Presenter at schools and libraries. *Exhibitions:* Original art exhibitions with the Society of Illustrators which included artwork from *Benny's Pennies* and *Dem Bones.*

Member

Art Directors Club of Boston.

Awards, Honors

Andy Award for Illustration, Children's International Book Fair, 1975, for *The Elephants' Visit;* Silver Honor Award, Parents' Choice, for *Dem Bones;* Pick of the Lists citation, American Booksellers Association, for *To Everything;* named San Francisco Library laureate, 2004.

Writings

SELF-ILLUSTRATED CHILDREN'S BOOKS

The Elephants' Visit, Little, Brown (Boston, MA), 1975.
Elephant Facts, Dutton (New York, NY), 1979.
The Elevator Escalator Book: A Transportation Fact Book, Doubleday (New York, NY), 1990.
The Bike Race, Houghton (Boston, MA), 1991.
How to Weigh an Elephant ("Start Smart Math" series), Bantam (New York, NY), 1995.
Space Race ("Start Smart Math" series), Bantam (New York, NY), 1995.
Too Many Dinosaurs ("Start Smart Math" series), Bantam (New York, NY), 1995.
Dem Bones, Chronicle Books (San Francisco, CA), 1996.
Dinosaurs Depart ("Start Smart Math" series), Bantam (New York, NY), 1996.
To Everything, Chronicle Books (San Francisco, CA), 1998.
Which Way to the Revolution?: A Book about Maps, Holiday House (New York, NY), 1998.
Bugs! Bugs! Bugs!, Chronicle Books (San Francisco, CA), 1999.
Fish Wish, Holiday House (New York, NY), 2000.
Walk the Dog, Chronicle Books (San Francisco, CA), 2000.
Dinosaur Bones, Chronicle Books (San Francisco, CA), 2001.
Stars!, Stars!, Stars!, Chronicle Books (San Francisco, CA), 2002.
Parade Day: Marching through the Calendar Year, Holiday House (New York, NY), 2003.
Bug Safari, Holiday House (New York, NY), 2004.
Penguins, Penguins, Everywhere!, Chronicle Books (San Francisco, CA), 2007.
Dinosaurs Roar, Butterflies Soar!, Chronicle Books (San Francisco, CA), 2009.
Bears! Bears! Bears!, Chronicle Books (San Francisco, CA), 2010.
The Day of the Dead/El día de los muertos, Spanish translation by Teresa Mlawer, Holiday House (New York, NY), 2010.

Alcatraz A to Z: A National Park ABC Book, Golden Gate National Parks Conservancy/Red Bridge Press (San Francisco, CA), 2011.
Animal Baths, Chronicle Books (San Francisco, CA), 2011.

ILLUSTRATOR

Eve Bunting, *We Need a Bigger Zoo!,* Ginn (Lexington, MA), 1974.
Van Aarle, *Don't Put Your Cart before the Horse Race,* Houghton (Boston, MA), 1980.
Patty Wolcott, *Double-Decker, Double-Decker, Double-Decker Bus,* Addison-Wesley (Reading, MA), 1980.
Joanne E. Bernstein, *Riddles to Take on Vacation,* Albert Whitman (Niles, IL), 1987.
Nat Segaloff, *Fish Tales,* Sterling (New York, NY), 1990.
Patricia Demuth, *Pick Up Your Ears, Henry,* Macmillan (New York, NY), 1992.
Pat Brisson, *Benny's Pennies,* Doubleday (New York, NY), 1993.
Patricia C. McKissack, *Where Crocodiles Have Wings,* Holiday House (New York, NY), 2005.
Traci N. Todd, *Wiggle, Waggle, Loop-de-loo!,* Kindermusik International (Greensboro, NC), 2006.
J. Patrick Lewis, *Big Is Big (and Little Little): A Book of Contrasts,* Holiday House (New York, NY), 2007.

Sidelights

Based in San Francisco, California, Bob Barner is the illustrator of numerous picture books, including many which he wrote himself. His first stories, *Elephant Facts* as well as the fanciful story in *The Elephants' Visit,* were sparked by his interest in pachyderms, and his range of interests have widened since then. Barner's books on dinosaurs, bugs, penguins, bears, dogs, and fish also explore fun yet factual topics that he brings to life in mixed-media art combining pen-and-ink, watercolor, and cut-and torn-paper collage. He also takes on a more unusual topic in *The Day of the Dead/El día de los muertos,* a bilingual picture book that focuses on a well-known Latin-American holiday. Recommending the work as "ideal for group sharing," *Booklist* contributor Andrew Medlar added that *The Day of the Dead* features brightly colored illustrations that "are celebratory and never spooky," while *School Library Journal* critic Roberto Zapata concluded that Barner's "festive and detailed" images "add to the authentic feel of the book."

Born in Arkansas, in 1947, Barner grew up in the Midwest and graduated from Ohio's Columbus College of Art and Design. He worked as an art therapist before shifting to jobs as art director in advertising agencies and design studios, where he had the chance to assist noted cartoonist Al Capp with Capp's "Li'l Abner" comic strip. Barner turned his attention to children's book production in the 1970s, illustrating Eve Bunting's *We Need a Bigger Zoo!* before starting to create his own books. Highly influential in his career was his experience studying under Milton Glaser at New York City's School of Visual Arts.

One of Barner's early nonfiction books, *The Elevator Escalator Book: A Transportation Fact Book* finds a large brown dog attempting to deliver a package, encountering many different forms of transportation in the process. More facts are served up in his contribution to the "Start Smart Math" series: *Space Race, Too Many Dinosaurs, Dinosaurs Depart,* and *How to Weigh an Elephant.* Each book in this series is designed to get children from ages four to eight off to a good start in mathematics by blending humorous stories with activities inspired by accepted educational standards. Reviewing *Space Race* and *Too Many Dinosaurs* in *Publishers Weekly,* a contributor called Barner's colorful creature characters "painless purveyors of mathematical prowess."

Another playfully educational title by Barner is the award-winning *Dem Bones,* which uses a familiar folk song to introduce the bones of the human skeleton in a "highly original mixture," as a *Books for Keeps* reviewer described it. "Barner dives gleefully into this clever anatomy lesson," wrote the critic for *Publishers Weekly,* and indeed, each page of this picture book is illustrated with torn-paper collages featuring a jazzy skeleton band blowing horns and strumming guitars. Each line from the song is given its own spread, and additional text explains the form and function of the bones mentioned. For example, with the lyric "Leg bone connected to da knee bone," Barner provides information on how the knee joint functions like a hinge, allowing humans all sorts of movement possibilities. Reviewing *Dem Bones,* a critic for *Publishers Weekly* noted that Barner's "cut and torn collages are geared for tickling the funny bones of the early elementary set," while *Booklist* critic Carolyn Phelan recommended the picture book as a "snappy introduction to the human skeleton" that features collage art that is "bold in form and vibrant in color."

Barner introduces young readers to cartography in *Which Way to the Revolution?: A Book about Maps.* He employs a well-known historical event, Paul Revere's ride, as an introduction not only to making but also to interpreting maps. Two lights shine in the Old North Church tower, and now Paul must spread the news that the British are coming. But which way should he go? How can he find his way from Boston to Lexington? To his great good fortune, in Barner's take on the story, a clever band of mice is there to help him, armed with a map and knowledge of the route. The travelers must watch out for another enemy besides the British, however: a pack of rats that will do anything to stop Paul Revere. Barner supplies seven colorful and simple maps for young cartographers to follow the group's course in a story that "adds a fantastic—and appealing—element" to the revolutionary tale, according to *Horn Book* critic Mary M. Burns. Writing in *School Library Journal,* Lucinda Snyder Whitehurst recommended *Which Way to the Revolution?* as "an appealing concept book" that "takes a fresh direction that youngsters will enjoy."

Bob Barner's paper collage illustrations for Pat Brisson's **Benny's Pennies** *follows a boy as he spends five pennies on perfect gifts for his family.* (Illustration copyright © 1993 by Bob Barner. Reproduced by permission of Dragonfly Books, an imprint of Random House Children's Books, a division of Random House, Inc.)

Barner turns his attention to verses from Ecclesiastes, "To everything there is a season," in *To Everything*. A celebration of the sentiments of the original verse, as well as an exuberant and colorful piece of artwork in its own right, the book shares the timeless message that everything in life has its proper time. For the verse, "a time to cry, a time to laugh," for example, Barner depicts a lone monkey on a tree branch watching others play together on a nearby bough. In *Kirkus Reviews* a critic cited Barner's "quite different approach" to the famous verses, and praised the addition of "vivid collages that are playful, joyous, and happy." A *Publishers Weekly* contributor commended *To Everything*, citing the "snazzy cut-and torn-paper collages" that set the biblical verses "rocking to a jazzy beat."

Insects are the inspiration for *Bug Safari* and *Bugs! Bugs! Bugs!*, the latter "an enthusiastic book crawling with splashy bugs," according to a reviewer for *Publishers Weekly*. In *Bugs! Bugs! Bugs!* Barner collects some of children's favorite insects, including the spot-

ted ladybug, butterflies, grasshoppers, bumble bees, and rolypoly bugs, all depicted in brightly colored collage art and accompanied by light, whimsical verse. He also makes the book an educational experience by including an actual-size bug chart and a "bug-o-meter" which lists facts such as the number of legs on each bug, where it lives, how it moves, and if it stings or not. "Budding entomologists will fly to this book like bees to honey," Dawn Amsberry predicted in her *School Library Journal* review, concluding that the "bright colors and easy text will be a hit at story time." Lauren Peterson, writing in *Booklist*, likewise praised the "bold colors and rhyming text" in *Bugs! Bugs! Bugs!*

Barner continues his focus on interesting subjects in *Stars!, Stars!, Stars!, Bears! Bears! Bears!*, and *Penguins, Penguins, Everywhere!*, all which pair his colorful torn-paper art with a simple, fact-filled text. Readers are guided through the night sky in *Stars! Stars! Stars!*, which "provides a concise, attractive introduction to stars and planets that will work well for reading aloud," according to a *Kirkus Reviews* writer, while *Bears! Bears! Bears!* brings children face to face with eight bear species in addition to the giant panda. "Barner's brilliantly colored collages" for *Bears! Bears! Bears!* depict these creatures as "furry, cuddly" animals, giving them "broad appeal" to "the youngest learners," according to another contributor to *Kirkus Reviews.*

In *Penguins, Penguins, Everywhere!* Barner uses what *Booklist* critic Shelle Rosenfeld described as "vibrant hues and textured shapes to depict subtly diverse penguin groups, both chicks and adults." Seventeen penguin species are included, their differences spelled out in the artist's characteristic combination of rhyming text and facts. Reviewing *Penguins, Penguins, Everywhere!,* Patricia Manning noted in *School Library Journal* that "Barner's simple rhyming text" pairs well with his art, resulting in an "effervescent" book that "will be just the thing for youngsters" too little to appreciate a scientific approach.

Fish are at the center of things in *Fish Wish,* in which a young boy gazing at a clown fish in an aquarium is taken on an imaginary tour of a coral reef. The boy wonders what it would be like to be such a fish when suddenly he finds himself hosted by the clown fish an underwater journey. "A series of eye-popping images accompanies equally vivid language," wrote a reviewer for *Publishers Weekly,* who also found that the characters in the book, from starfish to sea horses, "come together in a visually dynamic and informative grand finale." Barner blends cut and torn paper for the artwork, along with buttons, foil, fabric, and beads for the collages. In *Booklist* Carolyn Phelan found *Fish Wish* to be a "well-designed picture book, as simple and pleasing as a sea star."

In *Dinosaurs Roar, Butterflies Soar!* Barner broadens the timeline of young dino fans to show that butterflies were spreading their wings at the same time that dinosaurs lumbered across the earth. Using both paper and pastels, he "introduce[s] a bright and dynamic world," according to *Booklist* critic Abby Nolan, and his "array of dinosaurs . . . and prettily patterned butterflies" are shown living in symbiotic harmony. Barner introduces youngsters to the way different creatures contribute to nature's balance, as well as exploring the concept of extinction, when an asteroid appears and causes the demise of one species but not the other. Calling *Dinosaurs Roar, Butterflies Soar!* "useful, engaging, and illuminating," Susan Weitz added in *School Library Journal* that "Barner's illustrations are, as always, fantastically bright" and "eyecatching."

Biographical and Critical Sources

BOOKS

Bob Barner and You, Libraries Unlimited (Westport, CT), 2006.

PERIODICALS

Booklist, December 1, 1996, Carolyn Phelan, review of *Dem Bones,* pp. 662-663; July, 1999, Lauren Peterson, review of *Bugs! Bugs! Bugs!,* p. 1948; February 1, 2000, Carolyn Phelan, review of *Fish Wish,* p. 1027; November 1, 2001, Carolyn Phelan, review of *Dinosaur Bones,* p. 479; February 15, 2003, Lauren Peterson, review of *Parade Day: Marching through the Calendar Year,* p. 1072; April 15, 2004, Karin Snelson, review of *Bug Safari,* p. 1443; April 1, 2007, Shelle Rosenfeld, review of *Penguins, Penguins, Everywhere!,* p. 55; October 1, 2009, Abby Nolan, review of *Dinosaurs Roar, Butterflies Soar!,* p. 48; September 15, 2010, Andrew Medlar, review of *The Day of the Dead/El día de los muertos,* p. 62.

Books for Keeps, March, 1997, review of *Dem Bones,* p. 19.

Horn Book, November-December, 1990, review of *The Elevator Escalator Book: A Transportation Fact Book,* pp. 774-775; July-August, 1998, Mary M. Burns, review of *Which Way to the Revolution?: A Book about Maps,* p. 506.

Kirkus Reviews, October 1, 1998, review of *To Everything,* p. 1454; April 15, 2002, review of *Stars! Stars! Stars!,* p. 561; January 1, 2003, review of *Parade Day,* p. 140; January 15, 2003, review of *Parade Day;* February 1, 2004, review of *Bug Safari;* May 15, 2009, review of *Dinosaurs Roar, Butterflies Soar!;* May 15, 2010, review of *Bears! Bears! Bears!;* August 15, 2010, review of *The Day of the Dead.*

Publishers Weekly, February 6, 1995, reviews of *Too Many Dinosaurs* and *Space Race,* both p. 86; September 16, 1996, review of *Dem Bones,* p. 81; October 19, 1998, review of *To Everything,* p. 79; May 31, 1999, review of *Bugs! Bugs! Bugs!,* p. 91; February 21, 2000, review of *Fish Wish,* p. 86; June 12, 2000, review of *Walk the Dog,* p. 72; July 9, 2001, review of *Dinosaur Bones,* p. 66; May 6, 2002, review of *Stars!, Stars!, Stars!,* p. 57; January 13, 2003, review of *Parade Day,* p. 58; January 26, 2004, review of *Bug Safari,* p. 253; February 26, 2007, review of *Penguins, Penguins, Everywhere!,* p. 88; May 25, 2009, review of *Dinosaurs Roar, Butterflies Soar!,* p. 56.

School Library Journal, November, 1996, Christine A. Moesch, review of *Dem Bones,* pp. 95-96; May, 1998, Lucinda Snyder Whitehurst, review of *Which Way to the Revolution?,* p. 129; November, 1998, Patricia Pearl Dole, review of *To Everything,* p. 102; August, 1999, Dawn Amsberry, review of *Bugs! Bugs! Bugs!,* p. 144; May, 2000, Margaret Rhoades, review of *Fish Wish,* p. 130; July, 2000, Janet M. Blair, review of *Walk the Dog,* p. 91; April, 2003, Rosalyn Pierini, review of *Parade Day,* p. 114; January, 2004, Joy Fleishhacker, review of *Which Way to the Revolution?,* p. 77; March, 2004, Jane Barrer, review of *Bug Safari,* p. 189; June, 2007, Patricia Manning, review of *Penguins, Penguins, Everywhere!,* p. 130; June, 2009, Susan Weitz, review of *Dinosaurs Roar, Butterflies Soar!,* p. 104; May, 2010, Melissa Smith, review of *Bears! Bears! Bears!,* p. 79; September, 2010, Roberto Zapata, review of *The Day of the Dead,* p. 142.

ONLINE

Bob Barner Home Page, http://www.bobbarner.com (January 10, 2012).*

*   *   *

BENDICK, Jeanne 1919-

Personal

February 25, 1919, in New York, NY; daughter of Louis Xerxes (an inventor) and Amelia Maurice (Hess) Garfunkel; married Robert Louis Bendick (a television and film producer-director), November 24, 1960 (died, 2008); children: Robert Louis, Jr., Karen Ann Watson Holton. *Education:* New York High School of Arts and Music; Parsons School of Design, B.A. 1939. *Politics:* Democrat. *Religion:* Jewish. *Hobbies and other interests:* Sailing, beachcombing, science, history and mysteries, cooking, Inuit art.

Addresses

Home—Guilford, CT.

Career

Author and illustrator. Illustrator for *Jack and Jill* magazine; textile designer, c. 1930s. Associate producer of documentary *Fight for Food,* for public television. Trustee, Rye Free Reading Room, Rye, NY. *Military service:* Volunteer in American Women's Voluntary Services during World War II.

Member

Authors Guild, Authors League of America, Writers Guild, National Science Teachers Association, American Library Association, Society of Children's Book Writers and Illustrators.

Awards, Honors

Boy's Club Junior Book Award, 1949, for *How Much and How Many: The Story of Weights and Measures,* and 1975; New York Academy of Sciences Children's Science Honor Book Award, 1943, for *Let's Find Out: A Picture Science Book,* 1947, for *The First Book of Space Travel,* and 1974, for *Discovering Cycles;* Eva L. Gordon Award, American Nature Society, 1975.

Writings

SELF-ILLUSTRATED NONFICTION

Electronics for Boys and Girls, McGraw (New York, NY), 1944, published as *Electronics for Young People,* 1947, sixth edition, with R.J. Lefkowitz, 1972.

Jeanne Bendick (Courtesy of Jeanne Bendick.)

(With husband Robert L. Bendick) *Making the Movies,* McGraw (New York, NY), 1945, revised as *Filming Works like This,* McGraw (New York, NY), 1970.

How Much and How Many: The Story of Weights and Measures, McGraw (New York, NY), 1947, third edition, F. Watts (New York, NY), 1989.

(With Robert L. Bendick) *Television Works like This,* McGraw (New York, NY), 1948, revised edition, 1965.

All around You: A First Look at the World, McGraw (New York, NY), 1951.

What Could You See? Adventures in Looking, McGraw (New York, NY), 1957.

(With Barbara Berk) *How to Have a Show,* F. Watts (New York, NY), 1957.

(With children Candy Bendick and Rob Bendick, Jr.) *Have a Happy Measle, a Merry Mumps, and a Cheery Chickenpox,* McGraw (New York, NY), 1958.

Lightning, Rand McNally (Chicago, IL), 1961.

(With Marcia Levin) *Take a Number; New Ideas + Imagination = More Fun,* McGraw (New York, NY), 1961.

Archimedes and the Door of Science, F. Watts (New York, NY), 1962, reprinted, Bethlehem Books (Warsaw, ND), 1995.

(With Marcia Levin) *Take Shapes, Lines, and Letters: New Horizons in Mathematics,* McGraw (New York, NY), 1962.

A Fresh Look at Night, F. Watts (New York, NY), 1963.

Sea So Big, Ship So Small, Rand McNally (Chicago, IL), 1963.

(With Marcia Levin) *Pushups and Pinups: Diet, Exercise, and Grooming for Young Teens,* McGraw (New York, NY), 1963.

(With Leonard Simon) *The Day the Numbers Disappeared,* McGraw (New York, NY), 1963.

The Wind, Rand McNally (Chicago, IL), 1964.

The Shape of the Earth, Rand McNally (Chicago, IL), 1965.

(With Marcia Levin) *Illustrated Mathematics Dictionary,* McGraw (New York, NY), 1965, revised edition published as *Mathematics Illustrated Dictionary: Facts, Figures, and People,* F. Watts (New York, NY), 1989.

(With Marcia Levin) *New Mathematics Workbooks: Sets and Addition; Sets and Subtraction; Sets and Multiplication; Sets and Division,* Grosset (New York, NY), 1965.

The Emergency Book, Rand McNally (Chicago, IL), 1967.

Shapes, F. Watts (New York, NY), 1967.

(With Marian Warren) *What to Do? Everyday Guides for Everyone,* McGraw (New York, NY), 1967.

The Human Senses, F. Watts (New York, NY), 1968.

Space and Time, F. Watts (New York, NY), 1968.

Living Things, F. Watts (New York, NY), 1969.

Why Can't I?, McGraw (New York, NY), 1969.

A Place to Live: A Study of Ecology, Parents' Magazine Press (New York, NY), 1970.

Adaptation, F. Watts (New York, NY), 1971.

How to Make a Cloud, Parents' Magazine Press (New York, NY), 1971.

Measuring, F. Watts (New York, NY), 1971.

Names, Sets, and Numbers, F. Watts (New York, NY), 1971.

What Made You You?, McGraw (New York, NY), 1971.

Motion and Gravity, F. Watts (New York, NY), 1972.

Observation, F. Watts (New York, NY), 1972.

Why Things Work: A Book about Energy, additional illustrations by Karen Bendick, Parents' Magazine Press (New York, NY), 1972.

Heat and Temperature, F. Watts (New York, NY), 1974.

Solids, Liquids, and Gases, F. Watts (New York, NY), 1974.

Ecology, F. Watts (New York, NY), 1974.

How Heredity Works: Why Living Things Are as They Are, Parents' Magazine Press (New York, NY), 1975.

How Animals Behave, Parents' Magazine Press (New York, NY), 1976.

The Mystery of the Loch Ness Monster, McGraw (New York, NY), 1976.

(With Robert Bendick) *Finding out about Jobs: TV Reporting,* Parents' Magazine Press (New York, NY), 1976.

Putting the Sun to Work, Garrard (Champaign, IL), 1980.

Super People: Who Will They Be?, McGraw (New York, NY), 1980.

Elementary Science (teacher's edition with activities book), Volume 6, Ginn (Boston, MA), 1980.

Scare a Ghost, Tame a Monster, Westminster Press (Philadelphia, PA), 1983.

Egyptian Tombs, F. Watts (New York, NY), 1987.

Tombs of the Early Americans, F. Watts (New York, NY), 1992.

(With Robert L. Bendick) *Markets: From Barter to Bar Codes,* F. Watts (New York, NY), 1995.

Along Came Galileo, Beautiful Feet (Sandwich, MA), 1999.

Galen and the Gateway to Medicine, Bethlehem (Warsaw, ND), 2003.

Herodotus and the Road to History, Bethlehem (Warsaw, ND), 2009.

NONFICTION

The Future Explorers' Club Meets Here, illustrated by Joan Paley, Ginn (Boston, MA), 1973.

Why Things Change: The Story of Evolution, illustrated by daughter Karen Bendick Watson, Parents' Magazine Press (New York, NY), 1973.

(With Robert L. Bendick) *The Consumer's Catalog of Economy and Ecology,* illustrated by Karen Benedick Watson, McGraw (New York, NY), 1974.

Ginn Science Program (teacher's edition for grades K-4), Volumes 1-3, Ginn (Boston, MA), 1975.

Exploring an Ocean Tide Pool, photographs by Robert L. Bendick, Garrard (Champaign, IL), 1976, revised and enlarged edition, Holt (New York, NY), 1992.

The Big Strawberry Book of Astronomy, illustrated by Sal Murdocca, Strawberry Books/Larouse (New York, NY), 1979.

The Big Strawberry Book of the Earth: Our Ever-Changing Planet, illustrated by M. Luppold Junkins, McGraw (New York, NY), 1980.

Caves! Underground Worlds, illustrated by Todd Telander, Henry Holt (New York, NY), 1995.

"FIRST BOOK" NONFICTION SERIES

(Illustrator) Campbell Tatham (pseudonym of Mary Elting), *The First Book of Boats,* F. Watts (New York, NY), 1945, new edition with text by Margaret Gossett, 1953.

(Illustrator) Campbell Tatham, *The First Book of Trains,* F. Watts (New York, NY), 1948, new edition with text by Russell Hamilton, 1956.

(Illustrator) Campbell Tatham, *The First Flying Book,* F. Watts (New York, NY), 1948, published as *The First Book of Flight,* 1958.

(Illustrator) Campbell Tatham, *The First Book of Automobiles,* F. Watts (New York, NY), 1949, new edition with text by Bendick, 1966, revised as *Automobiles,* 1984.

(Illustrator) Benjamin Brewster (pseudonym of Mary Elting), *First Book of Baseball,* F. Watts (New York, NY), 1950, revised edition with text by Franklin Folsom published as *Baseball by Benjamin Brewster,* 4th revised edition, 1970.

(And illustrator) *The First Book of Airplanes,* California State Department of Education (Sacramento, CA), 1950, revised edition, F. Watts (New York, NY), 1976, published as *Airplanes,* 1982.

(Illustrator) Benjamin Brewster, *The First Book of Firemen,* F. Watts (New York, NY), 1951.

(And illustrator) *The First Book of Space Travel,* F. Watts (New York, NY), 1953, revised edition published as *Space Travel,* 1969.

(Illustrator) *The First Book of Supermarkets,* F. Watts (New York, NY), 1954.

(Illustrator) *The First Book of Ships,* F. Watts (New York, NY), 1959.

(With Barbara Berk, and illustrator) *The First Book of Costume and Makeup,* F. Watts (New York, NY), 1960.

(With Barbara Berk, and illustrator) *The First Book of How to Fix It,* F. Watts (New York, NY), 1961.

(And illustrator) *The First Book of Time,* F. Watts (New York, NY), 1963.

(And illustrator) *The First Book of Fishes,* F. Watts (New York, NY), 1965.

"EARLYBIRD ASTRONOMY" NONFICTION SERIES

(And illustrator) *Artificial Satellites,* F. Watts (New York, NY), 1983, published as *Artificial Satellites: Helpers in Space,* Millbrook Press (Brookfield, CT), 1991.

Comets and Meteors: Visitors from Space, illustrated by Mike Roffe, Millbrook Press (Brookfield, CT), 1991.

(And illustrator) *Moons and Rings: Companions to the Planets,* Millbrook Press (Brookfield, CT), 1991.

The Planets: Neighbors in Space, illustrated by Mike Roffe, Millbrook Press (Brookfield, CT), 1991.

The Stars: Lights in the Night Sky, illustrated by Chris Forsey, Millbrook Press (Brookfield, CT), 1991.

The Sun: Our Very Own Star, illustrated by Mike Roffe, Millbrook Press (Brookfield, CT), 1991.

The Universe: Think Big! illustrated by Mike Roffe and Lynn Willey, Millbrook Press (Brookfield, CT), 1991.

"INVENTING" NONFICTION SERIES; ILLUSTRATED BY SAL MURDOCCA

Eureka! It's an Airplane, Millbrook (Brookfield, CT), 1992.

Eureka! It's an Automobile, Millbrook (Brookfield, CT), 1992.

Eureka! It's a Telephone, Millbrook (Brookfield, CT), 1993.

(With Robert Bendick) *Eureka! It's Television,* Millbrook (Brookfield, CT), 1993.

SELF-ILLUSTRATED FICTION

The Good Knight Ghost, F. Watts (New York, NY), 1956.

The Blonk from beneath the Sea, F. Watts (New York, NY), 1958.

ILLUSTRATOR

Carol Lynn, *Modeling for Money,* Greenberg (New York, NY), 1937.

Charles F. Martin and George M. Martin, *At West Point,* Heath (Boston, MA), 1943.

Mary Elting and Robert T. Weaver, *Soldiers, Sailors, Fliers, and Marines,* Doubleday (New York, NY), 1943.

Katherine Britton, *What Makes It Tick?,* Houghton (Boston, MA), 1943.

Mary Elting and Robert T. Weaver, *Battles: How They Are Won,* Doubleday (New York, NY), 1944.

Mary McBurney Green, *Everybody Has a House,* W.R. Scott (New York, NY), 1944.

Shirley Matthews, *The Airplane Book,* W. Roberts (Washington, DC), 1945.

Jeffrey Roberts, *The Fix-It Book,* W. Roberts (Washington, DC), 1945.

Eleanor Clymer, *The Grocery Mouse,* R. McBride (New York, NY), 1945.

Elizabeth Kinsey, *Teddy,* R. McBride (New York, NY), 1945.

Mary Elting and Margaret Gossett, *We Are the Government,* Doubleday (New York, NY), 1945.

Mary Elting, *The Lollypop Factory,* Doubleday (New York, NY), 1946.

Herman and Nina Schneider, *Let's Find Out: A Picture Science Book,* Scott (New York, NY), 1946.

Eleanor Clymer, *The Country Kittens,* McBride (New York, NY), 1947.

Herman and Nina Schneider, *Your Telephone and How It Works,* McGraw (New York, NY), 1947.

John Ernest Bechdolt, *Going Up: The Story of Vertical Transportation,* Abingdon-Cokesbury (New York, NY), 1948.

Will Rogow, *The Fix-It Book: Big Pictures and Little Stories about Carpenters, Mechanics, Welders, Tailors, and Lots of Others,* W. Roberts (Washington, DC), 1949.

Herman Schneider, *Everyday Machines and How They Work,* McGraw (New York, NY), 1950.

Herman Schneider, *Everyday Weather and How It Works,* McGraw (New York, NY), 1951.

Dorothy Canfield Fisher, *A Fair World for All,* McGraw (New York, NY), 1952.

Joseph Leeming, *Real Book about Easy Music-Making,* Garden City Books (New York, NY), 1952.

Lynn Poole, *Today's Science and You,* McGraw (New York, NY), 1952.

Herman and Nina Schneider, *Science Fun with Milk Cartons,* McGraw (New York, NY), 1953.

Glenn Orlando Blough, *The Tree on the Road to Turntown,* McGraw (New York, NY), 1953.

Glenn Orlando Blough, *Not Only for Ducks: The Story of Rain,* McGraw (New York, NY), 1954.

Julius Schwartz, *Through the Magnifying Glass,* McGraw (New York, NY), 1954.

Glenn Orlando Blough, *Wait for the Sunshine: The Story of Seasons and Growing Things,* McGraw (New York, NY), 1954.

Lynn Poole, *Diving for Science,* McGraw (New York, NY), 1955.

Glenn Orlando Blough, *Lookout for the Forest: A Conservation Story,* McGraw (New York, NY), 1955.

John Perry, *Our Wonderful Eyes,* McGraw (New York, NY), 1955.

Glenn Orlando Blough, *After the Sun Goes Down: The Story of Animals at Night,* McGraw (New York, NY), 1956.

Herman and Nina Schneider, *Let's Find Out,* W. Scott, 1956.

(With Bob Beane) William Harry Crouse, *Understanding Science,* McGraw (New York, NY), 1956, 4th edition, 1973.

Glenn Orlando Blough, *Who Lives in This House? A Story of Animal Families,* McGraw (New York, NY), 1957.

Glenn Orlando Blough, *Young People's Book of Science,* McGraw (New York, NY), 1958.

George Barr, *Young Scientist Takes a Walk: A Guide to Outdoor Observations,* McGraw (New York, NY), 1959.

Glenn Orlando Blough, *Soon after September: The Story of Living Things in Winter,* McGraw (New York, NY), 1959.

Earl Schenck Miers, *The Storybook of Science,* Rand McNally (Chicago, IL), 1959.

Glenn Orlando Blough, *Christmas Trees and How They Grow,* McGraw (New York, NY), 1961.

Glenn Orlando Blough, *Who Lives in This Meadow? A Story of Animal Life,* McGraw (New York, NY), 1961.

Glenn Orlando Blough, *Who Lives at the Seashore? Animal Life along the Shore,* McGraw (New York, NY), 1962.

Glenn Orlando Blough, *Bird Watchers and Bird Feeders,* McGraw (New York, NY), 1963.

Glenn Orlando Blough, *Discovering Plants,* McGraw (New York, NY), 1966.

Glenn Orlando Blough, *Discovering Insects,* McGraw (New York, NY), 1967.

Glenn Orlando Blough, *Discovering Cycles,* McGraw (New York, NY), 1973.

Sam and Beryl Epstein, *Saving Electricity,* Garrard (Champaign, IL), 1977.

Wiker, Benjamin, *The Mystery of the Periodic Table,* Bethlehem (Warsaw, ND), 2003.

OTHER

Author of filmstrips *The Seasons,* for the Society for Visual Education, and *You and Me and Our World, Monsters and Other Science Mysteries,* and *Dreams and Other Science Mysteries,* for Miller-Brody. Also author of multimedia educational program "Starting Points" for Ginn. Story editor and script writer of television programs for National Broadcasting Company (NBC-TV), including *The First Look,* 1965-66, and *Giant Step,* 1968; author of "Evolution/Creation," for *20/ 20,* American Broadcasting Companies (ABC-TV). Contributor to *Britannica Junior Encyclopaedia, Book of Knowledge,* and other publications.

Author's papers from 1951 to 1977 are located at the University of Oregon. The Grummond Children's Literature Collection, University of Southern Mississippi, holds Bendick's papers spanning 1949 to 1984.

Adaptations

Sidelights

An acclaimed author and illustrator of children's books, Jeanne Bendick is especially regarded for her introductory science books. Comprehensive research combined with clearly written text and simple illustrations mark her work, much of which clarifies time, shapes, numbers, media technology, ecology, astronomy, heredity, and science history for young readers and inspires further research.

Bendick, who grew up in New York City, was taught to draw at an early age by her Grandpa Charley, an artist who demanded her best efforts. In addition to drawing for her, on Sundays the pair often visited the American Museum of Natural History together. Bendick was also encouraged to read at a young age, and when her family spent summer vacation at a farm in the mountains, she was allowed to select books from the enormous library of a family friend.

When Bendick was still a teen, her family was hit hard by the Great Depression. To earn income, she taught a children's art class on the weekends and work illustrating children's magazine *Jack and Jill* helped pay her tuition to Parsons School of Design. Benedick graduated in 1939, winning a scholarship to study in Paris for a year; but with war raging in Europe, she decided against leaving home. Instead she became engaged to Robert Bendick, whom she married a year later. Her husband, a photographer, entered the field of television by becoming one of the first three cameramen at the emerging CBS-TV network. Both Bendick and her husband were involved in the war effort and they collaborated on a project while he was stationed overseas: *Making the Movies,* which they rewrote twenty-five years later as *Filming Works like This.* Through the years, Bendick has worked with her husband on other projects, as well as collaborating with her son and her daughter Karen Benedick Watson, who is also an illustrator.

While her husband was in the service Bendick developed an interest in the new science of electronics. Lack of a simple, instructive book on the subject prompted her to write *Electronics for Boys and Girls,* which she has subsequently revised to keep pace with advancing technology. Bendick also became involved with Franklin Watts's "First Book" science series for children and was story editor and script writer for NBC-TV's spin-off telelvision series *The First Look.* Other series work includes the "Early Bird Astronomy" and "Inventing" series for Millbrook Press as well as three volumes for Ginn's science series. Author and/or illustrator of more than one hundred books, Bendick has not only helped to introduce young readers to the field of science, but she has helped to make that field less intimidating as well.

In an essay in *Science and Children,* Bendick expressed her belief that "text and pictures should complement, not duplicate each other," adding that "one of the best things any illustrator can give to a picture is his own viewpoint—the special way he sees things." Before she attempts to illustrate a scientific principle, she always builds a model of what she will be drawing to make sure that it really works. Although she admitted that she is "certainly not the best artist in the world," children respond well to her illustrations.

In a review of *A Place to Live: A Study of Ecology,* Bendick's book about conservation and the environment, Della Thomas wrote in *School Library Journal* that, "as usual, this author's simple but expressive pictures of active children keep readers' attention and help them to better appreciate the ideas in the text." Beryl B. Beatley concluded in her *Appraisal* review of *How Animals Behave* by noting that "Bendick is a born teacher for she knows how to stimulate interest and make a book both interesting and attractive without boring the reader." Carolyn Phelan, writing in *Booklist,* recommended Bendick's collaboration with her husband, *Markets: From Barter to Bar Codes,* as having "strengths for social studies units."

In addition to science books, Bendick has written and illustrated several biographies of notable ancient scientists and scholars for children, including *Archimedes and the Door of Science, Galen and the Gateway to Medicine, Along Came Galileo,* and *Herodotus and the Road to History.* Recommending the book for use in Christian home schools, Alicia Van Hecke wrote in *Love2Learn* online that *Herodotus and the Road to History* is "a brief, engaging and heavily illustrated biography of the world's first historian." Calling the same book "amazing," Lady Meriwen added in *Squeaky Clean Reviews* online that Bendick "makes ancient history as practical and exciting as it really is."

Biographical and Critical Sources

BOOKS

Books for Children, 1960-65, American Library Association (Chicago, IL), 1966.
Children's Bookshelf, Child Study Association of America/Bantam (New York, NY), 1965.
Children's Literature Review, Volume 5, Gale (Detroit, MI), 1983.

Fisher, Margery, *Matters of Fact: Aspects of Non-Fiction for Children,* Harper (New York, NY), 1972.
Good Books for Children, edited by Mary K. Eakin, Phoenix Books (Chicago, IL), 1966.
Hopkins, Lee Bennett, *Books Are by People,* Citation Press (New York, NY), 1969.
Illustrators of Children's Books: 1957-1966, Horn Book (Boston, MA), 1968.
Larrick, Nancy, *A Teacher's Guide to Children's Books,* Merrill (Columbus, OH), 1966.
Larrick, Nancy, *A Parent's Guide to Children's Reading,* 3rd edition, Doubleday (New York, NY), 1969.
Sutherland, Zena, *The Best in Children's Books,* University of Chicago Press (Chicago, IL), 1973.
Sutherland, Zena, Diane L. Monson, and May Hill Arbuthnot, *Children and Books,* 6th edition, Scott, Foresman (Glenview, IL), 1981.

PERIODICALS

Appraisal, spring, 1977, Beryl Beatley, review of *How Animals Behave,* pp. 12-13.
Booklist, August, 1992, Carolyn Phelan, review of *Exploring an Ocean Tide Pool,* p. 2005; August, 1993, Ilene Cooper, review of *Tombs of the Ancient Americas,* p. 2052; February 1, 1996, Stephanie Zvirin, review of *Caves,* p. 927; September 1, 1997, Carolyn Phelan, review of *Markets: From Barter to Bar Codes,* p. 108.
Bulletin of the Center for Children's Books, October, 1983, review of *Scare a Ghost, Tame a Monster,* p. 22; April, 1989, review of *Egyptian Tombs,* p. 188; November, 1992, review of *Eureka! It's an Airplane!,* p. 68.
School Library Journal, November, 1970, Della Thomas, review of *A Place to Live: A Study of Ecology,* p. 96.
Science and Children, April, 1973, Jeanne Bendick, "Illustrating Science Books for Children," pp. 20-21.
Science Books and Films, March-April, 1981, review of *Super People,* p. 212.

ONLINE

Love2Learn Web site, http://www.love2learn.net/ (October 21, 2009), Alicia Van Hecke, review of *Herodotus and the Road to History.*
Squeaky Clean Reviews Web site, http://www.squeakycleanreviews.com/ (November 17, 2011), Lady Meriwen, review of *Herodotus and the Road to History.*

Autobiography Feature

Jeanne Bendick

Jeanne Bendick contributed the following autobiographical essay to *SATA:*

For as long as I can remember, I have had a life list. It's not like the life list birdwatchers keep, on which they check off specimens observed, any time, any place. Mine is more like a marketing list of wishes—a list of things I want and things I want to do. As wishes are granted I cross them off, the way I cross off the items on my marketing list as I take them from the supermarket shelves and put them into the cart. As with all marketing lists, it is ongoing. Wishes are granted and new wishes are added.

Most of my wishes have come true, but like the lady in the story who is granted three wishes and ends up with a sausage on the end of her nose, they often turn out to be less than romantic and unexpectedly funny. With a twist. Like the wish I have had since I was a kid, to see the tidal bore roaring up the Bay of Fundy, in Nova Scotia. I did get to see it. The day I saw it the bore was a bore—a ripple about six inches high, making its lazy way upstream to the murmur of the assembled anticipatory crowds hissing to each other, "Is that it? It can't be it! It is it."

And then there was the wish about climbing up the secret passage through the Great Pyramid of Cheops. The day we made our climb turned out to be an Egyptian holiday and everyone in Egypt who was not milling around outside offering camel rides or photographs was climbing with us. There was a barely moving row going up and a molasses-flowing row squeezing past us on the way down, all closer than lovers, all bent double (the passage is very low), all sweating and cringing under the imagined weight of millions of rock tons over our heads.

And about that romantic gondola ride through the canals of Venice. The tide was low; the water was smelly. The gondolier didn't sing softly. He had an awful cold and sneezed and sniffled our way through the canals. Then, when we returned to base, a garbage scow had pulled up to the steps where the gondolier had to moor. So we scrambled ashore over the assorted garbage of Venice.

I am lucky. Most of my wishes come true. The ones that turn out funny are doubtless a projection of the

Jeanne Bendick, 1986 (Courtesy of Jeanne Bendick.)

books and books of O. Henry stories I assimilated when I was growing up. He was my favorite author. It had to rub off.

I have been lucky in a lot of ways and at a lot of times. All things considered, good luck would have been at the top of my wish list if I had thought I could wish it for myself.

*

Like so many American families, mine came together from all directions. My father's mother and father, Fanny and Max Garfunkel, were European, though both came to the United States when they were very young. Some of my mother's family came to America from France to settle in the Louisiana Territory while it was still French. Her father's family had settled in Pennsylvania before the Civil War. Both my mother's grandfathers fought in the Civil War, one with Pickett's Cavalry one in the Pennsylvania Regulars.

Dot, Lou, Bobby, and Jeanne Garfunkel, about 1922 (Courtesy of Jeanne Bendick.)

My mother's given name was Amelia Maurice Hess, but she was never called anything but Dot. The Hesses moved to New York City from Mobile, Alabama, when she was about sixteen, and the youngest member of the family, Caroline, was a small child. They moved because her older brother, Arthur, had a job in an architect's office in New York and my grandparents felt that families should be together. (Arthur Hess, who was never called anything but "Brother," became a well-known and successful architect.) Dot met my father, Louis Xerxes Garfunkel, while he was a student at the Columbia School of Journalism.

He graduated in the class of 1917—one of the most famous classes in the school's history. Lou wanted to write; my grandfather wanted him to go into the family restaurant business. So Max made a canny (and unfair) bargain; he would stake him to a year, and then if Lou hadn't started to make it as a writer, he would come into the business. Lou made the bargain. When you're young, what can't you accomplish in a year? Certainly you can become a writer in a year. He didn't. And being an honorable person he became a restaurant man and a writer on the side. A year! His friends and classmates who became famous—George Gershwin, Larry Hart, Irwin Edman, Morrie Ryskind, Muriel Rukeyser, Max Schuster, Herman Mankiewicz, George Sokolsky, and the others—never made it in a year either. Besides, he had met my mother in his last year at college; he wanted to get married and supporting a wife on a non-published writer's non-salary was impractical. It never occurred to him, at any time, to go back on his bargain. He loved my being a writer. He said it was the next best thing.

I'm not sure how it started, but my sister Bobby—she's a year and a half younger than I am—and I have al-

ways called our parents Dot and Lou. Dot had been brought up to believe, like most Southern women of her generation, that in social situations thirty seconds of silence was a disaster that reflected on one's ability to entertain. Actually, she was not a social person; she was perfectly content with her immediate family and nothing was too much for her to do for us. My father, on the other hand, was a professional public angel and was famous for it. He would plunge out into the night to find a dentist for some acquaintance who had a dental twinge, or to locate a peach in November (in those days, that was comparable to searching for the Holy Grail), if someone was incautious enough to express a yearning for a peach. It gave him enormous satisfaction to accomplish seemingly impossible small things. I think it was because he never accomplished the big thing he always wanted to do, being a writer. He wrote a lot—poems, lyrics, short stories—but he never had anything published except for a book about how to run a restaurant, a job he was very good at, but which he detested.

*

My grandfathers were enormously different, yet they liked and respected each other. They were even friends.

My mother's father, Charley Hess, was born in Philadelphia during the Civil War; he was a third-generation

Sarah and Charley Hess, 1911 (Courtesy of Jeanne Bendick.)

American. His name was not Charles; it was, simply, Charley. Clarence was the name he had been given, but one day when he was in the first grade he came home in tears and said he hated his name; the other boys kept teasing him about it and he wanted to change it. My great-grandfather said he would take him straight down to the city clerk to do the changing; on the way, Clarence was to decide on his new name. When they got to the city clerk's office, my great-grandfather said, "This boy wants to change his name."

The clerk got out the records and asked my grandfather what name he wanted. "Charley."

"You mean Charles."

"No, Charley."

"How do you spell that?"

"C-H-A-R-L-E-Y."

"There's no such name."

"There is now," my great-grandfather said firmly. And Charley it was ever after that.

My other grandfather, Max Garfunkel, came to America alone in 1888 before he was fourteen. He had been helping in his family's farm-hardware business since he was ten. When he was thirteen he announced to his astonished family that America was the land of opportunity and so he was off to America. He had saved enough money to permit him to enter the United States without a sponsor. So the immigration officer attached him to a childless couple in the line, whose name was Garfunkel. "Now, that's your name, too," he told Max. Max accepted the name. Whatever his name had been in the old country was behind him. He spent his first night sleeping in an empty wagon on the New York waterfront. The next day, with all of his possessions in a small bundle under his arm, he roamed lower Manhattan looking for work. By night he had a job in a saloon, working behind the free-lunch counter, and a home with the old German saloon owner.

Max learned English quickly, saved his money carefully, and by the time he was nineteen he had saved the unbelievable sum of $7,000. He married my grandmother Fanny and started in the restaurant business for himself. His idea was a place for no-frills eating—a place where working men (there were very few working women) could buy lunch for a few pennies, instead of carrying it in a lunch pail. In 1896 he opened Max's Busy Bee. Sandwiches were two cents, coffee was two cents, cakes were a penny and so was lemonade. This first cafeteria helped to change the eating habits of America. Before Max, only the rich, who could afford a dollar or two for lunch, ate out.

Max himself became rich enough to eat anywhere. By 1928 he had fifteen Busy Bees. He was a big man with a big voice and a very big temper. We were a little afraid of him.

I adored Grandpa Charley. He was a wonderful artist. He had wanted to be a professional artist, but that was not considered a reasonable career choice in the late nineteenth century, particularly in Mobile, Alabama, where he had lived since he was in his teens. Obediently, he went into the family's tobacco business, but art was always his great love. While he lived in Mobile he spent his spare time designing floats for the Mardi Gras. Later, in New York, he spent patient hours drawing for us. He made marvelous cardboard houses with tissue-paper windows, wallpaper on the walls, painted woodwork outside. He did beautiful calligraphy for all occasions, even in silly notes to us. Grandpa Charley taught me how to draw and was firm about my getting it right. Sometimes I got angry about being corrected and refused to go on.

"Why not?"

"I'm not in the mood," I would say loftily. "It's my artistic temperament." (I don't know where I got that.)

"There's no such thing," he would say. "That's just an excuse for being lazy. Or wanting to have your own way."

Max and Fanny Garfunkel in Venice, c. 1920s (Courtesy of Jeanne Bendick.)

Bobby and Jeanne with Grandpa Charley. "Grandpa Charley took us on all kinds of expeditions, real and make-believe." (Courtesy of Jeanne Bendick.)

Charley was a perfectionist and getting things exactly right, whether it was in pictures or words, became second nature to me. "Keep at it," he would say, "until you are absolutely comfortable with what you've done." (Our daughter Karen, who is a super-successful illustrator, would have made Grandpa Charley very, very happy.)

My grandmothers got along well, too, but they were never really friends. There was no way they could relate to one another. Fanny (we called her "Little Grandma") was a tiny, imperious woman who had Max completely under her thumb. She loved to travel and sailed to Europe every year, accompanied by a pair of enormous wardrobe trunks and sometimes by a reluctant Max. We always went to the boat to see them off and then, with greater anticipation, to welcome them home. Little Grandma loved to shop and she always brought presents—elaborate sets of china for my mother and my father's sister, Rose; Sulka ties and sweaters for my father and his younger brother, Dick; dolls and clothes for Bobby and me. We loved the dolls and wore the clothes inappropriately. Both of us were tomboys and tubby. We must have been a rare spectacle, riding our bikes or playing marbles in Riverside Park in pleated chiffons or embroidered silks.

When Fanny or the restaurant business or life in general became too much for Max, he took to the sea in his own way. He would engage a cabin on the Albany Night Boat, which sailed up the Hudson River. We came down to see him off just as solemnly as we saw Little Grandma off on her more elaborate voyages. Max would sail up the Hudson to Albany and back, returning from his trip relaxed and almost calm. Almost.

My grandmother Hess (we called her "Grandma Mama") was perpetually astonished by the relationship between Max and Fanny. Sarah had been born and raised in Mobile where gentlemen were gentlemen who took gallant care of their wives who, in turn, never

questioned their authority. She was helpmate, cook, loving mother, and grandmother, and her place was at home, whether in the house in Mobile or in an apartment in New York City. She hadn't transplanted well. She missed the South and in New York she never did some of the things she had enjoyed in her other life. She was an excellent rider but she was too timid to ride in Central Park. She was also an expert telegrapher. When we were walking with her in New York, sometimes she would stop outside a Western Union office where they were clicking away on a telegraph key and translate the messages for us.

Because Grandpa Charley was a perfectionist, Sarah's life wasn't always easy. We were at their house for lunch one day when she tried a daring innovation. Tired of ironing the yard-square napkins that accompanied every meal, she set the table with a new invention— paper napkins. Charley picked his up between thumb and forefinger, held it away from himself as if it were a dead mouse, and asked, "What, may I ask, is this?" I never saw a paper napkin there again.

Grandma Mama was ninety-five when she died. She was soft, innocent, always yielding and dependent in the old tradition of Southern ladies. Little Grandma was exactly the opposite. She was ingenious in getting her own way. Once, when she couldn't persuade my Aunt Rose to stop wearing a hat Fanny detested, she simply sat on it.

I like to think back to those ladies and to the two grandfathers. Grandpa Charley was my hero; an educated Southern gentleman who had tended the wounded in the Spanish-American War; who was a scholar and

Jeanne, about 1924. "I'd already opted for the sea." (Courtesy of Jeanne Bendick.)

an artist, gentle, patient, full of humor, and endlessly generous with his time. Max was tough and tempery. He treated us like interesting pets. I'm not sure that he ever read a book, though he set great store by the tabloids of the day. Yet never in his life did Charley have the courage to do the things he really wanted to do. And Max, with no family, no traditions, and no education, moved mountains.

*

In many ways, growing up in New York City in the 1920s wasn't too different from growing up in any neighborhood, anywhere. Our neighborhood was the big apartment house where we lived. Instead of going down the block or around the corner to our friends' houses, we went upstairs or downstairs in the elevator. There were twenty floors in the block-square house, perhaps 200 apartments with children in most of them. One winter the whole house had whooping cough. (This was before the vaccine that has almost wiped out that disease.) We were all out of school for about two months and we had a wonderful time in our whoopless hours. The treatment for whooping cough was a vaporizer puffing out fumes of tincture of benzoin and the entire building reeked of it—you got the first blast the instant you entered the dignified marble lobby. Rene, the elevator man, was patient with all of us, ferrying us between floors all day long until he came down with whooping cough himself. His temporary replacement was not so patient. We took revenge by doubling our vertical travels.

We went to our neighborhood school, carrying our lunch boxes, just like children in any other neighborhood across the country. After school we rode our bikes, roller-skated, played marbles in Riverside Park in the spring, and went sleigh-riding there and in Central Park in the winter.

And there were expeditions. Once in a while, before daybreak, we went down to the New York wholesale produce markets with Lou and watched while he bought food for the stores. There were separate markets for fruits and vegetables; for meat; for staples like butter, coffee, sugar, flour. The Fulton fish market on the East River was a real adventure, with ships unloading fresh fish and shellfish from all up and down the East Coast. Sometimes, on Sunday, we went with Grandpa Charley to his tobacco store. Then Lou would open the Busy Bee down the block and we would go behind the soda fountain and make ourselves fantastic ice-cream concoctions.

But usually, on Sunday, Grandpa Charley escorted Bobby and me to the American Museum of Natural History. Bobby got impatient with the expeditions after a while and took to the park instead, but I never got tired of the Museum. I think I was beginning to be a science sponge, even then. Room by room, over the years, we explored the massive building. Much later,

Jeanne and Bob Bendick on their wedding trip, December 1940 (Courtesy of Jeanne Bendick.)

when I was given the Nature Study Society's writing award in one of the bird halls of the Museum, I felt absolutely at home.

In the summer, my folks rented a house in Neponset, on the beach. It was too far for my father to come home every night so he stayed in our apartment during the week—sweltering in the city (no air-conditioning in those days)—and came out to the shore with the rest of the fathers in the neighborhood for weekends. Now Neponset is a part of New York City and an easy daily commute by subway.

One summer Dot decided that she would surprise my father and learn how to drive. She certainly surprised him. During her second lesson she drove into the garage and straight out through the back and that was the end of it. She was a most unmechanical person and never did learn how to drive. Some things that she had learned, she dismissed as being no longer interesting. Once, in her forties, she astonished us by sitting down at Lou's piano and playing some songs she had learned to play when she was growing up in Mobile. "Didn't like the piano," she said. "When Papa saw that I was never going to like it, he let me stop. That day to this,

The end of the honeymoon, 1940. "Our ancient car gave up the ghost and we had to come home by train (we were on our way back, anyway)." (Courtesy of Jeanne Bendick.)

I've never played. I just wanted you to know that I have some surprises in me." We regarded her absence at the piano all those years as a secret blessing. Lou loved the piano and played for at least two hours every day. He had no musical ear at all. That seems to be a family trait. I'm told that one night, when I was very small, George Gershwin was at the house, playing _An American in Paris,_ which he had just written. I put my hands over my ears, said firmly, "Too noisy!" and marched out of the room.

Occasionally in the summer we would go up to a farm in the mountains for a few weeks. It was the same kind of mothers-and-children, fathers-on-weekends arrangement. The farm was a big, old one that had been in the Meyers family since before the American Revolution, when all the families around there were Dutch settlers. It had a secret staircase that went down to some whitewashed cells under the house. We played settlers-and-Indians games in the cells. Sometimes the Indians were prisoners; sometimes the settlers howled behind the bars. Aunt Lucy Meyers, then in her eighties, would tell us tall tales about the old days while she laid out the thinnest, most delicious ginger cookies on the long slate kitchen table.

*

I made a special friend while we stayed at the farm. Miss Jessie Hasbrouck lived about a quarter of a mile down the road in a raspberry-colored brick house, built by a pre-Revolutionary Hasbrouck. It was a big house and she lived alone. Miss Jessie was white-haired, straight and angular as a picket fence. It seemed to me that she had another, inside life. One inside person recognizes another. On summer afternoons when I was tired of playing with the other kids in the barn or I

didn't feel like going down to the creek to swim with the rest of the gang, I would walk up the road to Miss Jessie's house where I played outside with her white cat and the blind white horse who lived in the pasture behind the house. Sometimes Miss Jessie asked me in to join her in lemonade and a cookie. She had a wonderful library, and after she watched me making love to the books she said that I could come any time I wanted. I was free to come into the library and even to play the player piano there but I was not to disturb her by wandering around the rest of the house.

I came often. I liked the feeling of getting away from the other children at the farm. I would slink off, dodging artfully from tree to tree up the lane. Then I would run along the newly paved county road, spread with hay to keep the concrete from drying out or buckling, open the big door quietly and slip into the dim library which smelled of lemon oil and spicy, sweetish, mildewed things. I would sit down at the player piano and play my two favorite songs: "The Japanese Sandman" and "When the Red, Red Robin Comes Bob, Bobbin' Along." One day I discovered that I could lock the music in place and read while the piano was playing. I read my way up one shelf and down another. I read books I understood and books whose meanings only glimmered in my head, but I loved the words.

I came again and again that summer, feeling like somebody different from my everyday, pudgy, ordinary self the minute I got into the dim and magic room, dreaming that when I was old I would be my own person, the

Bob Bendick in Burma. "Some of that mail has to be chapters of Making the Movies." (Courtesy of Jeanne Bendick.)

way Miss Jessie was. Sometimes I would meet her as I was coming or going, but she always pretended that she didn't see me.

*

When Bobby was eleven and I was twelve. Dot and Lou decided it would be good for us to go away to summer camp, to Camp Truda, in Maine. Bobby was in her element and I was in misery. Summer camp, at least in the beginning, is no place for a loner. I enjoyed my misery by going off by myself, which was not allowed. Later I capitalized on it and became a semi-famous camp poet, reading, at the weekly campfires, the sad and depressing poems I wrote during my solitude.

The Great Depression had begun. Max had long since retired. My father closed all the stores except one. Every day, behind that store, he ran a private breadline; there was no such thing, then, as government help for people who had no jobs, no money, no food. There were more customers in the breadline than in the store, but nobody was ever turned away. I still meet people who say that Max's Busy Bee saved their lives, when they had no place else to turn. Once, years later, we were in the car when my father was stopped for speeding. When the officer saw his name on the license he said, "I can't give you a ticket. Once, you were all I had."

We moved from our big apartment to a small hotel apartment with a kitchen that was smaller than one of our closets had been. Dot never complained and Lou never stopped being cheerful. We three women took turns cooking. Dot was fine with the fancy things, like gumbo and omelets. Bobby and I experimented with the rest. Both of us have loved to cook ever since.

*

When it was high school time I went to a new high school, which was to become the High School of Music and Arts the year we graduated. While I was there it was an annex of an old high school called Wadleigh, which was miles away in another part of Manhattan. The only time we got together with our main school was for our senior prom, and that was an event. Mary Ellington was in the senior class and her brother, Duke Ellington, volunteered himself and his band for the prom. We were the envy of every school in New York.

In those days there were no coeducational public high schools in New York City. Boys and girls were not supposed to be able to learn together. The people in our crowd were scattered in high schools all over the city. Mostly, we went to school by subway. Subways were an easy, inexpensive, hassle-free way to get around, and we all used them independently even before we were in our teens.

Almost the best thing about growing up in Manhattan was that you had so many choices—choices of schools, choices of things to do, choices of friends. Bobby and I never had the same friends, even though our friends were friendly. Like teenagers everywhere, our crowd paired and unpaired and gradually settled into more permanent couples. Over the years, Bob Bendick, one of my friends, got to be more than a friend. He was two years older than I was and before I finished high school he had started NYU on his way to become an engineer (engineers ran in his family), decided that that wasn't what he wanted, and left in favor of the Clarence White School of Photography. By the time I finished high school and made my brain-wringing decision to go to Parsons to study illustration instead of going to Wellesley, he and two of his classmates had opened a photography studio of their own.

Times were still hard when I started Parsons, so I worked my way through part of my tuition. Regularly, I helped teach a Saturday morning art class for children. Occasionally, the school sent me out on other jobs. One I liked best was restoring an enormous set of Italian tempera murals that were set into the dining-room walls of the president of the school. His chauffeur would pick me up at school in his cane-bodied Rolls Royce. What grandeur! (In those days, even a taxi was grand.) The murals were old and water-stained. At first, I was almost afraid to touch them, but the braver I got the more fun I had, and when I was finally finished I couldn't tell, myself, what parts were old Italian and what parts were me.

I picked up other jobs. One was illustrating a little book for one of my father's School-of-Journalism friends,

Jeanne exploring the Maine coast with her children, Karen and Rob
(Courtesy of Jeanne Bendick.)

now a publisher. The editor told me (kindly, of course) that I had absolutely no talent and suggested that I plan for marriage and a family.

The most important job for me during those years was doing some illustration for a children's magazine called *Jack and Jill,* which was published by the Curtis Publishing Company. Tina Lee, the art editor, was endlessly patient. We were learning grand things in school, but what we weren't learning was the ordinary, technical business of preparing art for printing—Benday, color separations, overlays. Tina Lee walked me through all the technicalities instead of simply throwing up her hands and calling in an experienced artist.

Tina Lee said that she wasn't sure why she liked my pictures; the people looked as if they were made of spaghetti. But children sometimes write to me saying that they like my pictures because I've drawn things the way *they* would draw them. Children do see things in another way from adults. I think that's because they look for different things. So when I draw and when I write, I try to look at the world their way and my way so that I end up with *our* way of seeing the world around us.

*

We moved out of the hotel to a bigger apartment again. Things were getting better for people in the United States, but worse in other parts of the world. Two of the boys in my class went off to fight in Spain and Hitler was on the rise in Europe. The year I graduated I won the coveted Parsons Paris scholarship; a year to study in Paris. I had dreamed about it and wished for it but it was another one of those wishes. The year was 1939, not exactly an auspicious time to be in Europe. Perhaps I wouldn't have gone even in the best of times. After

A farewell dinner party as the Bendicks leave for California: Jeanne Schaffner, game show producer Gil Fates, Jeanne Bendick, Bob Bendick, film director Franklin Schaffner, and Faye Fates, 1953 (Courtesy of Jeanne Bendick.)

years of being friends, Bob and I took a happy turn and became engaged. Weighing that against Paris, Paris seemed not worth a year away.

When I got out of Parsons I had two jobs. For two days a week, I designed stripes for a company that made men's shirting. It was hardly illustration. Under a magnifying glass I counted threads and made stripes of different widths and colors. After those days I dreamed stripes all night.

The other three days I worked for a well-known fabric designer, Margarita Mergantine, designing materials to be used in rooms at the 1939 New York World's Fair. I drew purple fish skeletons, Pennsylvania Dutch hearts and flowers, and bold replicas of presidential signatures. Between the signatures there were stripes. I couldn't get away from them. Fabric design was better than shirt stripes, but it still wasn't illustration. I kept plugging my portfolio, with not much luck.

Meanwhile, Bob was plugging his photography portfolio. One day he was sitting in the waiting room of a large advertising agency, next to a somewhat agitated man who asked, while they were waiting, to see Bob's pictures. He liked them. He asked if Bob knew anything about motion pictures. Bob, who didn't, said, "Certainly."

The man, Bob Edge, was about to make a publicity film for the Canadian Government and now, at the last minute, his cameraman was sick. Would Bob like to take his place? "Well, yes, Sure!"

Bob rushed out, hired a movie camera, and we spent the next week practicing. On the trip, the filming went well. The agency was happy, Canada was happy, Edge was happy, and he and Bob got to be friends. Edge was on the verge of a fascinating new job. CBS was going to begin experimental television broadcasting. He was to be sports director. Would Bob Bendick be interested in being a television cameraman?

The job came through. Bob was one of the first three television cameramen for CBS-TV, a network being born. And we got married.

Soon after, I had a real illustration assignment: to do pictures for a science book called *What Makes It Tick?* A science book? Unusual. In 1944, children's books were hardly ever science books. I was working on *What Makes It Tick?* on Pearl Harbor Day. The book was hardly history, but it made me a science-book illustrator. Maybe if the book had been about what I scornfully called robins in aprons I would have spent the rest of my illustrating-life drawing cute animals. But I doubt it.

The next year or so was hectic. Television news was valiantly trying to cover the war. From a studio, of course. There was no such thing as a remote broadcast. And I was working with Mary Elting (who was writing

Bob Bendick, Jeanne Bendick, Jeanne Schaffner (front); Franklin Schaffner, Faye Fates, and Gil Fates (back). "Twenty-five years later, here we are again—and in 1986, still together, when we can be." (Courtesy of Jeanne Bendick.)

under the name Campbell Tatham) on the illustrations for a book called *The First Flying Book,* which was a rebus—pictures took the place of some of the words. And it became the first of the Franklin Watts "First Book" series. After the *First Book of Boats* we abandoned the rebus format; it was too clumsy and confining.

That *First Flying Book* has had many incarnations over more than forty years and it's fun for me to compare the first and latest versions. I have written all except that first one. One thing about being a science writer—you have to be prepared to update your books as things change. Technology changes fast. Inventions build on inventions and new discoveries make some old ways of doing things and thinking about things obsolete. This is usually truer of technology than it is in the natural sciences, but new ideas there, too, can make something that was regarded as fact suddenly wrong. In 1965 I wrote a book for Rand McNally called *The Shape of the Earth.* It was reviewed as an excellent, accurate introduction to the evolution of earth geology. A few years later, along came the theory of plate tectonics and the way the earth in my book changed shape wasn't accurate any more.

Part of the fascination of science is that things are always changing. Scientists don't say, "This is how it is, and that's final." They say, "Maybe this is how it is. Let's see." When you're writing science, that has to be part of your working philosophy and you have to be willing to change what you've written. People ask if that's not a nuisance and a bore, but it's not. There is pleasure in refining anything and making it right. Keeping up to date keeps your brain awake, too. Along the

way you learn a lot and you also have a chance to make the whole book better. I have completely rewritten *The First Book of Space Travel* six times over the last thirty years. The first time I wrote it, nobody had even orbited the earth. Many people thought that the very idea of space travel was fantastic—something that happened only in science fiction or in the comics.

*

When World War II was not too old, CBS-TV went off the air for the duration and all personnel were assigned to radio. Bob began to get itchy and when the itch and his conscience got too troublesome, he enlisted in the U.S. Air Force. He was assigned to the Tenth Combat Camera Unit which, after some special training, was to operate in the China-Burma-India Theater. (The stateside adjutant of the unit was an actor named Ronald Reagan.)

When the unit left for overseas I gave up our apartment, Dot and Lou took a bigger one, and I moved in with them. The apartment overlooked the Hudson River, in Manhattan. At night, all during the war, I could see the convoys forming in the river and the hundreds of tanks moving down the parkway alongside toward their embarkation point. It was going to be a long war.

During a war the population seems to separate into two groups: the people overseas and the people at home. Even though they all have the same objective, they grow farther apart until they might be living on different planets. Bob and I decided that it would be good to have a binder, some tangible connection that would involve us both. A book seemed like a fine project. So I went to Helene Frye, the editor-in-chief at Whittlesey

Brigitte Bardot, Bob Bendick, and Dave Garroway in Paris. "Fantastic. I am at home with Karen and Rob and the measles." (Courtesy of Jeanne Bendick.)

House, the first Junior Book division of McGraw-Hill. I had already illustrated one book for them. I said, "I would like to write a book myself. About making the movies." And without blinking or asking what my writing credentials were, she said, "Well, do it."

Helene Frye was certainly one of the most important people in my working life. She had unflappable faith when I had an idea and she never punctuated her go-aheads with conditions. She also had a wonderful sense of humor which she brought to her relationships with authors. She was friend as well as editor.

Editors, like authors, have different styles, and authors who work for a number of editors learn to adapt to those styles without changing the way their own work looks in the end. Helene Frye and her successor, Eleanor Nichols, were completely hands-off editors. Alice Dickinson, at Franklin Watts, with whom I worked for many years, made her own clearheaded suggestions and then sat back and watched what I did with them. Lillian McClintock, who was my editor first at Rand McNally and then at Parents Magazine Press, was a totally involved, hands-on editor. Occasionally a manuscript would come back to me cut apart and reassembled line by line. This was disconcerting and often maddening until I cooled down and reassessed my masterpiece through her eyes. Of the dozen or so books that she edited over the years, I can't think of one that wasn't improved by her strip-mining of my original drafts.

So Bob and I wrote *Making the Movies* from hemisphere to hemisphere. I would write a chapter, send it to him; he would add, change, and criticize. In the course of the writing we acquired a third team-member, the CBI censor. All mail coming out of the area passed through the censor, who read every line. Personal letters sometimes had whole paragraphs scissored out but the manuscripts came and went intact, with the added comments of the censor in the margins. Once, when Bob wrote that something wasn't clear, the censor wrote underneath, "It's perfectly clear to me." Sometimes he would write. "This paragraph needs a little work." He even made suggestions of his own. At the end of the war, when Bob was home again, we pulled our long-distance book together and *Making the Movies* was published. I wish I had known who the censor was; he certainly deserved an acknowledgement.

Twenty-five years later, in 1970, we rewrote the book for young filmmakers. It was called *Filming Works like This.*

During the war my mother, the stay-at-home-wife (neither my grandfather nor my father ever agreed to her having a job), came into her own. She joined the American Women's Voluntary Services (called the AWVS), a group organized to do many kinds of work on the home front. Dot became an officer and eventually an aide to General Drum, who was the commandant of troop movements in the Port of New York. Dot left the house

every morning for someplace and came back in time for dinner. It was a marvel. She, who chattered about everything, who never could keep a secret, said not one word about where she went or what she did until the war was over. I think it was the best time of her life.

I was an AWVS volunteer, too. As the war progressed I found a niche of my own. We had a service booth on one of the Hudson River piers, through which soldiers and sailors funneled, rotating from overseas. They were not allowed to leave the pier, but a lot of them wanted to bring gifts to their wives or their girls. I was the designated shopper. The number-one gift request was for lingerie, preferably black. Clutching a list of sizes and a huge wad of bills, I plunged across town to Saks Fifth Avenue, where I became famous as "the underwear lady."

By this time the news was full of mysterious references to "electronic devices." I was so curious about these that I tried to do some research but I couldn't find a thing on a level I could understand. So back I went to Helene Frye.

"Electronics is a coming thing," I told her. "But everything I can find about it is too complicated for a layman and certainly too complicated for kids. There needs to be something on a simpler level."

"So write it," she said.

We had some senior scientist friends who had spent the war working on these secret things and they were enormously helpful. One of them even pinned a special

Jeanne Bendick, story editor, and Bob Bendick, director-producer, on the set of The First Look, *1965-66 (Courtesy of Jeanne Bendick.)*

clearance pass on me and walked me through a plant where they were manufacturing that thing called RADAR. If I had had the sense to realize how complicated the whole subject was I never would have tackled it, but since I didn't, I did.

I am not, by training, a scientist. Maybe what I am is a translator. I enjoy taking a complex science concept, breaking it down into components simple enough for me to understand, and then writing it that way for young people.

The result of that first experiment in simplifying was *Electronics for Boys and Girls,* which was published in 1944 and included a section on the energy in atoms. Not long after the book was published the atom bomb was dropped on Japan. I found myself an instant expert on atomic energy, with newspapers asking for interviews and publishing sections from the book. I felt like a charlatan. In the next edition the book became *Electronics for Young People.* It has been translated into more than twenty languages and has come through six editions, each one getting bigger and more complicated until the material could no longer be contained in one book and I could no longer contain or explain everything that has been happening in the field.

Writing, illustrating, and working for the AWVS kept me busy all during the war. I also managed to keep up with what Bob was doing in the CBI by reading the funny papers. One of the officers in the U.S. First Air Commandos was Colonel Philip Cochran, a good friend of cartoonist Milton Caniff who wrote and illustrated a popular comic strip called "Terry and the Pirates." One of the heroes of the strip was an Air Force officer called Flip Corkin, who was serving in the CBI. I still don't know by what mysterious method Mr. Caniff got his news, but the activities of Flip Corkin mirrored the activities of Colonel Cochran and the Tenth Air Force. So I knew about the first glider invasion into Burma and whatever else was going on—things that could not be told in letters—even before the news came out in the papers.

When Bob came home from overseas in the autumn of 1945, after the war with Japan was over, I was still living with Dot and Lou and so, then, was he. We searched for an apartment for months, more desperately as time went on and I was about to produce a baby boomer. There were no apartments anywhere. All the returning servicemen and their wives were in the same boat. Hopeless. Then my Aunt Rose, a staunch believer in the Power of Positive Thinking, told me, firmly, what my problem was. I wasn't thinking positively. She instructed me to fix in my mind *exactly* what I wanted and to concentrate on it. So I marched around New York, eyes glazed with concentration, mumbling to myself, "Four rooms and a terrace. Four rooms and a terrace."

One night at a party we met two other couples who were in the same fix. They had given up on finding anything and had arranged to buy a brownstone which

Writers' day at the Rye Free Reading Room: Steve Birmingham, Jeanne Bendick, John K. Hutchens, and David Dempsey. "We had fun." (Courtesy of Jeanne Bendick.)

had just been made into apartments. "We don't have anybody, yet, for the top floor," they said. "If you're interested, it has four rooms and a terrace."

The first time my Aunt Rose visited she panted up the three steep flights and said, indignantly, "You forgot to think of an elevator!"

The terrace was really a roof that opened off our bedroom. We whitewashed the brick wall that formed one side and I painted a big tree on it. We lived there until Rob was three and Karen was a year old. Two excursions a day up and down the stairs and out to the park were a real hassle, along with my work. Besides, I had been working in the living room and I really needed more space. So we moved out of town. We have never lived in a real city since then.

*

When I was doing more illustrating than writing I was very lucky in my authors and I learned a lot from them. From Nina and Herman Schneider, I learned to be careful and methodical in building the subject of a book, so that each step was a logical outcome of the step before it. I also learned that where there were investigations or experiments involved, to do them myself before I tried to illustrate them. When a reader tries to build something from pictures and finds that it can't be built, or that an investigation just doesn't work, that's a breach of faith. The placement of a tack or a paper clip or the thickness of a rubber band can make the difference between a working model and a disappointment, or a successful investigation and a confusion. In working out investigations I've always been partners with kids; after all, they are the ones who are going to try those investigations. I've always written my own captions, too, step-by-step, even for books I was only illustrating.

Of course all this home industry meant a lot of hands-on messiness, but the results were worth it. My favorite result was a soapbox car we made ourselves, while I was writing *The First Book of Automobiles.* All four of us scandalized the neighbors in Beverly Hills by coasting down the street in our conglomeration of wooden boxes, old wheels, and other found objects.

Over a period of twenty years, even after I was mostly an author myself, I illustrated a series of books with Dr. Glenn O. Blough, and we were a good team. I think that it is an illustrator's obligation to get on paper the pictures in the writer's head. Nobody should come between author and illustrator—not editor or agent or even the post office, if it can be avoided. Books come together with a wholeness when there is a real exchange of ideas. That's why I feel so lucky to be author and illustrator, exchanging ideas with myself.

I probably learned more about writing from Dr. Blough than from anyone else. He was, at the time, Specialist in Elementary Education in the U.S. Office of Education and was not only an author but a lecturer and, above all, a teacher. He could fascinate an entire audience of elementary-school children into spellbound silence—a feat of mammoth proportions. The Schneiders' books made technology understandable. Glenn Blough's books made the workings of the natural world more familiar and less mysterious.

That's what I've tried to do in so many of the books I've written for young children, starting with *All around You* in 1955. It's a particular platform of mine that at the lower elementary-school ages, children are the most curious, the most open to ideas, the most challenged by the world around them.

Everything they learn about that world is another piece they can fit into a giant puzzle. Where does each piece

Jill and Bob Bendick, Jr., on their wedding day (Courtesy of Jeanne Bendick.)

fit to make the picture clearer? One part of the job I set for myself is to make those young readers see that everything is connected to everything—that science isn't something apart. It's a part of everyday life. Another aim is to involve them directly in the text so they will ask themselves questions and try to answer them. If they can't answer, that's not really important. Science, like life, is open-ended and nobody knows all the answers. Questions are more important than answers.

Who knows, in science, what will happen next to change everything? If I were a fairy godmother, my gift to every child would be curiosity.

*

For several years, while Bob was the director of CBS-TV News, Sports, and Special Events, we lived in Fresh Meadows, a huge development on Long Island that was actually part of New York City. When we moved there, Fresh Meadows was an enclave almost entirely inhabited by ex-servicemen and their families. The place was like a living "Peanuts" comic strip. There was a wonderful nursery school and kindergarten, headed by Marguerita Rudolph, a Bank Street School expert and a great proponent of hands-on science. She was the first person I knew who believed that science teaching should begin in nursery school and kindergarten, and I have shared her soap box ever since.

In 1952 Bob was coaxed away from CBS by Lowell Thomas and Merian Cooper, to work in a new medium called *Cinerama.* Friends in the CBS News and Special Events department gave him a big surprise party when he left. Ed Murrow was the emcee.

Cinerama was the first wide-screen movie process and it changed the shape of the movies. The night *This Is Cinerama* opened in New York they were, literally, still pasting the pieces together. When it became evident that Bob wasn't going to have time to come home to

Karen and Peter Holton on their wedding day (Courtesy of Jeanne Bendick.)

Fresh Meadows to dress, he asked me to bring his evening clothes to the city when I came in. It was not one of my finer moments as a helpmate. I saw the suspenders dangling under the jacket and assumed that they were attached to trousers. Wrong. After some frantic telephoning to tall friends, we located trousers long enough, from the kids' doctor, Ben Spock. No shoes, though. Bob shared the ovations in borrowed pants and sneakers.

During the next few years we ricocheted from coast to coast, from movies to television. It didn't interfere with my work at all; I could write and draw wherever we were. Bob did another Cinerama, the *Today* show, *Wide Wide World, Today* again, and all kinds of specials. He was away a lot so my evenings were free to work in—a habit I found hard to displace later. I was doing book after book, feeling efficient and prolific, though at one point when he was in Paris with *Today,* and I was at home with Karen and Rob, both engulfed in measles, I certainly felt put upon. But a book called *Have a Happy Measle, a Merry Mumps, and a Cheery Chickenpox* came out of that, with the three of us working together. Kids make good science writers if they are interested and involved in a subject. They write simply. I try to do that, too. Almost thirty years later, I still find that book in libraries and I still get letters from children who have fun with it. Measles and mumps aren't around much any more, but funny stories are.

Finally we were back East to stay. During our bounces between California and the East we acquired and parted with houses and boats. (We have always had boats. Away from the sea, we are like lemmings.) We made friends all over the world and loved them all. (I have long ago ceased being a loner.)

And we had dogs. Dogs! First there was Taffy, a beagle whose favorite food was furniture legs, whose favorite drink was anything in a glass on the floor, and whose favorite pal was a parakeet named Pete, who had the fly of the house. Then there was Guido, ancestry unknown, adopted from the pound when he was an adorable ball of gray-brown fluff. Guido grew exponentially until he was the size of a bear, with a disposition to match. He hated everyone, man and beast, who wasn't inside our house. The neighbors kept stats on the number of people he treed every year. He was awful, but we loved him. After Guido there was Jenny B., a German shorthair pointer who was very beautiful, very elegant, and very dumb. And finally, the best dog of all, Friday, the offspring of a family English sheepdog and the next-door gentleman English pointer, who had been no gentleman. Friday was huge, loveable, funny, smart, and we still mourn her.

*

Bob and I had never really worked together until we had an idea for a children's television program based on the "First Book" series. We called it *The First Look* and

Grandchildren Rebecca, Robin, and Eric Bendick. "Happily, they are all characters." (Courtesy of Jeanne Bendick.)

we did it for NBC for a year. He was producer-director; I was editor of all scripts and writer of some and we had a fine cast, headed by the folksinger Oscar Brand, who wrote the music while I wrote the lyrics.

In 1968, I received a call from Mike Atkin (more formally known as J. Myron Atkin), dean of the Department of Science Teacher Training at the University of Illinois. He asked me to meet him to discuss a project he hoped I would be interested in. (I had known Mike many years before, when he was Rob's first-grade science teacher.) Now he was conceptualizing and coordinating a big project: a new science textbook series for Ginn & Company. Would I like to be involved in writing the kindergarten and the lower elementary grades? Isaac Asimov and Roy Gallant were going to write grades four through seven. My first reaction was to run fast in the other direction; I knew the project would take years. But what a challenge! The idea was that each of us, three science writers for young people, with three different styles and philosophies, would be free to handle the material in our own ways. Who could resist?

The science series was the first time I was a writer only. Other artists were going to do the illustrations. I was so accustomed to thinking of text and pictures as complementary parts of whatever I was writing that at first the idea made me uneasy. Then I was grateful. Each was a full-time job.

Writing a science textbook series is an enormous, coordinated team affair. It involves many kinds of editors, teachers, scientists in different fields, reading specialists, psychologists, people who design investigations and experiments, book designers, artists, and eventually, during a testing period, the children and their classroom teachers at the levels for which the books are written. We all read each other's work. Chapters were changed and changed again. Strands were included, dropped, emphasized, and deemphasized.

There has been a great deal written about how textbook publishers shy away from controversy and that is somewhat true. A textbook series is such an enormously expensive production that there is big pressure on publishers not to offend any large group or any small but powerful group in any state that is considering the adoption of those textbooks. During the years we were working on the science series, Xerox bought Ginn & Company but the team remained intact. We got to know each other better than some families do.

We produced everything first in pamphlet form and those versions were tested at all grade levels across the country. One of our goals, of making the children (and the teachers) reach a bit for the material, took something of a beating. Teachers said the reading level was too high so we wound up moving all the material up a grade. The kindergarten level became grade one and I wrote a new kindergarten level to put under the others.

As always, the children in our neighborhood helped to set up my investigations. For one project we made a very big terrarium that was to become the marshland/

woodland community we were studying. We inhabited it with chameleons, a toad and two frogs, a turtle, a salamander, and a tree frog. The human creators and observers came in every day to watch; to see whose territory was whose, who was fighting or eating whom. We kept a diary that became part of the science book. It was full of surprises.

We *knew* that the chameleons had to be a male and a female because two males would fight and one would probably wind up dead. Our happy pair lived happily, even after we discovered that they were both males. I love surprises!

Bob took a lot of the photographs for the books. We made a six-week drive across the country taking pictures so the children in the pictures and the places where they lived were a true cross-section. It was a wonderful experience because everyone wanted to help when they heard what we were doing. A state trooper took time off to drive up a canyon to show us where a pair of golden eagles had chicks in a cliff nest. A whole elementary school in the Tetons took two days out to work with us. Strangers fed us, put us up for the night, and passed us on to other people in other places. Everywhere, children appeared, magically, to be in the pictures. When Dr. James Ashley, the senior editor of the series, asked how we always happened to find children in the right places, Bob told him that we carried a set of blow-up children in the car to use when we needed them.

Jeanne Bendick on Jump, 1986 (Courtesy of Jeanne Bendick.)

"Key deer visiting the house in Big Pine." (Courtesy of Jeanne Bendick.)

Bob and I like working together even though sometimes we have some heated discussions. (At least, that's what we call them. Once when the Writers Guild was striking the Directors Guild, we built a chair barricade across our studio.) Though we often go our separate work ways, we have had a good time doing things as a team. One project was a filmstrip series (two series really), for Miller-Brody/Random House, titled *Monsters and Other Science Mysteries* and *Dreams and Other Science Mysteries*. Our idea was to lure reluctant students into science by baiting the hook with the mysteries they love. *The Mystery of the Loch Ness Monster* is really about changing ecosystems and extinctions, and so is *The Mystery of the Abominable Snowman*. *The Bermuda Triangle* is about latitude, longitude, and weather systems; *Atlantis* is about earthquakes and volcanoes; *Astrology* is about astronomy, and so on.

A really exciting joint project for me—Bob has long been used to round-the-world jaunts—was two one-hour documentaries for public television that explored the reasons for world hunger. Filming took us to Europe, Africa, Asia, and Latin America. Bob was producer-director and I was part writer, part unit-manager. (When a writer acquaintance asked me enviously how I landed such an exciting job, I told her that I slept with the producer.)

Some of our projects, now, are not-for-money. We have been doing a video history of Paget Farm, a fishing village on Bequia, an island in the Grenadines. Once the great whaling ships stopped at Bequia and picked up the men from Paget Farm to be sailors and harpooners. The Paget Farm fishermen still build the same small boats the whalers put out. They are proud of their tradition and we are proud to help them preserve it.

During all these years Bob, Jr. (we don't call him Rob any more) and Karen were growing up. Bob went to Williams College, then to NYU to study city planning. He married Jill Rice; they had gone together since they were in high school and we had always hoped it would happen. Now, Bob is the director of the Department of Environmental Management for the state of Rhode Island and Jill is a systems analyst. They have three children, Rebecca, Robin, and Eric, and they live in our next-door state. Happy for us. My sister's children and grandchildren all live in California.

Daughter Karen Watson dropped in and out of college and art schools, married, divorced, and is now married to Peter Holton, who is a physicist. It's a good mix. Along the way she was a house builder, gardener, baker, practical nurse, waitress, and finally came into her own as a very good artist. Karen and Peter live in Massachusetts. Close by, happy for us.

A funny thing happened to me on my way through my sixties. Sixty-ish seems to be some kind of boundary. You're certainly not young, but these days you're not really old, either.

You've had a lot of life experiences.

You've succeeded, exceeded, or failed at your life work.

Your wishes and dreams have come true or they haven't.

Your children are probably grown and, hopefully, are on their own.

Most of your obligations have dropped away.

Parsley (Courtesy of Jeanne Bendick.)

It's a time when you don't have to compromise. You can do things exactly the way you want to do them. You can even be eccentric, if that pleases you.

It's a time when mistakes hardly matter. Unless they are fatal.

It's a time when some people worry about fitting into the world, about accepting new, unfamiliar ideas. It doesn't really matter if you accept them or not; you and the world will both get along. For stubborn years I have put books together like collages, editing with scissors and Scotch tape. Now I have a word processor and rewriting is pure pleasure. I'm trying new things. I even like them.

Now's the time to catch up on the things I've always wanted to do.

So I'm writing an adult mystery.

Writing only the books that really challenge or especially interest me.

Teaching students to get their thoughts on paper in some kind of logical, organized way.

Helping elementary schoolteachers see that they don't have to panic at the idea of teaching science. Even if they don't know all the answers, saying, "Let's see if we can figure this out together," is one of the most satisfactory answers there is.

I don't really want to have a secure, pleasant, safe decline. Luckily, neither does Bob. It's a time to see what's on the blue highways, off the express roads; to take detours, drop into new niches, try on different costumes, have adventures. Adventures can last an hour, a month, or the rest of your life. When you're my age, your children may shake their heads and worry, but your grandchildren will brag about you. And think of all the things you'll have to write in your memoirs!

*

Bendick contributed the following update to her autobiographical essay in 2011:

Well, it's 2011 and I still haven't gotten to my memoirs, or even finished the mystery. A lot has happened on the way into my nineties. The years have been very full. I've lived in different houses in new places. I've seen new things in other countries, had new ideas, written a couple dozen new books, and illustrated more. Most important, I have a splendid and bigger family: In-laws I love, grandchildren, and even great-grandchildren.

As life moved along, everyone was growing up and moving around. Rob is with the Nature Conservancy now and lives mostly in Washington, DC. He and Jill also spend some time living in Jamestown, Rhode Island, and some time in Florida. My grandchildren all went in different directions—Becky went to Yale, Robin went to Smith, Eric went to Brown, and they are all married now. Becky is a geophysicist and a professor at the University of Montana in Bozeman. Earthquakes are her specialty and she tracks them in far places. (Becky and I have done a series of posters together, explaining earthquakes, how to build for them, and what to do in an earthquake emergency. They hang in public places in Himalayan earthquake zones and in Haiti.) Becky is married to Grant Kier and they have a daughter, Fiona. Robin is a teacher, when she's not busy being a mom to Aiden and Rory. She is married to Jim Plaziak and they live in Narragansett, Rhode Island. Eric is a nature filmmaker. He and Suzanne have a daughter, Talia, and they live in Bozeman. I'm four times a great-grandma. It's hard for me to believe.

Karen and Peter Holton are still happily in Lexington, Massachusetts. Karen is well known for her beautiful collages and Peter does his physics with nuclear medicine. Their son, Jamie, is in nursing school. He has been an EMT since he started college and has always had a passion for emergency medicine. Their daughter, Emily, is at Lyndon State College in Vermont. She manages everything so well that she will be anything she wants to be!

One of my earliest wishes—even before I could spell the word—was to be an archaeologist. We have done a lot of traveling in Egypt, in Greece, and in both Americas. Studying early civilizations deepened my respect for and curiosity about the ancient world, about how those long-ago people learned what they knew and made what they made, to leave us the bricks on which our world today is built. I have never had a chance to do my digging in the ground, but I'm deep in the past just the same. I do my digging in books, maps, and in the myths those people invented to try to explain what was happening in the world around them.

When did science begin? At first, people made up the answers to their questions. They imagined super beings who directed the action in the world around them. These myths were the only explanations until some of the most curious and thoughtful set about trying to *prove* their answers. While researching these ancient thinkers, I fell in love with the Greek scientist, Archimedes, who was born in Sicily in 287 B.C. I asked Franklin Watts if I could do something different from the kind of books I'd been doing for years. What I had been doing was *explaining* what we now know about how the world works, about the things we have found out, bit by bit, atom by atom, over thousands of years. So we have thousands or millions of answers now. We don't have to think about things *from the beginning.*

Imagine what this means. In Archimedes's day there were only ideas and wild guesses. Archimedes gave the world a logical way of thinking about things—of putting them in order so he could prove (or disprove) his ideas as he went along. He was a mathematician, a physicist and an inventor. (When Bob and I were in Egypt we saw farmers still using one of his inventions, Archimedes' screw, to lift water from the Nile for irrigating their fields.)

Archimedes and the Door of Science was first published by Franklin Watts in 1962 and it's been translated into many languages. Then, somewhere along the way, I wasn't paying attention and the copyright lapsed. (Authors should never be that absentminded.) In 1995 I got a letter from Bethlehem Books, saying that since *Archimedes* was now in the common domain, they would like to reissue it as a paperback. Generously (they were not obliged to do it) they would pay me

standard royalties. And would I be interested in doing a new book for them? Yes, I would! I could hardly wait to get back to the Greeks.

I had a wonderful time browsing through the very long list of Greek wise men (Oh, my, what we have learned from those ancient Greeks!) and decided on Galen, a physician who lived in the second century. (The Greek Hippocrates was a much-more-famous medical name from an even older time, but nobody is sure about Hippocrates. Was he one person, or was he a line of doctors whose medical prowess was shared by generations of Hippocrateses, by family lore, passed from generation to generation?) Galen was physician to emperors and gladiators. He was famous in his own time and his ideas were so respected that they were taught in medical schools for 1,500 years. Some of his ideas turned out to be wrong, but he was on the path to medicine today.

I also did a book about Herodotus, my almost-favorite of the ancient Greeks, who lived 2,500 years ago. He wasn't exactly a scientist, but he was a great traveler, an acute observer, and a faithful recorder of what he saw, what he learned about the wars of his time, and the kinds of people he met on his journeys around the known world. You might call him the first war correspondent. You might call him the first historian.

*"**Winter view from our house in Guilford.**"* (Courtesy of Jeanne Bendick.)

He is often called the Father of History. (A few of his contemporaries called him the Father of Lies; some of his stories were hard to believe.)

My archaeology also took me to Galileo, who lived later, and then back to ancient Egypt and into the civilizations of the Americas. Almost the best part of a book for me is doing research for the illustrations. I had to imagine what Herodotus looked like and design a cart for him to travel in. How might Archimedes have drawn his diagrams? What kind of medical instruments did Galen use? Some of the research I did in maps and books. Some of it I did up close, looking at the real thing. I am very lucky to have been in the Egyptian and Mayan tombs of ancient kings; lucky to climb their pyramids, and sail their seas. I have stood on a street in Thera (now called Santorini), an island in Greece, which was destroyed by a volcano in prehistoric times, and I have wandered through the mazes in Crete where the Minotaur was supposed to live. (Actually, the maze is what's left of the hundred-room castle of a long-ago king of Crete.) It is eerie to stand on the street of an ancient city and imagine living there.

Luck is a fine thing. If you are lucky enough to live in New England, (I live in Guilford, Connecticut) winters are usually special. Snow is beautiful and we have always loved having a fire to dream by or to read or play *Scrabble* by. And for many years, we had the Florida Keys, too. We found our house there by accident. Years ago, driving around Big Pine Key, we saw a homey-looking house, right on the water. (Of course, everything is on the water there.) Tacked onto a gnarled tree was a sign: "Can Be Rented during Winter." We never even looked inside. We called the owner and then rented it for a month every winter for sixteen years. Big Pine Key is wild. Most of it is a wildlife refuge for Key deer, which are very small. But Key West, a different kind of adventure, is not too far away, and parts of it seem like a city out of another time. The town dock at Key West is a gathering place at sunset. Everyone there faces west, looking across the water to watch the sun go down. When the last red sliver of light disappears over the horizon there is a concert of applause. The world has made it through another day!

Bob Bendick (Courtesy of Jeanne Bendick.)

At Big Pine we had a little boat for fishing and exploring. We called it *Parsley,* because it was an extra touch. One year, on my birthday, we decided to do a little fishing before going into Key West to celebrate. The water between some small keys is very shallow, and taking what we thought was a short cut, we got stuck in the sand. We were safe, but high and dry for hours until the tide turned. Our birthday dinner was four Fig Newtons, but it was a lovely night and the stars were beautiful.

At home in Connecticut I have enjoyed working with teachers to help students put their ideas on paper. That seems difficult for some of them these days, because they are used to expressing themselves on the Internet in bursts of three or four words. You can give a name, or a location, or make a date in a very few words, but you can't *think* that way. Thinking begins with asking a meaningful question, then experimenting with ways to answer it. So I asked the students to each write a short science-fiction story, describing an imaginary planet, its landscape, and why it looked the way it looked, how the people there looked (and why), and how they behaved (and why). There were howls about extra homework, but over the course of our once-a-week sessions, we wound up with some wonderful, logical stories. Some of them were pages long.

"Kokopelli, our last boat." (Courtesy of Jeanne Bendick.)

Bob died in 2008. We had been married for sixty-seven years and lived a great life together. He became an excellent carver after he retired from the world of television and film, and I had a fine time painting some of his carvings. The house is full of things we collaborated on. Lately, I've been painting a lot, translating some of our adventures to look like ancient Greek murals. Cars become chariots, jeans become togas, water spouts become Scylla and Charybdis. In one painting we stand in line with the Egyptian gods and goddesses to visit the pyramids.

So many things have changed in all my years. I began my writing career on a typewriter and was very proud to get my newly modern word processor, which repeatedly became obsolete, replaced by computers of all shapes and sizes. When we lived in California (centuries ago!), I had a chance to see the first RAND computer. It was a city block square.

Once, it was considered odd to be an author of science books for children. I am happy that I was one of those early ones. And I'm happy that, now, we are so many!

*   *   *

BERNE, Jennifer

Personal

Born in New York, NY; married Nick Nickerson. *Education:* Attended Parsons School of Design and New School for Social Research.

Addresses

Home—Copake, NY. *Agent*—Caryn Wiseman, Andrea Brown Literary Agency; caryn@andreabrownlit.com. *E-mail*—jberne@fairpoint.net.

Career

Author and copywriter. Advertising copywriter in New York, NY, c. 1970s; freelance copywriter, 1980-89, 1991-2005. Teacher of advertising writing at School of Visual Arts, New York, NY.

Member

Society of Children's Book Writers and Illustrators.

Awards, Honors

Numerous awards for advertising campaigns; Distinguished Achievement Award, Association of Educational Publishers, for short story "Water Works"; Best Children's Books designation, Society of Illustrators—New York, CYBILS Award nomination, Wilde Award for Picture Books, 2008, and Teacher's Choice designation and Children's and Young-Adult Book Award, both International Reading Association, both 2009, and several state awards, all for *Manfish* illustrated by Éric Puybaret; CYBILS Award nomination for picture book, 2010, for *Calvin Can't Fly.*.

Writings

Manfish: The Story of Jacques Cousteau, illustrated by Éric Puybaret, Chronicle Books (San Francisco, CA), 2008.

Calvin Can't Fly: The Story of a Bookworm Birdie, illustrated by Keith Bendis, Sterling (New York, NY), 2010.

Under Blankets of Stars, illustrated by David Walker, Sterling (New York, NY), 2012.

On a Beam of Light: A Story of Albert Einstein, illustrated by Vladimir Radunsky, Chronicle Books (San Francisco, CA), 2013.

Contributor to periodicals, including *Nick, Jr.*

Sidelights

Jennifer Berne examines the life of a pioneering oceanographer and activist in her debut picture book, *Manfish: The Story of Jacques Cousteau,* a "poetic profile of a doer and a dreamer," according to a *Kirkus Reviews* critic. A former advertising copywriter who created one of the most popular slogans of the 1970s and 1980s—" When E.F. Hutton talks, people listen"—Berne has also written *Calvin Can't Fly: The Story of a Bookworm Birdie,* which focuses on the adventures of a studious starling.

In *Manfish* Berne depicts Cousteau's childhood fascination with the sea and his passion for filmmaking, both which proved instrumental during the French scientist's revolutionary underwater explorations. She also highlights Cousteau's inventive and curious nature, discussing his development of the world's first SCUBA-diving gear and his voyages aboard the *Calypso,* his research vessel. "Berne gently leads readers to Cousteau's passion for saving the underwater environment," Nicki Clausen-Grace remarked in a *School Library Journal* review of *Manfish,* and Gillian Enberg noted in *Booklist* that "in a final, inspiring message, Berne calls for young people to become caring stewards of Earth."

A wise bird puts his knowledge to good use in *Calvin Can't Fly.* Too busy reading to learn how to fly, Calvin the starling finds himself at a disadvantage when it comes time to migrate. After his family members devise an intricate way to tow him along, Calvin returns the favor by advising them on the best way to navigate through a storm. A writer in *Kirkus Reviews* described *Calvin Can't Fly* as an "irresistible story," and a *Publishers Weekly* contributor praised Berne's skill in describing the "valuable experiences to be found both inside and outside books."

Biographical and Critical Sources

PERIODICALS

Booklist, June 1, 2008, Gillian Engberg, review of *Manfish: The Story of Jacques Cousteau,* p. 104.

Kirkus Reviews, May 15, 2008, review of *Manfish*; September 1, 2010, review of *Calvin Can't Fly: The Story of a Bookworm Birdie.*

New York Times Book Review, May 10, 2009, Lawrence Downes, review of *Manfish,* p. 16.

Publishers Weekly, August 23, 2010, review of *Calvin Can't Fly,* p. 47.

School Library Journal, November, 2008, Nicki Clausen-Grace, review of *Manfish,* p. 105; November, 2010, Ieva Bates, review of *Calvin Can't Fly,* p. 65.

ONLINE

Jennifer Berne Home Page, http://www.jenniferberne.com (January 15, 2012).

Publishers Weekly Online, http://www.publishersweekly.com/ (October 27, 2011), Marc Schultz, "*Calvin Can't Fly* Takes off with Educators."

*   *   *

BICK, Ilsa J.

Personal

Married; has children. *Religion:* Jewish. *Hobbies and other interests:* Hiking, biking, swimming, gardening.

Addresses

Home—WI.

Career

Child psychiatrist, film scholar, and writer. *Military service:* Served in U.S. Air Force.

Awards, Honors

Braceland Award, Hartford Psychiatric Society, 1985; William Zeller Award, Institute of Living, 1986, 1987; Paul N. Graffagnino Award, Hartford Child Psychiatry Training Consortium, 1986; Laughlin fellowship, American College of Psychiatrists, 1987; grand prize, *Star Trek: Strange New Worlds II* short-story competition, 1998; second prize, Writers of the Future award, 1999; second prize, *Star Trek: Strange New Worlds IV* short-story competition, 2000; third prize, SEAK Medical Fiction-Writing Competition, 2003; Westchester Fiction Award, and Best Children's Books of the Year selection, Bank Street College of Education, both 2011, both for *Draw the Dark.*

Writings

Draw the Dark, Carolrhoda Lab (Minneapolis, MN), 2010.
Ashes (first novel in trilogy), Egmont (New York, NY), 2011.
Drowning Instinct, Carolrhoda Lab (Minneapolis, MN), 2012.

Contributor of fiction to anthologies, including *Star Trek: Strange New Worlds II,* edited by Dean Wesley Smith, John Ordover, and Paula M. Block, Simon & Schuster (New York, NY), 1999; *Be Mine,* edited by L. Marie Wood, Cyber-Pulp (Houston, TX), 2004; and *Crime Spells,* edited by Martin H. Greenberg and Loren L. Coleman, DAW Books (New York, NY), 2009. Contributor of nonfiction to anthologies, including *Mythologies of Violence in Postmodern Media,* edited by Christopher Sharrett, Wayne State University Press (Detroit, MI), 1999; contributor to periodicals, including *Challenging Destiny, Cinema Journal, Journal of the American Psychoanalytic Association, Paradox, Psychoanalytic Review,* and *Talebones.*

FICTION; BASED ON "STAR TREK" TELEVISION SERIES

Well of Souls ("Star Trek: The Lost Era" series), Pocket Books (New York, NY), 2003.
Lost Time (e-book; "Star Trek: Starfleet Corps of Engineers" series; also see below), Pocket Books (New York, NY), 2005.
Wounds (e-book; "Star Trek: Starfleet Corps of Engineers" series), two volumes, Pocket Books (New York, NY), 2005.
Ghost (e-book; "Star Trek: Starfleet Corps of Engineers" series), Pocket Books (New York, NY), 2007.
(With others) *Wounds* ("Star Trek: Starfleet Corps of Engineers" series; contains *Wounds* and *Lost Time*), Pocket Books (New York, NY), 2008.

"MECHWARRIOR: DARK AGE" NOVEL SERIES

Daughter of the Dragon, New American Library/WizKids (New York, NY), 2005.
Blood Avatar, Roc (New York, NY), 2005.
Dragon Rising, New American Library (New York, NY), 2007.

Sidelights

A versatile author who pens young-adult novels, science fiction, and scholarly works about cinema, Ilsa J. Bick has received critical acclaim for *Draw the Dark,* a supernatural mystery, and *Ashes,* a dystopian thriller. Bick, a child psychologist who lives in rural Wisconsin, explained that *Draw the Dark,* her debut work for teen readers, was based in part on the history of the region she calls home, a region that housed a camp for German prisoners during World War II. As Bick stated on her home page, these prisoners "were moved often, mostly to eliminate manpower shortages on farms and in factories because all the American men were off fighting the war. Most of the camps were so far out in the boonies that people had no idea the German P[O]Ws were there—and the government was happy to keep it that way."

Draw the Dark focuses on Christian Cage, a seventeen-year-old Wisconsinite who possesses the curious ability to sketch other people's thoughts and fears, sometimes with tragic consequences. After he defaces a neighbor's barn with swastikas in his sleep, Christian begins to channel the visions of a young Jewish boy from the 1940s who is witnessing a terrifying murder involving a town business leader using German prisoners of war for labor. *Draw the Dark* "is chock-full of action and vivid characterization," as Robbie L. Flowers commented in *Voice of Youth Advocates,* and a *Kirkus Reviews* writer observed that "Bick's tight plotting drives the action forward, and dream drawing sequences provide tantalizing clues." As Leah J. Sparks maintained in *School Library Journal, Draw the Dark* "brilliantly strikes a compelling balance between fantasy and contemporary fiction."

In *Ashes* Bick introduces Alex, an orphaned, terminally ill teenager who has survived the global disaster that followed an electromagnetic pulse that shut down the communication grid. Although almost all the adults were killed, the pulse transformed some adolescents into flesh-eating zombies. Along with two other survivors—Ellie, a strong-minded youngster, and Tom, a soldier on leave—Alex makes her way to Rule, a small community led by cultish religious elders. "This is an affecting postapocalyptic tale that divides its time between survival story and horror," *Booklist* contributor Cindy Welch remarked. A critic in *Kirkus Reviews* noted that in *Ashes,* the first work in her planned trilogy, Bick leaves readers "with a thrilling, terrifying cliffhanger and a number of unresolved mysteries."

Biographical and Critical Sources

PERIODICALS

Booklist, October 1, 2010, Daniel Kraus, review of *Draw the Dark,* p. 82; September 15, 2011, Cindy Welch, review of *Ashes,* p. 63.

Kirkus Reviews, September 15, 2010, review of *Draw the Dark*; July 1, 2011, review of *Ashes;* January 1, 2012, review of *Drowning Instinct.*

Kliatt, July, 2004, Hugh Flick, Jr., review of *Well of Souls,* p. 26.

Publishers Weekly, October 4, 2010, review of *Draw the Dark,* p. 48; July 11, 2011, review of *Ashes,* p. 59.

School Library Journal, November, 2010, Leah J. Sparks, review of *Draw the Dark,* p. 104; October, 2011, Heather M. Campbell, review of *Ashes,* p. 130.

Voice of Youth Advocates, December, 2010, Robbie L. Flowers, review of *Draw the Dark,* p. 464.

ONLINE

Ilsa J. Bick Home Page, http://www.ilsajbick.com (January 15, 2012).

Inis Magazine Online, http://www.inismagazine.ie/ (July 11, 2011), Sarah Rees Brennan, interview with Bick.*

*　　*　　*

BONWILL, Ann

Personal

Born in MD; married; children: one son. *Education:* College of William & Mary, degree (psychology); M.S.W. *Hobbies and other interests:* Traveling, baking, spending time with family.

Addresses

Home—VA. *Agent*—Marietta B. Zacker, Nancy Gallt Literary Agency, 273 Charlton Ave., South Orange, NJ 07079; marietta@nancygallt.com. *E-mail*—annbonwill @gmail.com.

Career

Writer. Worked as a clinical social worker, Montessori teacher, and autism therapist.

Member

Society of Children's Book Writers and Illustrators.

Writings

Pocket's Christmas Wish, illustrated by Russell Julian, Oxford University Press (Oxford, England), 2009, Barron's (Hauppauge, NY), 2010.

Bug and Bear: A Tale of True Friendship, illustrated by Layn Marlow, Marshall Cavendish Children (New York, NY), 2011.

Naughty Toes, illustrated by Teresa Murfin, Tiger Tales (Wilton, CT), 2011.

I Don't Want to Be a Pea!, illustrated by Simon Rickerty, Atheneum Books for Young Readers (New York, NY), 2012.

Sidelights

A former therapist and social worker, Ann Bonwill is the author of *Pocket's Christmas Wish, I Don't Want to Be a Pea!,* and several other picture books. First published in England, where Bonwill once lived, *Pocket's Christmas Wish* centers on a tiny bunny that discovers the spirit of the holiday season. On Christmas morning Pocket follows some footprints in the snow to a lovely cabin, where he shares his gift of a carrot with a hungry mouse. Writing in *School Library Journal,* Eva Mitnick commented that "the bunny's holiday quest" in Bonwill's story "has a quiet appeal for older preschoolers."

Two pals learn the value of an apology in Bonwill's *Bug and Bear: A Tale of True Friendship.* As Bear heads home for a nap, energetic Bug decides to tag along but quickly becomes an annoyance. After Bear yells at her friend, she feels so guilty that she cannot sleep. Bear soon sets off in search of her missing friend, finding Bug in a most surprising location. "Friendship is always a popular topic," Amy Lilien-Harper remarked in her *School Library Journal* review of *Bug and Bear*, "and the final solution and acknowledgment that both characters were wrong is refreshing."

Based in part on the author's childhood experiences, *Naughty Toes* focuses on Chloe, a spirited youngster whose unorthodox talents challenge her ballet teacher. With its artwork by Tesa Murfin, *Naughty Toes* presents young readers with "a refreshing take on the need to follow one's own heart-or feet," observed a writer in *Kirkus Reviews*.

Bonwill explores the theme of compromise in *I Don't Want to Be a Pea!* While preparing for a fancy gala, Hugo Hippo and Bella Bird cannot agree on an appropriate costume: Bella refuses to dress as a pea to accompany Hugo's princess, and Hugo will not disguise himself as a rock for Bella's mermaid to sit upon. After angrily going their separate ways, each has a change of

heart and they both arrive at the ball in spectacular fashion. The author "peppers her gentle friendship story with bits of knowing humor," wrote a critic in reviewing *I Don't Want to Be a Pea!* for *Publishers Weekly*.

Biographical and Critical Sources

PERIODICALS

Booklist, May 1, 2011, Andrew Medlar, review of *Bug and Bear: A Tale of True Friendship,* p. 90.

Kirkus Reviews, September 1, 2010, review of *Pocket's Christmas Wish*; March 1, 2011, review of *Bug and Bear*; August 1, 2011, review of *Naughty Toes;* December 1, 2011, review of *I Don't Want to Be a Pea!*

Publishers Weekly, December 19, 2011, review of *I Don't Want to Be a Pea!,* p. 49.

School Librarian, summer, 2011, Rudolf Loewenstein, review of *Bug and Bear,* p. 89; winter, 2011, Prue Goodwin, review of *I Don't Want to Be a Pea!,* p. 217.

School Library Journal, October, 2010, Eva Mitnick, review of *Pocket's Christmas Wish,* p. 69; May, 2011, Amy Lilien-Harper, review of *Bug and Bear,* p. 72.

Ann Bonwill's story in* Pocket's Christmas Wish *comes to life in Russell Julian's engaging acrylic paintings. (Illustration copyright © 2009 by Russell Julian. Reproduced by permission of Oxford University Press UK.)

ONLINE

Ann Bonwill Home Page, http://www.annbonwill.com (January 15, 2012).

Oxford University Press Web site, http://www.oup.com/ (January 15, 2012), "Ann Bonwill."*

* * *

BOUDREAU, Hélène 1969-

Personal

Born 1969, in Isle Madame, Nova Scotia, Canada; married; has children. *Education:* B.S. (biology). *Hobbies and other interests:* Walking.

Addresses

Home—Markham, Ontario, Canada. *Agent*—Lauren E. MacLeod, Strothman Agency, 197 8th St., Flagship Wharf 611, Charlestown, MA 02129. *E-mail*—helene@heleneboudreau.com.

Career

Writer and artist. *Exhibitions:* Paintings exhibited at Toronto Public Library, Toronto, Ontario, Canada.

Member

Canadian Society of Children's Authors, Illustrators, and Performers, Writers Union of Canada, Canadian Children's Book Center.

Awards, Honors

Surrey International Writing Contest shortlist, 2007, for short story "With Measured Breath"; second place, Writers' Federation of New Brunswick Literary Award, 2008, and Hackmatack Children's Choice Book Award shortlist, 2009-10, both for *Acadian Star;* Crystal Kite Member Choice Award finalist, 2011, for *Real Mermaids Don't Wear Toe Rings;* Ontario Arts Council grant.

Writings

FICTION

Acadian Star, Nimbus Publishing (Halifax, Nova Scotia, Canada), 2008.

Keep Out!, Nimbus Publishing (Halifax, Nova Scotia, Canada), 2010.

Water Hazard, Nimbus Publishing (Halifax, Nova Scotia, Canada), 2010.

Real Mermaids Don't Wear Toe Rings, Sourcebooks Jabberwocky (Naperville, IL), 2010.

NONFICTION

Crimebusting and Detection, Crabtree Publishing (New York, NY), 2009.

Miraculous Medicines, Crabtree Publishing (New York, NY), 2009.

Swimming Science, Crabtree Publishing (New York, NY), 2009.

Life in a Fishing Community, Crabtree Publishing (New York, NY), 2010.

Life in a Residential City, Crabtree Publishing (New York, NY), 2010.

Contributor to periodicals, including *Know* magazine.

Adaptations

Real Mermaids Don't Wear Toe Rings was adapted as an audiobook, Dreamscape, 2010.

Sidelights

Canadian author Hélène Boudreau writes fiction and nonfiction for children and young adults. Her debut novel, *Acadian Star,* explores a disturbing episode from

Cover of Hélène Boudreau's imaginative middle-grade novel Real Mermaids Don't Wear Toe Rings, *featuring cover art by Jennifer Jackman.*
(Sourcebooks Jabberwocky, 2010. Jacket art copyright © by JenniferJackman.com. Reproduced by permission of Sourcebooks, Inc.)

Canadian history: *Le grande dérangement,* in which thousands of individuals of French-Acadian descent were forcibly expelled from Canada by British authorities.

Acadian Star centers on Meg Gallant, an Acadian youngster who finds herself transported to the mid-eighteenth century and forced to face a critical decision: whether to return to her own time or rescue a new friend who is about to be deported. "The backdrop of the story happens to be the Acadian Deportation because it was a time in history I really wanted to learn about and share with my daughters," Boudreau told *All Things Girl* on-line interviewer Brigita Pavshich. "My main goal in telling this story, though, was to entertain my reader by putting my character in an unlikely situation and giving her big choices to make."

A teen discovers that she has inherited a most unusual condition in Boudreau's fanciful novel *Real Mermaids Don't Wear Toe Rings.* While soaking in the tub one day, a surprised Jade sprouts a mermaid's tail and her dad finally reveals an incredible secret: Jade's mom, presumed drowned a year earlier, was a part-fish, part-human "Pesco-sapien." Soon, the teen learns that her mother is still alive, kidnapped by nefarious merfolk, and she embarks on a rescue mission to reunite her family. "The first-person narrative brings Jade's experiences up close and personal for readers," Cindy Welch noted in her *Booklist* review of *Real Mermaids Don't Wear Toe Rings.* A critic in *Kirkus Reviews* also applauded the work, stating that Boudreau's "appealing heroine, zippy prose and a preposterous plot make entertainment for young teens."

Biographical and Critical Sources

PERIODICALS

Booklist, December 15, 2010, Cindy Welch, review of *Real Mermaids Don't Wear Toe Rings,* p. 50.

Canadian Review of Materials, October 16, 2009, Barbara McMillan, reviews of *Crimebusting and Detection* and *Miraculous Medicines.*

Kirkus Reviews, November 1, 2010, review of *Real Mermaids Don't Wear Toe Rings.*

Resource Links, February, 2010, Susan Prior, review of *Life in a Fishing Community,* p. 22.

School Library Journal, February, 2010, Anne Chapman Callaghan, review of *Life in a Fishing Community,* p. 99; January, 20111, Mandy Lawrence, review of *Real Mermaids Don't Wear Toe Rings,* p. 100.

ONLINE

All Things Girl Web site, http://allthingsgirl.com/ (November-December, 2009) Brigita Pavshich, interview with Boudreau.

Hélène Boudreau Home Page, http://www.heleneboudreau. com (January 15, 2012).

Yorkregion.com, http://www.yorkregion.com/ (November 21, 2008), Simone Joseph, "Writer, Painter Makes the Grade: 10 Minutes with Hélène Boudreau."*

*   *   *

BOYDEN, Linda 1948-

Personal

Born July 6, 1948, in Attleboro, MA; daughter of Ray and Marie Simmons; married John P. Boyden (an engineer), 1988; children: A. Rachel, Eámon, Maeve; (stepchildren) Luanne, John, Jr. *Ethnicity:* "Caucasian/Native American." *Education:* Framingham State College, B.S. Ed., 1970; University of Virginia, M.Ed., 1992. *Hobbies and other interests:* Hiking in national parks, reading, sewing.

Addresses

Home—Redding, CA.

Career

Storyteller and writer. Elementary schoolteacher, 1970-97; full-time writer, beginning 1997. Teacher of writing at private middle school in HI; Sylvan Learning, Redding, CA, tutor, 2004-08; Redding School District, gifted and talented enrichment teacher, 2009—. Volunteer at Makawao Public Library.

Member

Society of Children's Book Writers and Illustrators, Wordcraft Circle of Native American Writers and Storytellers.

Awards, Honors

New Voices Award, Lee & Low Books, 2000, Wordcraft Circle of Native American Writers and Storytellers' Book of the Year in Children's Literature, 2002-03, and Paterson Prize, and Choices selection, Cooperative Children's Book Center, both 2003, all for *The Blue Roses;* Pleasanton (CA) Poetry Festival prizes; International Book Award finalist designations, 2011, for *Giveaways.*

Writings

The Blue Roses, illustrated by Amy Córdova, Lee & Low Books (New York, NY), 2002.

(Self-illustrated) *Powwow's Coming,* University of New Mexico Press (Albuquerque, NM), 2007.

(Self-illustrated) *Giveaways: An ABC Book of Loanwords from the Americas,* University of New Mexico Press (Albuquerque, NM), 2010.

Work represented in anthologies, including *Through the Eye of a Deer*, Auntlute Books, 1999; *Woven on the Wind*, Houghton Mifflin (Boston, MA), 2001; *Birthed from Scorched Hearts: Women Respond to War*, edited by MariJo Moore, Fulcrum Publishing (Golden, CO), 2008; and *The People Who Stayed Southeastern Indian Writing after Removal*, edited by Geary Hobson, Janet McAdams, and Kathryn Walkiewicz, University of Oklahoma Press (Norman, OK), 2010.

Sidelights

A respected storyteller who specializes in Native-American myths, Linda Boyden is the author of *The Blue Roses*, an award-wining tale about a youngster's relationship with her grandfather, as well as of the self-illustrated *Giveaways: An ABC Book of Loanwords from the Americas*. Boyden, who is of Cherokee and French-Canadian ancestry, has also spent more than thirty years in the classroom as an educator and literacy advocate. "I have spent most of my adult life leading children to literacy," she noted on her home page. "I enjoy performing at schools and working with students, encouraging them to play in their own sandboxes of words."

In *The Blue Roses* Boyden addresses an emotion-laded topic: the death of a loved one. Cared for by her grandfather while her mother works, Rosalie learns how to tend a garden under the man's tutelage, particularly a series of magnificent rose bushes. When "Papa" dies, Rosalie dreams of him standing in a wondrous garden, surrounded by the blue roses that will later grow up to bloom at his gravesite. "Boyden's prose is filled with color and imagery," according to a writer in *Kirkus Reviews*, and *Booklist* critic Lauren Peterson applauded Boyden for creating a "touching story, which clearly shows what healthy grieving is like."

"A traditional Cherokee myth says that the first stories came to people in dreams," Boyden noted on her home page. "My first book is based on a dream I had after my maternal grandfather passed on. I was thirty at the time, about to have my third child, and I couldn't travel the long distance to my grandfather's funeral. I was heartbroken. One night, Grandpa came to me in a dream. He stood in a beautiful garden (gardening had been his life-long hobby). Grandpa told me he was happy and to stop my carrying-on. It sounds strange, but I awoke with a new-found sense of contentment.

"Until then, death had terrified me. Seeing how happy he was changed that. Later I thought how poorly death is explained to most children. Wouldn't gardening be a great metaphor to help kids understand, to give them comfort and hope? These thoughts led to my book."

In her abecedary, *Giveaways*, Boyden presents twenty-six American English words that were derived from the languages of indigenous tribes in North, Central, and South America. She opens the work with "abalone", the sea creature called aulon by the Muwekma Ohlone Na-

Linda Boyden's imaginative self-illustrated books for children include **Giveways: An ABC Book of Loanwords from the Americas.** (Illustration copyright © 2010 by Linda Boyden. Reproduced by permission of University of New Mexico Press.)

tion of what is now Northern California. While Boyden discusses a host of familiar terms, including "canoe" and "maize", she also examines less-well-known words such as "hooghan" and "pogonip", offering a fact-filled history that extends the reader's knowledge of each. *Giveaways* serves as "an ebullient and salutary . . . reminder of our cultural and linguistic heritage," observed a *Kirkus Reviews* contributor.

"For as long as I can remember, I have loved words," Boyden once commented. "Before I could read, I told myself stories to fall asleep or stories for my dolls to enact. The first most important discovery of my life was learning how to read. It changed everything! I still loved to make up my own stories, but now I could enjoy what others had imagined, too.

"Kids are still as hungry for good books as I was. Leading them to their own literacy is what I enjoy doing most, next to writing. Children have stories to tell. Teaching them to express their words aloud or on paper and to enjoy the written words of others empowers them and enriches the world."

Biographical and Critical Sources

PERIODICALS

Booklist, May 15, 2002, Lauren Peterson, review of *The Blue Roses*, p. 1600.
Children's Bookwatch, December, 2007, review of *Pow-wow's Coming.*

Kirkus Reviews, April 1, 2002, review of *The Blue Roses,* p. 486; October 15, 2010, review of *Giveaways: An ABC Book of Loanwords from the Americas.*

School Library Journal, March, 2001, profile of Boyden, p. 22; June, 2002, Kathy Piehl, review of *The Blue Roses,* p. 88; February, 2011, Jayne Damron, review of *Giveaways,* p. 93.

ONLINE

Anderson Valley Post Online, http://www.andersonvalley post.com/ (November 3, 2009), Tracye Dethero, profile of Boyden.

Lee & Low Books Web site, http://www.leeandlow.com/ (January 15, 2012), "BookTalk with Linda Boyden, Author of *The Blue Roses.*"

Linda Boyden Home Page, http://www.lindaboyden.com (January 15, 2012).*

*   *   *

BROUGHAM, Jason 1971(?)-

Personal

Born c. 1971; father a sculptor and manager of automobile design sculptors; married Sandra Bache (a painter and photographer). *Education:* University of Michigan, B.F.A. (painting; with honors), 1993; Indiana University, M.F.A. (painting), 1997. *Hobbies and other interests:* Travel, Renaissance painting.

Addresses

Home—Brooklyn, NY. *Office*—American Museum of Natural History, Central Park W. at 79th St., New York, NY 10024-5192.

Career

Painter, illustrator, and dinosaur species sculptor. American Museum of Natural History, New York, NY, senior principal preparator/museum exhibit artist, beginning 1998.

Illustrator

Andra Serlin Abramson and Carl Mehling, *Inside Dinosaurs,* Sterling Innovation (New York, NY), 2010.

Biographical and Critical Sources

PERIODICALS

New York Times, April 25, 2006, Lily Koppel, "Inspired by Da Vinci . . . and Foghorn Leghorn," p. B2.

School Library Journal, December, 2010, Heather Acerro, review of *Inside Dinosaurs,* p. 133.

Science Scope, April-May, 2011, David Gillam, review of *Inside Dinosaurs,* p. 68.

ONLINE

American Museum of Natural History Web site, http:// research.amnh.org/ (December 13, 2011), "Jason Brougham."

Jason Brougham Home Page, http://www.jasonbrougham. com (January 15, 2012).*

*   *   *

BROWN, Tami Lewis

Personal

Born in WV. *Education:* Attended Smith College; Vermont College of Fine Arts, M.F.A. *Hobbies and other interests:* Aviation.

Addresses

Home—Washington, DC. *Agent*—Sarah Davies, Greenhouse Literary Agency; (703) 865-4990. *E-mail*—tami@ tamilewisbrown.com.

Career

Writer and librarian. Has worked an attorney; Sheridan School, Washington, DC, librarian and writer in residence.

Member

Society of Children's Book Writers and Illustrators.

Awards, Honors

Amelia Bloomer Project listee, American Library Association, and Notable Social Studies Trade Book for Young People selection, Children's Book Council/ National Council for the Social Studies, both 2011, both for *Soar, Elinor!;* work-in-progress grant, Society of Children's Book Writers and Illustrators, 2011, for *The Map of Me.*

Writings

Soar, Elinor!, illustrated by François Roca, Farrar, Straus & Giroux (New York, NY), 2010.

The Map of Me (novel), Farrar, Straus & Giroux (New York, NY), 2011.

Sidelights

Tami Lewis Brown profiles a little-known aviation pioneer in *Soar, Elinor!,* a picture-book biography aimed at middle-grade readers. *Soar, Elinor!* tells the story of

Elinor Smith, a Long Island native who took her first plane ride at the age of six and, just ten years later, became the youngest person in the United States to earn a pilot's license. In 1928, Smith gained fame and silenced those who doubted women's flying skills by guiding a stunt plane beneath all four of New York City's East River bridges. "The *New Yorker* magazine called her a 'feminist,' and pilots named her the 'Best Woman Pilot in America' beating Amelia Earhart and others," Brown told *Cynsations* online interviewer Cynthia Leitich Smith. "She was just a teenager, but nobody ever doubted she was a top flight pilot again. Elinor's determination to break through other people's barriers made her a great example for young people in the 1920s and for our time, too."

"Inspiration soars from every page" of the biography, John Peters commented in his review of *Soar, Elinor!* for *Booklist,* and a *Publishers Weekly* contributor described Brown's story as "a stirring tale of determination and moxie." According to Donna Cardon in *School Library Journal,* the author's "narration is fluent, engaging, and full of dialogue," and a *Kirkus Reviews* writer similarly observed that that the "prose is crystalline, lively and reads well aloud."

In *The Map of Me,* Lewis's debut novel, two sisters embark on an adventure-filled search for their missing parent. When twelve-year-old Margie and younger sister Peep arrive home from school one day, they discover a cryptic note from their mother that announces the woman's departure. Convinced that their mom, an avid collector of chicken memorabilia, is headed to the annual Rooster Romp at the International Poultry Hall of Fame, Margie and Peep seek help from their busy and disinterested father before deciding to take matters into their own hands. Stealing the family car, the girls set off for the poultry festival, mirroring their mom's own adventure. Brown "combines pathos and humor for an emotionally resonant story," a critic remarked in *Publishers Weekly,* and Corrina Austin noted in *School Library Journal* that in *The Map of Me* Lewis's "dialogue rings true and carries the story along."

Biographical and Critical Sources

PERIODICALS

Booklist, December 15, 2010, John Peters, review of *Soar, Elinor!,* p. 40.

Kirkus Reviews, September 15, 2010, review of *Soar, Elinor!*

Publishers Weekly, October 11, 2010, review of *Soar, Elinor!,* p. 42; June 20, 2011, review of *The Map of Me,* p. 53.

School Library Journal, November, 2010, Donna Cardon, review of *Soar, Elinor!,* p. 90; January, 2012, Corrina Austin, review of *The Map of Me,* p. 106.

ONLINE

Cynsations Web log, http://cynthialeitichsmith.blogspot.com/ (October 13, 2010), Cynthia Leitich Smith, interview with Brown.

Greenhouse Literary Agency Web site, http://greenhouseliterary.com/ (January 15, 2012), interview with Brown.

Tami Lewis Brown Home Page, http://www.tamilewisbrown.com (January 15, 2012).

Tami Lewis Brown Web log, http://tamilewisbrown.livejournal.com/ (January 15, 2012).

Teenreads.com, http://www.teenreads.com/blog/ (September 12, 2011), Tami Lewis Brown, "Tami Lewis Brown: Fact or Fiction?"

*   *   *

BURNE, Cristy

Personal

Born in New Zealand; married; children: two sons. *Education:* Murdoch University, B.S. (biotechnology); Australian National University, graduate diploma (science communication); Deakin University, graduate certificate (professional writing), 2004, M.A. (professional communication), 2007.

Addresses

Home—Perth, Western Australia, Australia. *E-mail*—cj@cristyburne.com.

Career

Science writer and editor and novelist. Taught high-school English near Osaka, Japan, for two years; Tsukuba Science City (biotechnology company), Japan, former technical editor; *Scientriffic* (children's science magazine), Canberra, Australian Capital Territory, Australia, former editor; *International Science Grid This Week* (weekly e-zine), Geneva, Switzerland, former editor in chief. Also worked as a performer for Shell Questacon Science Circus, Australia.

Member

Children's Book Council of Australia, Society of Children's Book Writers and Illustrators.

Awards, Honors

Young and Emerging Writer fellowship, Varuna House, 2006, and Voices on the Coast writing competition winner, 2008, both for *One Weekend with Killiecrankie;* Frances Lincoln Diverse Voices Children's Book Award, 2009, and Booktrust Booked Up selection, 2010, both for *Takeshita Demons.*

Writings

"TAKESHITA DEMONS" NOVEL SERIES; ILLUSTRATED BY SIKU

Takeshita Demons, Frances Lincoln Children's Books (London, England), 2010.
The Filth Licker, Frances Lincoln Children's Books (London, England), 2011.
Monster Matsuri Frances Lincoln Children's Books (London, England), 2012.

OTHER

Contributor of fiction and nonfiction to periodicals, including *Perth Woman*, *Metropolis*, *Kansai Time Out*, *Panorama*, *Helix*, *ScienceMax*, *Outdoor Australia*, *Cosmos*, *Cravings*, and *DestinAsian*.

Sidelights

A science writer who has lived in Japan, Switzerland, and Australia, among other locales, Cristy Burne is the creator of the "Takeshita Demons" series of fantasy

Cristy Burne teams up with sequential artist Siku on the fantastical graphic novel Takeshita Demons. (Illustration copyright © 2010 by Siku. Reproduced by permission of Frances Lincoln Children's Books.)

tales, which are drawn from Japanese folklore. In *Takeshita Demons,* her award-winning debut, Burne introduces Miku Takeshita, a Japanese school girl who does battle with a host of supernatural creatures. A contributor in *Kirkus Reviews* applauded the novel, describing it as "chock-full of authentic Japanese demons and gleefully entertaining."

Burne spent several years in Japan working as a teacher and editor, and during this time she took an interest in Japanese culture, particularly the beliefs in ghosts and demons, known as *yokai.* "There are dozens of supernatural yokai that most Japanese people will be familiar with," the author noted in an interview with Geraldine Brennan for *Paper Tigers* online. "They appear over and over again in all kinds of stories. Some are benign, some are nasty and some you're just not quite sure about. The demons that Miki has to deal with include the *nukekubi,* a kind of child-eating flying-head demon, and the *noppera-bo,* a faceless demon that can take on other personae."

In *Takeshita Demons* Miku moves to London, England, with her family after the death of her grandmother, a woman who had always protected them from demons. Unfortunately, evil creatures have followed the family to their new home and, led by a nukekubi disguised as one of Miku's teachers, they now kidnap Takeshita's younger brother, Kazu. With help from her new schoolmate, Cait O'Neill, Miku attempts a bold rescue, facing down a noppera-bo as well as the malevolent Woman of the Wet. According to Laura Ciftci in *School Librarian,* the "dialogue" in *Takeshita Demons* "helps the reader to formulate vivid images of each spooky demon, whilst maintaining a fast-paced adventure story." Burne continues Miku's story in *The Filth Licker,* in which the demons haunt Miku and her classmates at a school camp.

"I write because I love reading," Burne commented on her home page. "It's SO MUCH FUN to create stories and ideas in my head and share them with other people. I can't imagine my life without all the intrigues and mysteries of reading."

Biographical and Critical Sources

PERIODICALS

Bookseller, May 1, 2009, "Burne Wins First Frances Lincoln Award," p. 10.
Journal (Newcastle, New South Wales, Australia), May 5, 2009, Barbara Hodgson, "Memorable Year for Author Cristy"; June 8, 2010, Barbara Hodgson, "Double Celebration at Children's Books Centre."
Kirkus Reviews, November 1, 2010, review of *Takeshita Demons.*
School Librarian, winter, 2010, Laura Ciftci, review of *Takeshita Demons,* p. 225; autumn, 2011, Mary Crawford, review of *The Filth Licker,* p. 161.

ONLINE

Booked Up Web site, http://www.bookedup.org.uk/ (January 15, 2012), Cristy Burne, "My Top Five Interview Questions for Me."

Cristy Burne Home Page, http://www.cristyburne.com (January 15, 2012).

Cristy Burne Web log, http://cristyburne.wordpress.com (January 15, 2012).

Deakin University Web log, http://www.deakin.edu.au/ (January 15, 2012), "Alumni in Profile: Cristy Burne."

PaperTigers.org, http://www.papertigers.org/ (January 15, 2012), Geraldine Brennan, interview with Burne.

*   *   *

BUYEA, Rob 1976-

Personal

Born 1976, in NY; married; wife's name Beth; children: three daughters. *Education:* College degree.

Addresses

Home—Mount Hermon, MA. *E-mail*—rbuyea@rob buyea.com.

Career

Educator and author. Taught third-and fourth-grade math in Bethany, CT, for six years; Northfield Mount Hermon School, Mount Hermon, MA, biology teacher and football and wrestling coach. Presenter at schools.

Member

Society of Children's Book Writers and Illustrators.

Awards, Honors

New Voices selection, Association of Booksellers, and CYBILS Middle-Grade Award finalist, both 2010, and E.B. White Honor Book selection, and several state award nominations, all 2012, all for *Because of Mr. Terupt.*

Writings

Because of Mr. Terupt, Delacorte Press (New York, NY), 2010.

Mr. Terupt Falls Again, Delacorte Press (New York, NY), 2012.

Sidelights

A teacher of mathematics and biology who is based in New England, Rob Buyea became an author after a stray idea blossomed into his middle-grade novel *Because of Mr. Terupt.* Buyea's story takes place at a fic-

tional school in Vermont and is narrated by a group of preteens who chronicle their fifth-grade experience. The students in the class of fictional teacher Mr. Terupt were inspired by "bits and pieces of my former students combined with my imagination," as the author explained on his home page.

In *Because of Mr. Terupt* Buyea takes readers to Snow Hill School, where a new teacher finds a way to enrich the lives of the students in his fifth-grade class. Luke is the class brain and Peter is his trouble-making alter ego. Mousy Anna stays under the radar so that no one will ask about her home life, while Danielle is the designated target of school bullies. New to the school, Jessica excels at her studies but has trouble making friends, while Alexia has trouble keeping friends due to her aggressive personality and lack of loyalty. And Jeffrey would rather not be at school at all. As Mr. Terupt builds a relationship with his class, he also wins over each of these students by challenging them to excel and making school fun. There are those who disapprove of the teacher's innovative techniques, however, and when he is sidelined due to a playground accident both parents and students are left to evaluate his impact.

Cover of Rob Buyea's inspirational middle-grade novel Because of Mr. Terupt, *featuring cover art by Harry Bliss.* (Jacket art copyright © 2010 by Delacorte. Reproduced by permission of Delacorte Press, an imprint of Random House Children's Books, a division of Random House, Inc.)

Noting that Buyea's use of short chapters in *Because of Mr. Terupt* "keep[s] the story moving," Heather Booth praised the novel as "compelling" and "meditative," adding that it leaves readers with "much to ponder on the power of forgiveness." "The characters are authentic," added *School Library Journal* contributor Cheryl Ashton, and the seven student narratives "are skillfully arranged to keep readers moving headlong toward the satisfying conclusion." *Because of Mr. Terupt* is a good choice for teachers looking for points of discussion, suggested a reviewer in *Publishers Weekly;* Buyea's choice of "characters and conflicts . . . will be familiar to any middle-school student."

Biographical and Critical Sources

PERIODICALS

Booklist, October 15, 2010, Heather Booth, review of *Because of Mr. Terupt,* p. 63.

Bulletin of the Center for Children's Books, December, 2010, Karen Coats, review of *Because of Mr. Terupt,* p. 175.

Kirkus Reviews, September 15, 2010, review of *Because of Mr. Terupt.*

Publishers Weekly, October 18, 2010, review of *Because of Mr. Terupt,* p. 49.

School Library Journal, December, 2010, Cheryl Ashton, review of *Because of Mr. Terupt,* p. 104.

ONLINE

Northfield Mount Hermon School Web site, http://www.nmhschool.org/ (January 15, 2012), "Rob Buyea."

Rob Buyea Home Page, http://robbuyea.com (January 15, 2012).*

C

CHOAT, Beth 1964-

Personal

Born 1964. *Education:* Williams College, B.A. (history). *Hobbies and other interests:* Mountain biking, swimming, running.

Addresses

Home—NV. *E-mail*—BethChoat@TheInternational SportsAcademy.com.

Career

Police officer and writer. Worked as a sports journalist for two decades, including at *Sports Illustrated;* freelance radio journalist in South Africa, c. 2002. Las Vegas Metropolitan Police Department, patrol officer, beginning c. 2009.

Writings

Soccerland, Marshall Cavendish (Tarrytown, NY), 2010.

Sidelights

With a passion for athletic competition that encompasses her own time as a competitive cross-country skier, Beth Choat worked as a sports journalist for nearly two decades, chronicling Olympic and other world-class competitions in print as well as on radio broadcasts for National Public Radio and the British Broadcasting Corporation, among others. "I was perfectly happy writing news and sports stories," Choat explained on her home page, "but over time I realized that I had this incredible wealth of knowledge about what it's like to be a young elite female athlete. I also knew there were no smart sports books for and about girls who play sports." With this in mind, she was in-spired to write her first novel, *Soccerland.* She was also inspired to change her vocation, relocating from New York City to Nevada and beginning a new career as a police officer at the same time that *Soccerland* hit bookstore shelves.

Beth Choat channels her love of women's athletics into her sports-themed coming-of-age novel Soccerland. (Jacket photography copyright © 2010 by Robert Beck. Reproduced by permission of Marshall Cavendish Corporation.)

In *Soccerland* readers meet fourteen-year-old Flora Dupre, a talented soccer player who has become the star of her Maine high-school team. Flora's mother has always supported her playing, and since her tragic death from cancer two years ago the teen has dealt with the loss by focusing on a single goal: winning a spot on the U.S. Women's National Soccer League's Under-15 team. Her efforts win her a scholarship at Colorado's co-ed International Sports Academy, but here challenges face her both on and off the soccer field. As the best of the best, Flora's teammates provide her with true competition and the coaches are relentless in their demands. Socially, she must also deal with aggressive classmates, and her growing affection for a cute fellow athlete also sends the teen into uncharted territory.

In reviewing *Soccerland* for *Kirkus Reviews,* a writer noted that the book's focus on "the dedication, effort and sacrifice" of young athletes will be "riveting and inspiring" to Choat's intended audience. The author's experience following the career of professional athletes is also apparent, asserted Kim Dare, the *School Library Journal* reviewer classing *Soccerland* with the sports-themed novels of YA authors Mike Lupica and John Feinstein and recommending the novel as a good choice for librarians "looking to expand female representation" in the genre.

Biographical and Critical Sources

PERIODICALS

Kirkus Reviews, September 15, 2010, review of *Soccerland.*

Las Vegas Sun, June 7, 2011, Jackie Valley, "One Metro Officer's Passion: Fighting Crime, Penning Teen Literature."

School Library Journal, November, 2010, Kim Dare, review of *Soccerland,* p. 108.

ONLINE

International Sports Academy Web site, http://theinternationalsportsacademy.com/ (January 15, 2012), "Beth Choat."

Second Act Web site, http://www.secondact.com (June 22, 2011), Tracey Chang, "She Became a Cop at 46."

*   *   *

CLARE, Cassandra 1973-

Personal

Born July 31, 1973, in Tehran, Iran; daughter of American parents; married. *Education:* Earned college degree.

Addresses

Home—Brooklyn, NY. *E-mail*—cassandraclare@gmail.com.

Career

Journalist, short-story writer, and novelist. Journalist for entertainment magazines and tabloid newspapers, including *National Enquirer* and *Hollywood Reporter.*

Awards, Honors

Locus Award for Best First Novel finalist, 2007, and Teens' Top Ten selection, American Library Association (ALA), 2008, Georgia Peach Book Award Honor Book designation, Georgia Library Media Association, 2009-10, and Abraham Lincoln Award, Illinois School Library Media Association, and Young Readers Choice Award, Pacific Northwest Library Association, both 2010, all for *City of Bones;* ALA Teens' Top Ten selection, 2009, and Young Adults' Choices selection, International Reading Association, 2010, both for *City of Ashes;* ALA Teens' Top Ten selection, 2010, and Teen Choice Book of the Year finalist, Children's Book Council, both for *City of Glass;* numerous honors from state reading associations.

Writings

"MORTAL INSTRUMENTS" YOUNG-ADULT FANTASY SERIES

City of Bones, Margaret K. McElderry Books (New York, NY), 2007.

City of Ashes, Margaret K. McElderry Books (New York, NY), 2008.

City of Glass, Margaret K. McElderry Books (New York, NY), 2009.

The "Mortal Instruments" (omnibus), Margaret K. McElderry Books (New York, NY), 2009.

City of Fallen Angels, Margaret K. McElderry Books (New York, NY), 2011.

"INFERNAL DEVICES" YOUNG-ADULT FANTASY TRILOGY

Clockwork Angel, Margaret K. McElderry Books (New York, NY), 2010.

Clockwork Prince, Margaret K. McElderry Books (New York, NY), 2011.

OTHER

Contributor to anthologies, including *Turn the Other Chick,* edited by Esther Friesner, Baen Books, 2005; *So Fey,* edited by Steve Berman, Haworth Press, 2007; *Magic in the Mirrorstone,* edited by Berman, Mirrorstone Books, 2008; *Vacations from Hell,* HarperTeen, 2009; and *Teeth,* edited by Ellen Datlow and Terri Windling, Harper, 2011.

Author's books have been translated into several languages.

Adaptations

City of Bones, City of Ashes, City of Glass, and *Clockwork Angel* were adapted for audiobook, Simon & Schuster Audio.

Sidelights

With her debut novel, *City of Bones,* Cassandra Clare introduces a complex cast of characters and a vibrant, supernatural otherworld that has proved popular not only with readers but with reviewers as well. The works in her "Mortal Instruments" urban fantasy series and its steampunk prequels, the "Infernal Devices" novels, have found their way onto numerous bestseller lists and earned a host of honors from the American Library Association and the International Reading Association, among other organizations. "My goal for my books is that I hope they are read and enjoyed by many people," Clare stated on her home page. "I would like for readers to enjoy my books the way I have enjoyed favorite books in the past."

In the "Mortal Instruments" series, which is aimed at a young-adult audience, Clare crafts a shadow world populated by nephilim (descendants of angels) and demons, along with vampires, werewolves, and fairies. The first three novels—*City of Bones, City of Ashes,* and *City of Glass*—chronicle the struggles of a group of teenage demon-killers—known as Shadowhunters—against a ruthless villain with magical powers who is intent on world domination. Clare's *Clockwork Angel,* the first book in her "Infernal Devices" trilogy, is set in Victorian England. This prequel series mixes steampunk elements into the Shadowhunter world familiar to fans of her "Mortal Instruments" books.

Clare's family traveled the world and moved often during her childhood. An only child, she was born to American parents in Teheran, Iran, and as a toddler she spent a month in her father's backpack while her parents hiked through the Himalayas. By early elementary school, she had lived in France, England, and Switzerland. On her home page, Clare admitted that moving so often made her childhood "somewhat lonely," but she also credits it with developing a strong attachment to books. "I was the quiet kid in the corner, reading a book," she recalled of her school days in an online interview with Cynthia Leitich Smith for *Cynsations.* "In elementary school, I read so much and so often during class that I was actually forbidden from reading books during school hours by my teachers." Clare's love of reading eventually grew into a desire to write. "Getting lost in fictional worlds, realizing the power of narrative," she commented on her home page, "made me want to create fictional worlds of my own."

By high school, Clare's family had settled in Los Angeles, California, and the teen was busy writing stories and sharing them with her classmates. After graduating from college, she worked as a journalist, writing for entertainment magazines and supermarket tabloids such as the *National Enquirer.* In 2006, she left reporting behind to write fantasy fiction full time.

The idea for the "Mortal Instruments" books came to Clare while visiting a tattoo parlor in New York City, where the artists had created a stunning mural on the ceiling with their footprints. On her home page, she remembered that "it looked like some fabulous supernatural battle had been fought there by beings who'd left their footprints behind. I started thinking about a magical battle in a New York tattoo shop and the idea of a secret society of demon-hunters whose magic was based on an elaborate system of tattooed runes just sprang into my mind. When I sat down to sketch out the book, I wanted to write something that would combine elements of traditional high fantasy—an epic battle between good and evil, terrible monsters, brave heroes, enchanted swords—and recast it through a modern, urban lens."

City of Bones, the opening book of the series, introduces fifteen-year-old New Yorker Clary Fray. After witnessing a bizarre murder in which the killers simply vanished from sight, Clary learns that her mother has been kidnapped by demonic creatures. As Clary searches for her missing parent, she discovers an alternate shadow city existing within Manhattan. The Downworld, which remains unseen by humans (called mundanes), is populated by the nephilim, warriors descended from angels who are entrusted with protecting the world

Cover of Cassandra Clare's fantasy novel City of Fallen Angels, *part of her "Mortal Instruments" series and featuring cover art by Cliff Nielsen.* (Margaret K. McElderry Books, 2011. Jacket art copyright © 2011 by Cliff Nielsen. Reproduced by permission of Cliff Nielsen.)

from demons. These Shadowhunters have elaborate tattoos, known as runes, that are imbued with magical, protective qualities. With the help of Simon, a mundane, and Jace, a demon hunter, Clary battles a mastermind named Valentine who seeks the Mortal Cup, one of three "Mortal Instruments" that will give him ultimate power over the Shadowhunters. A *Publishers Weekly* reviewer praised the atmospheric setting in *City of Bones,* calling it "spot-on" and "informed equally by neo-gothic horror films and the modern fantasy leanings of Neil Gaiman." A *Kirkus Reviews* critic observed that "the story's sensual flavor comes from the wealth of detail" included in its descriptions of the werewolves, fairies, and vampires that inhabit the Downworld.

In *City of Ashes,* the second installment in the series, Clary seeks a cure to save her mother from a magically induced coma while also learning to harness her new-found abilities as a Shadowhunter. Valentine, who has been revealed as Clary's long-lost father, becomes the prime suspect in a series of grisly Downworlder murders as well as in the theft of the Soul-Sword, the second of the Mortal Instruments. Jennifer-Lynn Draper, writing in *School Library Journal,* called *City of Ashes* "well written in both style and language" and added that Clare's "human characters are well developed and quite believable."

Clary completes her hero's journey in *City of Glass* by traveling to Idris, the land of the Shadowhunters, in search of a cure for her mother. In this new realm she finds herself in the middle of an epic battle in which the nephilim have formed an uneasy alliance with the Downworlders, while both are threatened by Valentine's ruthless ambition. Clary's father has only to obtain the final Mortal Instrument, a mirror, to make himself invincible. Eliza Langhans, writing for *School Library Journal,* called the plot of *City of Glass* predictable, but added that Clare has a "talent for mixing hip, modern humor with traditional fantasy."

While *City of Glass* was originally intended to conclude Clare's fantasy series, she has since planned three additional novels. The first of these, *City of Fallen Angels,* continues the story of Clary and Jace by focusing on their relationship with Simon, who is now a vampire. When Simon comes under attack from unknown forces, he turns to Jace for protection. Writing in *Voice of Youth Advocates,* Stacey Hayman described *City of Glass* as "a fun read with plenty of action and tender emoting, plus a doozy, cliff-hanger of an ending."

Clockwork Angel the first installment in Clare's "Infernal Devices" trilogy, is set in Victorian London some 130 years before the events of the "Mortal Instruments" books. The novel focuses on Tessa Gray, a sixteen-year-old American who travels to England at the invitation of her older brother, Nathaniel. Tessa is kidnapped upon her arrival by the Dark Sisters, who are acting at the behest of a mysterious figure known as the Magister. During her captivity, Tessa learns that she has a unique

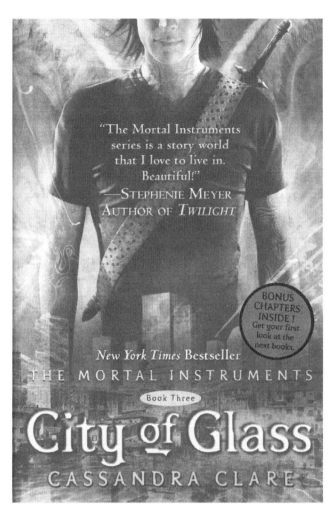

A young demon hunter prepares for an epic confrontation in City of Glass, *the final installment in Clare's "Mortal Instruments" trilogy.* (Margaret K. McElderry Books, 2009. Jacket art copyright © 2009 by Cliff Nielsen. Reproduced by permission of Cliff Nielsen.)

shape-shifting ability which her captors wish to exploit. After she is rescued by Shadowhunters Will Herondale and Jem Carstairs, Tessa helps the duo search for her adversary. Heather M. Campbell, reviewing *Clockwork Angel* in *School Library Journal,* wrote that "Clare has made each character unique," and the novel's "action-heavy plot takes off from the first page, propelling readers toward a dramatic conclusion." A *Publishers Weekly* reviewer also applauded the book's "authentic characters, who fight their own flaws and tragic pasts as often as they do evil."

Tessa's adventures continue in *Clockwork Prince,* the second installment in the "Infernal Devices" series. After finding safety at the London Institute under the protection of the Shadowhunters, Tessa hopes to discover the source of her unusual abilities. She also finds herself falling in love with both Will, a brave yet troubled individual, and Jem, Will's sickly yet devoted friend. Hoping to unlock the secrets to the Magister's sinister plans, Tessa uncovers a connection to her own hidden past, as well as a horrible secret involving Nathaniel. According to *School Library Journal* reviewer Caroline

Tesauro, *Clockwork Prince* "offers mystery, adventure, and, most importantly, a delicious love triangle." Susan Carpenter noted in the *Los Angeles Times* that "Clare . . . leaves no mossy stone unturned as readers travel from the chilly confines of the Shadowhunters' mansion to the tawdry inner-city underbelly of warlock opium dens and quasi-brothels in this lead-up to a major show-down."

Staying connected to her audience has been an essential part of Clare's writing career, and her decision to become a young-adult author has personal meaning. As she stated in a *Powells.com* interview, "I write books for teenagers because when I was a teenager, that was the best reading time of my life. It was the time I experienced reading the most intensely and read the most widely and with the most excitement. I wanted a chance to experience that again through writing for teens."

Biographical and Critical Sources

PERIODICALS

Booklist, March 1, 2009, Cindy Welch, review of *City of Glass,* p. 46; August 1, 2010, Lynn Rutan, review of *Clockwork Angel,* p. 45; July 1, 2011, Lynn Rutan, review of *City of Fallen Angels,* p. 58; November 15, 2011, Lynn Rutan, review of *Clockwork Prince,* p. 54.

Bulletin of the Center for Children's Books, June, 2007, April Spisak, review of *City of Bones,* p. 408; April, 2008, Spisak, review of *City of Ashes,* p. 327.

Kirkus Reviews, March 1, 2007, review of *City of Bones,* p. 218; February 15, 2008, review of *City of Ashes;* February 1, 2009, review of *City of Glass;* July 1, 2010, review of *Clockwork Angel.*

Los Angeles Times, December 4, 2011, Susan Carpenter, review of *Clockwork Prince.*

Magpies, November, 2007, Jo Goodman, review of *City of Bones,* p. 40.

New Zealand Herald, April 30, 2011, Stephen Jewell, "Magical Tales Take on Life of Their Own."

Publishers Weekly, April 9, 2007, review of *City of Bones,* p. 55; July 19, 2010, review of *Clockwork Angel,* p. 131.

School Library Journal, May, 2007, Heather M. Campbell, review of *City of Bones,* p. 130; August, 2008, Jennifer-Lynn Draper, review of *City of Ashes,* p. 116; July, 2009, Eliza Langhans, review of *City of Glass,* p. 80; October, 2010, Heather M. Campbell, review of *Clockwork Angel,* p. 110; January, 2012, Caroline Tesauro, review of *Clockwork Prince,* p. 108.

Voice of Youth Advocates, April, 2007, Sara Squires, review of *City of Bones,* p. 62; June, 2008, review of *City of Ashes,* p. 158; July 1, 2009, Eliza Langhans, review of *City of Glass,* p. 80; October, 2010, Sarah Hill, review of *Clockwork Angel,* p. 364; August, 2011, Stacey Hayman, review of *City of Fallen Angels,* p. 286; December, 2011, Suanne Roush, review of *Clockwork Prince,* p. 507.

ONLINE

Blogcritics Web site, http://blogcritics.org/ (May 8, 2007), Katie Trattner, interview with Clare.

Cassandra Clare Home Page, http://cassie-claire.com (January 15, 2012).

Cassandra Clare Web log, http://cassandraclare.livejournal.com (January 15, 2012).

Cynsations Web log, http://cynthialeitichsmith.blogspot.com/ (March 8, 2008), Cynthia Leitich Smith, interview with Clare.

Infernal Devices Web site, http://www.theinfernaldevices.com (January 15, 2012).

Mortal Instruments Web site, http://www.mortalinstruments.com (January 15, 2012).

Powells.com, http://www.powells.com/ (January 15, 2012), interview with Clare.

Publishers Weekly Online, http://www.publishersweekly.com/ (March 5, 2009), Donna Freitas, interview with Clare; (July 19, 2009) Sarah Moroz, "Saturday in the Park with Cassie."

Seventeen Online, http://www.seventeen.com/ (January 15, 2012), Cheryl Brody, "Cassandra Clare."

Simon & Schuster Web site, http://www.simonandschuster.com/ (January 15, 2012), "Author Revealed: Cassandra Clare."

TeensReadToo.com, http://www.teensreadtoo.com/ (January 15, 2012), Jen Wardrip, interview with Clare.*

*   *   *

CORDELL, Matthew 1975-

Personal

Born September 11, 1975, in Greenville, SC; son of Barney Stephen Cordell and Janet Jones; married Julie Halpern (a writer), 2003; children: Romy (daughter).

Addresses

Office—P.O. Box 8583, Gurnee, IL 60031. *Agent*— Rosemary Stimola, Stimola Literary Studio, 308 Livingston Ct., Edgewater, NJ 07020. *E-mail*—matthew@matthewcordell.com.

Career

Illustrator and graphic artist. *Exhibitions:* Work exhibited at galleries in Chicago, IL, and at Society of Illustrators Original Art showcase, 2009.

Awards, Honors

International Reading Association/Children's Book Center Children's Choice selection, 2010, and Honor Book selection, Florida Reading Association Children's Book Award, 2011, both for *Trouble Gum.*

Writings

SELF-ILLUSTRATED

Trouble Gum, Feiwel & Friends (New York, NY), 2009.
Another Brother, Feiwel & Friends (New York, NY), 2012.

ILLUSTRATOR

Julie Halpern, *Toby and the Snowflakes,* Houghton Mifflin (Boston, MA), 2004.

Amy Gordon, *Return to Gill Park,* Holiday House (New York, NY), 2006.

Amy Gordon, *The Gorillas of Gill Park,* Holiday House (New York, NY), 2007.

Jay M. Harris, *The Moon Is La Luna: Silly Rhymes in English and Spanish,* Houghton Mifflin (Boston, MA), 2007.

Rachel Vail, *Righty and Lefty: A Tale of Two Feet,* Scholastic Press (New York, NY), 2007.

James Preller, *Mighty Casey,* Feiwel & Friends (New York, NY), 2008.

Phyllis Root, *Toot Toot Zoom!,* Candlewick Press (Somerville, MA), 2009.

Rachel Vail, *Justin Case: School, Drool, and Other Daily Disasters,* Feiwel & Friends (New York, NY), 2010.

Lauren Thompson, *Leap Back Home to Me,* Margaret K. McElderry Books (New York, NY), 2011.

Julie Sternberg, *Like Pickle Juice on a Cookie,* Amulet Books (New York, NY), 2011.

Michelle Meadows, *Itsy-bitsy Baby Mouse,* Simon & Schuster Books for Young Readers (New York, NY), 2012.

Lynne Berry, *What Floats in a Moat?,* Simon & Schuster Books for Young Readers (New York, NY), 2013.

Sidelights

The first picture book Matthew Cordell illustrated was *Toby and the Snowflakes,* which featured a text by his wife, author Julie Halpern. Published in 2004, *Toby and the Snowflakes* jump-started Cordell's career in chil-

Cover of Rachel Vail's **Righty and Lefty,** *which features Matthew Cordell's whimsical watercolor art.* (Illustration copyright © 2007 by Matthew Cordell. Reproduced by permission of Scholastic, Inc.)

dren's books, and he has since brought to life stories by writers ranging from Phyllis Root to Rachel Vail to Michelle Meadows. In 2009 Cordell created his first original self-illustrated story for children, *Trouble Gum,* and has added to his list of writings with *Another Brother.*

In *Trouble Gum* Cordell introduces two young pigs named Ruben and Julius, who become fascinated with chewing gum after they are given a piece by their doting grandmother. Being the older of the two, Ruben quickly shows his expertise with the sticky substance, orchestrating the unauthorized acquisition of more sticks of gum and ultimately landing both piggy brothers in a bathtub. Using tones of gray, red, and pink, "Cordell mingles retro elements effectively," observed a *Kirkus Reviews* writer, and his illustrations provide readers with "much detail to pore and giggle over." The book's "simple story line and liberal use of white space" help "Cordell's winsome art . . . generate laughs," according to *Booklist* reviewer Ian Chipman, while in *School Library Journal* Lisa Glasscock recommended that the "humorous illustrations" in the onomatopoeic text for *Trouble Gum* be shared "one-on-one where the many mischievous details can be appreciated."

In *Toby and the Snowflakes* Halpern tells a story about a lonely young boy who spends the winter playing with snowflakes and is saddened when spring comes and the snowflakes melt away. As brought to life in Cordell's gently colored cartoon art, a new, human friend replaces the snow when another boy moves into a house in Toby's neighborhood. In *School Library Journal,* Margaret R. Tassia wrote that Cordell's use of "soft, muted colors and expansive white spaces" in his cartoon illustrations for *Toby and the Snowflakes* "add to the lonely feeling expressed in the story and create interest." A *Publishers Weekly* critic agreed, writing that the artist "makes intelligent use of white space as he demonstrates the simple pleasures to be found in winter pastimes." Calling *Toby and the Snowflakes* a "slow, quiet story," a *Kirkus Reviews* writer concluded that Cordell and Halpern's picture book "should appeal to kids with both real and imaginary friends."

In his work for Vail's *Righty and Lefty: A Tale of Two Feet,* Cordell contributes cartoon art that brings to life the quirky story about a pair of feet in which left and right have decidedly different ideas about what to wear and where to go. The "large expanses of white space" on the pages "showcase [Cordell's] . . . humorous pen-and-ink and pastel watercolors," noted *School Library Journal* contributor Maryann H. Owen in a review of *Righty and Lefty,* and in *Kirkus Reviews* a critic concluded that the illustrator's "understated watercolors help by lending the tale a soft, humorous tone."

Other illustration projects by Cordell include James Preller's picture book *Mighty Casey* as well as *The Gorillas of Gill Park* and *Return to Gill Park,* two humorous chapter books by Amy Gordon that find a seventh grader the owner of a public park after a millionaire dies and wills him the property. Reviewing *Mighty Casey* in *Kirkus Reviews,* a contributor wrote that the artist's "simply drawn cartoons of geeky, distracted children . . . suit this lightweight remake" of Ernest Thayer's popular turn-of-the-twentieth-century poem, and *Booklist* critic Ernie Cox asserted that Cordell's "illustrations add comic punch."

Teaming up with Julie Sternberg to create the chapter book *Like Pickle Juice on a Cookie,* the artist shifts gears slightly; here his "winsome cartoon drawings complement" Sternberg's "simple, poignant story" about a girl who misses her best friend, according to *Booklist* contributor Kara Dean. The "halftone cartoons" the artist creates for the chapter book "convey the story's pathos and humor," asserted a *Publishers Weekly* contributor, and in *School Library Journal* Terrie Dorio concluded of *Like Pickle Juice on a Cookie* that "Cordell's pen-and-ink drawings effectively illustrated the ups and downs" of a young girl's emotions.

Dubbed "a deceptively simple instant classic" by a *Kirkus Reviews* writer, *Leap Back Home to Me* features a text by Lauren Thompson that relates a rhyming story about a mother frog's affection for her young bouncy young frogling. In this book "Cordell's nimble line-and-watercolor illustrations are loose-limbed, unaffected and suitably silly," according to *New York Times* contributor Leonard S. Marcus, while a *Publishers Weekly* reviewer praised the artist's "marvelous . . . illustrations" in *Leap Back Home to Me* for capturing "the small frog's increasing confidence and joy in its independence." In *Booklist* Randall Enos noted that "the simplicity of the illustrations" pairs with "the brevity and repetition of [Thompson's] . . . lively text" to make *Leap Back Home to Me* "a natural for group sharing," and *School Library Journal* critic Marge Loch-Wouters concluded that the "author/illustrator team brings a light touch to a weighty subject."

Biographical and Critical Sources

PERIODICALS

Booklist, May 15, 2006, Todd Morning, review of *Return to Gill Park,* p. 140; April 1, 2009, Ernie Cox, review of *Mighty Casey,* p. 43; October 15, 2009, Ian Chipman, review of *Trouble Gum,* p. 57; March 1, 2010, Andrew Medlar, review of *School, Drool, and Other Daily Disasters,* p. 71; February 15, 2011, Kara Dean, review of *Like Pickle Juice on a Cookie,* p. 74; April 1, 2011, Randall Enos, review of *Leap Back Home to Me,* p. 74.

Bulletin of the Center for Children's Books, December, 2004, Deborah Stevenson, review of *Toby and the Snowflakes,* p. 157; December, 2007, Deborah Stevenson, review of *Righty and Lefty: A Tale of Two Feet,* p. 191.

Horn Book, May-June, 2010, Betty Carter, review of *School, Drool, and Other Daily Disasters,* p. 94; May-June, 2011, Susan Dove Lempke, review of *Like Pickle Juice on a Cookie,* p. 105.

Kirkus Reviews, July 1, 2004, review of *Toby and the Snowflakes,* p. 630; March 15, 2006, review of *Return to Gill Park,* p. 290; October 1, 2007, review of *Righty and Lefty;* January 15, 2009, review of *Mighty Casey;* July 15, 2009, review of *Trouble Gum;* April 15, 2010, review of *School, Drool, and Other Daily Disasters;* April 1, 2011, review of *Leap Back Home to Me.*

New York Times Book Review, June 19, 2011, Leonard S. Marcus, review of *Leap Back Home to Me,* p. 17.

Publishers Weekly, November 1, 2004, review of *Toby and the Snowflakes,* p. 61; November 5, 2007, review of *Righty and Lefty,* p. 62; March 2, 2009, review of *Mighty Casey,* p. 61; July 6, 2009, review of *Trouble Gum,* p. 50; April 19, 2010, review of *School, Drool, and Other Daily Disasters,* p. 53; January 24, 2011, review of *Like Pickle Juice on a Cookie,* p. 153; February 7, 2011, review of *Leap Back Home to Me,* p. 54.

School Library Journal, May, 2003, Barbara Auerbach, review of *The Gorillas of Gill Park,* p. 152; October, 2004, Margaret R. Tassia, review of *Toby and the Snowflakes,* p. 114; November, 2007, Maryann H. Owen, review of *Righty and Lefty,* p. 102; March, 2009, Ieva Bates, review of *Mighty Casey,* p. 126; May, 2009, Blair Christolon, review of *Toot Toot Zoom!,* p. 88; August, 2009, Lisa Glasscock, review of *Trouble Gum,* p. 72; May, 2010, Rachel Vail, review of *School, Drool, and Other Daily Disasters,* p. 93; March, 2011, Marge Loch-Wouters, review of *Leap Back Home to Me,* p. 136; April, 2011, Terrie Dorio, review of *Like Pickle Juice on a Cookie,* p. 154.

Tribune Books (Chicago, IL), December 29, 2007, Mary Harris Russell, review of *Righty and Lefty,* p. 12.

ONLINE

Matthew Cordell Home Page, http://www.mathewcordell. com (January 9, 2012).*

*   *   *

CORDEROY, Tracey

Personal

Born in Wales; married; children: two daughters. *Education:* Degree (education; with first-class honours), 1987.

Addresses

Home—Gloucestershire, England. *Agent*—Eve White Literary Agency, 54 Gloucester St., London SW1V 4EG, England. *E-mail*—me@traceycorderoy.com.

Career

Children's author. Formerly worked as a teacher. Literacy advocate.

Awards, Honors

Hillingdon Picture Book of the Year Award, 2011, for *The Grunt and the Grouch.*

Writings

PICTURE BOOKS

The Grunt and the Grouch, illustrated by Lee Wildish, Stripes (London, England), 2010.

Star Friends, illustrated by Alison Edgson, Little Tiger Press (London, England), 2010.

The Little White Owl, illustrated by Jane Chapman, Good Books (Intercourse, PA), 2010.

It's Potty Time!, illustrated by Caroline Pedler, Good Books (Intercourse, PA), 2011.

It's Mine!, illustrated by Caroline Pedler, Good Books (Intercourse, PA), 2011.

Brave Little Penguin, illustrated by Gavin Scott, Little Tiger Press (London, England), 2011.

Hubble Bubble, Granny Trouble!, illustrated by Joe Berger, Nosy Crow, 2011.

Oh, Dylan!, illustrated by Tina Macnaughton, Good Books (Intercourse, PA), 2011.

Just One More!, illustrated by Alison Edgson, Good Books (Intercourse, PA), 2012.

Monty and Milli, illustrated by Tim Warnes, Good Books (Intercourse, PA), 2012.

Never Say No to a Princess!, illustrated by Kate Leake, Alison Green Books (London, England), 2012.

Frog and Mouse, illustrated by Anna Popescue, Meadowside Children's Books (London, England), 2012.

"THE GRUNT AND THE GROUCH" READER SERIES; ILLUSTRATED BY LEE WILDISH

Beastly Feast!, Stripes (London, England), 2010.

Big Splash!, Stripes (London, England), 2010.

Pick 'n' Mix!, Stripes (London, England), 2010.

Freaky Funfair!, Stripes (London, England), 2011.

"WILLOW VALLEY" READER SERIES

The Big Bike Race, Scholastic (London, England), 2012.

Spooky Sleepover, Scholastic (London, England), 2012.

Hide and Seek, Scholastic (London, England), 2012.

Birthday Fun, Scholastic (London, England), 2012.

Biographical and Critical Sources

PERIODICALS

Booklist, December 1, 2010, Hazel Rochman, review of *The Little White Owl,* p. 66.

Kirkus Reviews, September 15, 2010, review of *The Little White Owl.*
School Library Journal, November, 2010, Tanya Boudreau, review of *The Little White Owl,* p. 68.

ONLINE

Little Tiger Press Web site, http://www.littletigerpress.com/ (January 11, 2012), interview with Corderoy.
Tracey Corderoy Home Page, http://www.traceycorderoy.com (January 20, 2012).

*   *   *

COSTANZA, Stephen

Personal

Male. *Education:* Attended Syracuse University; attended Philadelphia College of Art.

Addresses

Home—Belfast, ME. *Agent*—Lori Nowicki, Painted Words; lori@painted-words.com.

Career

Illustrator and graphic designer. *Exhibitions:* Work exhibited at Children's Book Fair, Bologna, Italy, 2000; and Society of Illustrators Original Art Show, New York, NY, 2003.

Writings

SELF-ILLUSTRATED

Mozart Finds a Melody, Henry Holt (New York, NY), 2004.
Vivaldi and the Invisible Orchestra, Henry Holt (New York, NY), 2012.

ILLUSTRATOR

April Pulley Sayre, *Noodle Man: The Pasta Superhero,* Orchard Books (New York, NY), 2002.
Nancy Gow, *Ten Big Toes and a Prince's Nose,* Sterling (New York, NY), 2010.
Trinka Hakes Noble, *A Christmas Spider's Miracle,* Sleeping Bear Press (Ann Arbor MI), 2011.

Contributor to periodicals, including *American Prospect* and *Cricket.*

Sidelights

Stephen Costanza, a respected designer and illustrator who studied music theory and composition in college, brings these interests to bear in his self-illustrated picture books *Mozart Finds a Melody* and *Vivaldi and the Invisible Orchestra.* In the former, Costanza offers a fictionalized version of an incident from the life of Wolfgang Amadeus Mozart, the celebrated eighteenth-century Austrian composer and conductor. Faced with writer's block one day, the young Mozart enlists the help of his pet starling, Miss Bimms, whose melodious chirping piques his interest. When the bird escapes from its cage, however, Mozart must give chase through the streets of Vienna, discovering further inspiration in the sounds of the busy city. "Costanza uses a mix of acrylics, gouache and colored pencils to create dreamlike illustrations that suggest the elusive imagination at work," a contributor for *Publishers Weekly* noted. Jennifer Mattson, writing in *Booklist,* also applauded the artwork, stating that Costanza's "paintings offer an ingenious view of eighteenth-century Vienna."

An orphaned girl provides assistance to groundbreaking Italian composer Antonio Vivaldi in Costanza's *Vivaldi and the Invisible Orchestra,* "a pleasing interpretation of the creative process and the power of art to connect individuals," according to a *Kirkus Reviews* writer. Working as a copyist at Venice's Ospedale della Pietá orphanage, renowned for its all-girl orchestra, young Candida begins jotting down her lyrical musings in the margins of Vivaldi's sheet music, stirring the artist's imagination and inspiring his famous "The Four Seasons." "There is a lovely melodic quality to the text," Linda Ludke commented in *School Library Journal,* and a *Publishers Weekly* reviewer observed of *Vivaldi and the Invisible Orchestra* that "Costanza's velvety pastel pictures, with their doll-like characterizations, . . . lends a fairy tale feel to the story."

In addition to his self-illustrated titles, Costanza has provided the artwork for tales by other authors. In *Noodle Man: The Pasta Superhero* April Pulley Sayre recounts the adventures of Al Dente, a bumbling businessman whose portable pasta maker comes in handy during a number of emergencies. When the town's streets flood, people spring over the water on Dente's fusilli, and he quickly creates a slide of lasagna noodles that helps the inhabitants of a burning building reach safety. "Costanza's cartoonlike watercolor illustrations take full advantage of the pasta motif," Kay Weisman noted in *Booklist.* A *Publishers Weekly* critic observed that the "shifting perspectives of people bouncing on fusilli above the rooftops, and streets that twist like spaghetti strands escalate the fun, frivolous mood" of *Noodle Man.*

In Nancy Gow's *Ten Big Toes and a Prince's Nose* a pair of royals finds love after learning to embrace their oh-so-obvious physical imperfections. "The saturated colors and folk-like feel of the artwork are just right for this jaunty tale," a writer for *Kirkus Reviews* maintained. In the words of *Booklist* contributor Carolyn Phelan, "Costanza's large-scale pastels illustrate the story with sweeping, curved lines and warm, softly applied colors."

Based on a Ukrainian folk tale, Trinka Hakes Noble's *A Christmas Spider's Miracle* celebrates the spirit of giving. During a harsh winter, a mother spider huddles her babies in a small fir tree. When a woman moves the tree inside her impoverished home to cheer her three children, Mother Spider is so grateful that she creates a decorative surprise for the woman on Christmas morning. A writer in *Kirkus Reviews* described *A Christmas Spider's Miracle* as an "appealing story with a magical aura spun by the shimmering illustrations and memorable story," and *School Library Journal* contributor Linda Israelson remarked that Noble's tale "is enriched by the visual magic of Costanza's colorful, textured compositions."

Biographical and Critical Sources

PERIODICALS

Booklist, February 15, 2002, Kay Weisman, review of *Noodle Man: The Pasta Superhero,* p. 1021; November 1, 2004, Jennifer Mattson, review of *Mozart Finds a Melody,* p. 498; October 15, 2010, Carolyn Phelan, review of *Ten Big Toes and a Prince's Nose,* p. 58.

Kirkus Reviews, February 15, 2002, review of *Noodle Man,* p. 265; August 15, 2004, review of *Mozart Finds a Melody,* p. 803; September 15, 2010, review of *Ten Big Toes and a Prince's Nose*; September 1, 2011, review of *A Christmas Spider's Miracle*; December 15, 2011, review of *Vivaldi and the Invisible Orchestra.*

Publishers Weekly, April 8, 2002, review of *Noodle Man,* p. 226; November 8, 2004, review of *Mozart Finds a Melody,* p. 55; September 26, 2011, review of *A Christmas Spider's Miracle,* p. 72; December 5, 2011, review of *Vivaldi and the Invisible Orchestra,* p. 73.

School Library Journal, March, 2002, Gay Lynn Van Vleck, review of *Noodle Man,* p. 200; November, 2004, Susan Lissim, review of *Mozart Finds a Melody,* p. 94; November, 2010, Mary N. Oluonye, review of *Ten Big Toes and a Prince's Nose,* p. 70; October, 2011, Linda Israelson, review of *A Christmas Spider's Miracle,* p. 96; January, 2012, Linda Ludke, review of *Vivaldi and the Invisible Orchestra,* p. 71.

ONLINE

Painted Words Web site, http://www.painted-words.com/ (January 15, 2012), "Stephen Costanza."*

* * *

CREMER, Andrea 1978-

Personal

Born August 1, 1978, in Ashland, WI; father a minister, mother a choir director; married; husband's name William. *Education:* Northland College, B.A. (history and English); Butler University, M.A.; University of Minnesota, Ph.D. (early American history), 2007. *Hobbies and other interests:* Computer gaming.

Addresses

Home—Minneapolis, MN. *Office*—Old Main 300, Macalester College, St. Paul, MN 55105; robertsona macalester.edu. *Agent*—Charlie Olsen, InkWell Management, 521 5th Ave., 26th Fl., New York, NY 10175; charlie@inkwellmanagement.com. *E-mail*—andreacre merwrites@gmail.com.

Career

Writer and educator. Macalester College, St. Paul, MN, assistant professor of history, beginning 2007.

Writings

"NIGHTSHADE" YOUNG-ADULT NOVEL TRILOGY

Nightshade, Philomel Books (New York, NY), 2010.
Wolfsbane, Philomel (New York, NY), 2010.
Bloodrose, Philomel Books (New York, NY), 2012.

Sidelights

A history professor at Macalester College, Andrea Cremer offers a feminist take on the teen werewolf genre in her "Nightshade" novel trilogy, which focuses on the relationship between Calla Tor, the alpha female of a pack of shape-shifting wolves, and Ren Laroche, an alpha male that she is destined to marry. "Calla inspired the story," Cremer remarked in an interview on the Macalester College Web site. "I had a girl in my head who was strong, a leader, a warrior. My favorite characters have always been strong women who take charge of their lives and can fight for themselves."

Cremer's trilogy, which includes *Wolfsbane* and *Bloodrose,* was also influenced by her explorations of the woods surrounding her childhood home. "Werewolves have been depicted as ugly, cursed mutations, half-animal, half-human, beastly and horrid," the author told Mary Ann Grossmann in the *St. Paul Pioneer Press.* "I grew up in the middle of the Chequamegon National Forest in northern Wisconsin, a magical wilderness where wolves were an essential part of that mystery. They are intelligent, social, forming incredibly tight packs. I thought they were a good metaphor for a human relations hierarchy."

In *Nightshade,* Cremer introduces Calla, her fierce seventeen-year-old protagonist, and the members of her pack, who are both fully human and fully wolf. Calla has long known that she will be mated to Ren as soon as they graduate from high school, and together they will rule a pack assigned to guard the sacred sites be-

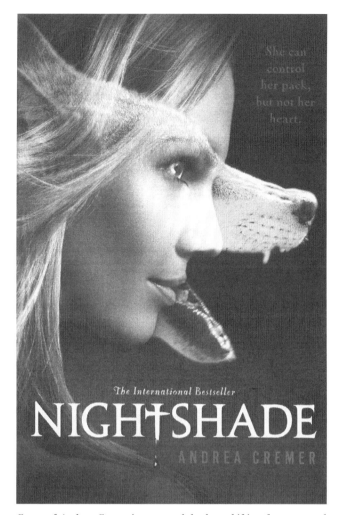

Cover of Andrea Cremer's young-adult shapeshifting fantasy novel Nightshade, *the first novel in her "Nightshade" trilogy.* (Jacket photograph copyright © 2011 by Gabrielle Revere. Reproduced by permission of Philomel Books, a division of Penguin Young Readers Group, a member of Penguin Group (USA), 345 Hudson Street, New York NY 10014. All rights reserved.)

longing to the Keepers, a cadre of powerful witches that controls the wolves. However, when Calla falls for Shay, a classmate whose life she spares, she begins to question the Keepers' laws as well as her allegiance to Ren. "Cremer's debut brings mystery and passion to a journey of self-determination," a critic observed in *Publishers Weekly,* and a *Kirkus Reviews* writer noted that the author "builds a compelling world, moving her plot forward with well-paced drive that easily holds readers' interest."

Having transformed Shay into a boy-wolf, Calla finds herself at odds with the merciless Keepers in *Wolfsbane,* the second installment of the "Nightshade" series.

To save Ren and her pack, Calla must enter an alliance with the Searchers, mortal enemies of the Keepers. "Those who are already invested in Cremer's world will enjoy the strong female protagonist and breakneck action," Tara Kehoe remarked in *School Library Journal.*

Cremer concludes her trilogy with *Bloodrose,* in which Calla engages in an epic battle against the Keepers while reconciling her romantic feelings for both Ren and Shay. A *Kirkus Reviews* contributor stated of *Bloodrose* that "the saga's clever surprise ending intimates that Calla's long-sought freedom comes with limitations."

Biographical and Critical Sources

PERIODICALS

Booklist, August 1, 2010, Debbie Carton, review of *Nightshade,* p. 49.

Kirkus Reviews, September 1, 2010, review of *Nightshade;* May 15, 2011, review of *Wolfsbane;* January 1, 2012, review of *Bloodrose.*

Publishers Weekly, October 4, 2010, review of *Nightshade,* p. 50.

St. Paul Pioneer Press (St. Paul, MN), October 29, 2010, Mary Ann Grossmann, "Local Author Cries Wolf, and Teens Start to Howl."

School Library Journal, December, 2010, Karen Alexander, review of *Nightshade,* p. 110; September, 2011, Tara Kehoe, review of *Wolfsbane,* p. 148.

Star Tribune (Minneapolis, MN), January 4, 2012, Laurie Hertzel, "Macalester Historian Writes Her Third Historical Fantasy," p. E1.

Voice of Youth Advocates, August, 2011, Amy Sisson, review of *Wolfsbane,* p. 286.

ONLINE

Andrea Cremer Home Page, http://www.andreacremer.com (January 15, 2012).

Andrea Cremer Web log, http://blurredhistory.blogspot.com (January 15, 2012).

Macalester College Web site, http://www.macalester.edu/ (November 4, 2010), "With Her First Novel, *Nightshade,* History Professor Andrea Cremer Introduces a New Fantasy Female, and Earns a Spot on the *New York Times* Bestseller List."*

D

DEMPSEY, Kristy

Personal

Born in SC; married; children: three. *Education:* Furman University, B.A. (health and exercise science). *Hobbies and other interests:* Running.

Addresses

Home—Belo Horizonte, Brazil. *E-mail*—kdempsey@ campusoutreach.org.

Career

Educator and poet/writer. American School, Belo Horizonte, Brazil, teacher and librarian, beginning 2010. Freelance writer, beginning 2005.

Member

International Reading Association, American Library Association, Society of Children's Book Writers and Illustrators.

Writings

PICTURE BOOKS

Me with You, illustrated by Christopher Denise, Philomel Books (New York, NY), 2009.
Mini Racer, illustrated by Bridget Strevens-Marzo, Bloomsbury Children's Books (New York, NY), 2011.
Surfer Chick, illustrated by Henry Cole, Abrams Books for Young Readers (New York, NY), 2012.

Sidelights

Kristy Dempsey grew up in South Carolina, and many of her fondest childhood memories involve sunny days spent on her grandfather's farm. Now a teacher and li-

brarian living in Belo Horizonte, Brazil, Dempsey divides her time between working with children and writing stories for them. Among them her picture-book texts are *Me with You, Mini Racer,* and *Surfer Chick,* the last a tale about a little chick's effort to master an unusual sport that has been paired with artwork by Henry Cole.

Kristy Dempsey teams up with illustrator Christopher Denise to create the multigenerational picture book Me with You.

Dempsey originally wrote the poem that became *Me with You* for her husband, then recognized that it would also make the perfect picture-book text. Paired with full-color illustrations by Christopher Denise, the multi-generational story in *Me with You* focuses on the affection between a young female bear and her grandfather, showing the pair as they play baseball, garden, take a stroll in the woods, and otherwise spend time together. Along with what *Booklist* critic Randall Enos described as "enticing, picturesque scenes [that] will make readers want to climb right into the pages," of Dempsey's story, *Me with You* features a rhyming text that "describes all of the ways" the two bears "play, spend time together, and support one another," according to *School Library Journal* critic Amy Lilien-Harper.

Inspired by Dempsey's rambunctious children and illustrated by Bridget Strevens-Marzo, *Mini Racer* introduces a dozen small race cars that are lined up for a cross-country competition. Each vehicle is driven by a different animal, and their passage along the twisty, turny race course is animated by a simple text fueled by high-action vocabulary. Featuring equally animated artwork by Strevens-Marzo that evokes the work of Richard Scarry, *Mini Racer* "has definite appeal for youngsters" due to its "zooming action and fender-bender drama," according to a *Kirkus Reviews* writer. Dempsey's "lively rhyming text provides an exciting play-by-play commentary," asserted *Booklist* contributor Enos, and in *School Library Journal* Marge Loch-Wouters recommended *Mini Racer* as a story perfect for "kids with a need for speed and a love of vehicles."

Biographical and Critical Sources

PERIODICALS

Booklist, May 15, 2009, Randall Enos, review of *Me with You,* p. 46; December 15, 2010, Randall Enos, review of *Mini Racer,* p. 59.
Children's Bookwatch, May, 2011, review of *Mini Racer.*
Kirkus Reviews, November 1, 2010, review of *Mini Racer.*
School Library Journal, June, 2009, Amy Lilien-Harper, review of *Me with You,* p. 82; January, 2011, Marge Loch-Wouters, review of *Mini Racer,* p. 72.

ONLINE

Kristy Dempsey Home Page, http://www.kristydempsey. com (January 9, 2012).
Kristy Dempsey Web log, http://kristydempsey.livejournal. com (January 9, 2012).*

*　　　*　　　*

DOUGLAS, David
See TUTT, Keith

DUEY, Kathleen 1950-

Personal

Born November 8, 1950. *Hobbies and other interests:* Singing, playing guitar, songwriting, horses, gardening, travel, blogging, learning anything, politics, sociology.

Addresses

Home—San Diego, CA. *E-mail*—kathleen@kathleen duey.com.

Career

Writer.

Member

Authors Guild, Society of Children's Book Writers and Illustrators.

Awards, Honors

Young Hoosier's Award nominee, 1999, for *Train Wreck: Kansas, 1892;* Golden Duck Award, 2001, for *Rex;* National Book Award finalist in Young People's Literature, 2007, for *Skin Hunger.*

Writings

Double-Yuck Magic, Morrow/Avon (New York, NY), 1991.
Mr. Stumpguss Is a Third Grader, Morrow/Avon (New York, NY), 1992.
The Third Grade's Skinny Pig, illustrated by Gioia Fiammenghi, Avon (New York, NY), 1993.
The Big Blue Easter Egg, Nesak International (Delray Beach, FL), 1996.
The Easter Morning Surprise, Nesak International (Delray Beach, FL), 1996.
(With Karen A. Bale) *Three of Hearts,* Morrow/Avon (New York, NY), 1998.
CX Ultimate Asteroid Book: The Inside Story on the Threat from the Skies, Sagebrush (Minneapolis, MN), 1998.
(With Ron Berry) *Allowance System Tool Kit: Easy-to-Use Tools That Teach Kids Money, Values, and Responsibilities,* Smart Kids Publishing (Carlsbad, CA), 2000.
(With Mary Barnes) *Freaky Facts about Natural Disasters,* Aladdin (New York, NY), 2000.
(With Mary Barnes) *More Freaky Facts about Natural Disasters,* Aladdin (New York, NY), 2001.
Terremoto, Planeta Publishing (Miami, FL), 2002.
Spider-Man Ultimate Picture Book, photographs by Robert Gould, illustrations by Eugene Epstein, Big Guy Books (Carlsbad, CA), 2002.
X-Men Ultimate Picture Book, photographs by Robert Gould, illustrations by Eugene Epstein, Big Guy Books (Carlsbad, CA), 2003.
Escapade Johnson in Mayhem at Mount Moosilauke, photographs by Robert Gould, illustrations by Eugene Epstein, Big Guy Books (Carlsbad, CA), 2006.

(With Bernadette Bailie) *100 Easy Ways to Get Your Kids Reading: A Busy Mom's Guide,* Big Guy Books (Carlsbad, CA), 2006.

Author's work has been translated into several languages, including French and German.

"BEASTY BUDDIES" PICTURE BOOK SERIES

Hogger the Hoarding Beastie, Smart Kids Publishing (Carlsbad, CA), 1999.
Moogie the Messy Beastie, Smart Kids Publishing (Carlsbad, CA), 1999.
Crassy the Crude Beastie, Smart Kids Publishing (Carlsbad, CA), 2001.
Glumby the Grumbling Beastie, Smart Kids Publishing (Carlsbad, CA), 2001.

"ALONE IN THE DARK" SERIES

Beware the Alien Invasion!, Smart Kids Publishing (Carlsbad, CA), 2000.
Nowhere to Run, Nowhere to Hide!, Smart Kids Publishing (Carlsbad, CA), 2000.
Stay out of the Graveyard!, Smart Kids Publishing (Carlsbad, CA), 2000.
Bogeyman in the Basement!, Smart Kids Publishing (Carlsbad, CA), 2000.

"AMERICAN DIARIES" SERIES

Emma Eileen Grove: Mississippi, 1865, Aladdin (New York, NY), 1996.
Mary Alice Peale: Philadelphia, 1777, Aladdin (New York, NY), 1996.
Sarah Anne Hartford: Massachusetts, 1651, Aladdin (New York, NY), 1996.
Anisett Lundberg: California, 1851, Aladdin (New York, NY), 1996.
Willow Chase: Kansas Territory, 1847, Aladdin (New York, NY), 1997.
Ellen Elizabeth Hawkins: Mobeetie, Texas, 1886, Aladdin (New York, NY), 1997.
Evie Peach: St. Louis, 1857, Aladdin (New York, NY), 1997.
Alexia Ellery Finsdale: San Francisco, 1905, Aladdin (New York, NY), 1997.
Celou Sudden Shout: Idaho, 1826, Aladdin (New York, NY), 1998.
Summer MacCleary: Virginia, 1749, Aladdin (New York, NY), 1998.
Agnes May Gleason: Walsenberg, Colorado, 1933, Aladdin (New York, NY), 1998.
Amelina Carrett: Bayou Grand Coeur, Louisiana, 1863, Aladdin (New York, NY), 1999.
Josie Poe: Palouse, Washington, 1943, Aladdin (New York, NY), 1999.
Rosa Moreno: Hollywood, California, 1928, Aladdin (New York, NY), 1999.

Nell Dunne: Ellis Island, 1904, Aladdin (New York, NY), 2000.
Maddie Retta Lauren: Sandersville, Georgia, 1864, Aladdin (New York, NY), 2000.
Francesca Vigilucci: Washington, DC, 1913, Aladdin (New York, NY), 2000.
Janey G. Blue: Pearl Harbor, 1941, Aladdin (New York, NY), 2001.
Zellie Blake: Lowell, Massachusetts, 1834, Aladdin (New York, NY), 2002.

"SURVIVAL!" SERIES; WITH KAREN A. BALE

San Francisco Earthquake, 1906, Aladdin (New York, NY), 1998.
Cave-in: St. Claire, Pennsylvania, 1859, Aladdin (New York, NY), 1998.
Stranded: Death Valley, 1850, Aladdin (New York, NY), 1998.
Flood: Mississippi, 1927, Aladdin (New York, NY), 1998.
Blizzard: Estes Park, Colorado, 1886, Aladdin (New York, NY), 1998.
Fire: Chicago, 1871, Aladdin (New York, NY), 1998.
Shipwreck: The Titanic, April 14, 1912, Aladdin (New York, NY), 1998.
Hurricane: Open Seas, 1844, Aladdin (New York, NY), 1999.
Train Wreck: Kansas, 1892, Aladdin (New York, NY), 1999.
Swamp: Bayou Teche, Louisiana, 1851, Aladdin (New York, NY), 1999.
Forest Fire: Hinckley, Minnesota, 1894, Aladdin (New York, NY), 1999.
Hurricane: New Bedford, Massachusetts, 1784, Aladdin (New York, NY), 1999.

"UNICORN'S SECRET" CHAPTER-BOOK SERIES; ILLUSTRATED BY OMAR RAYYAN

Moonsilver, Aladdin (New York, NY), 2001.
The Silver Thread, Aladdin (New York, NY), 2001.
The Silver Bracelet, Aladdin (New York, NY), 2002.
Mountains of the Moon, Aladdin (New York, NY), 2002.
The Sunset Gates, Aladdin (New York, NY), 2002.
True Heart, Aladdin (New York, NY), 2003.
Castle Avamir, Aladdin (New York, NY), 2003.
The Journey Home, Aladdin (New York, NY), 2003.

"ROBERT GOULD'S TIME SOLDIERS" SERIES; PHOTOGRAPHS BY ROBERT GOULD; ILLUSTRATED BY EUGENE EPSTEIN

Rex, Big Guy Books (Carlsbad, CA), 2001.
Rex Two, Big Guy Books (Carlsbad, CA), 2001.
Patch, Big Guy Books (Carlsbad, CA), 2002.
Arthur, Big Guy Books (Carlsbad, CA), 2004.
Mummy, Big Guy Books (Carlsbad, CA), 2005.
Samurai, Big Guy Books (Carlsbad, CA), 2006.

"SPIRIT OF THE CIMARRON" SERIES

Spirit: Stallion of the Cimarron (adapted from the motion picture), Penguin Putnam (New York, NY), 2002.
Esperanza, Penguin Putnam (New York, NY), 2002.

Bonita, Penguin Putnam (New York, NY), 2002.
Sierra, Penguin Putnam (New York, NY), 2002.

"HOOFBEATS" CHAPTER-BOOK SERIES

Katie and the Mustang, Book One, Puffin (New York, NY), 2003.
Katie and the Mustang, Book Two, Puffin (New York, NY), 2003.
Katie and the Mustang, Book Three, Puffin (New York, NY), 2003.
Katie and the Mustang, Book Four, Puffin (New York, NY), 2003.
Lara and the Gray Mare, Dutton (New York, NY), 2005.
Lara and the Moon-Colored Filly, Dutton (New York, NY), 2005.
Lara at Athenry Castle, Dutton (New York, NY), 2005.
Lara and the Silent Place, Dutton (New York, NY), 2005.
Silence and Lily: Boston, 1773, Puffin (New York, NY), 2007.
Margret and Flynn: Colorado, 1875, Puffin (New York, NY), 2008.

"RESURRECTION OF MAGIC" YOUNG-ADULT NOVEL TRILOGY

Skin Hunger, Atheneum Books for Young Readers (New York, NY), 2007.
Sacred Scars, Atheneum Books for Young Readers (New York, NY), 2009.

"FAERIES' PROMISE" CHAPTER-BOOK SERIES; ILLUSTRATED BY SANDARA TANG

Silence and Stone, Aladdin (New York, NY), 2010.
Following Magic, Aladdin (New York, NY), 2010.
The Full Moon, Aladdin (New York, NY), 2011.
Wishes and Wings, Aladdin (New York, NY), 2011.

Adaptations

Sacred Scars was adapted for audiobook, Recorded Books, 2010.

Sidelights

Kathleen Duey is the author of more than seventy books for children and young adults. She is perhaps best known for her works of historical fiction, which are featured in the "American Diary" and "Hoofbeats" series, as well as for the fantasy tales in her "Unicorn's Secret" and "Faeries' Promise" chapter books. In 2007 Duey earned a National Book Award nomination for her young-adult novel *Skin Hunger,* part of her "Resurrection of Magic" teen fantasy series. "I believe that literacy—the ability to pass on stories and facts through writing and reading—is a pillar of civilization," the author remarked to Cynthia Leitich Smith in a *Cynsations* online interview. "The human need for story seems endless," she added. "That happy fact diminishes my chances of ever needing a day job."

While growing up in Colorado, Duey developed a love of reading and writing. At age seventeen she left home and moved to an isolated cabin near Aspen, where she spent more than two decades living without electricity, learning to grind flour by hand, milk a goat, and cook on a woodstove. "Living lightly on the earth was a conscious choice and one that I am glad I made," Duey later told *Suite 101.com* interviewer Sue Reichard. "There are many people who did it. I treasure the experience. It informs every historical novel I write."

Duey began her career as a children's book author in the early 1990s with such titles as *Mr. Stumpguss Is a Third-Grader* and *The Third Grade's Skinny Pig.* In 1996 she produced *Emma Eileen Grove: Mississippi, 1865,* one of the first books in her ongoing "American Diary" series for readers in grades four to six. Each work in the series takes place over the course of a single day and begins and ends with a diary entry. *Mary Alice Peale: Philadelphia, 1777* chronicles the household dramas of a well-to-do girl whose father is loyal to British monarch George III but whose older brother has joined those fighting for colonial independence. *Sarah Anne Hartford: Massachusetts, 1651* details the experience of a twelve year old living in a Puritan family as she worries about her widowed father's impending marriage to a coldly righteous woman. "The story is exciting and the characters are sympathetic," wrote Connie Parker in her *School Library Journal* review of the latter story, while *Booklist* critic Karen Hutt stated that *Sarah Anne Hartford* "personalizes the social mores and everyday life of Puritan New England."

Duey has won praise for providing a wealth of historical detail in her "American Diary" books, and she continues to do so in *Anisett Lundberg: California, 1851,* a story about a young girl living through the California Gold Rush. With her husband dead, Anisett's mother earns a living cooking for hard-working gold miners, and Anisett and her brother both help with this work. One day, after delivering food by mule to the mining camps, Anisett is kidnapped by a desperate miner after he overhears her describing an unusual rock she has found. Susan F. Marcus, writing in *School Library Journal,* noted that *Anisett Lundberg* portrays "the view of the gold-rush culture" and "highlights the courage of those who were part of it."

Celou Sudden Shout: Idaho, 1826 tells the story of a twelve-year-old girl whose mother is Shoshone and father is a fur trapper of French origin. When Celou's mother and brother are kidnaped by hostile Crow Indians while her father is away, she must follow the raiding party in order to save them. A Texas cattle ranch is the setting for *Ellen Elizabeth Hawkins: Mobeetie, Texas, 1886,* as Duey's heroine proves she can follow in her father's footsteps as a rancher, despite the fact that she is a girl. Ann W. Moore, writing in *School Library Journal,* called *Celou Sudden Shout* an "exciting adventure story [that] also conveys information about the Shoshone," while Sylvia V. Meisner wrote in the same periodical that *Ellen Elizabeth Hawkins* serves up a "satisfying story about a resourceful heroine" who has the "grit and determination [needed] to persevere against almost overwhelming odds."

Evie Peach: St. Louis, 1857 takes place before the U.S. Civil War. The title character was once a slave, but her owner's last will and testament freed both Evie and her father. Hoping to buy her mother's freedom, they save 750 dollars and set out for the estate where the woman now works, but Irish neighbors plot revenge for a trick Evie has played on them and the girl's parents are arrested as runaway slaves. Reviewing *Evie Peach*, *Booklist* writer Denia Hester cited Duey's novel for its "good balance of warm, winning moments and well-plotted dramatic turns."

The U.S. Civil War era is the setting for *Amelina Carrett: Bayou Grand Coeur, Louisiana, 1863*, which finds orphaned Amelina living with her war-profiteering uncle in a Cajun swamp community. After gunfire erupts, she discovers an injured Union Army soldier and helps him despite the Cajuns' strong animus toward Northerners. In *School Library Journal* Janet Gillen deemed *Amelina Carrett* to be "written with insight and sensitivity" and full of interesting details about "Cajun life in the Louisiana bayou." The critic also commended Duey's young protagonist for her "courage and fortitude."

The American immigrant experience is voiced in *Nell Dunne: Ellis Island, 1904*. As her fictional diary relates, Nell sails from Ireland with her family, and the journey is hardly a luxurious one: the cabins for such passengers are cramped, and there are few facilities for washing. However, Nell gains a sense of magic upon catching her first glimpse of the imposing New York City skyline. In writing *Nell Dunne*, according to *School Library Journal* critic Alison Grant, Duey "captures the experience of thousands of immigrants seeking freedom and fortune" on the North American continent.

The glamorous world of early Hollywood is the setting of *Rosa Moreno: Hollywood, California, 1928*, which spans the years 1928 to 1934. Rosa's late father was a Mexican actor, and she and her mother are now determined that Rosa will achieve motion-picture stardom as well. The girl takes elocution lessons, visits a hair salon to achieve a set of curls similar to those of popular child star Shirley Temple, and auditions frequently. When she meets a female film director, Rosa thinks she might like to direct, too. "Duey portrays Rosa's life vividly and realistically," wrote Susan Knell in her *School Library Journal* review of *Rosa Moreno*, the critic adding praise for Duey's focus on the rigors endured by child actors early in the motion-picture era.

The experiences of Japanese Americans provides the subplot of *Janey G. Blue: Pearl Harbor, 1941*. A Kansas native, Janey lives with her family near the Hawai'i military base where her father works. She befriends Akiko Fujiwara, a shy and quiet neighbor near her own

Kathleen Duey's fantasy stories for younger readers includes **Silence and Stone,** *a story featuring artwork by Sandara Tang.* (Aladdin, 2010. Illustration copyright © 2010 by Sandara Tang. Reproduced by permission of Sandara Tang.)

age, when the two are thrown together during the confusion following the Japanese attack on Pearl Harbor. In *School Library Journal* Elaine Lesh Morgan noted of *Janey G. Blue* that "the mood of fear and uncertainty is well maintained, and information about the attack is neatly interwoven" into Duey's tale.

Duey also mixes fiction with history in her "Hoofbeats" chapter-book series, which focus on the perennial love affair between preteen girls and horses. The first four books of the series focus on Katie Rose, an orphan living in Iowa during the late 1800s who develops a strong bond with a wild horse. *Margret and Flynn, 1875* finds twelve-year-old orphans Margret and Libby staying with Mrs. Fredriksen, who lives in a sod house in rural Colorado. When an injured horse is discovered near the home following a violent storm, Margret sets about caring for it, finding a new friend and gaining a sense of permanence in the process. The "Hoofbeats" series also includes *Silence and Lily: Boston, 1773*, in which preteen Silence determines to find out who has been riding her beloved white mare after dark at the same time that her wealthy parents prepare for war to break out near their Boston home.

Reviewing *Katie and the Mustang, Book One, Booklist* critic Kay Weisman praised the first installment in the "Hoofbeats" series as "realistic in both tone and subject." "Duey draws a convincing portrayal of Silence's family life," wrote Phelan in her appraisal of *Silence and Lily* for the same periodical. Duey continues to mix girls and horses in *Lara and the Gray Mare*, one of four books in the series that are set in medieval Ireland and focus on a determined nine year old. According to *Booklist* contributor Carolyn Phelan, *Lara and the Gray Mare* mixes together "a convincing setting, a thoroughly likable heroine, and a strong narrative" about a pre-teen's efforts to help her beloved mare through a difficult foaling.

Moonsilver introduces Duey's "Unicorn's Secret" series of chapter books. In the story, Heart Avamir is living on her own in a feudal village when she befriends a wounded unicorn and its colt. The author "has written a beguiling story of love and healing in an easy-to-read style," noted Susan Dove Lempke in her *Booklist* review of *Moonsilver,* and Catherine Threadgill recommended the story in *School Library Journal* as "a good alternative for children who have outgrown easy-readers but who are not quite ready for longer, denser works of fiction." Duey continues Heart's story in seven other books, including *Mountains of the Moon* and *Castle Avamir.* She "shows impressive skill at weaving an intriguing fantasy with strongly realized characters and setting," Lempke remarked in a review of *Mountains of the Moon,* and *School Library Journal* contributor Elaine E. Knight predicted of *Castle Avamir* that "the unicorn theme and the multi-book serial will appeal" to young readers.

Fantasy comes into play in Duey's "Faeries' Promise" chapter books, as well as in her "Resurrection of Magic" novels for older readers. The "Faeries Promise" stories follow the adventures of a faery named Alida as she escapes from a long captivity and goes in search of her family and include *Silence and Stone, Following Magic, The Full Moon,* and *Wishes and Wings,* all illustrated by Sandara Tang. Praising *Silence and Stone,* a *Kirkus Reviews* writer described Duey's "lovely, sincere faerie story" as one that "tempers sadness with joy," while in *School Library Journal* Teri Markson predicted that the "simple fantasy will engage young readers and leave them eager" for further adventures in the "Faeries' Promise" series.

Skin Hunger, the first work in Duey's "Resurrection of Magic" trilogy, concerns Sadima, a young woman who has the ability to speak with animals, and Hahp, a wizard's apprentice. Employing a dual narrative, Duey follows Sadima as she joins the household of Somiss, an exiled wizard seeking to use the power of song to restore magic to the world with the help of his devoted servant, Franklin. In a parallel story set years in the future, Hahp enrolls at a magician's academy run by the cruel, now elderly Somiss. "Both tales are compelling enough to have been novels in their own right," as-

serted *Kliatt* reviewer Cara Chancellor, "and Duey's magical combination will appeal to nearly any semi-advanced audience." "The pacing in this page-turner accelerates as the stories progress and links between them emerge," observed Diana Tixier Herald in her *Booklist* review of *Skin Hunger.* "Duey's view of magic is incisive and morally complex," noted *Locus* reviewer Gary K. Wolf, and "if the remainder of the 'Resurrection of Magic' plays out at this level of intensity, it will easily take its place among those YA trilogies that ought to earn the attention of fantasy readers of any age."

Somiss is living in exile in a cave when readers again encounter him in *Sacred Scars.* Still in love with Franklin, Sadima does Somiss's bidding, transcribing songs from ancient documents and watching silently as he kidnaps street urchins and teaches them to write so that they can assist her. After rising up against this wrong and helping the children to escape from the caves, Sadima must find a new home in a seaside community, her knowledge of her former life magically erased by Somiss. Years later, Hahp is still a student of the elderly Somiss, and now he and friend Gerrard seek a way to thwart the man's brutal teachings and find a way to release his hold on magic.

Reviewing *Sacred Scars,* a *Kirkus Reviews* writer asserted that the second installment in the "Resurrection of Magic" saga is "thrumming with dense, meaningful tension from first page to last," and in *Horn Book* Anita L. Burkham described Duey's story as an "exquisitely suspenseful fantasy." Although *School Library Journal* contributor Corinda J. Humphrey recommended the novel "for serious readers with long attention spans," Andy Sawyer asserted in *School Librarian* that *Sacred Scars* ranks within the "canon of dark fantasy" as a novel "that pushes the genre far beyond the romantic escapades of werewolves and vampires" and features language that is both "passionate and vivid."

Asked by Reichard why she writes for a young audience, Duey replied: "The answer keeps changing. Right now, I write for kids because I hope to influence the future of my species. I hope to keep them believing that the world is not hopeless, that they can build a human culture that enjoys and tolerates differences and makes room for every kind of intelligence." The author concluded, "I want them to live lives that matter."

Biographical and Critical Sources

PERIODICALS

Booklist, May 15, 1996, Karen Hutt, review of *Sarah Anne Hartford: Massachusetts, 1651,* p. 1585; March 1, 1997, Lauren Peterson, review of *Willow Chase: Kansas Territory, 1847,* p. 1164; February 1, 1998, Carolyn Phelan, reviews of *Blizzard: Estes Park, Colorado, 1886* and *Earthquake, 1906,* both p. 917;

February 15, 1998, Denia Hester, review of *Evie Peach: St. Louis, 1857*, p. 1011; January 1, 2002, Susan Dove Lempke, review of *Moonsilver*, p. 856; March 1, 2002, Susan Dove Lempke, review of *The Silver Thread*, p. 1136; June 1, 2002, Karen Hutt, review of *Sierra*, p. 1722; September 1, 2002, Susan Dove Lempke, review of *The Mountains of the Moon*, p. 123; March 1, 2003, Susan Dove Lempke, review of *The Sunset Gates*, p. 1197; June 1, 2004, Kay Weisman, reviews of *Katie and the Mustang: Book One* and *Katie and the Mustang: Book Two*, both p. 1725; February 1, 2005, Carolyn Phelan, review of *Lara and the Gray Mare*, p. 960; July, 2005, Carolyn Phelan, review of *Lara at the Silent Place*, p. 1924; June 1, 2007, Diana Tixier Herald, review of *Skin Hunger*, p. 62; October 1 2007, Carolyn Phelan, review of *Silence and Lily: Boston, 1773*, p. 59; August 1, 2009, Krista Hutley, review of *Sacred Scars*, p. 60.

Bulletin of the Center for Children's Books, May, 1996, Elizabeth Bush, review of *Sarah Anne Hartford*, pp. 297-298; April, 1998, Elizabeth Bush, review of *Earthquake*, p. 278.

Horn Book, July-August, 2007, Anita L. Burkam, review of *Skin Hunger*, p. 393; September-October, 2009, Anita L. Burkam, review of *Sacred Scars*, p. 557.

Kirkus Reviews, June 15, 2007, review of *Skin Hunger*; July 1, 2009, review of *Sacred Scars*; June 1, 2010, review of *Silence and Stone*.

Kliatt, July, 2007, Cara Chancellor, review of *Skin Hunger*, p. 12.

Locus, February, 2008, Gary K. Wolfe, review of *Skin Hunger*.

Publishers Weekly, March 18, 1996, review of *Sarah Anne Hartford*, p. 70; May 17, 2004, review of *Katie and the Mustang: Book One*, p. 51; July 23, 2007, review of *Skin Hunger*, p. 70.

School Librarian, summer, 2010, Andy Sawyer, review of *Sacred Scars*, p. 110.

School Library Journal, June, 1996, Connie Parker, review of *Sarah Anne Hartford*, p. 120; December, 1996, Jane Gardner Connor, review of *Mary Alice Peale: Philadelphia, 1777*, and Susan F. Marcus, review of *Anisett Lundberg: California, 1851*, both p. 122; April, 1997, Rebecca O'Connell, review of *Willow Chase*, p. 137; August, 1997, Sylvia V. Meisner, review of *Ellen Elizabeth Hawkins: Mobeetie, Texas, 1886*, p. 157; March, 1998, Peggy Morgan, review of *Blizzard*, Robin L. Gibson, review of *Evie Peach*, and Mary M. Hopf, review of *Earthquake*, all pp. 211-212; April, 1998, Denise Furgione, review of *Alexia Ellery Finsdale: San Francisco, 1905*, p. 131; June, 1998, Ann W. Moore, review of *Celou Sudden Shout: Idaho, 1826*, p. 143; September, 1998, Joan Zaleski, reviews of *Shipwreck: The Titanic, April 14, 1912* and *Fire: Chicago, 1871*, both p. 200; December, 1998, Elaine Lesh Morgan, review of *Flood: Mississippi, 1927*, and Janet Gillen, review of *Summer MacCleary: Virginia, 1749*, both pp. 121-122; January, 1999, Coop Renner, review of *Agnes May Gleason: Walsenberg, Colorado, 1933*, p. 124; September, 1999, Janet Gillen, review of *Amelina Carrett: Bayou Grand Coeur, Louisiana, 1863*, p. 222; June, 2000, Susan Knell, review of *Rosa Moreno: Hollywood, California, 1928*, p. 143; October, 2000, Alison Grant, review of *Nell Dunne:*

Ellis Island, 1904, p. 156; April, 2001, Betsy Barnett, review of *Francesca Vigilucci: Washington, DC, 1913*, p. 139; October, 2001, Elaine Lesh Morgan, review of *Janey G. Blue: Pearl Harbor, 1941*, p. 154; December, 2001, Catherine Threadgill, review of *Moonsilver*, p. 99; April, 2002, Louise L. Sherman, review of *Sierra*, p. 146; October, 2002, Elaine Fort Weischedel, review of *Zellie Blake: Lowell, Massachusetts, 1834*, and Carol Schene, reviews of *Bonita* and *Esperanza*, both p. 162; February, 2004, Elaine E. Knight, review of *Castle Avamir*, p. 111; October, 2004, Tim Wadham, review of *Arthur*, p. 112; March, 2007, H.H. Henderson, review of *Rex*, p. 163; November, 2007, Corinda J. Humphrey, review of *Skin Hunger*, p. 120; November, 2009, Corinda J. Humphrey, review of *Sacred Scars*, p. 104; September, 2010, Teri Markson, review of *Silence and Stone*, p. 122.

ONLINE

Cynsations Web site, http://cynthialeitichsmith.blogspot.com/ (September 13, 2007), Cynthia Leitich Smith, interview with Duey.

Kathleen Duey Home Page, http://www.kathleenduey.com (January 1, 2012).

Kathleen Duey Web log, http://kathleenduey.blogspot.com (January 20, 2012).

National Book Award Web site, http://www.nationalbook.org/ (April 1, 2008), Rita Williams-Garcia, interview with Duey.

Suite 101.com, http://www.suite101.com/ (September 1, 2003), Sue Reichard, "Kathleen Duey: Writer Extraordinaire."

Unicorn's Secret Web site, http://www.theunicornssecret.com/ (January 1, 2012).

*   *   *

DUFF, Hilary 1987-

Personal

Born September 28, 1987, in Houston, TX; daughter of Bob (a retail executive) and Susan (a business manager) Duff; married Michael Comrie (a professional hockey player), August 14, 2010; children: Luca Cruz (son).

Career

Actor, singer, and songwriter. Television appearances include: *Chicago Hope*, 2000; *Lizzie McGuire*, 2001-04; *George Lopez*, 2005; *Ghost Whisperer*, 2009; and *Community*, 2010. Film appearances include: *Human Nature*, 2001; *Agent Cody Banks*, 2003; *The Lizzie McGuire Movie*, 2003; *Cheaper by the Dozen*, 2003; *A Cinderella Story*, 2004; *Raise Your Voice*, 2004; *The Perfect Man*, 2004; *Cheaper by the Dozen 2*, 2005; *Material Girls*, 2006; *War, Inc.*, 2008; *Stay Cool*, 2009; *What Goes Up*, 2009; *According to Greta*, 2009; *Gossip Girl*, 2009; *Bloodworth*, 2010; and *Beauty and the Briefcase*, 2010. Vocal recordings include: (with others) *The Santa Clause 2* (soundtrack), 2002; *Santa Claus Lane*,

Hilary Duff (Photograph © 2005 by Lisa OConnor/ZUMA/Corbis.)

2002; *Metamorphosis,* 2003; (with others) *The Lizzie McGuire Movie* (soundtrack), 2003; *Hilary Duff,* 2004; (with others) *A Cinderella Story* (soundtrack), 2004; (with others) *Raise Your Voice* (soundtrack), 2004; *Most Wanted,* 2005; (with others) *Material Girls* (soundtrack), 2006; (with others) *Bring It On: In It to Win It* (soundtrack), 2007; *Dignity,* 2007; (with others) *War, Inc.* (soundtrack), 2008; *Best of Hilary Duff,* 2008; and (with others) *What Goes Up* (soundtrack), 2009.

Awards, Honors

Young Hollywood Award, 2004; several viewer choice awards.

Writings

NOVELS

(With Elise Allen) *Elixir,* Simon & Schuster Books for Young Readers (New York, NY), 2010.
(With Elise Allen) *Devoted* (sequel to *Elixir*), Simon & Schuster Books for Young Readers (New York, NY), 2011.

Sidelights

Hilary Duff became a household name and a worldwide phenomenon thanks to her starring role in the wildly popular Disney television series *Lizzie McGuire.* With her wholesome blonde looks and exuberant personality, Duff stepped into the part of the likable middle-schooler with ease and parlayed that success into a thriving film and television career before making her mark as a singer. In 2010 Duff expanded her creative efforts to writing, producing the paranormal romance *Elixir.*

In *Elixir,* co-written with Elise Allen, Duff introduces Clea Raymond, a gifted young photojournalist who travels the world on assignment. After Clea's father, a renowned heart surgeon, vanishes while on a humanitarian mission in Brazil, an eerie figure appears in the background of several of her photographs. She also has a series of terrifying dreams of past lives in which the same shadowy individual appears and the dream ends in her death. With help from longtime friend Ben, Clea discovers the identity of the stranger, whose name is Sage, and she soon finds herself drawn into a conflict involving a secret society charged with protecting an ancient elixir, the key to immortality. An "entertaining" debut, *Elixir* "has a good mix of romance and suspense with a little reincarnation thrown in for good measure," Traci Glass remarked in *School Library Journal,* and Rachel Wadham noted in *Voice of Youth Advocates* that Duff's novel "is quite exciting and keeps you reading."

Clea makes a return appearance in *Devoted,* the sequel to *Elixir.* While searching for Sage, from whom she is currently estranged, Clea learns that members of two powerful organizations, the Cursed Vengeance and the Saviors, want Sage dead so that they can possess the elixir he carries in his body. To protect her beloved, Clea enlists the help of an immortal, Amelia, who suggests that she strike a deal with the Cursed Vengeance to prevent the Saviors from creating a race of evil immortals. "The sense of adventure and urgency are compelling," Lynn Rashid commented in her *School Library Journal* review of Duff's second novel.

Biographical and Critical Sources

PERIODICALS

Booklist, October 15, 2010, Courtney Jones, review of *Elixir,* p. 59.
Kirkus Reviews, September 15, 2010, review of *Elixir.*
Publishers Weekly, September 20, 2010, review of *Elixir,* p. 67.
School Library Journal, December, 2010, Traci Glass, review of *Elixir,* p. 112; January, 2012, Lynn Rashid, review of *Devoted,* p. 110.
Voice of Youth Advocates, December, 2010, Rachel Wadham, review of *Elixir,* p. 468; December, 2011, Rachel Wadham, review of *Devoted,* p. 509.

ONLINE

Hilary Duff Home Page, http://hilaryduff.com (January 15, 2012).
People Online, http://www.people.com/ (January 15, 2012), "Hilary Duff."*

*   *   *

DYER, Brooke

Personal

Born in Northampton, MA; daughter of Tom and Jane (an author and illustrator) Dyer; married; husband's name Ayr; children: Clementine, Blue. *Education:* School of the Museum of Fine Arts/Tufts University, joint B.F.A.

Addresses

Home—Lincoln, MA.

Career

Illustrator.

Writings

(Compiler and illustrator) *Lullaby Moons and a Silver Spoon: A Book of Bedtime Songs and Rhymes,* Little, Brown (New York, NY), 2003.

ILLUSTRATOR

Karma Wilson, *Mama Always Comes Home,* HarperCollins (New York, NY), 2005.
Amy Krouse Rosenthal, *Cookies: Bite-Size Life Lessons,* HarperCollins (New York, NY), 2006.
Amy Krouse Rosenthal, *Christmas Cookies: Bite-Size Holiday Lessons,* HarperCollins (New York, NY), 2006.
Jane Yolen and Heidi E.Y. Stemple, *Sleep, Black Bear, Sleep,* HarperCollins (New York, NY), 2007.
(With mother, Jane Dyer) Amy Krouse Rosenthal, *Sugar Cookies: Sweet Little Lessons on Love,* Harper (New York, NY), 2009.
(With Jane Dyer) Amy Krouse Rosenthal, *One Smart Cookie: Bite-Size Lessons for the School Years and Beyond,* Harper (New York, NY), 2010.
(With Jane Dyer) Frederich H. Heider and Carl Kress, *There's a Train out for Dreamland,* Harper (New York, NY), 2010.

Sidelights

Brooke Dyer, the daughter of children's book illustrator Jane Dyer, has followed in her mother's footsteps by providing the artwork for a number of stories for young readers, including *Sleep, Black Bear, Sleep* by mother-daughter team Jane Yolen and Heidi E.Y. Stemple. In her self-illustrated picture-book debut, *Lullaby Moons and a Silver Spoon: A Book of Bedtime Songs and Rhymes,* Dyer presents twenty-one selections from such acclaimed writers as Eve Merriam, Malachy Doyle, and Margaret Wise Brown. A *Kirkus Reviews* writer praised the "elegant, understated, richly colored illustrations" that appear throughout this work. Writing in *School Library Journal,* Jane Marino applauded in particular the illustration Dyer pairs with Mary Jane Carr's poem "Shop of Dreams," which features "soft green hillsides with grazing sheep, a cozy thatch-roofed shop, and a rosy-cheeked moon floating over the horizon."

Dyer also contributed the illustrations to *Mama Always Comes Home,* a picture book by Karma Wilson that explores the loving relationship between mothers and their children. The artist's "colors are as bright and clear as early summer," wrote a critic in *Kirkus Reviews,* and Susan Weitz ranked the images in *School Library Journal* as "insightful." In *Sleep, Black Bear, Sleep* Yolen and Stemple follow the activities of a group of woodland animals as each prepares to hibernate for the winter. "Dyer's consistently adorable watercolors especially stand out when she finds comic inspiration in the hallmark qualities of her animal cast," a *Publishers Weekly* critic wrote of *Sleep, Black Bear, Sleep,* and Weitz observed that the illustrator "deftly inserts details of pattern and personality using gentle, appealing colors."

In her work as an illustrator, Dyer collaborates with her mother on several works. *Sugar Cookies: Sweet Little Lessons on Love* by Amy Krouse Rosenthal offers definitions for a host of words—including "selfless", "considerate", and "endearment"—that are associated with love. *Booklist* reviewer Ilene Cooper stated that "the Dyers' fabulous artwork . . . extend[s] the definitions" of Rosenthal's text. A companion volume, *One Smart Cookie: Bite-Size Lessons for the School Years and Beyond,* offers Rosenthal's take on such terms as "persevere" and "curious". "Old-fashioned images in bright watercolor illustrations invite readers to look twice," Carolyn Phelan maintained in her *Booklist* review of this collaborative picture book.

The Dyers also combine their talents on *There's a Train out for Dreamland,* which features lyrics to a popular 1947 song recorded by the legendary Nat King Cole. In the picture-book version of the song (written by Frederich H. Heider and Carl Kress), a group of children are invited by a cuddly bear to board a blue train that rides along peppermint rails through the wintry countryside. Highlights of the lyrical story include "the roly-poly animals and charming children in soft-focus watercolors," according to a writer in *Kirkus Reviews.*

Biographical and Critical Sources

PERIODICALS

Booklist, April 15, 2003, GraceAnne A. DeCandido, review of *Lullaby Moons and a Silver Spoon: A Book of*

Brooke Dyer joins her mother, Jane Dyer, in creating the illustrations for Frederich H. Heider and Carl Kress's picture book There's a Train out for Dreamland. (Illustration copyright © 2010 Jane Dyer and Brooke Dyer. Reproduced by permission of Harper, an imprint of HarperCollins Childrens, a division of HarperCollins Publishing and Curtis Brown, Ltd.)

Bedtime Songs and Rhymes, p. 1473; November 15, 2006. GraceAnne A. DeCandido, review of *Sleep, Black Bear, Sleep,* p. 56; February 1, 2010, Ilene Cooper, review of *Sugar Cookies: Sweet Little Lessons on Love,* p. 52; September 1, 2010, Carolyn Phelan, review of *One Smart Cookie: Bite-Size Lessons for the School Years and Beyond,* p. 113.

Childhood Education, winter, 2005, Patti Gardner, review of *Mama Always Comes Home,* p. 113; spring, 2008, Susana M. Abreu, review of *Sleep, Black Bear, Sleep,* p. 172.

Kirkus Reviews, April 1, 2003, review of *Lullaby Moons and a Silver Spoon,* p. 533; March 15, 2005, review of *Mama Always Comes Home,* p. 361; September 15, 2010, review of *There's a Train out for Dreamland.*

Publishers Weekly, March 21, 2005, review of *Mama Always Comes Home,* p. 50; December 18, 2006, review of *Sleep, Black Bear, Sleep,* p. 61.

School Library Journal, May, 2003, Jane Marino, review of *Lullaby Moons and a Silver Spoon,* p. 135; May, 2005, Susan Weitz, review of *Mama Always Comes Home,* p. 105; February, 2007, Susan Weitz, review of *Sleep, Black Bear, Sleep,* p. 98; September, 2010, Mary Elam, review of *One Smart Cookie,* p. 133; October, 2010, Julie Roach, review of *There's a Train out for Dreamland,* p. 99.

ONLINE

HarperCollins Web site, http://www.harpercollins.com/ (January 15, 2012), "Brooke Dyer."*

F-G

FERRER, Barbara
See FERRER, Caridad

*   *   *

FERRER, Caridad
(Barbara Ferrer)

Personal

Born in New York, NY; married; children: two. *Ethnicity:* "Cuban-American." *Education:* Attended Florida State University, 1985-90. *Hobbies and other interests:* Music, reading, cooking and collecting cookbooks, photography.

Addresses

Home—Seattle, WA. *Agent*—Adrienne Rosado, PMA Literary & Film Management, 45 W. 21st St., Ste. 401, New York, NY 10010; adrienne@pmalitfilm.com. *E-mail*—barbaracaridadferrer@gmail.com.

Career

Writer.

Member

Society of Children's Book Writers and Illustrators.

Awards, Honors

Rita Award for Best Contemporary Single Title Romance, Romance Writers of America, 2007, and Popular Paperbacks for Young Adults designation, American Library Association, both for *Adiós to My Old Life;* International Latino Book Award, 2010, for *When the Stars Go Blue.*

Writings

Adiós to My Old Life, MTV Books (New York, NY), 2006.

It's Not about the Accent, MTV Books (New York, NY), 2007.
When the Stars Go Blue, Thomas Dunne Books (New York, NY), 2010.

Contributor to *Fifteen Candles: Fifteen Tales of Taffeta, Hairspray, Drunk Uncles, and Other Quinceañera Stories,* edited by Adriana Lopez, HarperCollins (New York, NY), 2007. Author of adult fiction under name Barbara Ferrer.

Sidelights

Cuban-American writer Caridad Ferrer explores Latino culture in her award-winning young-adult novels, among them *When the Stars Go Blue.* Discussing her debut title, *Adiós to My Old Life,* in a *Bildungsroman* online interview, Ferrer stated: "One thing I really wanted to try to show, in some small way, how many different flavors of Latin there are and they're not all created the same although there are definitely some universalities that cross all borders."

In *Adiós to My Old Life* Ferrer introduces Alegría Montero, a gifted seventeen-year-old singer and guitarist hoping to make it big in the music industry. Selected to appear on the reality television show *Oye Mi Canto,* a Latino version of *American Idol,* Alegría finds herself at odds with her strict, traditional Cuban-American father, a professor of music. As the competition heats up and her fame soars, Alegría struggles to stay grounded, seeking guidance from Jaime Lozano, a cute production assistant. "The main characters are appealing and down to earth," a critic observed in a *Kirkus Reviews* appraisal of *Adiós to My Old Life,* and Hazel Rochman noted in *Booklist* that there is "a real story here, with frenetic action, romance . . ., pop-scene fantasy, and surprises to the very end."

The musical element of *Adiós to My Old Life* was important to Ferrer, a talented vocalist who also plays piano, trumpet, and French horn and who dabbled in percussion as a member of a drum corps. As she remarked to Jen Wardrip in a *Teensreadtoo.com* interview, "I suppose my greatest constant and certainly a huge factor in this particular story, is music. I've been a musician my entire life and I let so much of my love for music come out in this particular story."

It's Not about the Accent, Ferrer's second novel for teens, focuses on Caroline Darcy, a bored small-town girl who adopts a new identity. Before heading to college, Darcy decides to pattern her life after that of her gorgeous, fiery great-grandmother, Nana Ellie. Renaming herself "Carolina" and announcing that she is half Cuban, the freshman theater major dyes her hair, upgrades her wardrobe, and sports a flirty personality. When her relationship with Erik, a smug frat boy, takes a distressing turn, Darcy turns to Peter, a Cuban classmate, for help, and he encourages her to investigate her great-grandmother's past. As she does so, a *Publishers Weekly* critic noted, *It's Not about the Accent* "achieves a real richness: [Darcy] not only learns unexpected secrets about Nana Ellie, but hears many revealing life stories."

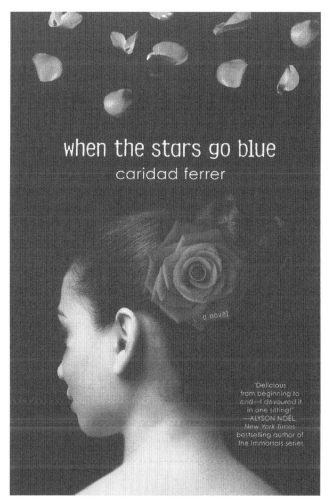

Cover of Caridad Ferrer's novel When the Stars Go Blue, *a modern retelling of Bizet's classic opera* Carmen. (Cover photographs by Andreas Kuehn/Getty Images (woman); TS Photography/Getty Images (rose); Scott Kleinman/Getty Images (rose petals).)

Another Cuban-American teen is at the heart of *When the Stars Go Blue,* a retelling of George Bizet's celebrated opera *Carmen.* Soledad Reyes, a high-school senior pondering a career in dance, receives an intriguing offer from schoolmate Jonathan Crandall to portray Carmen, the beautiful but doomed gypsy, in his competitive drum and bugle corps. As the summer progresses, Soledad and Jonathan fall in love, but their relationship is threatened after Soledad meets Taz, a soccer player who also steals her heart. In her *Booklist* review of *When the Stars Go Blue,* Frances Bradburn applauded the novel's "contemporary characters and . . . engaging story line," and Shawna Sherman concluded in *School Library Journal* that Ferrer's romantic story "satisfies with a climactic ending."

Biographical and Critical Sources

PERIODICALS

Booklist, September 15, 2006, Hazel Rochman, review of *Adiós to My Old Life,* p. 69; November 15, 2010, Frances Bradburn, review of *When the Stars Go Blue,* p. 45.
Kirkus Reviews, November 1, 2010, review of *When the Stars Go Blue.*
Kliatt, September, 2006, Olivia Durant, review of *Adiós to My Old Life,* p. 22.
Publishers Weekly, August 27, 2007, review of *It's Not about the Accent,* p. 91.
School Library Journal, June, 2011, Shawna Sherman, review of *When the Stars Go Blue,* p. 116.
Voice of Youth Advocates, Feburary, 2011, Susan Hampe and Julia Inglesby, review of *When the Stars Go Blue,* p. 552.

ONLINE

Bildungsroman Web log, http://slayground.livejournal.com/ (July 4, 2006), interview with Ferrer.
Caridad Ferrer Home Page, http://caridadferrer.com (January 15, 2012).
Teensreadtoo.com, http://www.teensreadtoo.com/ (January 15, 2012), Jen Wardrip, interview with Ferrer.*

*   *   *

GLIORI, Debi 1959-

Personal

Born February 21, 1959, in Glasgow, Scotland; daughter of Lionel (a musical instrument maker) and Josephine (a tax inspector) Gliori; married George Karl Carson, August 2, 1976 (divorced, February 14, 1978); married Jesse Earl Christman (a furniture maker), June 21, 1991 (divorced, 1999); companion of Michael Holton (a company secretary); children: (first marriage) Rowan Gliori; (second marriage) Benjamin, Patrick, Sophie Christman; (with Holton) Katie Rose. *Education:* Edinburgh College of Art, B.A. (with honors), 1984, postgraduate diploma (illustration). *Politics:* "Left of center."

Addresses

Home and office—Scotland. *Agent*—Penny Holroyde, Caroline Sheldon Literary Agency, 71 Hillgate Pl., London W8 7SS, England; pennyholroyde@caroline sheldon.co.uk.

Career

Author and illustrator. Debi Gliori, Ltd., E. Lothian, Scotland, director. Children's writer-in-residence, Shetland Islands, UK.

Awards, Honors

British Children's Book Award, 1997; Kate Greenaway Medal shortlist, 1997; Scottish Arts Council Award shortlist, 2001, for *Pure Dead Magic;* Kate Greenaway Medal shortlist, and Green Prize for Sustainable Literature, Santa Monica (CA) Library, both 2010, both for *The Trouble with Dragons.*

Writings

SELF-ILLUSTRATED

New Big Sister, Walker Books (London, England), 1990, Bradbury Press (New York, NY) 1991.
New Big House, Walker Books (London, England), 1991, Candlewick Press (Cambridge, MA), 1992.
My Little Brother, Candlewick Press (Cambridge, MA), 1992.
What a Noise, Creative Edge, 1992.
When I'm Big, Walker Books (London, England), 1992.
The Snowchild, Bradbury (New York, NY), 1994.
A Lion at Bedtime, Hippo (London, England), 1994.
Willie Bear and the Wish Fish, Macmillan Books for Young Readers (New York, NY), 1995, published as *Little Bear and the Wish-Fish,* Frances Lincoln (London, England), 1995.
The Snow Lambs, Scholastic (New York, NY), 1996.
The Princess and the Pirate King, Kingfisher (New York, NY), 1996.
Can I Have a Hug?, Orchard Books (New York, NY), 1998.
Tickly under There, Orchard Books (New York, NY), 1998.
No Matter What, Harcourt (San Diego, CA), 1999.
Polar Bolero: A Bedtime Dance, Scholastic (London, England), 2000, Harcourt (San Diego, CA), 2001.
Flora's Blanket, Orchard Books (New York, NY), 2001.
Debi Gliori's Bedtime Stories: Bedtime Tales with a Twist, Dorling Kindersley (New York, NY), 2002.
Penguin Post, Harcourt (San Diego, CA), 2002.

Flora's Surprise, Orchard Books (New York, NY), 2003.
Where Did That Baby Come From?, Harcourt (Orlando, FL), 2005.
Goodnight, Baby Bat, Doubleday (London, England), 2007.
The Trouble with Dragons, Walker Books (London, England), 2008.
Stormy Weather, Walker & Company (New York, NY), 2009.
The Scariest Thing of All, Walker & Company (New York, NY), 2012.

"MR. BEAR" SERIES; SELF-ILLUSTRATED

Mr. Bear Babysits, Artists & Writers Guild, 1994.
Mr. Bear's Picnic, Golden Books (New York, NY), 1995.
Mr. Bear Says I Love You, Little Simon (New York, NY), 1997.
Mr. Bear Says Good Night, Little Simon (New York, NY), 1997.
Mr. Bear Says Peek-a-Boo, Little Simon (New York, NY), 1997.
Mr. Bear Says a Spoonful for You, Little Simon (New York, NY), 1997.
Mr. Bear Says "Are You There, Baby Bear?", Orchard (New York, NY), 1999.
Mr. Bear's New Baby, Orchard Books (New York, NY), 1999.
Mr. Bear to the Rescue, Orchard Books (New York, NY), 2000.
Mr. Bear's Vacation, Orchard Books (New York, NY), 2000.

"PURE DEAD" MIDDLE-GRADE NOVEL SERIES;

Pure Dead Magic, Knopf (New York, NY), 2001.
Pure Dead Wicked, Knopf (New York, NY), 2002.
Pure Dead Brilliant, Knopf (New York, NY), 2003.
Deep Trouble, Doubleday (London, England), 2004, published as *Pure Dead Trouble,* Knopf (New York, NY), 2005.
Deep Water, Doubleday (London, England), 2005, published as *Pure Dead Batty,* Knopf (New York, NY), 2006.
Deep Fear, Doubleday (London, England), 2006, published as *Pure Dead Frozen,* Knopf (New York, NY), 2007.

"WITCH BABY" SERIES; SELF-ILLUSTRATED

Witch Baby and Me, Corgi Books (London, England), 2008.
Witch Baby and Me after Dark, Corgi Books (London, England), 2009.
Witch Baby and Me at School, Corgi Books (London, England), 2009.
Witch Baby and Me on Stage, Corgi Books (London, England), 2010.

ILLUSTRATOR

Roger McGough and Dee Reid, *Oxford Children's ABC Picture Dictionary,* Oxford University Press (Oxford, England), 1990.

Margaret Donaldson, *Margery Mo,* Deutsch (London, England), 1991.

Stephanie Baudet, *The Incredible Shrinking Hippo,* Hamish Hamilton (London, England), 1991.

Roger McGough, *Oxford 123 Book of Number Rhymes,* Oxford University Press (Oxford, England), 1992.

Sue Stops, *Dulci Dando,* Holt (New York, NY), 1992.

Sue Stops, *Dulcie Dando, Disco Dancer,* Scholastic (New York, NY), 1992.

Margaret Donaldson, *Margery Mo's Magic Island,* Scholastic (New York, NY), 1992.

Sue Stops, *Dulcie Dando, Soccer Star,* Holt (New York, NY), 1992.

Lisa Bruce, *Oliver's Alphabets,* Bradbury Press (New York, NY, 1993.

David Martin, *Lizzie and Her Puppy,* Candlewick Press (Cambridge, MA), 1993.

David Martin, *Lizzie and Her Dolly,* Candlewick Press (Cambridge, MA), 1993.

David Martin, *Lizzie and Her Kitty,* Candlewick Press (Cambridge, MA), 1993.

David Martin, *Lizzie and Her Friend,* Candlewick Press (Cambridge, MA), 1993.

Poems Go Clang!: A Collection of Noisy Verse, Candlewick Press (Cambridge, MA), 1997.

Joyce Dunbar, *Tell Me Something Happy before I Go to Sleep,* Harcourt (New York, NY), 1998, published with CD, Picture Corgi (London, England), 2007.

Christina Rossetti, *Give Him My Heart,* new edition, Bloomsbury (London, England), 1998, published as *What Can I Give Him?,* Holiday House (New York, NY), 1998.

Joyce Dunbar, *The Very Small,* Harcourt (San Diego, CA), 2000.

The Dorling Kindersley Book of Nursery Rhymes, Dorling Kindersley (New York, NY), 2001, published with CD, 2005.

Joyce Dunbar, *Tell Me What It's Like to Be Big,* Harcourt (San Diego, CA), 2001.

Alan Durant, *Always and Forever,* Harcourt (Orlando, FL), 2004.

OTHER

A Present for Big Pig, illustrated by Kate Simpson, Candlewick Press (Cambridge, MA), 1995.

The Candlewick Book of Bedtime Stories, Candlewick Press (Cambridge, MA), 2003.

Author's works have been translated into Spanish.

Adaptations

Pure Dead Magic and *Pure Dead Wicked* were adapted for audiocassette by Recorded Books (Frederick, MD), 2002.

Sidelights

Scottish author and illustrator Debi Gliori has earned plaudits on both sides of the Atlantic for her bright and whimsical picture books as well as for her humorous novels and chapter books, all which feature a touch of magic. Gliori's ink-and-watercolor artwork brings to life dozens of original stories and also graces the pages of numerous children's books by other writers, including Joyce Dunbar, Christina Rossetti, Alan Durant, and David Martin. Gliori's palette ranges in tone from pastels to brilliantly saturated color, and the use of intriguing perspectives and an attention to detail are considered hallmarks of her work.

Many of Gliori's books center on the everyday concerns of youngsters, such as being afraid of the dark, accepting new siblings, outgrowing the family home, dealing with bullies, and making friends. Featuring what *School Library Journal* critic Piper L. Nyman called a "funny and rhythmic perspective," *Where Did That Baby Come From?* casts a tiger cub in place of a small human child and poses a logical question: Why do parents open their home to the turmoil that a new baby brings? Books of this type are inspired by Gliori's own experience as the mother of five children. "I've never questioned my motivation for writing—it is as essential a part of my life as breathing and eating," she once told *SATA.* "With five children, the option of working away from home was unthinkable. I want to be around my kids and to watch and marvel as they grow up. Writing for children is a natural extension of this process."

Gliori's first books feature human characters and portray changes in families. Adorned with "charming, humorous" illustrations, to quote *School Library Journal* critic Lucy Young Clem, *New Big Sister* describes the changes a pregnant mother undergoes while awaiting the arrival of twins from a young girl's viewpoint. A *Books for Keeps* reviewer called the title "refreshing" and expressed similar praise for *New Big House,* which also treats the challenges of an expanding family. In *New Big House* a house-hunting family decides to add on to their existing home instead of moving. *Booklist* contributor Hazel Rochman praised this picture book for its emotive illustrations, while *School Library Journal* reviewer Virginia E. Jeschelnig noted its verisimilitude.

Another early self-illustrated work by Gliori, *My Little Brother,* recounts how an older sister tries to get rid of her exasperating toddler brother and concludes with what a *Books for Keeps* reviewer called a "delightful ending." Conversely, *When I'm Big* describes a young boy's fantasies about growing older in what *School Librarian* contributor Elizabeth J. King called a "funny, jokey" manner.

Other titles by Gliori treat childhood fears. For example, the very real fear of monsters under the bed is the subject of *A Lion at Bedtime,* in which the fearless Ben shows he is not afraid by dressing his under-bed

Debi Gliori acts as both writer and illustrator on the picture book **Where Did That Baby Come From?** (Harcourt, Inc., 2005. Reprinted by permission of Houghton Mifflin Harcourt Publishing Company, and The Random House Group Ltd.)

lion in his father's pajamas. While acknowledging the Scottish author/illustrator's debt to Maurice Sendak, G. English praised *A Lion at Bedtime* for its "witty style" in a *Books for Your Children* review. London *Observer* reviewer Kate Kellaway also appreciated the work for its style and what she termed its "wonderful" illustrations.

The Snowchild deals with another fear: bullies. Introverted young Katie experiences the unkindness of her peers, but she finally makes friends when other children join her in crafting small snow people. While *Booklist* critic Julie Walton found the writing "uneven," she praised Gliori's "appealing" artwork for *The Snowchild.* Janet Sims predicted in *School Librarian* that the book would be "useful" in discussions about self-esteem and bullies, while a *Books for Keeps* contributor deemed *The Snowchild* "thought-provoking."

Gliori addresses another common childhood concern—dark, blustery nights—in *Stormy Weather,* a bedtime tale. Her self-illustrated work opens on an anxious young fox whose mother offers a reassuring presence as a storm rages outside. Readers then visit a host of animal parents, from polar bears to snails to rabbits, who also provide comfort to their young ones by protecting them from the elements. "Gliori's familiar characters assist the straightforward narrative through expressive faces, completing a unified package," Meg Smith observed in her *School Library Journal* review of *Stormy Weather.*

Gliori's *The Trouble with Dragons,* which was shortlisted for the prestigious Kate Greenaway Medal, offers a lyrical story about caring for planet Earth. In the tale, a world overpopulated by dragons that care about little other than themselves soon finds itself on the brink of environmental collapse. When the dragons turn to other creatures for help, they discover the importance of reforestation and recycling. "What could have been heavy-handed is magical, thanks to the playful artwork and bouncy rhymes," Kathleen Kelly MacMillan observed in *School Library Journal,* and a *Publishers Weekly* critic similarly noted that the "conversational writing style" in *The Trouble with Dragons* "scores points without sounding preachy." A writer in *Kirkus Reviews* applauded Gliori's artwork for the book, stating that her pictures of "brilliant orange dragons in chaotic urban scenes . . . help to foster a sense of urgency."

Gliori features a host of affable bruins in her "Mr. Bear" series of board-and picture books. In *Mr. Bear Babysits* the good-natured bear does just that by babysitting the neighbor cubs. *Mr. Bear's Picnic* finds him taking his own unappreciative cubs on an outing, and *Mr. Bear's New Baby* recounts how the house is thrown into disarray in preparation for the new arrival. In *Mr. Bear to the Rescue,* another volume in the series, Papa Bear rises to the occasion when disaster strikes. Reviewing *Mr. Bear's Picnic* for *School Library Journal,* Lynn Crockett described Gliori's characters as "lovable" and apt for story time. Another bear character makes his debut in *Little Bear and the Wish Fish,* a cautionary tale that explains what can happen when we get what we supposedly want.

Standards in the oeuvre of most children's-book illustrators include alphabet books and compilations of nursery rhymes and poems. In her work for *Oliver's Alphabets* by Lisa Bruce, Gliori serves as illustrator, detailing a young boy's world, replete with "pleasing minutae" in the opinion of *School Library Journal* critic Mary Lou Budd. In her own *Poems Go Clang!: A Collection of Noisy Verse* she includes fifty classic verses, making up what Jean Pollock deemed a "serviceable" collection in her *School Library Journal* review. Mother Goose gets a new look in Gliori's version of fifty rhymes and poems, with explanatory annotations. The combination of "beguiling artwork" and "fascinating tidbits of information" in *Debi Gliori's Bedtime Stories: Bedtime Tales with a Twist* results in a better-than-average work of its kind, according to a *Kirkus Reviews* contributor.

Although Gliori first earned a reputation as an author and illustrator of picture books, she has also turned to writing works for older readers. Her "Pure Dead" series, which includes *Pure Dead Magic, Pure Dead Trouble,* and *Pure Dead Frozen,* introduces readers to the eccentric Strega-Borgia family. Laced with bits of Scots dialect, the stories combine fantasy, high technology, action, and humor in what a *Kirkus Reviews* critic described as a "nonstop farce." In the debut novel, *Pure Dead Magic,* the three Strega-Borgia children are left to rescue their kidnapped father while their mother attends graduate school for witches. Eva Mitnick predicted in *School Library Journal* that the novel would appeal to fans of children's authors J.K. Rowling and Lemony Snicket, and she determined as well that "any plot defi-

ciencies" are offset by the work's farcical tone. In *Booklist* Ilene Cooper held a similar opinion, stating that although the plot is "occasionally tedious," *Pure Dead Magic* is "original" and provides "plenty of laughs."

The travails of the Strega-Borgia siblings continue in *Pure Dead Wicked,* which a *Kirkus Reviews* critic dubbed a "pedal-to-the-metal page turner." Here family members find refuge at the Auchenlochtermuchty Arms after the roof collapses on Strega-Schloss, their ancestral family castle in Scotland. Dubbed "another fast-paced, grossly hilarious adventure" by *Booklist* contributor Kay Weisman, *Pure Dead Brilliant* follows a group of visiting witches as they throw the family household into turmoil; meanwhile Titus discovers that the massive fortune he has inherited from his mafia-boss grandfather may have strings attached. In *Pure Dead Trouble* the Strega-Borgias find themselves threatened when a newly hired butler turns out to be a demon intent upon blowing up a nearby corporate headquarters. Fortunately, the children's nanny, Flora McLachlan, is quick to assess the threat and peg it as a demonic presence searching for the powerful Chronostone. Noting

Gliori presents a family saga of a creepy sort in the series that includes **Pure Dead Batty,** *featuring cover art by Jimmy Pickering.* (Reproduced by permission of Yearling, an imprint of Random House Children's Books, a division of Random House, Inc.)

Gliori's self-illustrated chapter book Witch Baby and Me after Dark *is the first installment in her "Witch Baby" series.* (Published by Corgi Books. Reprinted by permission of The Random House Group Ltd.)

that the series contains an ever-expanding cast list, *Booklist* critic Abby Nolan wrote that *Pure Dead Trouble* features "humor [that] is darker . . . than in Gliori's previous books, and includes enough "details about the workings of Hell" to fascinate preteen readers.

Published in England as *Deep Water, Pure Dead Batty* finds Titus, Pandora, and Damp worried over Nanny McLachlan's disappearance. When their father is arrested as the nanny's possible murderer, the children are on their own in interpreting the strange omens they hope will lead them to Flora McLachlan and win Don Luciano Strega-Borgia's freedom. The battle with demonic forces continues in *Pure Dead Frozen,* as the family—which now includes a newborn changeling—unites against the hoards of assembled evil creatures hoping to acquire the powerful Chronostone against all odds. "The madness and the antics are as crazed as ever" in *Pure Dead Batty,* according to *School Library Journal* contributor Saleena L. Davidson, the critic citing the "Pure Dead" books as "perfect for fantasy readers who want humor with their magic."

Gliori's "Witch Baby" series of self-illustrated chapter books focuses on the MacRae family, whose youngest member—one-year-old Daisy—possesses incredible magical powers that enable her to levitate a refrigerator, transform a human into a slug, and conjure up an invisible (and smelly) canine, among other things. Trouble

is, only nine-year-old Lily is able to bear witness to these astounding events, and her parents refuse to believe her account of Daisy's exploits. In *Witch Baby and Me,* the first installment in the series, Lily and Daisy are tasked with visiting their new neighbors to deliver party invitations for a soiree that could prove disastrous should the youngster cast any spells. A writer in *Kirkus Reviews* noted that Gliori "applies the same ebullient and wacky sense of humor" to her "Witch Baby" titles as she did to her "Pure Dead" series.

Witch Baby and Me after Dark takes place on Halloween. With help from her friend, Vivaldi, Lily brings Daisy trick-or-treating but finds it impossible to stop her sister from transforming into a variety of spooky creatures. To make matters worse, Daisy's odiferous pooch, WayWoof, has gone missing and Lily must now track him down. "Gliori's story brims with humor," remarked *Booklist* reviewer Kay Weisman. In *Witch Baby and Me on Stage* Lily prepares to play her grandfather's bagpipes at a school concert while the Sisters of Hiss—the three Scottish witches who secretly created Daisy—bargain for her return, noting specifically that the toddler is not yet toilet trained. "Gliori's humor, as always in this series, is much concerned with the kind of adorable grossness common to small children," a writer in *Kirkus Reviews* stated.

Biographical and Critical Sources

PERIODICALS

Booklist, February 1, 1991, Hazel Rochman, review of *Mr. Bear's New Baby,* p. 979; May 15, 1992, Hazel Rochman, review of *New Big House,* p. 1687; December 1, 1992, Leone McDermott, review of *Dulcie Dando, Soccer Star,* pp. 677-678; December 15, 1994, Julie Walton, review of *The Snowchild,* p. 757; November 15, 1996, Karen Morgan, review of *The Snow Lambs,* p. 584; February 1, 1998, Hazel Rochman, review of *Mr. Bear Says Peek-a-Boo,* p. 922; September 1, 1998, Hazel Rochman, review of *What Can I Give Him?,* p. 132; November 15, 1999, Tim Arnold, review of *No Matter What,* p. 635; May 15, 2000, Marta Segal, review of *Mr. Bear's Vacation,* pp. 1, 48; November 15, 2000, Marta Segal, review of *Mr. Bear to the Rescue,* p. 648; December 15, 2000, Lauren Peterson, review of *The Very Small,* p. 825; April 1, 2001, Hazel Rochman, review of *The Dorling Kindersley Book of Nursery Rhymes,* p. 1474; May 1, 2001, Shelle Rosenfeld, review of *Polar Bolero: A Bedtime Dance,* p. 1690; May 15, 2001, Ilene Cooper, review of *Flora's Blanket,* p. 1757; August, 2001, Ilene Cooper, review of *Pure Dead Magic,* p. 2118; June 1, 2002, Ilene Cooper, reviews of *Can I Have a Hug?* and *Tickly under There,* both p. 1713; September 15, 2002, Susan Dove Lempke, review of *Pure Dead Wicked,* p. 231; December 15, 2002, Connie Fletcher, review of *Penguin Post,* p. 766; November 1, 2003, Kay Weisman, review of *Pure Dead Brilliant,* p. 496; March 1, 2005, Connie Fletcher, review of *Where Did That Baby Come From?,* p. 1203; October 1, 2005, Abby Nolan, review of *Pure Dead Trouble,* p. 57; August 1, 2006, Ilene Cooper, review of *Pure Dead Batty,* p. 70; September 1, 2010, Kay Weisman, review of *Witch Baby and Me*, p. 108; September 1, 2011, Kay Weisman, review of *Witch Baby and Me on Stage*, p. 116.

Books for Your Children, spring, 1994, G. English, review of *A Lion at Bedtime*, p. 8.

Bulletin of the Center for Children's Books, May, 1994, Roger Sutton, review of *Mr. Bear Babysits*, p. 287; February, 1997, Lisa Mahoney, review of *The Snow Lambs*, pp. 204-205; February, 2002, review of *Pure Dead Magic*, p. 204; March, 2003, review of *Flora's Surprise!*, p. 274.

Children's Playmate, October-November, 1994, review of *Mr. Bear Babysits*, p. 19.

Horn Book, fall, 1995, Sheila M. Geraty, reviews of *Willie Bear and the Wish Fish* and *Mr. Bear's Picnic*, both p. 95; spring, 1997, Martha Sibert, reviews of *The Princess and the Pirate King* and *The Snow Lambs*, both p. 29; fall, 2001, Sheila M. Geraty, reviews of *Flora's Blanket*, *Mr. Bear to the Rescue*, and *Polar Bolero*, all p. 231.

Junior Bookshelf, February, 1993, review of *When I'm Big*, p. 12; April, 1995, review of *A Present for Big Pig*, p. 66; August, 1995, review of *Little Bear and the Wish Fish*, p. 128.

Kirkus Reviews, June 1, 1994, review of *Mr. Bear Babysits*, pp. 774-775; January 15, 1999, review of *Mr. Bear's New Baby*, p. 144; November 1, 1999, review of *No Matter What*, p. 1741; February 1, 2001, review of *The Dorling Kindersley Book of Nursery Rhymes*, pp. 182-183; July 1, 2001, review of *Pure Dead Wicked*, p. 955; August 1, 2001, review of *Pure Dead Magic*, p. 1122; August 15, 2001, review of *Tell Me What It's Like to Be Big*, p. 1211; October 1, 2002, review of *Penguin Post*, p. 1470; December 15, 2002, review of *Flora's Surprise!*, p. 1850; July 1, 2005, review of *Pure Dead Trouble*, p. 735; July 1, 2006, review of *Pure Dead Batty*, p. 677; July 1, 2007, review of *Pure Dead Frozen*; September 15, 2008, review of *The Trouble with Dragons*; October 15, 2009, review of *Stormy Weather*; July 1, 2010, review of *Witch Baby and Me*; July 1, 2011, review of *Witch Baby and Me on Stage*.

Kliatt, July, 2004, Mary Purucker, review of *Pure Dead Brilliant*, p. 55; July, 2005, Paula Rohrlick, review of *Pure Dead Trouble*, p. 11.

Library Journal, August, 2001, Maria Otero-Boisvert, review of *No Matter What*, p. S60.

Magpies, November, 1998, Joan Zahnleiter, review of *Give Him My Heart*, p. 27.

Observer (London, England), November 28, 1993, Kate Kellaway, review of *A Lion at Bedtime*, p. 11.

Publishers Weekly, August 24, 1992, review of *My Little Brother*, p. 78; May 2, 1994, review of *Mr. Bear Babysits*, p. 306; June 5, 1995, review of *Mr. Bear's Picnic*, p. 62; September 9, 1996, review of *The Princess and the Pirate King*, p. 82; October 28, 1996, review of *The Snow Lambs*, pp. 80-81; September 28, 1998, review of *What Can I Give Him?*, pp. 58-59, and *Tell Me Something Happy before I Go to Sleep*, p. 101; February 15, 1999, review of *Mr. Bear's New Baby*, p. 106; November 8, 1999, review of *No Matter What*, p. 66; October 2, 2000, review of *The Very*

Small, p. 80; March 12, 2001, review of *The Dorling Kindersley Book of Nursery Rhymes*, p. 93; April 9, 2001, review of *Flora's Blanket*, p. 73; May 7, 2001, review of *Polar Bolero*, p. 246; July 2, 2001, review of *Tell Me What It's Like to Be Big*, p. 74; August 27, 2001, review of *Pure Dead Magic*, p. 85; July 8, 2002, review of *Pure Dead Wicked*, p. 51; March 21, 2005, review of *Where Did That Baby Come From?*, p. 50; August 18, 2008, review of *The Trouble with Dragons*, p. 61.

School Librarian, February, 1993, Elizabeth J. King, review of *When I'm Big*, p. 15; November, 1994, Janet Sims, review of *The Snowchild*, p. 146; August, 1995, Jane Doonan, review of *Little Bear and the Wish-Fish*, p. 103; February, 1997, Carolyn Boyd, review of *Mr. Bear to the Rescue*, and Chris Stephenson, review of *The Princess and the Pirate King*, both p. 18.

School Library Journal, February, 1992, Lucy Young Clem, review of *New Big Sister*, p. 72; August, 1992, Virginia E. Jeschelnig, reviews of *New Big Sister*, p. 72, and *New Big House*, pp. 135-136; January, 1993, Virginia E. Jeschelnig, review of *My Little Brother*, p. 76; April, 1993, Lori A. Janick, review of *Dulcie Dando, Soccer Star*, pp. 102-103; December, 1993, Mary Lou Budd, review of *Oliver's Alphabets*, p. 80; August, 1994, Lauralyn Persson, review of *Mr. Bear Babysits*, p. 130; December, 1994, Margaret A. Chang, review of *The Snowchild*, pp. 74-75; July, 1995, Martha Gordon, review of *Willie Bear and the Wish Fish*, p. 61; August, 1995, Lynn Cockett, review of *Mr. Bear's Picnic*, p. 122; March, 1998, Jean Pollock, review of *Poems Go Clang!*, pp. 200-201; October, 1998, Anne Connor, review of *What Can I Give Him?*, p. 41; November 1, 1998, Judith Constantinides, review of *Tell Me Something Happy before I Go to Sleep*, pp. 83-84; March, 1999, Dawn Amsberry, review of *Mr. Bear's New Baby*, p. 175; November, 1999, Marlene Gawron, review of *No Matter What*, p. 116; January, 2000, Selene S. Vasquez, review of *Mr. Bear Says, Are You There, Baby Bear?*, p. 96; March, 2000, Faith Brautigam, review of *Mr. Bear's Vacation*, p. 197; November, 2000, Joy Fleishhacker, review of *The Very Small*, p. 119, and Jody McCoy, review of *Mr. Bear to the Rescue*, p. 120; June, 2001, Helen Foster James, review of *Polar Bolero*, p. 114; July, 2001, Christina F. Renaud, review of *Flora's Blanket*, p. 81, and JoAnn Jonas, review of *The Dorling Kindersley Book of Nursery Rhymes*, p. 94; September, 2001, Alison Kastner, review of *Tell Me What It's Like to Be Big*, p. 188, and Eva Mitnick, review of *Pure Dead Magic*, p. 225; June, 2002, Teresa Bateman, review of *Pure Dead Magic*, pp. 70-71; August, 2002, Lynn Evarts, review of *Pure Dead Wicked*, p. 184; October, 2003, Elaine Baran Black, review of *Pure Dead Brilliant*, p. 164; April, 2005, Piper L. Nyman, review of *Where Did That Baby Come From?*, p. 98; August, 2005, Saleena L. Davidson, review of *Pure Dead Trouble*, p. 125; August, 2006, Saleena L. Davidson, review of *Pure Dead Batty*, p. 120; September, 2007, Walter Minkel, review of *Pure Dead Frozen*, p. 196; November, 2008, Kathleen Kelly MacMillan, review of *The Trouble with Dragons*, p. 88; December, 2009, Meg Smith, review of *Stormy Weather*, p. 82; September, 2010, Delia Carruthers, reviews of *Witch Baby and Me* and *Witch Baby and Me after Dark,* both p. 154.

Times Educational Supplement, June 28, 1996, Susan Young, "Bend Them, Shake Them, Any Way You Want Them"; October, 1996, Melissa Hudak, review of *The Snow Lambs,* p. 94; November 20, 1998, review of *Give Him My Heart.*

ONLINE

Debi Gliori Home Page, http://www.debiglioribooks.com (January 15, 2012).

Random House Web site, http://www.randomhouse.com/ (June 1, 2008), autobiographical essay by Gliori.

Walker Books Web site, http://www.walker.co.uk/ (January 15, 2012), "Debi Gliori."

*   *   *

GOODMAN, Shawn 1970-

Personal

Born in 1970; married; children: two daughters. *Education:* Master's degree.

Addresses

Home—Ithaca, NY. *Agent*—Seth Fishman, Gernert Company, 136 E. 57th St., New York, NY 10022; sfishman@thegernertco.com. *E-mail*—shawn@shawn goodmanbooks.com.

Career

Writer and school psychologist. Worked variously as a cook, bicycle mechanic, and psychologist; former psychologist at girls' and boys' juvenile justice facilities in New York State. Advocate for juvenile justice reform and literacy; lecturer.

Member

Society of Children's Book Writers and Illustrators.

Awards, Honors

Delacorte Prize for Best Young-Adult Debut, 2009, and Best Fiction for Young Adults selection, American Library Association/YALSA, 2012, both for *Something like Hope.*

Writings

Something like Hope, Delacorte Press (New York, NY), 2011.

Former columnist.

Shawn Goodman (Photograph by Sonya Sones. Reproduced by permission.)

Sidelights

Shawn Goodman is a writer and school psychologist whose personal experiences working in a girls' juvenile detention facility inspired him to write his first novel, *Something like Hope.* Winner of the 2009 prize for best-young-adult novel debut awarded by Delacorte Press, *Something like Hope* is one of several ways Goodman has turned public attention to problems within the current U.S. juvenile justice system. He also continues to write and lecture on issues related to special education, foster care, and literacy.

Goodman grew up as a reluctant reader, but he credits a novel by Pat Conroy with changing his life at age fifteen. "Every day in English class, it was this slow death picking through irrelevant plots to find examples of symbolism, and foreshadowing," he recalled in an online interview with Cynthia Leitich Smith. "None of it meant anything to me. Which is why, as a YA writer/former reluctant reader, I have to keep in mind the thousand or so reasons kids have to not read."

Seventeen-year-old Shavonne, the central character in *Something like Hope,* has been in juvenile detention since middle school, and she worries what will happen when she is released from the system on her eighteenth birthday. Fortunately, Shavonne is in the care of Mr. Delpopolo, a counselor who is determined to help the young woman deal with the issues from her past that threaten her future behavior: a childhood living with a drug-addicted mother, her deep-seated guilt over her betrayal of her younger brother, being prostituted by a foster mother, and becoming pregnant at age fifteen. Life in detention also poses threats, as Shavonne must deal with a series of emotionally troubled roommates and an abusive guart who seems to have it in for her.

Goodman tells his story in a first-person narrative that "builds to a tense climax," as Hazel Rochman noted in her *Booklist* review of *Something like Hope.* Shavonne's voice is "witty, tender, explicit, and tough," added the critic, and it "will grab readers." The "gritty, frank" account of a teen trapped in a seemingly unjust justice system "doesn't shrink from the harshness of the setting," wrote a *Kirkus Reviews* writer, the critic adding that Shavonne's choices ultimately result in "much-needed redemption." In *Publishers Weekly* a reviewer asserted that the author's "delicate prose avoids sentimentality," and in *Something like Hope* Goodman effectively crafts "a searing" portrait of a troubled teen who readers will cheer as she begins to "claim the life long stolen from her."

Biographical and Critical Sources

PERIODICALS

Booklist, December 15, 2010, Hazel Rochman, review of *Something like Hope,* p. 45.
Bulletin of the Center for Children's Books, December, 2010, Karen Coats, review of *Something like Hope,* p. 186.
Kirkus Reviews, November 1, 2010, review of *Something like Hope.*
Publishers Weekly, November 1, 2010, review of *Something like Hope,* p. 45.

ONLINE

Cynsations Web log, http://cynthialeitichsmith.blogspot.com/ (March, 2011), interview with Goodman.
Elevensies Web log, http://2011debuts.livejournal.com/ (October 6, 2009), interview with Goodman.
Shawn Goodman Home Page, http://www.shawngoodmanbooks.com (January 9, 2012).*

*   *   *

GOSSELINK, John 1967-

Personal

Born 1967, in CA; mother a teacher; married; wife a librarian; children: three. *Education:* College degree.

Addresses

Home—Smithville, TX.

Career

Educator and author. Teacher of English at secondary and university level. Presenter at schools and festivals.

Writings

The Defense of Thaddeus A. Ledbetter, illustrated by Jason Rosenstock, Amulet Books (New York, NY), 2010.

Contributor to periodicals, including *Smithville (TX) Times;* contributor of biweekly humor column "Stumbling Forward" to *TexasEscapes.com,* 2003-06.

Sidelights

John Gosselink grew up in Texas, where he continues to make his home. In addition to working as a teacher of English and composition, Gosselink contributes humorous essays to his hometown newspaper that poke fun at everything from poetry readings to the U.S. Census, all with a heaping helping of personal anecdotes. He has also channeled his quirky humor into fiction for children, producing the engaging middle-grade novel *The Defense of Thaddeus A. Ledbetter.*

Illustrated by Jason Rosenstock, *The Defense of Thaddeus A. Ledbetter* finds the titular middle schooler in pretty big trouble. Half way into his seventh-grade studies, twelve-year-old Thaddeus decided to point out the flaws in the safety-drill system at Crooked Creek Middle School, but the policemen, firemen, and other first-responders who are called in to deal with his pretend emergency do not appreciate the boy's efforts. Now Thaddeus looks forward to an arduous six months of in-school detention, which means sitting in a room doing homework with only a bored teacher's aide to monitor

John Gosselink introduces a nerdy young hero in his middle-grade novel The Defense of Thaddeus A. Ledbetter, *featuring cover art by Jason Rosenstock.* (Jacket art copyright © 2010 by Jason Rosenstock. Reproduced by permission of Amulet Books, an imprint of Harry N. Abrams.)

him. The preteen quickly sizes up his options and decides to transform his punishment into an opportunity. With the help of friends, family, and the school's office equipment, Thaddeus begins to mount a defense of his actions, detailing the flaws he sees in the school's operation and engaging in a snarky series of letters with school administrators. Gosselink mimics the case-file nature of Thaddeus's activities by including the boy's notes, letters and e-mails, drawings and diagrams, and diary entries; from these clues they also slowly piece together the legitimate reason for the geeky adolescent's compulsive safety concerns.

The hero of *The Defense of Thaddeus A. Ledbetter* "is as weird and annoying as the students and faculty think he is," asserted a *Kirkus Reviews* writer, "but there is something endearing about him too." The "chaotic" nature of Gosselink's storyline requires patient reading, Amanda MacGregor noted, but the *Voice of Youth Advocates* critic added that such patience is "rewarded with hilarious situations told by a memorable narrator in a unique format." Calling Thaddeus "as deficient in social skills as he is clever and motivated," Kara Dean wrote in *Booklist* that the author's "original and entertaining" debut will appeal to fans of the "Wimpy Kid" novels by Jeff Kinney, and *School Library Journal* contributor Tina Martin predicted that the "sassy irreverent spirit" of Gosselink's young hero will inspire readers to "root him on as they identify with his frustrations."

Biographical and Critical Sources

PERIODICALS

Booklist, November 1, 2010, Kara Dean, review of *The Defense of Thaddeus A. Ledbetter,* p. 67.

Kirkus Reviews, September 15, 2010, review of *The Defense of Thaddeus A. Ledbetter.*

School Library Journal, November, 2010, Tina Martin, review of *The Defense of Thaddeus A. Ledbetter,* p. 116.

Voice of Youth Advocates, December, 2010, Amanda MacGregor, review of *The Defense of Thaddeus A. Ledbetter,* p. 454.

ONLINE

Texas Book Festival Web site, http://www.texasbook festival.org/ (January 11, 2012), "John Gosselink."

Texas Escapes Online, http://www.texasescapes.com/ (January 11, 2012), "John Gosselink."

*   *   *

GOW, Nancy

Personal

Born in Canada.

Addresses

Home—Montreal, Quebec, Canada. *E-mail*—gowster 2003@yahoo.ca.

Career

Poet. Former vocalist with rock group Software; yoga instructor.

Member

Canadian Society of Children's Authors, Illustrators, and Performers.

Writings

Ten Big Toes and a Prince's Nose, illustrated by Stephen Costanza, Sterling (New York, NY), 2010.

Sidelights

In addition to writing poetry, Canadian author Nancy Gow has worked as the lead singer in a rock-and-roll band as well as teaching yoga. By channeling her talent in wordsmithing with her skill as a storyteller, Gow created the entertaining text for her first picture book, *Ten Big Toes and a Prince's Nose.*

Illustrated by Stephen Costanza, *Ten Big Toes and a Prince's Nose* treats young readers to a fairy tale-type story in which a beautiful and kindly princess is having difficulty attracting a suitable partner because of her hugely oversized feet. In a separate and far-off kingdom, a good-natured prince has a similar dilemma: he finds it impossible to kindle the affections of a prospective wife due to his amazingly large nose. Because true love always finds a way, the prince and princess eventually meet on a ski-lift, where their unusual attributes are conveniently concealed beneath bulky winter clothing.

"The pleasant lilt of the rhyming, rhythmic text" in *Ten Big Toes and a Prince's Nose* results in what *Booklist* contributor Carolyn Phelan described as "an original prince-princess story with a nice message" that is also "a natural for reading aloud." Costanza's use of "saturated [pastel] colors and folk-like . . . artwork are just right for this jaunty tale," asserted a *Kirkus Reviews* writer, while in *School Library Journal* Mary N. Oluonye wrote that Gow's tale "carries an obvious but nonetheless important message of self-acceptance."

Biographical and Critical Sources

PERIODICALS

Booklist, October 15, 2010, Carolyn Phelan, review of *Ten Big Toes and a Prince's Nose,* p. 58.

Kirkus Reviews, September 15, 2010, review of *Ten Big Toes and a Prince's Nose.*

School Library Journal, November, 2010, Mary N. Oluonye, review of *Ten Big Toes and a Prince's Nose,* p. 70.

ONLINE

Authors Now Web site, http://www.authorsnow.com/ (January 9, 2012), "Nancy Gow."

Nancy Gow Home Page, http://www.nancygow.com (January 9, 2012).

*   *   *

GRABENSTEIN, Chris 1955-

Personal

Born September 2, 1955, in Buffalo, NY; married; wife's name Jennifer (a voice-over actress). *Education:* University of Tennessee, B.S. (communications).

Addresses

Home—New York, NY. *Agent*—Spieler Agency, 154 W. 57th St., Ste. 135, New York, NY 10019. *E-mail*—author@chrisgrabenstein.com.

Career

Writer. Formerly worked at a bank in New York, NY; comedian in New York City clubs; J. Walter Thompson (advertising agency), New York, NY, copywriter, 1984-88; Bates Worldwide (advertising agency), New York, NY, creative director, 1988-91; Young & Rubicam (advertising agency), New York, NY, group creative director, 1991-2001; Bart & Chris (radio creative services), New York, NY, and Seattle, WA, cofounder.

Member

Mystery Writers of America (president of New York City chapter), International Thriller Writers, Society of Children's Book Writers and Illustrators.

Awards, Honors

Anthony Award for Best First Mystery, 2006, for *Tilt a Whirl;* Anthony Award for Best Children's/Young-Adult Novel, 2009, and Agatha Award for Best Children's/Young-Adult Novel, 2008, both for *The Crossroads;* Agatha Award for Best Children's/Young-Adult Novel, 2009, for *The Hanging Hill.*

Writings

"JOHN CEEPAK" ADULT MYSTERY SERIES

Tilt a Whirl, Carroll & Graf (New York, NY), 2005.
Mad Mouse, Carroll & Graf (New York, NY), 2006.
Whack a Mole, Carroll & Graf (New York, NY), 2007.

Chris Grabenstein (Photograph by Tess Steinkolk. Reproduced by permission.)

Hell Hole, St. Martin's Minotaur (New York, NY), 2008.
Mind Scrambler, Minotaur Books (New York, NY), 2009.
Rolling Thunder, Pegasus Books (New York, NY), 2010.
Fun House, Pegasus Books (New York, NY), 2012.

Short story in series published in *Alfred Hitchcock Mystery Magazine.*

"CHRISTOPHER MILLER HOLIDAY THRILLER" ADULT NOVEL SERIES

Slay Ride, Carroll & Graf (New York, NY), 2006.
Hell for the Holidays, Carroll & Graf (New York, NY), 2007.

"HAUNTED MYSTERY" JUVENILE NOVEL SERIES

The Crossroads, Random House (New York, NY), 2008.
The Hanging Hill, Random House (New York, NY), 2009.
The Smoky Corridor, Random House (New York, NY), 2010.
The Black Heart Crypt, Random House (New York, NY), 2011.

OTHER

(With Ronny Venable) *The Christmas Gift* (screenplay), Columbia Broadcasting System (CBS), 1986.

The Curiosity Cat (play; produced in Knoxville, TN, 2010), Samuel French (New York, NY), 2010.

Riley Mack and the Other Known Troublemakers (novel), HarperCollins (New York, NY), 2012.

Author of movie and television scripts, including *Jim Henson's Little Muppet Monsters,* CBS. Contributor to periodicals and anthologies.

Sidelights

Chris Grabenstein first gained fame in the literary world with his "John Ceepak" mystery series, which follows the adventures of police officer John Ceepak, a veteran of the Iraq war who lives his life by a strict moral code. In 2008 Grabenstein branched out with his first effort for younger readers: *The Crossroads,* a ghost story that received both the Anthony Award and the Agatha Award. Since that time, the author has completed a number of sequels, including *The Hanging Hill* and *The Smoky Corridor.* "I think writing for kids is a blast," Grabenstein told *Kidsreads.com* contributor Amy Alessio. "I get to be a kid again and remember what it was like to be 10 and a nerd. I get to use more of my imagination."

Grabenstein graduated with a degree in communications from the University of Tennessee at Knoxville, where he spent his available time acting at the university's Clarence Brown Theatre. He then left Knoxville for New York City, working evenings during the early 1980s as an improvisational comedian in a troupe that included the well-known actor Bruce Willis. Grabenstein supported himself by day with a clerical job in a bank. However, writing was something he did from the time he was a child, and always with an eye to entertain. As a child, he had written plays, skits, and puppet shows for him and his brothers to perform for their parents, charging five cents admission per performance. In New York, he continued writing skits, this time for his friends, and they were performed at a small theater in Greenwich Village. From here Grabenstein moved on to writing scripts for Jim Henson's Muppets.

Grabenstein got his first steady writing job, working for the J. Walter Thompson advertising agency, by answering a unique ad placed in the newspaper by ad exec and future novelist James Patterson, the man who ultimately became Grabenstein's boss. The notice included a page-long writing-aptitude test that Patterson had created. Grabenstein responded and was the first person hired. For nearly two decades, he wrote commercials there and for Young & Rubicam. In 2001 he made the break to become a novelist by penning his crime tale *Tilt a Whirl,* which became the first of his "John Ceepak" adult mysteries. Other titles in the series include *Hell Hole* and *Rolling Thunder.*

Grabenstein kicked off his "Haunted Mystery" series with *The Crossroads.* The book follows the story of eleven-year-old Zack Jennings, whose mother has re-

cently passed away after a battle with cancer. Zack is convinced that his mom now haunts the New York City apartment where he and his father still live, and he is immensely disturbed by this. When Zack's father remarries and the new family moves to Connecticut, Zack feels a sense of relief, convinced he can now move on with his life without having his mother's ghost watching his every move. However, Zack's preoccupation with the dead does not end once he leaves the city.

In his new town, Zack meets Gerda Spratling, his neighbor and an older woman who is the last surviving member of the family that originally founded their town. Gerda still mourns for her husband, although the man has been dead for fifty years. Mr. Spratling died at the crossroads across from the Jennings' new home, and Gerda visits that place, where a tall oak tree grows, every week in homage to her late husband. Zack senses something evil about that oak tree, and after a freak lightning strike breaks the tree in half and strange things begin to happen all over town he is convinced that the oak has released something bad. With help from Gerda and a new friend, the preteen sets out to save the town

Cover of Grabenstein's middle-grade novel **The Smoky Corridor,** *featuring cover art by Scott Altmann.* (Jacket cover copyright © 2010 by Yearling. Reproduced by permission of Yearling Book, an imprint of Random House Children's Book, a division of Random House, Inc.)

he has adopted as his own. Jessica Miller, in a review for *School Library Journal*, declared Grabenstein's first effort for younger readers to be "a well-told ghost story with plenty of twists and chills." A writer in *Kirkus Reviews* remarked that the "fast-paced action chapters, tight plotting, . . . and a sympathetic main character" in *The Crossroads* "keep things moving." In *Booklist* Connie Fletcher applauded the novel's "creepy atmosphere, believable story, and suspense that engulfs readers from the very first page."

Grabenstein's "Haunted Mystery" series continues with *The Hanging Hill*, as Zack's ability to see ghosts once again draws him into an adventure. While attending a rehearsal of the play his stepmother, Judy, has written, the boy witnesses the appearance of a number of ghosts, and strange things start to derail the performance, upsetting the director. Zack then teams up with actress and classmate Meghan to investigate the supernatural occurrences. "Readers will race through terse sentences and demonically paced chapters to reach the satisfying, Indiana Jones-like . . . ending," a contributor in *Kirkus Reviews* observed. Robyn Gioia, in a review for *School Library Journal*, declared of *The Hanging Hill* that "the story line is hauntingly delicious as the fully fleshed-out creepiness comes tempered with humor."

In *The Smoky Corridor*, the third installment in the "Haunted Mystery" series, Zack does battle with a ghoul that lives beneath his haunted school. After meeting the ghosts of the Donnelly brothers, who died on the grounds years earlier in a mysterious fire, he learns that a brain-eating zombie guards Confederate treasure that is buried under the school, protecting it for a voodoo-practicing spirit that hopes to inhabit the body of a living human. The "well-constructed twists and turns, realistic (rather than slapstick) humor, [and] nifty puzzles" earned *The Smoky Corridor* praise from a contributor in *Kirkus Reviews*. According to Connie Tyrrell Burns, writing in *School Library Journal*, "Grabenstein is a riveting storyteller; most kids won't be able to put this book down."

In *The Black Heart Crypt* a gallery's worth of criminal-minded ghosts escape from their crypt and plan to wreak havoc, much to Zack's dismay. As Halloween approaches, thirteen members of the notorious Ickleby clan, including an eighteenth-century highwayman and a Prohibition-era gangster, break their confinement and set out to punish Zack, whose witchy great-aunts were the ones who cast the spell imprisoning the spirits. When the Icklebys take possession of the body of one of the spell casters' descendants, Zack is forced to seek help from his relatives to restore peace. In the words of a *Kirkus Reviews* critic, the "events [in *The Black Heart Crypt*] spiral to a suspenseful climax, and the mix of corpses and comedy add up to a faintly macabre tone." Hazel Rochman, writing in *Booklist*, complimented the "fast-paced action" in Grabenstein's novel, adding that "the horror is timeless."

Grabenstein notes that his training as an actor has benefited his work as an author. "I use my improv and acting every day as a writer," he told Alessio. "I come to the keyboard in character and act out the scenes in my head as I write them. I have a loose outline but use the improv techniques—create a character, put them in a situation, keep saying yes, keep moving forward, and see what happens—to get from point to point."

Biographical and Critical Sources

PERIODICALS

Booklist, September 1, 2005, Jenny McLarin, review of *Tilt a Whirl*, p. 69; May 1, 2006, Donna Seaman, review of *Mad Mouse*, p. 32; October 1, 2006, Allison Block, review of *Slay Ride*, p. 41; September 1, 2007, Thomas Gaughan, review of *Hell for the Holidays*, p. 61; May 1, 2008, Connie Fletcher, review of *Crossroads*, p. 51; March 1, 2009, Thomas Gaughan, review of *Mind Scrambler*, p. 29; April 1, 2010, Thomas Gaughan, review of *Rolling Thunder*, p. 27; August 1, 2011, Hazel Rochman, review of *The Black Heart Crypt*, p. 59.

Detroit Free Press, October 19, 2005, Ron Bernas, review of *Tilt a Whirl*.

Entertainment Weekly, December 15, 2006, Gilbert Cruz, review of *Slay Ride*, p. 92.

Kirkus Reviews, August 1, 2005, review of *Tilt a Whirl*, p. 818; May 1, 2008, review of *Crossroads*; May 1, 2009, review of *Mind Scrambler*; June 15, 2009, review of *The Hanging Hill*; July 1, 2010, review of *The Smoky Corridor*; June 1, 2011, review of *The Black Heart Crypt*.

Library Journal, September 15, 2005, Nicole A. Cooke, review of *Tilt a Whirl*, p. 60; June 1, 2006, review of *Mad Mouse*, p. 549; September 1, 2006, review of *Slay Ride*, p. 878; March 15, 2007, review of *Whack a Mole*.

Publishers Weekly, August 8, 2005, review of *Tilt a Whirl*, p. 216; May 8, 2006, review of *Mad Mouse*, p. 49; September 11, 2006, review of *Slay Ride*, p. 36; March 5, 2007, review of *Whack a Mole*, p. 42; September 17, 2007, review of *Hell for the Holidays*, p. 34; March 2, 2009, review of *Mind Scrambler*, p. 46; March 8, 2010, review of *Rolling Thunder*, p. 38.

School Library Journal, November 1, 2008, Jessica Miller, review of *The Crossroads*, p. 120; August 1, 2009, Robyn Gioia, review of *The Hanging Hill*, p. 103; July, 2010, Connie Tyrrell Burns, review of *The Smoky Corridor*, p. 88.

ONLINE

Beatrice, http://www.beatrice.com/ (September 29, 2005), Ron Hogan, interview with Grabenstein.

Bookreporter.com, http://www.bookreporter.com/ (September 26, 2009), Joe Hartlaub, reviews of *Tilt a Whirl*, *Mad Mouse*, *Slay Ride*, and *Mind Scrambler*.

Chris Grabenstein Home Page, http://www.chrisgraben stein.com (January 15, 2012).

Kidsreads.com, http://www.kidsreads.com/ (November, 2009), Amy Alessio, interview with Grabenstein.

Mystery Reader Web site, http://www.themysteryreader. com/ (June 4, 2007), Lesley Dunlap, review of *Tilt a Whirl,* and Kathy Sova, interview with Grabenstein.

Random House Web site, http://www.randomhouse.com/ (January 15, 2012), "Chris Grabenstein."

Spinetingler Online, http://www.spinetinglermag.com/ (March 22, 2010), Jack Getze, interview with Grabenstein.

*   *   *

GRANT, Katy

Personal

Born in Lewisburg, TN; married Eric Grant; children: Jackson, Ethan. *Education:* College degree.

Addresses

Home—Mesa, AZ. *E-mail*—katy@katygrant.com.

Career

Educator and author. Adjunct faculty at colleges, including and Maricopa County Community College District, Phoenix, AZ. Presenter at schools.

Writings

Hide and Seek, Peachtree Press (Atlanta, GA), 2010.

"SUMMER CAMP SECRETS" MIDDLE-GRADE NOVEL SERIES

Pranked, Aladdin Paperbacks (New York, NY), 2008.
Acting Out, Aladdin Paperbacks (New York, NY), 2008.
Friends Forever, Aladdin Paperbacks (New York, NY), 2008.
Tug-of-war, Aladdin (New York, NY), 2010.
Fearless, Aladdin (New York, NY), 2010.
Rumors, Aladdin (New York, NY), 2010.

Sidelights

Born and raised in Tennessee, Katy Grant now lives in Arizona, where she teaches college classes and writes stories for young readers. Although she wanted to be a writer since discovering the biography of *Little Women* author Louisa May Alcott at age eight, Grant opted for a career in teaching. In the early 1990s she decided to write a novel, doing so while teaching creative writing and English at nearby colleges. By 2008 Grant had become a published author: three of her books—the first three novels in her "Summer Camp Secrets" series—were available on bookstore shelves.

Grant's "Summer Camp Secrets" books focus on preteens' experiences at Camp Pine Haven for Girls. Each volume features a different girl experiencing the camping life differently, based on her unique personality, talents, and interests. In *Pranked,* for instance, Kelly Hedges worries about being popular with the in-crowd, and although she quickly makes friends with Melissa, she has her sights set on joining the group lead by stuck-up (but popular) twins Reb and Jennifer. Judith Duckworth is the star of *Acting Out,* and she uses her time at Camp Pine Haven to recreate herself into someone with a cool name and personality to match. In *Friends Forever* third-year camper Darcy Bridges has looked forward to spending time with camping buddy Nicole, but their friendship does not click the way it did in years past. Another friendship seems to be in trouble in *Tug-of-war,* while in *Fearless,* preteen equestrian Jordan Abernathy feels pressured by friend Molly to advance her riding skills a little too fast. Four weeks of summer camp means that Kayla Tucker has four weeks to figure out who started some mean-spirited gossip about her in *Rumors,* the sixth book in Grant's ongoing series.

Cover of Katy Grant's young-adult novel Hide and Seek, *in which a boy is drawn into mystery through his hobby of geocaching.* (Jacket cover copyright © 2010 by Peachtree Publishers. Reproduced by permission of Peachtree Publishers, Inc.)

Grant focuses on a popular pastime—geocaching—in her standalone novel *Hide and Seek,* which is also geared for preteens. Chase and his parents live in Arizona, where his mom and stepfather run a small resort and store for tourists, and geocaching—using his GPS to discover the location of hidden objects—is one of his favorite pastimes. During one geocache outing, the teen discovers a metal box containing a strange, scrawled message; on a second trip to the box he finds a plea for food. Worried that the person or persons writing these notes may be lost or in trouble, Chase attempts to track down the box's owner and ultimately finds himself drawn into a dangerous situation that he may not be able to deal with on his own. Recommending *Hide and Seek* for fans of stories by Jim Arnosky, *Booklist* critic Todd Morning added that Grant's "well-paced adventure novel" benefits from "her developed portrayal of Chase." A *Kirkus Reviews* writer also praised the story, noting that "an original premise and an appealing theme" add up to "first-rate suspense." Noting the coming-of-age elements in Grant's novel, Susan W. Hunter added in her *School Library Journal* review that *Hide and Seek* is a "readable survival story that . . . may also entice reluctant readers" with its engaging mix of "mystery and adventure."

Biographical and Critical Sources

PERIODICALS

Booklist, October 1, 2010, Todd Morning, review of *Hide and Seek,* p. 91.
Kirkus Reviews, July 1, 2010, review of *Hide and Seek.*
School Library Journal, September, 2010, Susan W. Hunter, review of *Hide and Seek,* p. 154.

ONLINE

Children's Literature Web site, http://www.childrenslit. com/ (January 15, 2012), "Katy Grant."
Katy Grant Home Page, http://www.katygrant.com (January 9, 2012).
Peachtree Publishers Web log, http://peachtreepub.blogspot .com/ (June 28, 2010), interview with Grant.*

*   *   *

GRAY, Serena
See SHELDON, Dyan

H

HARVEY, Sarah N. 1950-

Personal
Born 1950, in Chicago, IL; father a neurosurgeon; children: two. *Education:* Degree (English).

Addresses
Home—Victoria, British Columbia, Canada. *E-mail*—sarah@sarahnharvey.com.

Career
Writer and editor. University of Victoria Bookstore, Victoria, British Columbia, Canada, book buyer for fifteen years; children's book editor.

Member
Children's Writers and Illustrators of British Columbia.

Awards, Honors
Chocolate Lily Award, 2007, and Our Choice selection, Canadian Children's Book Centre (CCBC), both for *Puppies on Board;* Quick Picks for Reluctant Young-Adult Readers designation, and CCBC Best Books selection, both 2008, both for *Bull's Eye;* Sheila A. Egoff Children's Literature Prize finalist, Bolen Books Children's Book Prize, and Young-Adult Book Award finalist, Canadian Library Association, all 2009, all for *The Lit Report;* Bolen Books Children's Book Prize nomination, 2009, Chocolate Lily Award nomination, 2009-10, and CCBC Best Books for Kids and Teens selection, 2010, all for *The West Is Calling;* Bolen Books Children's Book Prize shortlist, and White Pine Award nomination, both 2011, both for *Death Benefits.*

Writings
Puppies on Board, illustrated by Rose Cowles, Orca Book Publishers (Victoria, British Columbia, Canada), 2008.

(With Leslie Buffam) *The West Is Calling: Imagining British Columbia,* illustrated by Dianna Bonder, Orca Book Publishers (Victoria, British Columbia, Canada), 2008.
(With Leslie Buffam) *Great Lakes and Rugged Ground: Imagining Ontario,* illustrated by Kasia Charko, Orca Book Publishers (Custer, WA), 2010.

Author of book reviews for Toronto *Globe and Mail,* 1988; columnist for *Times Colonist* (Victoria, British Columbia, Canada), and *Monday* magazine. Contributor to *Dropped Threads 2: More of What We Aren't Told,* edited by Carol Shields and Marjorie Anderson, Vintage Canada, 2003.

NOVELS

Bull's Eye, Orca Book Publishers (Victoria, British Columbia, Canada), 2007.
The Lit Report, Orca Book Publishers (Custer, WA), 2008.
Plastic, Orca Book Publishers (Custer, WA), 2010.
Death Benefits, Orca Book Publishers (Custer, WA), 2010.
Shattered, Orca Book Publishers (Custer, WA), 2011.

Sidelights
An award-winning Canadian writer, Sarah N. Harvey explores teen pregnancy, assisted suicide, and other complex topics in such works as *The Lit Report* and *Death Benefits.* In addition to her young-adult novels, Harvey has penned the children's book *Puppies on Board* as well as the regional poetry volumes *The West Is Calling: Imagining British Columbia* and *Great Lakes and Rugged Ground: Imagining Ontario.*

Bull's Eye, Harvey's young-adult fiction debut, centers on Emily, a high-school senior who discovers that the woman who raised her is not her biological mother. Upon learning that her late aunt—her mother's sister—actually gave birth to her, Emily feels betrayed and leaves home for a time, attempting to make sense of the stunning revelation. In *The Lit Report* a studious teen-

Sarah N. Harvey captures the relationship between a caring teen and the elderly man who depends on him in her young-adult novel **Death Benefits.** (Orca Book, 2010. Jacket photograph by Zoomstock/Masterfile. Reproduced by permission of Orca Book Publishers.)

ager tries to help a rebellious classmate hide an unplanned pregnancy. When Julia's best friend, Ruth, loses her virginity at a raucous party and later announces that she is pregnant, the girls team up to conceal the news from Ruth's fundamentalist Christian parents. Using knowledge gleaned from the midwife assisting Julia's stepmother, Julia and Ruth decide to deliver the baby themselves, then leave the infant at a church, "a plan that even a minimally astute young reader will recognize is doomed to fail from the start," observed *Quill & Quire* reviewer Dory Cerny. In her *Kliatt* review of *The Lit Report*, Claire Rosser applauded Harvey's portrayal of story narrator Julia, "a wonderful character with her mixture of practical wisdom and intelligence and her naiveté."

Harvey shines a spotlight on unethical cosmetic surgeons in *Plastic,* "a fast, funny, and interesting story," as Pam Klassen-Dueck remarked in the *Canadian Review of Materials.* Appalled that his best friend plans to undergo breast augmentation surgery—a birthday present from her mother—fifteen-year-old Jack decides to research the operation. After Jack meets a doctor who is willing to perform any procedure for a price, he

begins a campaign against unnecessary surgeries that goes national. *"Plastic,"* wrote Emily Chornomaz in *School Library Journal,* "does a good job of exploring an important societal issue while telling a timely tale."

Death Benefits focuses on Royce Peterson, a sixteen year old who agrees to care for his ailing and curmudgeonly grandfather, Arthur, a once-great cellist. Although Royce and Arthur initially find themselves at odds, they gradually come to respect each other, and when Arthur suffers a debilitating stroke he asks Royce to help him end his life. According to a *Kirkus Reviews* writer, "Harvey offers a realistic view of the aging process," and a *Publishers Weekly* contributor asserted that *Death Benefits* "sheds light on . . . family dynamics, and a person's ability to adapt to less than ideal circumstances."

In *Shattered* March Moser, a privileged teen, tries to change her life after committing an act of violence. In this novel Harvey delivers "some surprisingly old-fashioned ideas about atonement, thankfully delivered with a light touch in March's believable, acerbic voice," according to Kay Weisman in the *Canadian Review of Materials.*

In Harvey's picture book *Puppies on Board,* a youngster who lives on a houseboat must find homes for eleven tiny canines. "The lighthearted text doesn't shy away from the hard work attendant upon a litter of puppies," a critic in *Kirkus Reviews* stated. Coauthored with Leslie Buffam, Harvey's verse collections *The West Is Calling* and *Great Lakes and Rugged Ground* present a lyrical look at the wonders of Canada. "The haikus themselves . . . are surprising in their intricacy," Megan Moore Burns wrote in *Quill & Quire.*

Biographical and Critical Sources

PERIODICALS

Booklist, December 1, 2010, Francisca Goldsmith, review of *Death Benefits,* p. 53; March 15, 2010, Francisca Goldsmith, review of *Plastic,* p. 38.

Canadian Review of Materials, December 19, 2008, Ellen Heaney, review of *The West Is Calling: Imagining British Columbia;* February 26, 2010, Pam Klassen-Dueck, review of *Plastic;* September 30, 2011, Kay Weisman, review of *Shattered.*

Kirkus Reviews, October 15, 2005, review of *Puppies on Board,* p. 1138; September 15, 2010, review of *Death Benefits.*

Kliatt, November, 2007, Debra Kilcup, review of *Bull's Eye,* p. 18; November, 2008, Claire Rosser, review of *The Lit Report,* p. 24.

Publishers Weekly, October 25, 2010, review of *Death Benefits,* p. 51.

Quill & Quire, November, 2008, Dory Cerny, review of *The Lit Report;* November, 2010, Megan Moore Burns, review of *Great Lakes and Rugged Ground: Imagining Ontario.*

Resource Links, December, 2005, Adriane Pettit, review of *Puppies on Board,* p. 4.

School Library Journal, January, 2009, Adrienne L. Strock, review of *The Lit Report,* p. 104; July, 2010, Emily Chornomaz, review of *Plastic,* p. 90; January, 2011, Jennifer Barnes, review of *Death Benefits,* p. 108.

ONLINE

Sarah N. Harvey Home Page, http://www.sarahnharvey. com (January 15, 2012).*

*　　*　　*

HELAKOSKI, Leslie

Personal

Born in LA; married; children: three. *Education:* University of Louisiana, B.A. (advertising design); Northern Michigan University, B.A. (media illustration).

Addresses

Home and office—Lawton, MI. *E-mail*—leslie@ helakoskibooks.com.

Career

Author and illustrator. Worked previously in advertising.

Member

Society of Children's Book Writers and Illustrators (regional advisor of Michigan chapter, 2011).

Awards, Honors

Michigan Reads Picture Book, State of Michigan, 2007, and Great Lakes Great Books Award, both for *Big Chickens;* Great Lakes Book Award finalist, 2008, for *Woolbur;* numerous honors from state reading associations.

Writings

The Smushy Bus, illustrated by Sal Murdocca, Millbrook Press (Brookfield, CT), 2002.

Big Chickens, illustrated by Henry Cole, Dutton Children's Books (New York, NY), 2006.

Woolbur, illustrated by Lee Harper, HarperCollins (New York, NY), 2008.

Big Chickens Fly the Coop, illustrated by Henry Cole, Dutton Children's Books (New York, NY), 2008.

Big Chickens Go to Town, illustrated by Henry Cole, Dutton Children's Books (New York, NY), 2010.

(Self-illustrated) *Fair Cow,* Marshall Cavendish Children (Tarrytown, NY), 2010.

Sidelights

Author and artist Leslie Helakoski has earned critical acclaim for her energetic and often silly tales for young readers, including *Woolbur* and *Big Chickens Go to Town.* In addition to including an element of humor in her stories for young readers, Helakoski feels that it is important to combine learning with fun, a philosophy that was instilled in her at a young age by her parents,

Leslie Helakoski takes a humorous turn around the farmyard, courtesy of Henry Cole's fun-filled art, in the picture book **Big Chickens.** (Illustration copyright © 2006 by Henry Cole. Reproduced by permission of Dutton Children's Books, a division of Penguin Young Readers Group, a member of Penguin Group (USA), Inc., 345 Hudson Street, New York NY 10014. All rights reserved.)

Helakoski creates original illustrations for her humorous barnyard story **Fair Cow.** (Illustration copyright © 2010 by Leslie Helakoski. Reproduced by permission of Marshall Cavendish Corporation.)

both early childhood specialists. As she noted on her home page, "it's possible to say anything or tell any story, as long as you phrase it in a certain way."

A *Kirkus Reviews* critic praised *Big Chickens* as a frolicsome tale that includes "wordplay reminiscent of Margie Palatini at her best." In the story, four hens are frightened when they spot a wolf lurking around their henhouse and decide to escape to the woods in an attempt to hide from the wily predator. Once in the woods, however, the hens discover that there are more things to fear, including a group of grass-munching cows, a muddy puddle, and a lake. In *Booklist* Gillian Engberg wrote that Helakoski's humorous text "bolsters the slim story with infectious repetition and rhyme," encouraging young children to chant along.

The rambunctious quartet makes a return appearance in *Big Chickens Fly the Coop,* which depicts their comic efforts to locate the farmhouse. On the hens' first attempt, they mistakenly wind up angering the inhabitants of the farm's dog house, and they later have embarrassing encounters with a tractor and some livestock before reaching their closer-than-expected goal. "Much of the fun comes from Helakoski's memorable refrain, rhyming words, and rhythmic phrases," Carolyn Phelan

stated in *Booklist,* and Julie R. Ranelli noted in *School Library Journal* that the rhymes "move the story forward with just enough predictability to engage young listeners and beginning readers."

In *Big Chickens Go to Town* the feathered friends get more than they bargained for when they hop into the back of the farmer's pickup truck to peck at some feed. After the vehicle zooms off, the tailgate spills open and the four anxious hens find themselves forced to cross a busy road before dining on unusual fare in a café, dancing to the lively sounds of a jazz band, and encountering a flock of pigeons. "Helakoski's language is deliciously dense and tricky," Susan Weitz commented in *School Library Journal.*

A free-spirited sheep is the star of *Woolbur,* a tale that celebrates nonconformity. Marching oh-so-enthusiastically to the beat of his own drummer, the eponymous protagonist delights in carding his own wool (while it's still on his body), riding the spinning wheel, and cavorting with the dogs rather than standing still with the flock. When his parents insist that Woolbur act like every other sheep, however, the young lamb shows that he has one more trick up his fleecy sleeve. A contributor in *Kirkus Reviews* applauded the "surprising twists in a text full of repetitive language," and *School Library Journal* critic Kara Schaff Dean also praised Helakoski's theme "in which being different is not a struggle but a happy choice made in the spirit of fun."

Fair Cow was inspired by a documentary that showed how farmers prepare their cows for "Best in Show" competitions at state fairs. "I didn't realize all of these things they do like women going to the beauty parlor, competing against each other, doing their hair, getting highlights, having their nails done," Helakoski noted in an *MLive.com* interview with Linda S. Mah. In her picture book, the author introduces Effie, a cow that is determined to win a blue ribbon at the show and agrees to an extreme makeover from her friend, Petunia the pig. When Effie meets the other contestants, though, she feels so intimidated that she heads back to the barn, stopping along the way to graze on tasty grass, an old habit that ultimately earns her a great reward. "The blend of farmyard and trendy beauty rituals is a winning combination," Hazel Rochman noted in *Booklist*, and a critic wrote in *Kirkus Reviews* that Helakoski's self-illustrated debut "shows off her goofy acrylics, which are a terrific match for her frisky farm fable."

Biographical and Critical Sources

PERIODICALS

Booklist, October 15, 2002, Carolyn Phelan, review of *The Smushy Bus,* p. 412; February 1, 2006, Gillian Engberg, review of *Big Chickens,* p. 55; January 1, 2008, Carolyn Phelan, review of *Big Chickens Fly the Coop,* p. 90, and Abby Nolan, review of *Woolbur,* p. 96; January 1, 2010, Hazel Rochman, review of *Big Chickens Go to Town,* p. 96; September 1, 2010, Hazel Rochman, review of *Fair Cow,* p. 112.

Kirkus Reviews, December 15, 2005, review of *Big Chickens,* p. 1322; November 15, 2007, review of *Woolbur*; December 1, 2007, review of *Big Chickens Fly the Coop*; July 1, 2010, review of *Fair Cow.*

Publishers Weekly, December 10, 2007, review of *Woolbur,* p. 54; July 26, 2010, review of *Fair Cow,* p. 73.

School Library Journal, November, 2002, Mary Elam, review of *The Smushy Bus,* p. 124; February, 2006, Lauralyn Persson, review of *Big Chickens,* p. 103; January, 2008, Kara Schaff Dean, review of *Woolbur,* p. 88; June, 2008, Julie R. Ranelli, review of *Big Chickens Fly the Coop,* p. 104; February, 2010, Susan Weitz, review of *Big Chickens Go to Town,* p. 86; September, 2010, Iem Bates, review of *Fair Cow,* p. 125.

ONLINE

Children's Literature Network Web site, http://www.childrensliteraturenetwork.org/ (March 30, 2007), "Leslie Helakoski."

Kids Book Link Web site, http://www.kidsbooklink.org/ (November 29, 2006), Lindy Rymill, "Meet Author and Illustrator Leslie Helakoski."

Leslie Helakoski Home Page, http://www.helakoskibooks.com (January 12, 2012).

MLive.com, http://www.mlive.com/ (November 17, 2010), Linda S. Mah, "Picturing Beauty in *Fair Cow:* Writer Leslie Helakoski Offers Her First Book Illustrations."*

*   *   *

HILLS, Lia

Personal

Born in Wellington, New Zealand; married; children: two sons. *Education:* College degree.

Addresses

Home—Melbourne, Victoria, Australia. *Agent*—Booked Out Speaker's Agency, P.O. Box 580, South Yarra, Victoria 3141, Australia; bookings@bookedout.com.au.

Career

Poet, novelist, and storyteller. Worked variously as a camera operator, theatre director, and editor; teacher of English in Australia and at international schools. Presenter at conferences. Co-founder and editor of "Moving Galleries" (urban art/poetry project), Melbourne, Victoria, Australia.

Awards, Honors

IP Picks Best Poetry Award, 2008, for *The Possibility of Flight; New Zealand Post* Children's Book Award for Senior Fiction, 2010, for *The Beginner's Guide to Living.*

Writings

The Possibility of Flight (poetry), Book Group Australia, 2008.

The Beginner's Guide to Living, [Australia], 2009, Farrar, Straus & Giroux (New York, NY), 2010.

Translator of books, including *Tom Is Dead,* by Marie Darrieussecq, 2009.

Sidelights

Born in New Zealand and now living in Australia, poet, translator, and novelist Lia Hills is the author of *The Beginner's Guide to Living,* which chronicles the efforts of a grieving teen to come to terms with his mother's recent death. "I am passionate about encouraging young people to explore 'big ideas,' and to accept that there is no age to begin or end such investigations," Hills noted in discussing her writing on the Booked Out Speakers Agency Web site. "Also, I believe that literature remains a vital and important means of delving into what it means to be human, and that language is an integral part of this investigation."

Illustrated with Hills' photographs, *The Beginner's Guide to Living* finds seventeen-year-old Will left rudderless in the wake of his mother's tragic death in an accident caused by an intoxicated driver. Depressed and emotionally isolated from his friends and family, Will becomes numb to the world around him. When he sees Taryn at his mom's funeral, the high-school senior feels a spark of emotion and quickly falls in love with her. Taryn's friendship, along with the passage of time and a great deal of introspective thought on the young man's part, gradually helps Will find a purpose in embracing life. As chronicled in the pages of Hills' novel, the young man searches the works of poets, artists, and philosophers for this discovered meaning, and he also uses his camera to capture visual images that hint at something greater than meaninglessness and chaos.

Cover of Lia Hills' thought-provoking young-adult novel The Beginner's Guide to Living, *featuring cover art by Istvan Banyai.* (Jacket art copyright © 2010 by Istvan Banyai. Reproduced by permission of Farrar, Straus & Giroux.)

The Beginner's Guide to Living "explores grief, first love, and first sex with poetic frankness that . . . is also refreshing," asserted Gillian Engberg in her *Booklist* review of Hills' debut, and a *Kirkus Reviews* writer recommended the same novel as "a well-crafted story from a new voice." Citing the "cast of clever and convincing characters" that populate Will's coming-of-age story, *Voice of Youth Advocates* contributor Rachel Neururer-Frost added that "the harshest and most frank passages are richly lyrical." The addition of visual images in the form of black-and-white photographs makes *The Beginner's Guide to Living* "not just a book, but a work of art," Neururer-Frost added, and in *School Library Journal* Melyssa Kenney predicted that the Australian author's "beautifully written" novel "will appeal to teens who are deep thinkers and questioners." "Although this novel begins with a death . . . ," noted a *Publishers Weekly* contributor, *The Beginner's Guide to Living* is actually "a celebration of life, companionship, and love."

Biographical and Critical Sources

PERIODICALS

Booklist, October 15, 2010, Gillian Engberg, review of *The Beginner's Guide to Living,* p. 59.
Kirkus Reviews, September 15, 2010, review of *The Beginner's Guide to Living.*
Publishers Weekly, September 27, 2010, review of *The Beginner's Guide to Living,* p. 62.
School Library Journal, December, 2010, Melyssa Kenney, review of *The Beginner's Guide to Living,* p. 115.
Voice of Youth Advocates, December, 2010, Rachel Neururer-Frost, review of *The Beginner's Guide to Living,* p. 455.

ONLINE

Booked Out Speaker's Agency Web site, http://bookedout.com.au/ (January 11, 2012), "Lia Hills."
Macmillan Children's Publishing Group Web log, http://mackids.squarespace.com/ (January 6, 2011), "Lia Hills: Who Am I? What Am I?"*

*   *   *

HUGHES, Mark Peter

Personal

Born in Liverpool, England; immigrated to United States at age one; married; wife's name Karen; children: Evan, Lucía, Zoe.

Addresses

Home—MA.

Career

Writer. Presenter at schools and conferences.

Awards, Honors

Best Books for the Teen Age selection, New York Public Library, 2005, for *I Am the Wallpaper.*

Writings

YOUNG-ADULT NOVELS

I Am the Wallpaper, Delacorte Press (New York, NY), 2005.
Lemonade Mouth, Delacorte Press (New York, NY), 2007.
A Crack in the Sky, Delacorte Press (New York, NY), 2010.
Lemonade Mouth Puckers Up, Delacorte Press (New York, NY), 2012.

Sidelights

Mark Peter Hughes entertains preteens and young adults in his engaging novels *I Am the Wallpaper* and *A Crack in the Sky* as well as the companion novels *Lemonade Mouth* and *Lemonade Mouth Puckers Up.* Praised for creating realistic teen characters with realistic worries, fears, and foibles, Hughes also taps into adolescent ambitions with his focus on fitting in, being heard and acknowledged, and making a difference.

Hughes was born in England but moved with his family to the United States as a toddler, living in Massachusetts, then California, before settling in Barrington, Rhode Island, where he spent much of his childhood. He exhibited a talent for storytelling even as a young boy, and his childhood exploits have become fodder for the stories he now writes as an adult. Short for his age as a boy, Hughes retains particularly vivid memories of gym class, where he feared getting trampled by teammates whenever a game involved a ball.

Interestingly, Hughes's first young-adult novel, *I Am the Wallpaper,* focuses on a teenage girl. Thirteen-year-old Floey Packer feels like she is as invisible as wallpaper whenever her older, more vibrant sister, Lillian, is around. The summer after seventh grade Floey decides to remake herself into a newer, more noticeable Floey: she colors her hair purple, dons a black fedora hat, and attempts to act in a flamboyant manner in order to attract attention. These efforts seem to backfire, however, when Floey realizes that, in addition to failing to meet new friends, she is also alienating her old friends, even best friend Azra and current crush Calvin. A prank pulled on her by her cousins makes Floey reconsider her scheme in a novel that a *Kirkus Reviews* critic described as "an entertaining contribution to the current private-diary-made-public trend." In *School Library Journal* Rhona Campbell wrote of *I Am the Wallpaper* that Hughes's heroine "bursts right off the page with an engaging vivacity," and a *Publishers Weekly* critic cited the story's mix of "a well-orchestrated plot, hilarious scenarios, snappy dialogue and a vulnerable, believable heroine."

Five outcast teens in detention hall decide to team up and form a rock band in *Lemonade Mouth,* Hughes's second novel. The five new friends practice in the school's basement, where "geek" activities are relegated, and their shared goal helps them feel like a part of something special. They call their band Lemonade Mouth in honor of the frozen lemonade machine down the hall from their practice spot, and when the machine is replaced by a soda machine as part of a corporate sponsorship deal they lead a grassroots protest. Unfortunately, the reaction to their efforts sparks a riot and Lemonade Mouth is banned from appearing at an upcoming school talent contest until another school-wide protest supports the band's right to perform. As the band's saga plays out, Hughes shares diverse viewpoints by allowing each band member to tell his or her own story in parallel journal entries. *Booklist* contributor Debbie Carton commented that "Hughes's obvious musical knowledge contributes greatly to the verisimilitude" in *Lemonade Mouth,* while a *Publishers Weekly* critic predicted that "readers will delight in watching these well-developed characters stand up for what they believe in and, in the end, learn who they are." Corinda

Cover of Mark Peter Hughes's fantasy novel A Crack in the Sky, *featuring cover art by Per Haagensen.* (Jacket art copyright © 2011 by Per Haagensen. Reproduced by permission of Yearling Book, an imprint of Random House Children's Books, a division of Random House, Inc.)

J. Humphrey, in a review of the novel for *School Library Journal,* called Hughes's book "a tale of underdogs getting a break in the world."

Described by *Booklist* critic Krista Hutley as an "ecocrisis dystopia" set in the near future, *A Crack in the Sky* centers on Eli Papadopoulos, who lives in the domed city of Providence now that global warming has reduced Earth's surface population through parching heat, violent storms, and slow starvation. Eli's family controls InfiniCorp, which regulates the environment of domed cities like Providence and also attempts to lull residents into complacency by encouraging consumerism and promoting lies denying the continued degradation of the outside environment. Others have not been as lucky as Eli: some survivors have been left to forage in the greater wilderness, where the temperatures continue to rise in contrast to InfiniCorp's propaganda. Eli is unaware that there is a world outside his own, and he is being groomed for an eventual job in his family's business. Then he meets members of a group that is intent on breaking InfiniCorp's hold on society. His questions prompts Eli's removal to a retraining camp, where he meets Tabitha and is inspired to help stop the corporation from controlling society's future.

The first novel in Hughes's proposed "Greenhouse Chronicles" series, *A Crack in the Sky* benefits from what *School Library Journal* critic Krista Anderson described as "taut pacing and interesting characters." Noting that the novel "follows a familiar formula," Hutley added in *Booklist* that *A Crack in the Sky* "marks the beginning of a thought-provoking series" that is augmented by "a reading list and intelligent examples of how real science informed the story." A *Kirkus Reviews* writer predicted of the author's science-fiction thriller that "there's enough excitement in this story of gadgets and intelligent animal sidekicks . . . to keep readers turning pages."

Biographical and Critical Sources

PERIODICALS

Booklist, February 15, 2007, Debbie Carton, review of *Lemonade Mouth,* p. 71; July 1, 2010, Krista Hutley, review of *A Crack in the Sky,* p. 49.

Bulletin of the Center for Children's Books, September, 2005, Karen Coats, review of *I Am the Wallpaper,* p. 20; June, 2007, Karen Coats, review of *Lemonade Mouth,* p. 421.

Kirkus Reviews, May 1, 2005, review of *I Am the Wallpaper,* p. 539; January 15, 2007, review of *Lemonade Mouth,* p. 74; July 1, 2010, review of *A Crack in the Sky.*

Kliatt, May, 2005, Myrna Marler, review of *I Am the Wallpaper,* p. 14; March, 2007, Janis Flint-Ferguson, review of *Lemonade Mouth,* p. 14.

Publishers Weekly, June 20, 2005, review of *I Am the Wallpaper,* p. 77; March 12, 2007, review of *Lemonade Mouth,* p. 59; August 2, 2010, review of *A Crack in the Sky,* p. 47.

School Library Journal, May, 2005, Rhona Campbell, review of *I Am the Wallpaper,* p. 130; May, 2007, Corinda J. Humphrey, review of *Lemonade Mouth,* p. 134; October, 2010, Kristin Anderson, review of *A Crack in the Sky,* p. 119.

Voice of Youth Advocates, August, 2005, Ann T. Reddy-Damon, review of *I Am the Wallpaper,* p. 218; February, 2007, Robyn Guedel, review of *Lemonade Mouth,* p. 526.

ONLINE

Beatrice Web site, http://www.beatrice.com/ (April 10, 2007), interview with Hughes.

Cynsations Web Log, http://cynthialeitichsmith.blogspot.com/ (June 14, 2005), Cynthia Leitich Smith, review of *I Am the Wallpaper.*

Mark Peter Hughes Home Page, http://www.markpeterhughes.com (January 9, 2012).*

J-K

JENKINS, Ward 1968-

Personal

Born November 24, 1968; married; wife's name Andrea; children: Ava, Ezra. *Education:* Georgia State University, B.F.A. *Hobbies and other interests:* Painting, graffiti, collecting vintage books.

Addresses

Home and office—Portland, OR. *Agent*—Jennifer Laughran, Andrea Brown Literary Agency; jennL@andreabrownlit.com. *E-mail*—wardomatic@comcast.net.

Career

Animation director, illustrator, and designer. Worked in animation industry beginning 1996, including as animator at Click 3X, Atlanta, GA, animation director at Primal Screen, Atlanta, and LAIKA/house, Portland, OR. *Exhibitions:* Work exhibited at Grassyknoll Gallery, Portland, OR, 2008.

Member

Society of Children's Book Writers and Illustrators.

Writings

SELF-ILLUSTRATED

New York, Baby!, Chronicle Books (San Francisco, CA), 2012.
San Francisco, Baby!, Chronicle Books (San Francisco, CA), 2012.

ILLUSTRATOR

Michael Phelps and Alan Abrahamson, *How to Train with a T. Rex and Win Eight Gold Medals,* Simon & Schuster Books for Young Readers (New York, NY), 2009.

Sudipta Bardhan-Quallen, *Chicks Run Wild,* Simon & Schuster Books for Young Readers (New York, NY), 2011.

Sidelights

A respected illustrator and animator whose work has appeared on the Cartoon Network, Nickelodeon, and HGTV, Ward Jenkins has also provided the artwork for a number of children's books, including *How to Train with a T. Rex and Win Eight Gold Medals* and *Chicks Run Wild,* The former, coauthored by world-renowned athlete Michael Phelps, offers a humorous look at the swimmer's training regimen in preparation for the 2008 Summer Olympics in Beijing, China, during which Phelps won a record eight gold medals. Throughout the six years he prepared for the event—a period that the athlete compares to a kindergartner's lifetime—Phelps swam more than 12,000 miles, or three full lengths of the Great Wall of China, while in a single workout he would lift some 18,000 pounds, the weight equivalent of a Tyrannosaurus Rex and then some. "Digitally rendered artwork humorously depicts the action, making the book visually appealing," Maryann H. Owen commented in her *School Library Journal* review of *How to Train with a T. Rex and Win Eight Gold Medals.* A *Publishers Weekly* reviewer also applauded Jenkins' contribution, remarking that he depicts "Phelps as a cheerful, larger-than-life caricature."

In *Chicks Run Wild,* a story in verse by Sudipta Bardhan-Quallen, a quintet of rambunctious chicks refuses to settle down for the night until Mama devises a clever solution to tire them out. "Jenkins takes the story at full throttle . . . with plenty of double-page spreads popping with energy and good cheer," a writer stated in *Kirkus Reviews* in reviewing the picture book. According to a *Publishers Weekly* critic, the artist's "rambunctious, roly-poly chicks resemble fuzzy yellow Easter eggs," and Roxanne Burg maintained in *School Library Journal* that Jenkins' illustrations for Bardhan-Quallen's text "carry the folksy tale in an able fashion."

Ward Jenkins' illustration projects include creating the artwork for Sudipta Bardhan-Quallen's humorous picture book **Chicks Run Wild.** (Illustration copyright © 2011 by Ward Jenkins. Reproduced by permission of Simon and Schuster Books for Young Readers, an imprint of Simon & Schuster Children's Publishing Division.)

Biographical and Critical Sources

PERIODICALS

Booklist, January 1, 2011, Diane Foote, review of *Chicks Run Wild,* p. 112.
Kirkus Reviews, May 15, 2009, review of *How to Train with a T. Rex and Win Eight Gold Medals*; November 15, 2010, review of *Chicks Run Wild.*
Publishers Weekly, June 15, 2009, review of *How to Train with a T. Rex and Win Eight Gold Medals,* p. 48; November 1, 2010, review of *Chicks Run Wild,* p. 40.
School Library Journal, August, 2009, Maryann H. Owen, review of *How to Train with a T. Rex and Win Eight Gold Medals,* p. 92; January, 2011, Roxanne Burg, review of *Chicks Run Wild,* p. 69.

ONLINE

Drawn Web log, http://blog.drawn.ca/ (January 15, 2012).
Ward Jenkins Home Page, http://wardjenkins.com (January 15, 2012).
Ward Jenkins Web log, http://wardomatic.blogspot.com/ (January 15, 2012).*

*   *   *

KEYES, Pamela 1962(?)-

Personal

Born c. 1962; married Walt Keyes (an engineer with the National Park Service); children: Zach, one other. *Education:* University of Colorado at Boulder, B.A. (German), 1985; attended Universität Regensburg, 1983-84; attended University of Arizona, 1987-88; University of Washington, M.A. (architecture), 1995. *Hobbies and other interests:* Hiking, travel.

Addresses

Home—Tucson, AZ.

Career

Architect and author. Erickson Leader Associates, Tucson, AZ, registered architect, 1995-2006.

Writings

The Rune of Zachary Zimbalist, Blue Works, 2005.
The Legend of Zamiel Zimbalist, Blue Works, 2005.
The Jumbee, Dial Books (New York, NY), 2010.

Sidelights

Pamela Keyes honed her imagination by writing while growing up, and then worked for several years in her chosen career of architect before revisiting her love of storytelling. Keyes' first two books, *The Rune of Zachary Zimbalist* and *The Legend of Zamiel Zimbalist,* are part of her "Connedim" fantasy series and focus on a twelve-year-old boy and his uncle as they navigate a space between past and future and battle evil beings called Scatterers. She turns to the classics in the *The Jumbee,* a retelling of Gaston Leroux's serialized 1909 novel *The Phantom of the Opera* that shifts its setting from Paris, France, to an exotic Caribbean island with a troubled history.

Praised by *Booklist* contributor Jennifer Hubert as a "haunting romance," *The Jumbee* finds high-school senior Esti Legard moving to the island of Cariba with her newly widowed mom. Esthi's late father was a famous stage actor, and her own talent now gains her enrollment at a prestigious performing-arts high school on the island. Practicing alone on the school's stage, Esthi

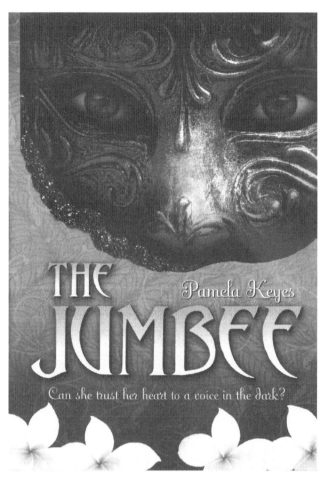

Cover of Pamela Keyes' young-adult novel The Jumbee, *a romantic adventure set on a tropical island.* (Jacket photograph by Shutterstock. Reproduced by permission of Dial Books, an division of Penguin Young Readers Group, a member of Penguin Group (USA), 345 Hudson Street, New York NY 10014. All rights reserved.)

is coached by a hidden teacher whose voice which quickly moves from unnerving to seductive. Although a handsome local teen named Rafe Solomon sparks her romantic interest, he does not share her passion for Shakespeare as does Alan, her mystery teacher. Esti's feelings for the unseen Alan grow stronger as he helps her prepare for an upcoming school performance of *Romeo and Juliet;* meanwhile a series of mishaps threatens the planned production. Ultimately, the approach of a tropical storm allows Esti to unearth information about her family's past as well as resolve her romantic dilemma by discovering Alan's true identity.

Reviewing *The Jumbee* in *School Library Journal,* Lalitha Nataraj praised Keyes for producing a "compelling retelling" of a classic mystery story, adding that her "evocative gothic tale will engage teens looking for an unconventional romance infused with suspense." The "lushly described" island setting "breaths new life into the classic . . . story line," asserted Hubert, and in *Kirkus Reviews* a contributor recommended *The Jumbee* as "a good way to introduce younger readers to themes from the classics."

Biographical and Critical Sources

PERIODICALS

Booklist, September 15, 2010, Jennifer Hubert, review of *The Jumbee,* p. 72.
Kirkus Reviews, September 15, 2010, review of *The Jumbee.*
School Library Journal, November, 2010, Lalitha Nataraj, review of *The Jumbee,* p. 119.

ONLINE

Orchard House Press Web site, http://www.orchardhouse press.com/ (January 11, 2012), "Pamela Keyes."
Pamela Keyes Home Page, http://www.pamelakeyes.com (January 11, 2012).*

*   *   *

KIM, Grace
See MACCARONE, Grace

*   *   *

KIMMEL, Elizabeth Cody
(Elizabeth Kimmel Willard)

Personal

Born in New York, NY; married; children: Emma. *Education:* Kenyon College, bachelor's degree. *Hobbies and other interests:* Reading, hiking, singing, rock climbing.

Addresses

Home—Hudson River Valley, NY. *E-mail*—cody kimmel@gmail.com.

Career

Children's book writer. Presenter at schools.

Writings

FICTION

In the Stone Circle, Scholastic (New York, NY), 1998.
Balto and the Great Race, illustrated by Nora Koerber, Random House (New York, NY), 1999.
Visiting Miss Caples, Dial (New York, NY), 2000.
My Wagon Will Take Me Anywhere, illustrated by Tom Newsom, Dutton (New York, NY), 2002.

Lily B. on the Brink of Cool, HarperCollins (New York, NY), 2003.

What Do You Dream?, illustrated by Joung un Kim, Candlewick Press (Cambridge, MA), 2003.

My Penguin Osbert, illustrated by H.B. Lewis, Candlewick Press (Cambridge, MA), 2004.

Lily B. on the Brink of Love, HarperCollins (New York, NY), 2005.

Lily B. on the Brink of Paris, HarperCollins (New York, NY), 2006.

The Top Job, illustrated by Robert Neubecker, Dutton Children's Books (New York, NY), 2007.

Glamsters, illustrated by Jackie Urbanovic, Hyperion Books for Children (New York, NY), 2008.

(Under name Elizabeth Kimmel Willard) *Mary Ingalls on Her Own,* HarperCollins (New York, NY), 2008.

Spin the Bottle, Dial Books for Young Readers (New York, NY), 2008.

My Penguin Osbert in Love, illustrated by H.B. Lewis, Candlewick Press (Cambridge, MA), 2009.

The Reinvention of Moxie Roosevelt, Dial Books for Young Readers (New York, NY), 2010.

Forever Four, Grosset & Dunlap (New York, NY), 2012.

Author of one-act play *Hudson Adrift,* produced 2009.

Author's books have been translated into several languages.

"ADVENTURES OF YOUNG BUFFALO BILL" CHAPTER-BOOK SERIES; ILLUSTRATED BY SCOTT SNOW

To the Frontier, HarperCollins (New York, NY), 2001.

One Sky above Us, HarperCollins (New York, NY), 2002.

In the Eye of the Storm, HarperCollins (New York, NY), 2003.

West on the Wagon Train, HarperCollins (New York, NY), 2003.

"SUDDENLY SUPERNATURAL" NOVEL SERIES

School Spirit, Little, Brown (Boston, MA), 2008.

Scaredy Kat, Little, Brown (New York, NY), 2009.

Unhappy Medium, Little Brown (New York, NY), 2009.

Crossing Over, Little, Brown (New York, NY), 2010.

NONFICTION

Ice Story: Shackleton's Lost Expedition, Clarion (New York, NY), 1999.

Before Columbus: The Leif Eriksson Expedition, Random House (New York, NY), 2003.

As Far as the Eye Can Reach: Lewis and Clark's Westward Quest, Random House (New York, NY), 2003.

The Look-It-Up Book of Explorers, Random House (New York, NY), 2004.

Ladies First: Forty Daring American Women Who Were Second to None, National Geographic (Washington, DC), 2005.

Dinosaur Bone War: Cope and Marsh's Fossil Feud, Random House (New York, NY), 2006.

Boy on the Lion Throne: The Childhood of the 14th Dalai Lama, foreword by His Holiness the Dalai Lama, Roaring Book Press (New York, NY), 2009.

Adaptations

The "Suddenly Supernatural" books were adapted for audiobook, ready by Allyson Ryan, Listening Library, 2009.

Sidelights

Elizabeth Cody Kimmel grew up in both New York and Brussels, Belgium. As a writer of fiction and nonfiction for children and young adults, she focuses on subjects she finds interesting: from Antarctica to ghost stories to medieval history to the life of the Dalai Lama. Several of Kimmel's nonfiction books, such as *Ice Story: Shackleton's Lost Expedition* and *As Far as the Eye Can Reach: Lewis and Clark's Westward Quest,* focus on explorers, while her young-adult novels deal with themes such as multi-generational friendships and being true to yourself while also introducing readers to engaging and upbeat characters. Kimmel also turns to the picture-book set in *The Top Job,* in which her humorous family-centered story is paired with artwork by Robert Neubecker to produce what a *Kirkus Reviews* critic dubbed "fizzy, fascinating and eminently kid-friendly."

The Lewis and Clark Expedition is the subject of *As Far as the Eye Can Reach,* which follows the explorers' efforts to locate a northern route to the Pacific

Elizabeth Cody Kimmel capture's a boy's pride in his father's work in her picture book **The Top Job,** *featuring artwork by Robert Neubecker.*

Ocean. Kimmel's book was described as "a well written, lively account for young readers" by a contributor to *Kirkus Reviews,* and *Booklist* critic Carolyn Phelan wrote that its "clearly written summary provides a useful overview for students." As Renee Steinberg commented in her review of *As Far as the Eye Can Reach* for *School Library Journal,* "a book such as this can excite young readers to delve further into U.S. history."

Kimmel focuses on a different sort of expedition in *Boy on the Lion Throne: The Childhood of the 14th Dalai Lama,* which chronicles the story of the 1937 search for the fourteenth reincarnation of Tibet's most revered spiritual leader. Featuring numerous photographs that bring to life the monks' search, as well as a foreword by His Holiness the Dalai Lama, *Boy on the Lion Throne* was praised by reviewers and a portion of its sales were donated to Tibet Aid.

Another nonfiction work by Kimmel, *Before Columbus: The Leif Eriksson Expedition,* introduces readers to the Viking exploration of the Americas. A *Kirkus Reviews* contributor characterized this book as "more a quick once-over than a systematic study," but added that *Before Columbus* is "well designed to stimulate an early interest" in its subject. Ginny Gustin, writing in *School Library Journal,* noted that the nonfiction text reads more like an historical novel, and acknowledged that "Kimmel's book will captivate and entertain young readers." More clearly designed as a reference resource, *The Look-It-up Book of Explorers* covers the expeditions of world explorers through the ages. Carol Wichman, writing in *School Library Journal,* deemed this work "a concise and useful guide to virtually all of the explorers usually studied in public schools."

In *Dinosaur Bone War: Cope and Marsh's Fossil Feud* Kimmel focuses on a different kind of exploration. In a text that Ilene Cooper characterized in *Booklist* as "lively," she surveys the facts surrounding a feud that existed between two scientists during the 1870s and 1880s. Edward Cope and Othniel "Charlie" Marsh were initially colleagues and friends, but their work excavating for prehistoric bones in the American West destroyed that friendship after trust was violated and supremacy was measured by the quantity of bones unearthed and species discovered. While discussing the many scientific discoveries that came about during these "Bone Wars"—Cope discovered eighty new species, while Marsh found fifty-six—Kimmel also steps back and allows readers to see the huge advances that occurred in the field of paleontology as a result of the competition between Cope and Marsh. A *Kirkus Reviews* writer characterized *Dinosaur Bone War* as "a straightforward chronological account" of two pioneering scientists, adding that "the drama of the . . . escalating quarrel . . . carries the reader along."

Turning to fiction, Kimmel entertains teens with her first novel-length work, *Visiting Miss Caples.* The book tells the story of thirteen-year-old Jenna, whose father abandons her family. To make things worse, the girl's best friend no longer speaks to her. Jenna assumes that a class project to visit Mrs. Caples, an elderly shut-in, will be just one more bad aspect of the year. However, she soon realizes that Mrs. Caples, despite her difference in age, understands a lot of what Jenna is going through. "Kimmel ably articulates a young person's experience," wrote Gillian Engberg in a *Booklist* review of the multigenerational novel.

Kimmel entertains 'tween readers with her "Lily B." and "Suddenly Supernatural" series, both of which find a spunky teen heroine coping with various misadventures. In *Lily B. on the Brink of Cool* Lily is convinced that her family is anything but up to date. When she meets distant cousin Karma and Karma's family, Lily is determined to fit in, becoming more sophisticated by proximity. However, it soon appears that Karma's family has more in mind than befriending Lily, and the teen ultimately learns that sometimes first impressions are deceiving. "Lily is a likable teen who wants more than she has, only to discover that what she has is pretty darn good," wrote Linda Binder in *School Library Journal.* A *Kirkus Reviews* contributor found Lily to be "a delightful heroine, sweeter than [other teen heroines] and hilarious," while a *Publishers Weekly* critic described her as, "by turns chirpy, sardonic, glib, and melodramatic—and always likable." Louise Bruggemann concluded her *Booklist* review by calling *Lily B. on the Brink of Cool* a "funny, fast-moving . . . novel."

Lily B. on the Brink of Love finds Lily serving as her middle school's newspaper advice columnist. As she soon learns, dealing with her own love life is more difficult than sorting out the romantic foibles of her classmates. In *Lily B. on the Brink of Paris* the thirteen year old joins seven friends on a trip to gay Paree, where the highlights include her efforts to begin writing a novel and the real-life drama of getting lost. "Lily's journal entries and advice columns . . . deliver laughs and substance," wrote Wendi Hoffenberg in a *School Library Journal* review of *Lily B. on the Brink of Love,* and a *Kirkus Reviews* contributor called the same book "heartwarming and funny." In *School Library Journal* Cheryl Ashton described Kimmel's third "Lily B." installment as "light, fun fiction" featuring the "detail-disoriented Lily," and a *Kirkus Reviews* writer concluded that, "as always, Lily's offbeat adventures are good for a laugh."

In the "Suddenly Supernatural" series readers meet Kat, a preteen who learns to cope with an unwanted new talent. When readers meet her in *School Spirit,* the seventh grader has just realized that by turning thirteen she has inherited her mother's ability to communicate with the deceased. She worries that this talent for talking to the dead will ruin her reputation in middle school, where being different is socially deadly. Through her friendship with Jac, a cello-playing teen with a similarly strange family situation, Kat gradually comes to terms with her talent and begins to embrace her gift as a bridge to the dearly departed.

A trip to an old house is the focus of *Scaredy Kat,* the second installment in the "Suddenly Supernatural" series, while in *Unhappy Medium* Kat and Jac travel to the haunted Whispering Pines Mountain House. Confident in her ability to talk with the dead, Kat attempts to persuade a ghost to pass along to the next realm, but her discussions are soon disrupted by something far more evil. *Crossing Over* finds the two friends taking a school field trip to the French-Canadian city of Montreal, and Kat takes the opportunity to attract the attention of a boy she is currently crushing on. She also attracts the attention of some local spectres, however, and their attentions take a toll on her love life.

Praising Kat as "a smart and witty narrator with a wry sense of humor," Kitty Flynn added in *Horn Book* that *School Spirit* is an "inviting" story that includes telling insights into "middle-school [life] and mother-daughter dynamics." In another review of *School Spirit,* a *Kirkus Reviews* writer deemed the book "a satisfying start to a new series," while *School Library Journal* critic Elaine E. Knight called the teen heroines in *Scaredy Kat* "an engaging team" whose "dialogue generally rings true." In *Unhappy Medium* "Kimmel includes some fascinating background movement about the [late-eighteenth-century] Spiritualist Movement," wrote Kathy Kirchoefer in another *School Library Journal* review.

In writing *Spin the Bottle,* Kimmel draws on her own mixed experiences acting in a school play during middle school. In the novel, Phoebe Hart has been stage-struck for her entire life, and she joins her middle school's Drama Club as soon as she gets the chance. The seventh grader also becomes love-struck when she sets eyes on classmate Tucker, and her twin distractions take energy away from her longstanding friendship with BFF Harper. "Kimmel perfectly blends the humor and angst experienced by most preteens" in Phoebe's entertaining narrative, wrote a *Kirkus Reviews* writer, the critic dubbing *Spin the Bottle* "great fun" for its intended readership. In *School Library Journal* Angela M. Reichert described the seventh grader's commentary as "funny and intelligent," while in *Booklist* Hazel Rochman observed that the young teen's "wry" insights illuminate both "the school hierarchy and adults who just don't get it" while also capturing "the rising excitement" generated by live theatre.

Another seventh grader is the focus of *The Reinvention of Moxie Roosevelt,* but Moxie's only dream is to break out of being perpetually ordinary. When her parents arrange for her to attend a private boarding school, the thirteen year old recognizes the move as an opportunity to reinvent herself. There are so many options, however, and Moxie finds it difficult to pin down her new persona. She goes from artsy to jock, from hippie-dippie Earth mother to ultra-cool and indifferent, depending on her mood and circumstances, and soon she has lost track of who, where, and why. New friends come to her aid, however, in a "sharply observed novel [that] reflects a keen understanding of the agony of self-

Cover of Kimmel's middle-grade novel Spin the Bottle, *featuring artwork by Natalie C. Sousa.* (Jacket art and design © 2008 by Natalie C. Sousa. Reproduced by permission of Dial Books for Young Readers, a division of Penguin Young Readers Group, a member of Penguin Group (USA), Inc. 345 Hudson Street, New York NY 10014. All rights reserved.)

definition that is adolescence," according to a *Kirkus Reviews* writer. "While her misadventures are hilarious," wrote Nancy P. Reeder in her review of *The Reinvention of Moxie Roosevelt* for *School Library Journal,* Kimmel's heroine "is an endearing, complex character" that will appeal to teens, and in *Booklist* Carolyn Phelan dubbed Moxie's first-person narration "witty" and "vibrant."

Along with nonfiction and novels, Kimmel has also crafted picture books, including *My Penguin Osbert* and its sequel, *My Penguin Osbert in Love,* both of which feature artwork by H.B. Lewis. *My Penguin Osbert* tells the story of a Christmas wish gone wrong: Joe wants a live penguin, but when Osbert is delivered by Santa, the boy realizes that having a pet penguin is not quite what he imagined. When Joe finally brings Osbert to a new home in the zoo, both boy and penguin end up happy. "Kimmel sneaks some sly humor into the well-told, nicely paced tale," wrote Cooper in a *Booklist* review of *My Penguin Osbert,* and a *Kirkus Reviews* contributor recommended the story as "salutary reading for all children campaigning for a pet." In *Horn Book* Lauren E. Raece deemed the picture book a "satisfying tale," and a *Publishers Weekly* critic predicted of *My Penguin Osbert* that readers would "find much to enjoy in this lighthearted fantasy with realistic holiday roots."

Joe and his penguin friend return in *My Penguin Osbert in Love.* Escaping from the zoo, Osbert and his gang of penguin friends ask the boy for help in getting to Antarctica in time to witness the southern lights. Traveling in a overcrowded helicopter, the group makes its way to the South Pole where it meets beautiful penguin Aurora Australis. Osbert is immediately smitten with this southern belle, leaving Joe to manage amid a sea of penguins in a story that features Lewis's "colorful and softly muted . . . watercolor, pastel, and digital" artwork, according to *School Library Journal* critic Kirsten Cutler. Also citing Lewis's art, Phelan praised Kimmel's ability to give Joe a "wonderfully evocative" narrative voice and concluded that *My Penguin Osbert in Love* is "a winner for winter storytimes."

Cover of Kimmel's middle-grade novel **The Reinvention of Moxie Roosevelt,** *in which a new school provides the chance for a young teen to reinvent herself.* (Jacket photograph copyright © 2011 by Barbara Cole. Reproduced by permission of Dial Books for Young Readers, a division of Penguin Young Readers Group, a member of Penguin Group (USA), 345 Hudson Street, New York NY 10014. All rights reserved.)

Featuring artwork by Jackie Urbanovic, *Glamsters* is another storyhour treat by Kimmel. Harriet Hamster worries that she is being overlooked while all the other hamsters awaiting adoption at Hamster World quickly find homes. Harriet finds a unique answer to her dilemma in a magazine: a rodent makeover that involves whisker extensions, fur volumizer, and claw polish. The hamster's efforts yield surprising results in a story that Mary Hazelton recommended in *School Library Journal* as "a starting point for discussions about popularity and love." "Kimmel makes the most of her [story's] silly premise," asserted a *Kirkus Reviews* writer, the critic calling *Glamsters* "a hoot and a half."

Biographical and Critical Sources

PERIODICALS

Booklist, May 15, 2000, Gillian Engberg, review of *Visiting Miss Caples,* p. 1739; January 1, 2003, Carolyn Phelan, "Lewis & Clark on the Road Again," p. 885; July, 2003, Roger Leslie, review of *Before Columbus: The Leif Eriksson Expedition,* p. 1882; October 1, 2003, Lauren Peterson, review of *What Do You Dream?,* p. 328; December 1, 2003, Louise Brueggemann, review of *Lily B. on the Brink of Cool,* p. 666; December 1, 2004, Ilene Cooper, review of *My Penguin Osbert,* p. 659; October 1, 2005, Anne O'Malley, review of *Lily B. on the Brink of Love,* p. 58; December 1, 2006, Ilene Cooper, review of *Dinosaur Bone War: Cope and Marsh's Fossil Feud,* p. 57; January 1, 2007, Ilene Cooper, review of *Lily B on the Brink of Paris,* p. 81; July 1, 2007, Debbie Carton, review of *The Top Job,* p. 61; May 1, 2008, Hazel Rochman, review of *Spin the Bottle,* p. 90; February 1, 2009, Carolyn Phelan, review of *My Penguin Osbert in Love,* p. 47; June 1, 2010, Carolyn Phelan, review of *The Reinvention of Moxie Roosevelt,* p. 76.

Bulletin of the Center for Children's Books, April, 2000, review of *Visiting Miss Caples,* p. 285; February, 2004, review of *Lily B. on the Brink of Cool,* p. 237.

Horn Book, November-December, 2004, Lauren E. Raece, review of *My Penguin Osbert,* p. 662; July-August, 2008, Kitty Flynn, review of *School Spirit,* p. 451; March-April, 2009, Kitty Flynn, review of *Scaredy Kat,* p. 198.

Kirkus Reviews, December 15, 2002, review of *As Far as the Eye Can Reach,* p. 1851; July 15, 2003, review of *Before Columbus,* p. 965; October 15, 2003, review of *Lily B. on the Brink of Cool,* p. 1272; November 1, 2004, review of *My Penguin Osbert,* p. 1051; August 1, 2005, review of *Lily B. on the Brink of Love,* p. 851; December 1, 2006, reviews of *Lily B. on the Brink of Paris* and *Dinosaur Bone War,* both p. 1222; March 15, 2008, review of *Spin the Bottle;* May 15, 2008, review of *School Spirit;* October 1, 2008, review of *Glamsters;* November 15, 2008, review of *My Penguin Osbert in Love;* May 15, 2010, review of *The Reinvention of Moxie Roosevelt.*

Kliatt, July, 2004, Sherri Ginsberg, review of *Lily B. on the Brink of Cool,* p. 53; September, 2005, Heidi Hauser Green, review of *Lily B. on the Brink of Cool,* p. 20.

Publishers Weekly, December 10, 2001, review of *Visiting Miss Caples,* p. 73; June 9, 2003, review of "Adventures of Young Buffalo Bill" series, p. 54; December 8, 2003, review of *Lily B. on the Brink of Cool,* p. 62; November 22, 2004, review of *My Penguin Osbert,* p. 60; July 23, 2007, review of *The Top Job,* p. 67.

School Librarian, autumn, 2004, Chris Brown, review of *Lily B. on the Brink of Cool,* p. 156.

School Library Journal, July, 2002, Anne Knickerbocker, review of *My Wagon Will Take Me Anywhere,* p. 94; March, 2003, Renee Steinberg, review of *As Far as the Eye Can Reach,* pp. 172, 253; October, 2003, Ginny Gustin, review of *Before Columbus,* p. 152, and Linda Binder, review of *Lily B. on the Brink of Cool,* p. 169; February 2004, Sanda Kitain, review of *What Do You Dream?,* p. 116; January, 2005, Wendi Hoffengberg, review of *Lily B. on the Brink of Love,* p. 104, and Carol Wichman, review of *The Look-It-up Book of Explorers,* p. 149; July, 2005, Wendi Hoffenberg, review of *Lily B. on the Brink of Love,* p. 104; January, 2007, Cheryl Ashton, review of *Lily B. on the Brink of Paris,* p. 130; September, 2008, Danielle Serra, review of *School Spirit,* p. 188; November, 2008, Mary Hazelton, review of *Glamsters,* p. 90; March, 2009, Elaine E. Knight, review of *Scaredy Kat,* p. 146; May, 2009, Kirsten Cutler, review of *My Penguin Osbert in Love,* p. 82; November, 2009, Kathy Kirchoefer, review of *Unhappy Medium,* p. 112; July, 2010, Nancy P. Reeder, review of *The Reinvention of Moxie Roosevelt,* p. 91.

Voice of Youth Advocates, August, 2000, review of *Ice Story,* p. 165; October, 2003, review of *Lily B. on the Brink of Cool,* p. 312.

ONLINE

Authors Unleashed Web log, http://authorsunleashed. blogspot.com/ (February 18, 2009), interview with Kimmel.

Elizabeth Cody Kimmel Home Page, http://www.codykim mel.com (January 15, 2012).

Kids Reads Web site, http://www.kidsreads.com/ (April 27, 2006), "Elizabeth Cody Kimmel."*

*   *   *

KINCH, Michael
(Michael P. Kinch)

Personal

Married; wife's name Marjorie (an artist); children: two daughters. *Education:* Portland State University, B.S. (biology); University of Washington, M.S. (biology); Oregon State University, M.S. (library science, history of science). *Hobbies and other interests:* Painting, paleontology, genealogy, books.

Addresses

Home—Corvallis, OR.

Career

Librarian and author. Oregon State University, Corvallis, science librarian, 1969-98; freelance writer. *Military service:* U.S. Army, served three years.

Writings

"BLENDING TIME" TRILOGY

The Blending Time, Flux (Woodbury, MN), 2010.
The Fires of New Sun, Flux (Woodbury, MN), 2012.

OTHER

Warts (juvenile nonfiction), Franklin Watts (New York, NY), 2000.

Contributor to periodicals, including *American Artist* and *Watercolor.*

Sidelights

Michael Kinch began writing while working as a science librarian at Oregon State University, and his first book, a work of juvenile nonfiction, was published as part of Franklin Watts's "My Health" series in 2000. Kinch's knowledge of library technology led to his appointment as workshop leader for a group of African librarians in Malawi, and the time he spent in that region of the world ultimately inspired his first young-adult novel, *The Blending Time.*

The Blending Time, the first book in Kinch's ongoing dystopian "Blending Time" trilogy, takes place in 2069, as societies are in the process of adapting to a world devastated by environmental catastrophes and disease. Jaym Johansen, Reya Delacruz, and D'Shay Green have grown up in what is now known as "NorthAm," a region under the sway of the Global Alliance. Now reaching age seventeen, each must choose—like all society's "s'teeners"—among four work options. Because those who choose the military, canal work, or street patrol do not live for long, each of the three chooses "Blender": being among those tasked to restore communities and repopulate parts of Africa where the native population has become infertile. As they become friends during their trip to the plateau continent, the three teens start to rethink their choice: scorched by solar flares and rife with violence sparked by warring factions, Africa is actually a brutal place and blenders are hated by the natives and eliminated. When the teens learn of the existence of a sanctuary in a remote mountain region, they must weigh the risk of abandoning their task and attracting the animus of Africa's totalitarian elite.

Cover of Michael Kinch's near-future novel The Blending Time, *in which teens are charged with restoring a ecologically devastated earth.*
(Jacket cover photographs copyright by Kevin Russ/iStockphoto.com (young man with brown hair); Nickola Mrdalj/iStockphoto.com (building and sky); Juan Estey/iStockphoto.com (woman); Eileen Hart/iStockphoto.com (young man wearing hat); Ricardo De Mattos/iStockphoto.com (sky). Reproduced by permission of Flux, an imprint of Llewellyn Worldwide, Ltd.)

While noting the growth in the dystopian genre, Jane Henricksen Baird wrote in *School Library Journal* that *The Blending Time* stands out. "Kinch's novel is a frighteningly clear vision of a very possible future," Hendricksen wrote, remarking on the violence that fuel's the story's "unrelenting pace." Comparing the book to works by Suzanne Collins and Cory Doctorow, *Booklist* critic Debbie Carton predicted that it would be popular among reluctant readers, calling *The Blending Time* "determinedly multiethnic, fast-paced, and with plentiful gore and violence." Narrated by each of the teens in turn, Kinch's text is "edgy and filled with descriptions of futuristic technology and a world spinning out of control," noted *Voice of Youth Advocates* author Florence Munat, and a *Kirkus Reviews* writer deemed *The Blending Time* "a compelling, realistic, and exciting thriller for more mature young readers."

The "Blending Time" saga continues in *The Fires of New Sun* as the three teens survive Africa's desolate desert landscape and Jaym and D'Shay lead a group from the Nswibe tribe to a safe haven. The young men rejoin Reya at New Sun, a hidden Blenders retreat. Discovered by renegades, New Sun is attacked and if its residents are unable to defend themselves it will likely mean death. While recommending that readers begin with *The Blending Time,* a *Kirkus Reviews* contributor noted the well-drawn characters and suspenseful plot in *The Fires of New Sun.* "Kinch makes the action truly exciting," asserted the critic, characterizing the second "Blending Time" novel as a "war story" that, for readers who enjoy "some great action, . . . can't be beat."

Biographical and Critical Sources

PERIODICALS

Booklist, June 1, 2000, Ellen Mandel, review of *Warts,* p. 1884; November 1, 2010, Debbie Carton, review of *The Blending Time,* p. 61.

Kirkus Reviews, September 15, 2010, review of *The Blending Time;* November 15, 2011, review of *The Fires of New Sun.*

School Library Journal, February, 2011, Jane Henriksen Baird, review of *The Blending Time,* p. 112.

Voice of Youth Advocates, December, 2010, Florence Munat, review of *The Blending Time,* p. 472.

ONLINE

Michael Kinch Home Page, http://www.michaelkinch.com (January 15, 2012).*

*   *   *

KINCH, Michael P.
  See KINCH, Michael

L

LEEDY, Loreen 1959-

Personal

Born June 15, 1959, in Wilmington, DE; daughter of James Allwyn (an auditor) and Grace Anne (a registered nurse and homemaker) Leedy; married Andrew Schuerger (a scientist), April 27, 2002. *Education:* Attended Indiana University—Bloomington, 1978-79; University of Delaware, B.A. (art; cum laude), 1981. *Hobbies and other interests:* Making beaded jewelry, hiking, gardening, art quilting, reading.

Addresses

Home—FL. *E-mail*—LJLart@bellsouth.net.

Career

Author and illustrator. Craftsperson, specializing in jewelry, 1982-84; freelance writer and illustrator, 1984—. Speaker at schools and conventions. *Exhibitions:* Work exhibited at Society of Illustrators' Original Art Show, 1994, 2003; Florida Illustrators show, 1997-99; Martin County Council for the Arts, 2000; Greensburgh Nature Center, Scarsdale, NY; and Visual Art Center of Northwest Florida and Art Institute of Fort Lauderdale, both 2011.

Member

Authors Guild, Society of Children's Book Writers and Illustrators.

Awards, Honors

Parents' Choice Award for Illustration, 1987, for *Big, Small, Short, Tall;* Parents' Choice Award in Learning and Doing, 1989, for *The Dragon Halloween Party;* Ezra Jack Keats Award for excellence in the arts, 1989; Best Books Award, *Parents* magazine, 1990, for *The Furry News: How to Make a Newspaper,* and 1992, for *The Monster Money Book;* Outstanding Science Trade Book designation, National Science Teacher's Association, 1993, for *Tracks in the Sand;* Parent's Choice Gold Award for Picture Books, 1998, for *Measuring Penny;* National Council for the Social Studies Notable Trade Book, 2001, for *Mapping Penny's World;* American Library Association Notable Book designation, and Notable Childrens Books in the English Language Arts designation, Children's Literature Assembly of National Council of Teachers of English, both 2004, both for *There's a Frog in My Throat!;* AAAS *Science Books & Films* award finalist, 2007, for *The Great Graph Contest;* Florida Book Awards Bronze Medal, 2008, and Chicago Public Library Best of the Best selection, 2009, both for *Missing Math.*

Writings

SELF-ILLUSTRATED

A Number of Dragons, Holiday House (New York, NY), 1985.

The Dragon ABC Hunt, Holiday House (New York, NY), 1986.

The Dragon Halloween Party, Holiday House (New York, NY), 1986.

Big, Small, Short, Tall, Holiday House (New York, NY), 1987.

The Bunny Play, Holiday House (New York, NY), 1988.

A Dragon Christmas: Things to Make and Do, Holiday House (New York, NY), 1988.

Pingo the Plaid Panda, Holiday House (New York, NY), 1988.

The Potato Party, and Other Troll Tales, Holiday House (New York, NY), 1989.

A Dragon Thanksgiving Feast: Things to Make and Do, Holiday House (New York, NY), 1990.

The Furry News: How to Make a Newspaper, Holiday House (New York, NY), 1990.

The Great Trash Bash, Holiday House (New York, NY), 1991.

Messages in the Mailbox: How to Write a Letter, Holiday House (New York, NY), 1991.

Blast off to Earth! A Look at Geography, Holiday House (New York, NY), 1992.

The Monster Money Book, Holiday House (New York, NY), 1992.

Postcards from Pluto: A Tour of the Solar System, Holiday House (New York, NY), 1993, revised edition, 2006.

The Race, Scott, Foresman (Glenview, IL), 1993.

Tracks in the Sand, Doubleday (New York, NY), 1993, revised e-book edition, 2011.

The Edible Pyramid: Good Eating Every Day, Holiday House (New York, NY), 1994, revised edition, 2007.

Fraction Action, Holiday House (New York, NY), 1994.

Who's Who in My Family?, Holiday House (New York, NY), 1995.

2 X 2 = Boo! A Set of Spooky Multiplication Stories, Holiday House (New York, NY), 1995.

How Humans Make Friends, Holiday House (New York, NY), 1996.

Mission Addition, Holiday House (New York, NY), 1997.

Measuring Penny, Henry Holt (New York, NY), 1997.

Celebrate the Fifty States!, Holiday House (New York, NY), 1999.

Mapping Penny's World, Henry Holt (New York, NY), 2000.

Subtraction Action, Holiday House (New York, NY), 2000.

Follow the Money!, Holiday House (New York, NY), 2002.

(With Pat Street) *There's a Frog in My Throat! 440 Animal Sayings a Little Bird Told Me,* Holiday House (New York, NY), 2003.

Look at My Book: How Kids Can Write and Illustrate Terrific Books, Holiday House (New York, NY), 2004.

The Great Graph Contest, Holiday House (New York, NY), 2005.

(With husband, Andrew Schuerger) *Messages from Mars,* Holiday House (New York, NY), 2006.

It's Probably Penny, Henry Holt (New York, NY), 2007.

Crazy like a Fox: A Simile Story, Holiday House (New York, NY), 2008.

Missing Math: A Number Mystery, Marshall Cavendish (New York, NY), 2008.

My Teacher Is a Dinosaur, and Other Prehistoric Poems, Jokes, Riddles, and Amazing Facts, Marshall Cavendish Children (Tarrytown, NY), 2010.

The Shocking Truth about Energy, Holiday House (New York, NY), 2010.

Seeing Symmetry, Holiday House (New York, NY), 2012.

ILLUSTRATOR

David A. Adler, *The Dinosaur Princess, and Other Prehistoric Riddles,* Holiday House (New York, NY), 1988.

Tom Birdseye, *Waiting for Baby,* Holiday House (New York, NY), 1991.

Sidelights

Loreen Leedy is an author and artist who crafts books that introduce important, life-navigating concepts to young readers. In *Fraction Action, Mission Addition,* and *Missing Math: A Number Mystery* early elementary graders learn useful math concepts, while *Celebrate the Fifty States!, Mapping Penny's World, Follow the Money!,* and *The Shocking Truth about Energy* help youngsters begin to independently explore the world outside their family home. Other nonfiction titles by Leedy, such as *The Edible Pyramid: Good Eating Every Day, Messages in the Mailbox: How to Write a Letter,* and *Look at My Book: How Kids Can Write and Illustrate Terrific Books,* encourage self-reliance and self-expression, while *There's a Frog in My Throat! 440 Animal Sayings a Little Bird Told Me* and *My Teacher Is a Dinosaur, and Other Prehistoric Poems, Jokes, Riddles, and Amazing Facts* are packed with useful information.

Leedy often weaves mathematical concepts into her humorously illustrated picture books, with effective results. In *Subtraction Action* for instance, she "creates an action-packed volume that is perfectly suited to its audience," according to a *Publishers Weekly* reviewer. *Measuring Penny, Mapping Penny's World,* and *It's Probably Penny* introduce a young girl named Lisa as she brings home concepts from school and attempts to apply them to her own life. Penny, Lisa's pet Boston terrier, is measured, weighed and otherwise sized up in *Measuring Penny,* while the pup's habitat is thoroughly mapped out in *Mapping Penny's World.* Probability is the concept behind *It's Probably Penny,* as Lisa and her pup calculate the odds of a number of likely—and unlikely—scenarios. Stephanie Zvirin, reviewing *Mea-*

A group of upbeat animals takes readers on a fascinating tour in Loreen Leedy's self-illustrated **The Edible Pyramid: Good Eating Every Day.**

suring Penny for *Booklist,* praised Leedy's story as a "creative introduction" to a sometimes perplexing subject, while Julie Cummins noted in the same periodical that *It's Probably Penny* "clearly and cleverly depicts . . . possibilities and choices" in Leedy's simply drawn and humorous sequential art.

In *Follow the Money!,* another math-based book by Leedy, readers can follow the path of a newly minted coin, a quarter fittingly named George, as it cycles from bank to piggy bank to purse to cash register, again and again. Called a "lighthearted travelogue" by a *Kirkus Reviews* writer, *Follow the Money!* also includes lessons in budgeting, saving, and making change. Noting the "lighthearted tone" in Leedy's guide to child-sized economics, a *Publishers Weekly* contributor also cited the author/illustrator's "playful mixed-media art, flippant asides . . . , and occasional puns." Describing another of the author/illustrator's fictional approaches to math, *The Great Graph Contest,* a *Kirkus Reviews* writer noted that "Leedy makes graphing simple and fun in this delightfully clever outing" about a toad and lizard that decide to see who can create the best graph.

Science takes center stage in Leedy's books *Postcards from Pluto: A Tour of the Solar System* and *Messages from Mars.* In both stories, readers blast off into space—and into the future—as a group of young space travelers reach a far-distant planetary (or in the case of Pluto, not-quite-planetary) destination and compare their new surroundings with those left behind on Earth. In *Messages from Mars* Leedy collaborates with scientist husband Andrew Schuerger, an astrobiologist whose research lab is located at the Kennedy Space Center and whose experience adds a fascinating dimension to the couple's fictional story. In *School Library Journal,* Mary Jean Smith praised Leedy's "colorful cartoons," and also noted the inclusion of "authentic photographs from NASA" and the wealth of "factual information" provided by the coauthors. Dubbing the same book "clever," Carolyn Phelan went on in her *Booklist* review to recommend *Messages from Mars* as "a good starting point for those intrigued by Mars."

More science facts are served up in *The Shocking Truth about Energy,* as Leedy's engaging cartoon-style illustrations draw readers along on a page-by-page study of what energy is and where different forms of energy come from. From arm muscles to wind power, from solar heat to fossil fuels, all are explained by the book's energetic narrator, a bright yellow bolt of energy named Erg. Praising the book's mix of cartoons, diagrams, speech bubbles, and energy facts, Grace Oliff noted in her *School Library Journal* review that *The Shocking Truth about Energy* benefits from artwork "featuring cheerful and appealing anthropomorphized appliances" and "chatty little asides uttered by toasters, hair dryers, [and] computers." "Leedy's experience selecting facts that are most relevant and engaging . . . is evident," noted Kathleen Isaacs in her *Booklist* review of the same book, while in *Kirkus Reviews* a writer asserted of

Leedy's nonfiction picture book **Follow the Money!** *follows the path of a shiny new quarter after it leaves the U.S. mint.* (Holiday House, 2002. Reproduced by permission of Holiday House, Inc.)

The Shocking Truth about Energy that the author/illustrator "presents difficult concepts in a way that even younger readers can understand."

In a mix of humorous digital art and story, *Crazy like a Fox: A Simile Story* turns reader attention to the power of words to transform one object into another. In her well-illustrated story, Rufus the fox illustrates how to "roar like a lion" when he frightens timid Babette, and the lamb responds by becoming as "mad a hornet" and leading readers on a simile-studded chase to a surprising ending. Leedy's artwork adds to the fun as the verbal comparisons yield physical transformation with each turn of the page. "Her vivid illustrations, filled with movement and wide-eyed creatures, will entertain readers," predicted *School Library Journal* contributor Jane Damron, while a *Kirkus Reviews* critic described *Crazy like a Fox* as a book "as welcome as springtime to teachers, aspiring writers and any who appreciate wordplay."

"I was inspired to become a children's book author/illustrator because picture books combine two of my favorite things: art and writing," Leedy once told *SATA.* "I majored in art in college, but didn't focus on children's books until three years after graduating. I enjoy creating books that put information in context so it's meaningful to young readers. I always learn something new with every project and have used a variety of media to create my illustrations: pen and ink, watercolor, colored pencil, or acrylics.

"In the late 1990s I learned to use my computer to create artwork. I had to become a student again and read a lot of how-to books. Eventually I was able to draw and paint with my wonderful digital tools. The computer opens up many new creative possibilities and allows me to experiment extensively with color and placement while working. I've also enjoyed incorporating photographs and real objects such as twigs and rocks into the illustrations."

Discussing her decision to focus her creative career on writing and illustrating children's books, Leedy—a former polymer clay jewelry maker—once noted: "Reading, writing, and creating art have been important to me throughout my lifetime. The picture book is a unique art form in which the words and images work together to tell the story or convey information. When developing a book, I go back and forth between the text and the illustrations to create a unified whole. My books generally incorporate humor to engage the young reader and include information children are learning in school.

"I choose a subject such as measuring, then think of characters and a setting where the story can take place. For *Measuring Penny,* I used a little girl who has a homework assignment to measure 'something,' and dogs because they come in so many sizes and shapes. The story takes place at school, at home, and in the park.

"The garden setting for *The Great Graph Contest* is close to the ground where bugs, slugs, and other small critters live. The toad and lizard competitors use materials at hand such as flowers, butterflies, and cookies left on a picnic table to create their graphs. Many of the objects and textures in the illustrations were photographs or scans of real objects. The toad's skin, for example, is derived from a photograph of an asphalt road.

Leedy takes readers on a tour of how modern life is powered in her self-illustrated picture book The Shocking Truth about Energy. (Jacket cover copyright by Holiday House. Reproduced by permission of Holiday House, Inc.)

"The fantastic photographs of the Red Planet taken primarily by NASA inspired *Messages from Mars.* My scientist husband compiled the images from a variety of Web sites. We worked together to develop a storyline to showcase as much information as possible about Mars and the missions that have explored it to date. The time is 100 years in the future, and the characters are kids from a variety of nationalities who have won a trip to visit Mars."

Biographical and Critical Sources

PERIODICALS

Booklist, October 15, 1997, Carolyn Phelan, review of *Mission Addition,* p. 74; April, 1998, Stephanie Zvirin, review of *Measuring Penny,* p. 1325; September 1, 1999, Ilene Cooper, review of *Celebrate the Fifty States!,* p. 136; July, 2000, Catherine Andronik, review of *Mapping Penny's World,* p. 2040; September 15, 2000, Carolyn Phelan, review of *Subtraction Action,* p. 246; April 15, 2002, Susan Dove Lempke, review of *Follow the Money!,* p. 1398; March 15, 2003, Ellen Mandel, review of *There's a Frog in My Throat! 440 Animal Sayings a Little Bird Told Me,* p. 1322; February 15, 2004, Kay Weisman, review of *Look at My Book: How Kids Can Write and Illustrate Terrific Books,* p. 1060; August, 2005, Todd Morning, review of *The Great Graph Contest,* p. 2029; September 15, 2006, Carolyn Phelan, review of *Messages from Mars,* p. 64; April 1, 2007, Julie Cummins, review of *It's Probably Penny,* p. 54; May 1, 2007, Hazel Rochman, review of *The Edible Pyramid: Good Eating Every Day,* p. 92; April 1, 2008, Carolyn Phelan, review of *Missing Math: A Number Mystery,* p. 55; April 15, 2010, Kathleen Isaacs, review of *The Shocking Truth about Energy,* p. 48; November 1, 2010, Carolyn Phelan, review of *My Teacher Is a Dinosaur, and Other Prehistoric Poems, Jokes, Riddles, and Amazing Facts,* p. 42.

Bulletin of the Center for Children's Books, September, 2000, review of *Mapping Penny's World,* p. 27; April, 2002, review of *Follow the Money!,* p. 285; April, 2003, review of *There's a Frog in My Throat!,* p. 319.

Horn Book, July-August, 1998, Marilyn Bousquin, review of *Measuring Penny,* p. 476; May-June, 2003, Roger Sutton, review of *There's a Frog in My Throat!,* p. 368.

Kirkus Reviews, March 1, 2002, review of *Follow the Money!,* p. 338; February 1, 2003, review of *There's a Frog in My Throat!,* p. 235; February 1, 2004, review of *Look at My Book,* p. 135; August 1, 2005, review of *The Great Graph Contest,* p. 852; August 1, 2006, review of *Messages from Mars,* p. 790; March 1, 2007, review of *It's Probably Penny;* September 1, 2008, review of *Crazy like a Fox: A Simile Story;* April 15, 2010, review of *The Shocking Truth about Energy;* August 15, 2010, review of *My Teacher Is a Dinosaur, and Other Prehistoric Poems, Jokes, Riddles, and Amazing Facts.*

Publishers Weekly, March 16, 1998, review of *Measuring Penny,* p. 63; January 11, 1999, review of *Mission Addition,* p. 74; February 4, 2002, review of *Follow the Money!,* p. 76; January 6, 2003, review of *There's a Frog in My Throat!,* p. 60.

School Library Journal, September, 1999, Jackie Hechtkopf, review of *Celebrate the Fifty States!,* p. 214; September, 2000, Holly T. Sneeringer, review of *Subtraction Action,* p. 219; May, 2002, Anne Chapman Callaghan, review of *Follow the Money!,* p. 139; April, 2003, Susan Marie Pitard, review of *There's a Frog in My Throat!,* p. 152; January, 2004, Joy Fleishhacker, review of *Mapping Penny's World,* p. 77; April, 2004, Jody Kopple, review of *Look at My Book,* p. 134; June, 2004, Steven Engelfried, review of *There's a Frog in My Throat!,* p. 57; September, 2004, Janet Dawson Hamilton, review of *Fraction Action,* p. 58; November, 2004, Alison Follows, review of *Look at My Book,* p. 65; September, 2005, Robyn Walker, review of *The Great Graph Contest,* p. 176; October, 2006, Mary Jean Smith, review of *Messages from Mars,* p. 138; May, 2007, Kathy Piehl, review of *The Edible Pyramid,* p. 120; June, 2007, Mary Jean Smith, review of *It's Probably Penny,* p. 135; June, 2008, Marian Creamer, review of *Missing Math,* p. 108; September, 2008, Jayne Damron, review of *Crazy like a Fox,* p. 153; May, 2010, Grace Oliff, review of *The Shocking Truth about Energy,* p. 98; January, 2011, Julie Roach, review of *My Teacher Is a Dinosaur, and Other Prehistoric Poems, Jokes, Riddles, and Amazing Facts,* p. 90.

ONLINE

Loreen Leedy Home Page, http://www.loreenleedy.com (January 9, 2012).
Loreen Leedy Web log, http://loreenleedybooks.blogspot. com (January 9, 2012).

*   *   *

LEWIS, Jon S.
See LEWIS, J.S.

*   *   *

LEWIS, J.S. 1972-
(Jon S. Lewis)

Personal

Born May 15, 1972; married; has children. *Education:* Arizona State University, B.S. (broadcast journalism). *Hobbies and other interests:* Movies, football, World War II history, comic books spending time with friends and family.

Addresses

Home—Phoenix, AZ. *Office*—P.O. Box 2431, Chandler, AZ 85244. *E-mail*—jslewis@greygriffins.com.

Career

Comic-book writer. Worked for Web-development companies.

Writings

"GREY GRIFFINS" NOVEL SERIES; WITH DEREK BENZ

The Revenge of the Shadow King, Orchard Books (New York, NY), 2005.
The Rise of the Black Wolf, Orchard Books (New York, NY), 2007.
The Fall of the Templar, Orchard Books (New York, NY), 2008.
The Brimstone Key ("Clockwork Chronicles" sequence), Little, Brown (New York, NY), 2010.
The Relic Hunters ("Clockwork Chronicles" sequence), Little, Brown (New York, NY), 2011.
The Paragon Engine ("Clockwork Chronicles" sequence), Little, Brown (New York, NY), 2012.

"C.H.A.O.S." NOVEL SERIES

(Under name Jon S. Lewis) *Invasion,* Thomas Nelson (Nashville, TN), 2010.
(Under name Jon S. Lewis) *Alienation,* Thomas Nelson (Nashville, TN), 2012.

OTHER

Free Realms (graphic novel; based on the Free Realms videogame), illustrated by John Buran, Wildstorm (La Jolla, CA), 2010.

Also author of comic-book texts, including for *Megamatric: Hero Within,* 2010.

Adaptations

The "Grey Griffins" story has been optioned for film. The "C.H.A.O.S." books were adapted as audiobooks.

Sidelights

As a writer, J.S. Lewis is best known for his collaboration with lifelong friend Derek Benz on the "Grey Griffins" novels, which are represented in a highly interactive Web site and include *The Revenge of the Shadow King, The Rise of the Black Wolf, The Fall of the Templar, The Brimstone Key, The Relic Hunters,* and *The Paragon Engine.* In *Invasion,* Lewis also introduces the teen hero in his "C.H.A.O.S." adventure series, publishing these books under the name Jon S. Lewis.

Raised in the Midwest, Lewis met Benz when his family moved to Des Moines, Iowa, and the boys started creating their own comic books in elementary school. Over time their collaborations switched from comic books to fantasy novels. Then, during college, the friends went their separate ways, Benz to a Midwestern college and Lewis to Arizona State University, where he earned a degree in broadcast journalism. Although Lewis embarked on a career that included journalism as well as radio production and voiceovers, graphic design. and Web development and marketing, he reconnected with Benz in his late twenties and the "Grey Griffins" series was born.

"A lot of the story is set in the woods in a fictional farming community in the Midwest . . . ," Lewis explained, describing the backdrop of the "Grey Griffins" saga to *Journal of Adolescent & Adult Literacy* interviewer James Blasingame. "Those woods, and the farm where the main character's grandmother lives, are basically the area where Derek grew up. We used to go on adventures in those woods and pretend that we were characters from [J.R.R. Tolkien's] *The Lord of the Rings.* Those were some of our favorite memories, and we wanted to use that as the backdrop for our series." As far as working on a collaborative venture with Benz,

Cover of J.S. Lewis and Derek Benz's collaborative history-themed adventure novel The Fall of the Templar, *featuring artwork by August Hall.* (Jacket cover illustration copyright © 2007 by August Hall. Reproduced by permission of Orchard Books, an imprint of Scholastic Inc.)

"there are definite advantages," Lewis noted. "I get to work with my best friend, making up stories that we've talked about our entire lives."

Lewis and Benz's "Grey Griffins" saga opens with *The Revenge of the Shadow King,* as Max Sumner and sixth-grade friends Ernie, Harley, and Natalia form a secret club in their Minnesota home town. When strange, goblin-like creatures begin to appear in Max's backyard, the four Grey Griffins realize that these mythic beings mirror the characters of an antique role-playing card game that they purchased at a local collectibles store and are now playing. With the help of a magical book—the likely cause of the problem—Max and his friends try to track down the source of the goblin and faery infestation, but when a local shopkeeper disappears and the Grey Griffins unearth a legend about the evil Shadow King, the stakes become much higher. The town's hidden history, which includes a 500-year-old Gothic temple and Max's destiny as a modern-day Templar knight fighting on the side of good, propels the plot of what a *Kirkus Reviews* critic described as an "entertaining series opener."

The adventures of the Grey Griffins continue in *The Rise of the Black Wolf,* as Max, Ernie, Harley, and Natalia travel to Scotland to spend Christmas vacation with Max's wealthy father at his family castle. When Lord Sumner disappears and a pack of vicious werewolves is seen patrolling the castle grounds, the sixth graders know that they are up against a new form of evil, one led by the witch Morgan la Fey in her search for a powerful talisman called the Spear of Ragnarok. Lord Sumner returns with that talisman in hand in *The Fall of the Templar,* but when he delves into its secrets he ushers in a new Ice Age. Joining other Templar knights, Max and the Griffins embark on a search for a relic powerful enough to stop the coming deep freeze, and this search takes them into the depths of the Underworld.

Describing *The Rise of the Black Wolf* as an "amalgam of Norse mythology, Arthurian legends, the Dracula story and others," a *Kirkus Reviews* writer added that Lewis and Benz's "fast-paced adventure" will appeal to fans of sword-and-sorcery fantasy. The Grey Griffins' "adventures are scary, exciting, and a bit gruesome—just what the young adventurer looks for in a fantasy/adventure/supernatural novel," asserted Linda Broughton in her *Journal of Adolescent & Adult Literacy* review of the same novel, while colleague Tara Lehmann concluded of *The Fall of the Templar* that "reading this book made me wish there had been a series like this around when I was a youngster: never-ending adventure, creatures around every corner, . . . and superhero powers."

Lewis and Benz create a new set of Grey Griffin adventures in the "Clockwork Chronicles" sequence, which finds Max, Ernie, Harley, and Natalie attending Iron Bridge Academy, a school that trains recruits to battle

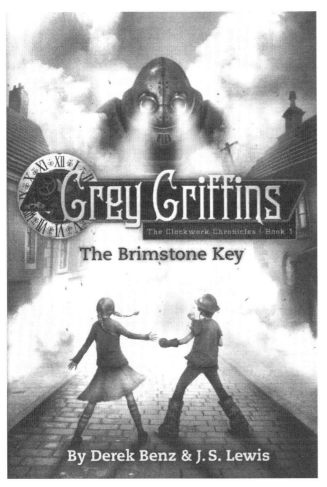

Lewis and Benz continue their "Grey Griffins" fantasy series in **The Brimstone Key.** (Jacket art copyright © 2011 by Vincent Chong. Reproduced by permission of Little, Brown and Company, an imprint of Hachette Book Group.)

evil in its many forms. When readers catch up with the young teens in *The Brimstone Key* the Griffins have attracted the attention of the Clockwork King, a powerful scientist and legendary foe of the Knights Templar. Intending to build a vast army of mechanical fighters, the Clockwork King also plans to enslave the souls of all humans who have supernatural abilities or faerie blood, and that includes the Griffins as well as their classmates. The Grey Griffins' adventures continue in *The Relic Hunters* and *The Paragon Engine* as they continue to thwart the efforts of Templar foes and save the worlds of both humans and benevolent supernatural beings. "Fans of the 'Grey Griffins' series will be thrilled to revisit their old friends in this action-packed adventure," predicted Heather M. Campbell in her *School Library Journal* appraisal of *The Brimstone Key,* while Blasingame cited the influences of both the steampunk genre and J.K. Rowling's "Harry Potter" series. *The Brimstone Key* "may act as a bridge to more complex works like those of J.R.R. Tolkien," the critic added, noting that Lewis and Benz's "Grey Griffins" stories are "as much about forging friendships as fighting monsters."

In *Invasion* Lewis branches out on his own, creating the first installment in his "C.H.A.O.S." novel series. At age sixteen, Colt McAlister's parents die in an automo-

bile accident and he is sent to Arizona to live with Grandfather Murdoch. Haunted by his parent's death, Colt becomes convinced that it may have been murder, and he becomes even more sure of this when he learns that his mother was investigating Trident Biotech, a corporation that had developed the ability to control thoughts, at the time of her death. As Colt starts to track his mom's investigation, helped by friends Danielle and Oz, he also attracts unwanted attention. Soon Colt learns things that he would rather not have known, things about alien shape shifters called the Thule and the threat they pose to all humanity. The teen's adventures continue in *Alienation,* as he and his friends are recruited by the U.S. government and enroll at the C.H.A.O.S. Military Academy, where someone or some thing is attempting to thwart his training by deadly means.

While noting that Lewis focuses more on action than character development in his "Chaos" novels, a *Publishers Weekly* critic wrote that *Invasion* will appeal to "breakneck-adventure addicts" due to its "brisk pace, aliens, and jet-packs and other cool-but-unlikely gizmos." and *School Library Journal* contributor Ryan Donovan predicted of the same novel that Lewis's "fast paced and well-defined world will keep readers glued to the pages."

Biographical and Critical Sources

PERIODICALS

Journal of Adolescent & Adult Literacy, November, 2007, Linda Broughton, review of *The Rise of the Black Wolf,* p. 286; May, 2008, Tara Lehmann, review of *The Fall of the Templar,* p. 691; May, 2010, James Blasingame, review of *The Brimstone Key,* p. 693, and interview with Lewis, p. 694.
Kirkus Reviews, January 1, 2006, review of *The Revenge of the Shadow King,* p. 37; December 15, 2006, review of *The Rise of the Black Wolf,* p. 1264; November 15, 2010, review of *Invasion.*
Publishers Weekly, November 8, 2010, review of *Invasion,* p. 62.
School Library Journal, April, 2006, Susan L. Rogers, review of *The Revenge of the Shadow King,* p. 134; March, 2007, Farida S. Dowler, review of *The Rise of the Black Wolf,* p. 203; March, 2008, Jennifer-Lynn Draper, review of *The Fall of the Templar,* p. 194; August, 2010, Heather M. Campbell, review of *The Brimstone Key,* p. 96; January, 2011, Ryan Donovan, review of *Invasion,* p. 110; July, 2011, Kathleen Meulen Ellison, review of *The Relic Hunters,* p. 92.
Voice of Youth Advocates, October, 2010, Lisa Martincik, review of *The Brimstone Key,* p. 361.

ONLINE

Grey Griffins Web site, http://www.greygriffins.com (January 9, 2012).

LINDNER, April 1962-

Personal

Born 1962, in North Merrick, NY; married Andre St. Amant; children: Eli St. Amant, Noah St. Amant. *Education:* University of New Hampshire, B.A., 1984; Sarah Lawrence College, M.F.A., 1989; University of Cincinnati, Ph.D., 1998. *Hobbies and other interests:* Cooking, rock music, playing guitar.

Addresses

Home—Havertown, PA. *E-mail*—alindner@sju.edu.

Career

Educator and author. St. Joseph University, Philadelphia, PA, associate professor, beginning 2001, currently professor of English. Speaker at schools.

Awards, Honors

Walt McDonald First Book Poetry Prize, Texas Tech University Press, 2001, for *Skin;* Pushcart Prize nomination, 2001.

Writings

NOVELS

Jane, Little, Brown (New York, NY), 2010.
Catherine, Little, Brown (New York, NY), 2013.

April Lindner (Photograph by Melissa Kelly. Reproduced by permission.)

OTHER

New Formalist Poets of the American West, Boise State University (Boise, ID), 2001.
Skin, Texas Tech University Press (Lubbock, TX), 2002.
Dana Gioia, second edition, Boise State University (Boise, ID), 2003.
Women Poets of the New Formalism, Textos Books (Cincinnati, OH), 2004.
(Editor with R.S. Gwynn) *Contemporary American Poetry: A Pocket Anthology,* Pearson/Longman (New York, NY), 2004.
This Bed Our Bodies Shaped, Able Muse Press (San Jose, CA), 2012.

Contributor to journals, including *Carolina Quarterly, Formalist, Hudson Review, Measure II, Mezzo Cammin, MiPoesias, Paris Review, Prairie Schooner,* and *Verse Daily.* Work included in anthologies *Good Poems,* edited by Garrison Keilor, Viking (New York, NY), 2002; *Poetry: A Pocket Reader,* 5th edition, edited by R.S. Gwynn, Longman (New York, NY), 2004; *Western Wind,* 5th edition, edited by John Frederick Nims and David Mason, McGraw Hill (New York, NY), 2005; *Three Genres,* 8th edition, edited by Stephen Minot, Prentice Hall (New York, NY), 2006; and *Literature: An Introduction,* 10th edition, edited by X.J. Kennedy and Dana Gioia, Longman, 2006.

Author's work has been translated into Russian and Spanish.

Sidelights

April Lindner is an award-winning poet as well as an editor and a professor of English at Philadelphia's Saint Joseph's University, and she has published literary criticism and poetry in a wide range of journals and anthologies. Lindner's two favorite literary classics inspired her first forays into fiction: *Jane* is a contemporary retelling of Charlotte Brontë's 1847 novel *Jane Eyre,* while *Catherine* is based on *Wuthering Heights,* a novel published by Charlotte's sister Emily Brontë in the same year. "A fierce intelligence sets Lindner's work apart," noted Ned Balbo in reviewing her highly acclaimed poetry collection *Skin* in the *Antioch Review.* "As an exploration of culture, custom, and biological drive," the poet has produced "a marvelous book, confident and unified."

Jane Moore is nineteen and about to abandon her studies at New York's Sarah Lawrence College in the wake of her parents' tragic death when readers are introduced to her in *Jane.* She leverages her academic achievements into a job as nanny to Maddy, the daughter of well-known rock star Nico Rathburn. Nico lives at Thornfield Park, where he hosts lavish parties for a steady stream of fans and well-connected friends to help fuel his career comeback. Although Jane does not normally act imprudently, her attraction to the moody but charismatic Nico is too much to resist, and she is surprised when her affection is returned. As does Mr. Rochester in the original novel, Nico proposes marriage to the young student and she accepts, only to realize that Thornfield Park contains many things that do not make sense . . . , until she learns the truth about Nico's hidden and tragic past.

In *Jane* Lindner "delivers an entrancing star-crossed relationship," noted *School Library Journal* contributor Emily Chornomaz, "and it is not necessary to be familiar with the original to enjoy it." For Frances Bradburn, reviewing the novel in *Booklist,* most impressive is the author's ability to "demonstrate . . . an organic understanding of rock culture" and "its over-the-top lifestyle," while a *Kirkus Reviews* critic wrote that the "distracting improbabilities" that come to mind in comparing the setting of the two novels are balanced by "flashes of originality, wit and vivid imagery." "Well-written and faithful to the original," according to a *Publishers Weekly* critic, Lindner's *Jane* treats teens to "a fresh and addictive adaptation" of a literary classic.

Lindner reimagines a classic of English literature in Jane, *a retelling of Jane Austen's nineteenth-century novel Jane Eyre.* (Jacket art copyright © 2010 by Margaret Malandruccolo. Reproduced by permission of Little, Brown and Company, an imprint of Hachette Book Group.)

Biographical and Critical Sources

PERIODICALS

Antioch Review, summer, 2003, Ned Balbo, review of *Skin,* p. 585.
Booklist, November 15, 2010, Frances Bradburn, review of *Jane,* p. 41.
Bulletin of the Center for Children's Books, January, 2011, Karen Coats, review of *Jane,* p. 245.
Kirkus Reviews, September 15, 2010, review of *Jane.*
Publishers Weekly, October 4, 2010, review of *Jane,* p. 50.
School Library Journal, January, 2011, Emily Chornomaz, review of *Jane,* p. 110.

ONLINE

April Lindner Home Page, http://www.aprillindner.com (January 15, 2012).
St. Joseph's University Web site, http://www.sju.edu/ (January 15, 2012), "April Lindner."

*   *   *

LOGAN, Bob 1968-

Personal

Born 1968, in Baltimore, MD; married; children: one son. *Education:* Edinboro University of Pennsylvania, B.F.A. (applied media arts).

Addresses

Home—Thousand Oaks, CA. *E-mail*—bobopoly@mac.com.

Career

Author/illustrator and story artist. Worked as an assistant director for television programming, beginning 1999; story artist for Film Roman, Disney Television, Sony Pictures Animation, and Imagi Studios, and Dreamworks Animation.

Writings

The Sea of Bath, Sourcebooks Jabberwocky (Naperville, IL), 2010.
Rocket Town, Sourcebooks Jabberwocky (Naperville, IL), 2011.

Biographical and Critical Sources

PERIODICALS

Kirkus Reviews, September 15, 2010, review of *The Sea of Bath;* July 1, 2011, review of *Rocket Town.*

Publishers Weekly, September 27, 2010, review of *The Sea of Bath,* p. 56.

ONLINE

Bob Logan Web log, http://www.bobloganillustration. blogspot.com (January 9, 2012).
Ventura County Star Online, http://www.vcstar.com (March 12, 2011), Rachel McGrath, "Thousand Oaks Man Publishing Children's Book of Drawings."

*　*　*

LORD, Cynthia

Personal

Born in Waltham, MA; married; children: two. *Education:* Attended college.

Addresses

Home—Brunswick, ME. *Agent*—Adams Literary, 7845 Colony Rd., C4 No. 215, Charlotte, NC 28226. *E-mail*—cindy@cynthialord.com.

Career

Educator and writer. Former teacher of first-and sixth-grade in New England public schools.

Member

Society of Children's Book Writers and Illustrators, Maine Writers' and Publishers' Alliance.

Awards, Honors

Society of Children's Book Writers and Illustrators work-in-process grant, 2004; *Smartwriters.com* contest winner; Newbery Honor Book designation, Schneider Family Book Award in middle-school category, Michigan Library Association Mitten Award, New York Public Library 100 Titles for Reading and Sharing inclusion, National Council of Teachers of English Notable Children's Book in the Language Arts designation, American Library Association Notable Book designation, and nominations for numerous child-selected state awards, all c. 2007, all for *Rules.*

Writings

Rules (middle-grade novel), Scholastic (New York, NY), 2006.
Hot Rod Hamster, illustrated by Derek Anderson, Scholastic Press (New York, NY), 2010.
Touch Blue, Scholastic Press (New York, NY), 2010.
Happy Birthday, Hamster, illustrated by Derek Anderson, Scholastic Press (New York, NY), 2011.

Cynthia Lord (Photograph by John Bald. Reprinted by the permission of Adams Literary as agents for the author.)

Also author of short fiction and of curriculums for educational publishers.

Sidelights

With her first book, former middle-school teacher Cynthia Lord achieved what many writers only dream of: earning an Honor Book designation from the prestigious Newbery Award committee. Lord's middle-grade novel *Rules,* was inspired by her experience raising her autistic son; Although "some incidents in the book came from real experience . . . ," she noted on her home page, "most of the events, details, and characters in *Rules* came from my imagination." "The first line I ever wrote on the first blank page was: 'At our house, we have a rule,' and the story, the characters, the title, all sprang from that seed."

Dubbed "a heartwarming first novel" by *Booklist* contributor Cindy Dobrez, *Rules* draws readers into the story of twelve-year-old Catherine, who lives with her parents and autistic younger brother David in coastal Maine. Although Catherine is a caring girl and loves David, she is embarrassed by some of the things the boy does, such as hugging strangers and dropping his toys into the family's fish tank. She also feels burdened by having to care for her little brother much of the time. To help David understand his surroundings and learn to navigate daily life, Catherine develops a series of simple rules for him to follow. Over the summer, sadness over a departed best friend, feelings of guilt over her anger that David takes the bulk of her parents' attention, the approach of adolescence, and her growing affection for a wheelchair-bound boy named Jason all combine to cause the girl confusion. To deal with her feelings, Catherine turns to art and also sets down a series of ground rules that she hopes will define her own world.

Ultimately, the preteen "begins to understand that normal is difficult, and perhaps unnecessary, to define," as Connie Tyrell Burns noted in a *School Library Journal* review of *Rules*. Referencing Catherine's conflicting feelings, a *Kirkus Reviews* writer predicted that "middle-grade readers will recognize her longing for acceptance," and in *School Library Journal* Connie Tyrrell Burns wrote that Lord's "endearing narrator . . . tells her story with both humor and heartbreak." In her novel the author "candidly capture[s] . . . the delicate dynamics" within a family coping with disability, Burns added, and a *Publishers Weekly* critic described *Rules* as "a rewarding story that may well inspire readers to think about others' points of view."

In *Touch Blue* Lord focuses on a slightly younger girl who also learns to accept things as they are rather than as she wishes they could be. When thirteen-year-old foster child Aaron Hamilton comes to life with Tess Brooks and her parents, the eleven year old is excited to have a new friend join her at her home off the Maine coast, especially since Aaron's presence means that the state will not close their small island school due to lack of enrollment. The troubled boy quickly shows that he will not fulfill all her expectations, however. A loner who is uncomfortable living the family's island lifestyle, he spends most of his time in his room. As Tess plots a way to help Aaron enjoy life the way she does, both children gradually come to change their perceptions and expectations in a story wherein a "tight-knit community and lobster-catching details make for a warm, colorful environment," according to *Booklist* contributor Krista Hutley. *Touch Blue* comes to life through its "realistic characters, humor, and a charming setting," asserted a *Kirkus Reviews* writer, while *School Library Journal* contributor Rebecca Webster predicted that readers "will feel an enormous amount of hope as they read Tess and Aaron's story." Lord's "thoughtful first-person narration" captures Tess's engaging humor, noted Jennifer M. Brabander in *Horn Book,* and *Touch Blue* readers can share the sights and sounds and smells of the place Tess loves and desperately doesn't want to leave."

With their high-energy stories and comic-book-style artwork by Derek Anderson, *Hot Rod Hamster* and *Happy Birthday, Hamster* are geared for younger readers, especially boys. In *Hot Rod Hamster* Lord introduces a scrappy little rodent that is determined to build a race car fast enough to beat the dogs at an upcoming race at the 4 Paws Speedway. Readers are allowed to help as the fluffy orange hamster trolls the junkyard searching for the best tires, fenders, and race-car accessories. "Young readers will love helping the irrepressible ham-

ster build his dream car," predicted Sara Paulson-Yarovoy in her *School Library Journal* review, and a *Publishers Weekly* critic praised Lord's "clever, rhythmic story." "Anderson's acrylics are boisterously large, colorful, and off-kilter," observed *Booklist* contributor Daniel Kraus, and in *Kirkus Reviews* a critic noted that the author's "rollicking" rhymes are "punctuated by questions" that help "move the story along without breaking the flow."

In an online interview with Debbi Michiko Florence, Lord discussed her thoughts on the writing life. "One personal rule I tell children who ask me for writing advice is *Read, write, learn, and dream,*" she told Florence. Her advice for beginning writers: "Don't be afraid to try something, even if you think it won't work. Sometimes I am not the best judge of what my story needs and trying a suggestion can open a new possibility."

Biographical and Critical Sources

PERIODICALS

Booklist, February 15, 2006, Cindy Dobrez, review of *Rules,* p. 98; December 1, 2009, Daniel Kraus, review

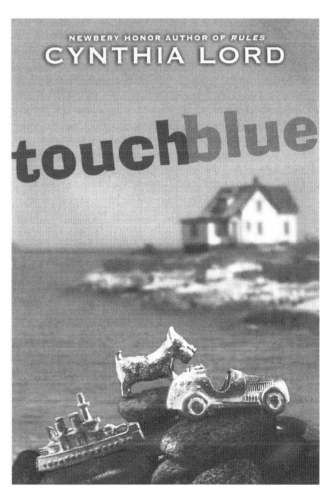

Cover of Lord's coming-of-age novel **Touch Blue,** *which takes place in Maine and features artwork by Marc Tauss.* (Jacket cover copyright © 2010 by Marc Tauss. Reproduced by permission of Scholastic, Inc.)

of *Hot Rod Hamster,* p. 50; August 1, 2010, Krista Hutley, review of *Touch Blue,* p. 56.

Bulletin of the Center for Children's Books, May, 2006, Deborah Stevenson, review of *Rules,* p. 411.

Horn Book, November-December, 2010, Jennifer M. Brabander, review of *Touch Blue,* p. 94.

Kirkus Reviews, March 1, 2006, review of *Rules,* p. 234; December 15, 2009, review of *Hot Rod Hamster*; July 1, 2010, review of *Touch Blue.*

Publishers Weekly, April 15, 2006, review of *Rules,* p. 188; January 11, 2010, review of *Hot Rod Hamster,* p. 46; August 9, 2010, review of *Touch Blue,* p. 53.

School Library Journal, April, 2006, Connie Tyrrell Burns, review of *Rules,* p. 142; January, 2010, Sara Paulson-Yarovoy, review of *Hot Rod Hamster,* p. 77; September 2010, Rebecca Webster, review of *Touch Blue,* p. 157.

ONLINE

Cynthia Lord Home Page, http://www.cynthialord.com (January 15, 2012).

Debbi Michiko Florence Web site, http://www.debbimichikoflorence.com/ (April, 2006), interview with Lord.

M

MACCARONE, Grace
(Grace Kim)

Personal

Children: Jordan (daughter). *Education:* Hobart & William Smith Colleges, B.A. (English and art history), 1974.

Addresses

Home—Westchester, NY. *Office*—Holiday House, 425 Madison Ave., New York, NY 10017.

Career

Editor and author. Scholastic, Inc., New York, NY, executive editor of Cartwheel Books imprint, 1979-2009; *Wireless Generation* (magazine), executive editor, 2009-10; Holiday House (publisher), New York, NY, executive editor, beginning 2010.

Awards, Honors

Children's Choice selections, International Reading Association/Children's Book Council, 1995, for both *Monster Math* and *My Tooth Is about to Fall Out,* and 1999, for *The Haunting of Grade Three.*

Writings

Mini-Mysteries Featuring Walt Disney's Mickey Mouse and Friends, illustrated by Bill Langley and Paul Edwards, Western Pub. Co. (Racine, WI), 1989.
Baby Visits Grandma and Grandpa, illustrated by Carol Hudson, Scholastic/Avon (New York, NY), 1990.
Baby's Toys, illustrated by Carol Hudson, Scholastic/Avon (New York, NY), 1990.
The Ghost on the Hill, illustrated by Kelly Oechsli, Little Apple Paperbacks (New York, NY), 1990.
Itchy, Itchy Chicken Pox, illustrated by Betsy Lewin, Scholastic (New York, NY), 1992.

The Sword in the Stone, illustrated by Joe Boddy, Scholastic (New York, NY), 1992.
Oink! Moo! How Do You Do? A Book of Animal Sounds, illustrated by Hans Wilhelm, Scholastic (New York, NY), 1994.
Pizza Party, illustrated by Emily Arnold McCully, Cartwheel Books (New York, NY), 1994.
Soccer Game!, illustrated by Meredith Johnson, Scholastic (New York, NY), 1994.
"What Is That?" Said the Cat, illustrated by Jeffrey Scherer, Scholastic (New York, NY), 1995.
Cars! Cars! Cars!, illustrated by David A. Carter, Scholastic (New York, NY), 1995.
(Under name Grace Kim) *She Sells Seashells: A Tongue Twister Story,* illustrated by Patricia Hammel, Scholastic (New York, NY), 1995.
The Silly Story of Goldie Locks and the Three Squares, illustrated by Anne Kennedy, Scholastic (New York, NY), 1996.
Three Pigs, One Wolf, and Seven Magic Shapes, illustrated by David Neuhaus, Scholastic (New York, NY), 1997.
I Shop with My Daddy, illustrated by Denise Brunkus, Scholastic (New York, NY), 1998.
The Haunting of Grade Three, Scholastic (New York, NY), 1999.
A Child Was Born: A First Nativity Book, illustrated by Sam Williams, Scholastic (New York, NY), 2000.
Mr. Rover Takes Over, illustrated by Meredith Johnson, Scholastic (New York, NY), 2000.
A Child's Good Night Prayer, illustrated by Sam Williams, Scholastic (New York, NY), 2001, board-book edition published as *Bless Me,* 2004.
Dinosaurs, illustrated by Richard Courtney, Scholastic (New York, NY), 2001.
I See a Leaf, illustrated by Laura Freeman, Scholastic (New York, NY), 2001.
The 100th Day, illustrated by Laura Freeman, Scholastic (New York, NY), 2002.
(With Ruby Bridges) *Let's Read about . . . Ruby Bridges,* illustrated by Cornelius Van Wright and Ying-Hwa Hu, Scholastic (New York, NY), 2003.
Graduation Day Is Here!, illustrated by Rick Brown, Scholastic (New York, NY), 2006.

Peter Rabbit's Happy Easter, illustrated by David McPhail, Scholastic (New York, NY), 2006.

I Am Blessed, illustrated by Jacqueline Rogers, Little Shepherd Books (New York, NY), 2008.

Bunny Race, illustrated by Ethan Long, Scholastic (New York, NY), 2009.

Six Super Easy-to-Read Stories, Scholastic (New York, NY), 2009.

Miss Lina's Ballerinas, illustrated by Christine Davenier, Feiwel & Friends (New York, NY), 2010.

The Gingerbread Family, illustrated by Louise Gardner, Little Simon (New York, NY), 2010.

Miss Lina's Ballerinas and the Prince, illustrated by Christine Davenier, Feiwel & Friends (New York, NY), 2011.

"SCHOOL FRIENDS" READER SERIES; WITH BERNICE CHARDIET

Brenda's Private Swing, illustrated by G. Brian Karas, Scholastic (New York, NY), 1990.

Merry Christmas, What's Your Name?, illustrated by G. Brian Karas, Scholastic (New York, NY), 1990.

The Best Teacher in the World, illustrated by G. Brian Karas, Scholastic (New York, NY), 1990.

Martin and the Tooth Fairy, illustrated by G. Brian Karas, Scholastic (New York, NY), 1991.

Bunny Runs Away, illustrated by G. Brian Karas, Scholastic (New York, NY), 1992.

Martin and the Teacher's Pets, illustrated by G. Brian Karas, Scholastic (New York, NY), 1995.

We Scream for Ice Cream, illustrated by G. Brian Karas, Scholastic (New York, NY), 1998.

The Snowball War, illustrated by G. Brian Karas, Scholastic (New York, NY), 1999.

"HELLO MATH READER" SERIES

Monster Math, illustrated by Marge Hartelius, Scholastic (New York, NY), 1995.

Monster Math School Time, illustrated by Marge Hartelius, Scholastic (New York, NY), 1997.

Monster Math Picnic, illustrated by Marge Hartelius, Scholastic (New York, NY), 1998.

Monster Money, illustrated by Marge Hartelius, Scholastic (New York, NY), 1998.

It Was Halloween Night: A Scary Math Story—with Tangrams!, illustrated by Matthew Straub, Scholastic (New York, NY), 2001.

"FIRST-GRADE FRIENDS" READER SERIES; ILLUSTRATED BY BETSY LEWIN

My Tooth Is about to Fall Out, Scholastic (New York, NY), 1995.

The Classroom Pet, Scholastic (New York, NY), 1995.

The Lunch Box Surprise, Scholastic (New York, NY), 1995.

Recess Mess, Scholastic (New York, NY), 1996.

The Gym Day Winner, Scholastic (New York, NY), 1996.

Sharing Time Troubles, Scholastic (New York, NY), 1997.

I Have a Cold, Scholastic (New York, NY), 1998.

The Class Trip, Scholastic (New York, NY), 1999.

Softball Practice, Scholastic (New York, NY), 2001.

The Sleep Over, Scholastic (New York, NY), 2003.

"MAGIC MATT" SERIES; ILLUSTRATED BY NORMAN BRIDWELL

Magic Matt and Skunk in the Tub, Scholastic (New York, NY), 2003.

Magic Matt and the Cat, Scholastic (New York, NY), 2003.

Magic Matt and the Jack-o'-lantern, Scholastic (New York, NY), 2003.

Magic Matt and the Dinosaur, Scholastic (New York, NY), 2004.

Sidelights

Grace Maccarone is a long-time editor of children's books whose career has spanned several New York City publishing houses but remained focused on picture books, beginning readers, and novelty books. In addition to her editing work, Maccarone is the author of dozens of original stories that have been brought to life by talented illustrators such as G. Brian Karas, Betsy Lewin, Ethan Long, Hans Wilhelm, David A. Carter, and Cornelius Van Wright. Reviewing *Cars! Cars! Cars!*, a book featuring Carter's humorous art, Hazel Rochman commented in *Booklist* that Maccarone's text "is a great way to introduce simple concepts to a young audience." Carolyn Phelan praised the author's easy-reading *I Shop with My Daddy* in the same periodical, calling it perfect for budding readers "looking for books that don't look babyish but have a simple vocabulary."

Among Maccarone's many books for beginning readers are her "Hello Reader" and "First-Grade Friends" series, the "Hello Math Reader" books, and her collaboration with well-known children's author/illustrator Norman Bridwell on the "Magic Matt" stories. Another collaboration, this time with artist Sam Williams, resulted in both *A Child Was Born: A First Nativity Book* and *A Child's Good Night Prayer*, the latter which a *Publishers Weekly* critic described as "an unusually gentle bedtime verse" in which Maccarone's "sweetly distilled prayer" is reflected in Williams' "warmly lit watercolors" with their "childlike perspective." *Monster Math Picnic*, which introduces the concept of number grouping to the "Monster Math Reader" series, was praised by Phelan as "a simple, cheerful book for children ready to take one step beyond counting."

Maccarone teams up with artist Christine Davenier to create the girl-centric picture books *Miss Lina's Ballerinas* and *Miss Lina's Ballerinas and the Prince*. With its powder-pink cover and focus on dancing, *Miss Lina's Ballerinas* introduces eight young dancers in Miss Lina's class. Standing in a single row, the students perform their steps in class, while in pairs of two they follow their teacher on walks around the city. When

Grace Maccarone's stories for children include **A Child Was Born,** *a biblical retelling that comes to life in pen-and-water color artwork by* **Sam Williams.** (Illustration copyright © 2000 by Sam Williams. Reproduced by permission of Scholastic, Inc.)

another student joins the class, walking two by two always leaves someone alone, and a subtle chaos reigns until Miss Lina solves the problem. The book cover shifts to lavender in *Miss Lina's Ballerinas and the Prince,* as another new student enters the class and again causes changes to be made. This time, the dancer is a young boy who will be dancing the role of the prince in the girls' upcoming recital. While the tutu'd dancers keep their cool, the future prince does not, and soon the pink-clad ballerinas must take to the streets to hunt for their shy costar.

Noting the "echoes of [Ludwig] Bemelmans' *Madeline*" in Maccarone's story, Phelan praised *Miss Lina's Ballerinas* in her *Booklist* review, writing that the mix of "math concept" and playful vocabulary makes "this picture book . . . a pleasure to read aloud and a beguiling choice for any young dancer." A *Kirkus Reviews* writer cited the same book for its "infectious text" and described Davenier's pastel-toned artwork as "filled with humor, movement and lovely shades of pink." "Maccarone has fashioned another charming story in rhyme for young readers," noted a *Kirkus Reviews* writer in reference to *Miss Lina's Ballerinas and the Prince,* and a *Publishers Weekly* critic hinted at both books' appeal by noting that "the girls' enthusiasm is undeniable infectious as they dance."

"Mostly, I write what I observe," Maccarone explained in an interview for the Scholastic Web site. "I have written about friends I had as a child. I have written about my daughter and her friends. And I have written about my adult friends as children. I find inspiration from life experiences, books, and conversations." "In the publishing company where I work at my day job, . . . there are gregarious sales people and publicists, creative artists and writers, fastidious people in manu-

facturing and finance, and editorial people who endeavor to please all of the above," she added, in discussing her editorial work. "When we're at our best, we cooperate and accomplish great things."

Biographical and Critical Sources

PERIODICALS

Booklist, January 15, 1995, Hazel Rochman, review of *Cars! Cars! Cars!,* p. 937; July, 1995, Ilene Cooper, review of *My Tooth Is about to Fall Out,* p. 1885; January 1, 1996, Carolyn Phelan, review of *The Lunch Box Surprise,* p. 850; August, 1996, Stephanie Zvirin, review of *The Gym Day Winner,* p. 1910; February 1, 1997, Hazel Rochman, review of *Recess Mess,* p. 950; May 1, 1997, Hazel Rochman, review of *Sharing Time Troubles,* p. 1504; May 1, 1998, Carolyn Phelan, review of *Monster Math Picnic,* p. 1525; July, 1998, Carolyn Phelan, review of *I Shop with My Daddy,* p. 1891; September 1, 2000, Susan Dove Lempke, review of *A Child Was Born: A First Nativity Book,* p. 134; October 1, 2001, Carolyn Phelan, review of *A Child's Good Night Prayer,* p. 337; November 1, 2010, Carolyn Phelan, review of *Miss Lina's Ballerinas,* p. 60.

Kirkus Reviews, September 15, 2010, review of *Miss Lina's Ballerinas;* August 15, 2011, review of *Miss Lina's Ballerinas and the Prince.*

Publishers Weekly, August 8, 1994, review of *Oink! Moo! How Do You Do? A Book of Animal Sounds,* p. 426; September 25, 2000, review of *A Child Was Born,* p. 68; August 27, 2001, review of *A Child's Good Night Prayer,* p. 82; February 13, 2006, review of *Peter Rabbit's Happy Easter,* p. 90; October 11, 2010, review of *Miss Lina's Ballerinas,* p. 40.

School Library Journal, October, 2000, review of *A Child Was Born,* p. 61; October, 2001, Patricia Pearl Dole, review of *A Child's Good Night Prayer,* p. 143; December, 2010, Rachel Kamin, review of *Miss Lina's Ballerinas,* p. 84.

ONLINE

Scholastic Web site, http://www.scholastic.com/ (January 15, 2012),* interview with Maccarone.

*   *   *

MacCOLL, Michaela

Personal

Born in NY; married; children: two daughters. *Education:* Vassar College, B.A.; Yale University, M.A. (Russian and Soviet history).

Addresses

Home—Westport, CT. *Agent*—George Nicholson, Sterling Lord Literistic, 65 Bleecker St., New York, NY 10012. *E-mail*—Michaela@michaelamaccoll.com.

Career

Writer. Technical writer and project manager for Internet design firms.

Awards, Honors

Amelia Bloomer Project nomination, American Library Association, 2011, for *Promise the Night*.

Writings

Prisoners in the Palace: How Victoria Became Queen with the Help of Her Maid, a Reporter, and a Scoundrel, Chronicle Books (San Francisco, CA), 2010.
Promise the Night, Chronicle Books (San Francisco, CA), 2011.

Sidelights

Michaela MacColl was inspired to become a writer due to her wide-ranging curiosity and interest in the ebb and flow of history. Raised in upstate New York, MacColl studied Russian and Soviet history in college, her studies enhanced by a visit to the then-USSR two years before the wall came down in 1989. Shortly thereafter, newly married, she moved to France, where she spent five years immersed in that country's dynamic history and technological advances. Since returning to the United States, MacColl and her family have settled in New England, where she has raised her children and also worked as a technical writer and project manager for Internet design companies. "I was always fascinated by stories of how famous people grew up to be that way," she admitted on her home page in discussing her move to fiction writing. She focuses on two famous people in her young-adult novels *Prisoners in the Palace: How Victoria Became Queen with the Help of Her Maid, a Reporter, and a Scoundrel* and *Promise the Night,* the latter which chronicles the childhood of noted aviatrix Beryl Markham, who grew up to became the first pilot to fly solo across the Atlantic from England to North America.

As its title suggests, *Prisoners in the Palace* portrays Princess Victoria of England as a teenager who feels trapped in a repressive life. When orphaned teen Liza gains a job as maid to the seventeen-year-old regent, she quickly becomes aware that Victoria's feelings about being trapped are well founded. Because the young woman is next in line for the crown of England (England has not had a king since the death of George III the year after Victoria was born), her widowed mother, German-born Princess Victoria of Saxe-Coburg-Saalfeld, and comptroller Sir John Conroy hope to wield influence over her when she attains the throne at age eighteen. With the help of Liza and Liza's fiancée, Victoria is able to avoid relinquishing her rights and also gains the independence of mind that will characterize her sixty-three-year-long reign.

While noting that *Prisoners in the Palace* takes an "alternative history" approach to Victoria's life during a pivotal year, a *Kirkus Reviews* writer described MacColl's tale as providing "a pleasurable portal into an historical event which is practically a Gothic novel even without the addition of fiction." The novel builds on history with "a riveting plot full of conspiracy, sexual abuse of servants, treachery, and a great love story," according to Corinne Henning-Sachs, the *School Library Journal* writer dubbing *Prisoners in the Palace* "a great read." "MacColl weaves enough goodness into Victoria that she never becomes a caricature," noted a *Publishers Weekly* contributor, the critic concluding that "court intrigue abounds" in the author's "delightful story."

Praised by another *Publishers Weekly* critic as "a rousing piece of historical fiction," *Promise the Night* meets up with aviator Beryl Markham when she is ten years old. Born Beryl Clutterbuck, Markham and her father lived in the highlands of British East Africa (now Kenya), where she grew up amid the Nandi tribe while her father raised horses. She found an outlet for her adventurous spirit through hunting and exploring the African wilderness, but she also faced the expectation of

Cover of Michaela MacColl's imaginative historical novel Prisoners in the Palace, *a novel that follows England's Queen Victoria on her path to the throne.* (Copyright © 2010 by Michaela MacColl. Reproduced by permission of Chronicle Books LLC, San Francisco. Visit chroniclebooks.com)

the British colonial community to behave as a proper young lady. In addition to telling the story about "a fiercely determined individualist," *Promise the Night* also addresses the deep-seated racial tensions that existed in Kenya during the early twentieth century, according to the *Publishers Weekly* reviewer. Employing portions of Markham's own memoirs as well as fictional news reportage, MacColl "portrays her headstrong protagonist . . . with fierce, exuberant spirits," asserted Anne O'Malley in *Booklist,* and a *Kirkus Reviews* writer cited *Promise the Night* for its "fluid prose" and its focus on "a life much stranger than fiction."

Biographical and Critical Sources

PERIODICALS

Booklist, October 1, 2011, Anne O'Malley, review of *Promise the Night,* p. 87.
Kirkus Reviews, September 15, 2010, review of *Prisoners in the Palace: How Victoria Became Queen with the Help of Her Maid, a Reporter, and a Scoundrel;* October 1, 2011, review of *Promise the Night.*
Publishers Weekly, October 4, 2010, review of *Prisoners in the Palace,* p. 48; October 31, 2011, review of *Promise the Night,* p. 57.
School Library Journal, December, 2010, Corinne Henning-Sachs, review of *Prisoners in the Palace,* p. 118.
Voice of Youth Advocates, October, 2011, Hilary Crew, review of *Promise the Night,* p. 386.

ONLINE

Authors Now Web site, http://www.authorsnow.com/ (January 9, 2012), "Michaela MacColl."
Michaela MacColl Home Page, http://www.michaelamaccoll.com (January 9, 2012).
YA Bookshelf Web site, http://www.yabookshelf.com/ (November, 2010), interview with MacColl.

*   *   *

MANDEL, Peter 1957-

Personal

Born June 7, 1957, in New York, NY; son of Paul (an author and associate editor of *Life* magazine) and Sheila (a writer and journalist) Mandel; married Kathryn Byrd (a tax accountant), June 13, 1981. *Education:* Middlebury College, B.A. (American literature), 1979; Brown University, M.A. (creative writing), 1981. *Hobbies and other interests:* Animals, birds, trees, ocean liners, travel, tennis, playing and watching baseball.

Addresses

Home—Providence, RI. *Agent*—Emilie Jacobson, Curtis Brown Ltd., 10 Astor Pl., New York, NY 10003. *E-mail*—pbmandel@cox.net.

Peter Mandel (Reproduced by permission.)

Career

Travel journalist, writer, and editor. Former publications editor at Brown University, Providence, RI; Bryant University, Smithfield, RI, former assistant to college president; freelance writer, beginning 1995. Teacher of adult education seminars. Presenter at schools and libraries; shipboard lecturer; speaker to numerous groups.

Member

Authors Guild, Society of Children's Book Writers and Illustrators, North American Travel Journalists Association.

Awards, Honors

Cat Medallion, Cat Writers Association, 1994, for best humor piece; American Bookseller Pick of the Lists selection, 1994, for *Red Cat, White Cat;* Lowell Thomas Bronze Award, Society of American Travel Writers, 2003, 2006, (two) 2007; Lowell Thomas Gold Award for Adventure Travel Article, 2005; Northern Lights Award, Canadian Tourist Board, 2006; Children's Indie Pick selection, American Booksellers Association, 2010, for *Bun, Onion, Burger.*

Writings

FOR CHILDREN

Red Cat, White Cat, illustrated by Clare Mackie, Henry Holt (New York, NY), 1994.
My Ocean Liner: Across the North Atlantic on the Great Ship Normandie, illustrated by Betsey MacDonald, Stemmer House (Owings Mills, MD), 2000.
Say Hey! A Song of Willie Mays, illustrated by Don Tate, Jump at the Sun/Hyperion Books for Children (New York, NY), 2000.

Boats on the River, illustrated by Edward Miller, Scholastic (New York, NY), 2004.

Planes at the Airport, illustrated by Edward Miller, Scholastic (New York, NY), 2004.

Bun, Onion, Burger, illustrated by Chris Eliopoulos, Simon & Schuster Books for Young Readers (New York, NY), 2010.

Jackhammer Sam, illustrated by David Catrow, Roaring Brook Press/Macmillan (New York, NY), 2011.

Zoo Ah-choooo, illustrated by Elwood H. Smith, Holiday House (New York, NY), 2012.

NOVELS; FOR YOUNG PEOPLE

Haunted House Mystery, Antioch, 1986.
Revenge of the Ghosts, Antioch, 1986.
Cry of the Wolf, Antioch, 1987.
Whisper's Secret Dream, Antioch, 1987.

OTHER

The Official Cat I.Q. Test, illustrated by June Otani, HarperCollins (New York, NY), 1991.

If One Lived on the Equator (poetry), Nightshade Press, 1993.

The Cat Dictionary, Penguin Books (Camberwell, Victoria, Australia), 1994.

The Official Dog I.Q. Test, Bonus Books, 1995.

Travel columnist for *Huffington Post* online, beginning 2011. Contributor to numerous periodicals, including *Boston Globe, Budget Travel, Chicago Tribune, Coastal Living, Cosmopolitan, Harper's, International Herald Tribune, Los Angeles Times, National Geographic Kids, Minneapolis Star Tribune, Reader's Digest, Toronto Star, Yankee,* and the *Washington Post.* Contributor to anthologies, including *Chicken Soup for the Cat and Dog Lover's Soul.* Former sports and book-review editor, *Brown Alumni Monthly,* Brown University.

Author's work has been translated into several languages, including Chinese, Danish, Dutch, German, Italian, Japanese, and Swedish.

Sidelights

In addition to his work as an award-winning travel writer, where his exploits include tracking penguins in their natural habitat, slashing through dense jungle terrain, paddling a kayak across New York harbor, hiking a suburban strip mall, and chartering a taxicab from Washington, DC, to Manhattan, Peter Mandel shares his witty take on life with younger readers in children's books that include *Red Cat, White Cat, Say Hey! A Song of Willie Mays, Bun, Onion, Burger, Jackhammer Sam,* and *Zoo Ah-choooo.* In addition to books, Mandel's work has appeared in such publications as the *Washington Post* and *Chicago Tribune* as well as magazines ranging from *Reader's Digest* to *National Geographic Kids.*

Haunted House Mystery and *Revenge of the Ghosts,* two of Mandel's early books for children, focus on characters from the television program *The Real Ghostbusters.* Writing these books was just like an assignment at school, the author once recalled. "The publishing house gave me the cast of characters. I had to write the story following various guidelines, just like an English class assignment, only with more rules. It was an interesting bridge between being in school and becoming a writer."

With *Red Cat, White Cat* Mandel began freelancing and suddenly had acres more creative latitude. He was inspired to write this particular story by his red-and-white tomcat, Chuck. A collaboration with British illustrator Clare Mackie, the book features a series of paired images of long-whiskered felines accompanied by appropriate rhymed, double-word captions representing the relevant antonyms and contrasts. With each turn of the page, readers discover cats in humorous circumstances and activities: Farm Cat dozes on the back of a cud-chewing cow while fishing with a cork tied to her tail, while Shy Cat attempts to woo his sweetheart with a paw-printed valentine. According to a *Bulletin of the Center for Children's Books* critic, Mandel's text in *Red Cat, White Cat* is "deft and appealing, with a controlled vocabulary that is accessible to the earliest beginning

Cartoonist Chris Eliopoulos makes his picture-book debut as the illustrator of Mandel's toddler-friendly Bun, Onion, Burger. (Illustration copyright © 2010 by Chris Eliopoulos. Reproduced by permission of Simon & Schuster Books for Young Readers, an imprint of Simon & Schuster Children's Publishing Division.)

readers," while a *Publishers Weekly* contributor cited "Mackie's loopy cartoon" drawings, with their "minute detail" and "perky extras."

Given his penchant for travel, it is not surprising that several of Mandel's picture books focus on transportation. In *My Ocean Liner: Across the North Atlantic on the Great Ship Normandie* illustrations by Betsey MacDonald are paired with his first-person story about a nine-year-old boy who, in 1939, sets off with his parents for a trip from New York to England and France aboard the *Normandie*. Colorful illustrations by Edward Miller bring to life Mandel's text for *Boats on the River* and *Planes at the Airport*, two board books that pair a simple, rhyming text with a plane or boat that has a special job to do. "Busy and bright, these larger-than-average board books whir with vehicles in motion," according to *Booklist* critic Gillian Engberg, and in *School Library Journal* Olga R. Khuarets predicted that their mix of "spare phrases" and "bold graphic illustrations will entice busy toddlers."

Mandel is a long-time fan of the New York Mets, and in *Say Hey!* he profiles one of the most legendary center fielders in baseball history. Illustrated with stylized artwork by Don Tate, the book takes readers back to the Alabama sandlot where Mays played his first games, then moves forward to his time in the Negro Leagues and his move to the New York Giants at a time when African Americans did not figure largely in professional sports. Praising Mandel's profile of one of baseball's most beloved hall-of-famers, Bill Ott wrote in *Booklist* that the author's "sing-along text" pairs well with Tate's "sharp-edged pictures" with their "vivid, sparkling colors and . . . vibrant immediacy." *Say Hey!* was included in an exhibit curated by the National Baseball Hall of Fame and staged at both the Museum of Natural History and the Smithsonian Institute.

Mandel's onomatopoeic text pairs with David Catrow's lively cartoon art in *Jackhammer Sam,* which introduces an exuberant construction worker as he brags about his work in folk-tale fashion. Another energetic storytime offering, *Zoo Ah-choooo* is illustrated by noted cartoon artist Elwood H. Smith and follows an explosive sneeze as it passes from animal to animal at the City Zoo.

Noting that "Sam's got swagger and enthusiasm to spare," Shelle Rosenfeld added in her *Booklist* review of *Jackhammer Sam* that Mandel's "bouncy rhyming text" teams with Catrow's "kinetic and colorful art" to produce "a peppy read with a tall-tale flair." "Like New York City itself, Sam is wonderful and overwhelming, rattling and mesmerizing," according to a *Publishers Weekly* critic, and a *Kirkus Reviews* writer praised *Jackhammer Sam* as "an endearing ode to an oft-grumbled-about profession."

Biographical and Critical Sources

PERIODICALS

Black Issues Book Review, July, 2000, Khafre Abif, review of *Say Hey! A Song of Willie Mays,* p. 73.
Booklist, February 15, 2000, Bill Ott, review of *Say Hey!,* p. 1115; May 15, 2004, Gillian Engberg, reviews of *Boats on the River* and *Planes at the Airport,* both p. 1622; November 15, 2011, Shelle Rosenfeld, review of *Jackhammer Sam,* p. 61.
Bulletin of the Center for Children's Books, November, 1994, review of *Red Cat, White Cat.*
Kirkus Reviews, October 15, 1994, review of *Red Cat, White Cat,* p. 1412; May 15, 2010, review of *Bun, Onion, Burger;* October 1, 2011, review of *Jackhammer Sam.*
Publishers Weekly, November 14, 1994, review of *Red Cat, White Cat,* p. 67; August, 2000, Blair Christolon, review of *Say Hey!,* p. 172; October 16, 2000, review of *My Ocean Liner: Across the North Atlantic on the Great Ship Normandie,* p. 76; June 14, 2010, review of *Bun, Onion, Burger,* p. 50; October 17, 2011, review of *Jackhammer Sam,* p. 66.
School Library Journal, December, 1994, review of *Red Cat, White Cat;* August, 2000, Blair Christolon, review of *Say Hey!,* p. 172; September, 2004, Olga R. Kuharets, reviews of *Boats on the River* and *Planes at the Airport,* both p. 173.

ONLINE

Peter Mandel Home Page, http://www.author-illustr-source.com/petermandel.html (January 15, 2012).

*   *   *

McTIGHE, Carolyn

Personal

Born in Canada; married Jim McTighe; children: William, Olivia, Benjamin, Emily. *Education:* Attended Thompson Rivers University, 1994-2000.

Addresses

Home—Alberta, British Columbia, Canada. *Agent*—Anne McDermid & Associates Literary Agency; info@mcdermidagency.com.

Career

Freelance journalist and author.

Awards, Honors

Alberta Book Publishing Children's Book Award finalist, and Best Book selection, Canadian Children's Book Centre, both 2008, both for *The Sakura Tree* illustrated by Karen Brownlee.

Writings

The Sakura Tree, illustrated by Karen Brownlee, Red Deer Press (Markham, Ontario, Canada), 2007.
How to Ruin Your Life, and Other Lessons School Doesn't Teach You, Red Deer Press (Markham, Ontario, Canada), 2010.

Contributor to periodicals, including *Airdrie Echo, Avenue, Calgary Herald, Elle Canada, Los Angeles Times, Ottawa Sun, San Diego Union Tribune,* and *Toronto Sun.*

Sidelights

Counting Ernest Hemingway and Laura Ingalls Wilder among her literary heroes, Carolyn McTighe is a journalist and author who lives and works in Canada, where she ferrets out writing while caring for her family. In addition to publishing her work in mainstream periodicals, McTighe engages middle-grade readers in her whimsically titled novel *How to Ruin Your Life, and Other Lessons School Doesn't Teach You.* She also entertains younger children with *The Sakura Tree,* a picture-book story that, paired with artwork by Karen Brownlee, describes three Japanese sisters from a poor village who are sent to Canada during the early twentieth century in order to secure husbands able to offer them a better life.

Nine-year-old Penelope Jane "PJ" Parker is the narrator of *How to Ruin Your Life, and Other Lessons School Doesn't Teach You,* and her fourth-grade perspective is relayed in a voice that a *Kirkus Reviews* writer described as "believable and often a little funny." With a talent for running, PJ is confident that she will win the sprint competition during her school's upcoming Track & Field Day. Not wanting to intimidate running pal and best friend Katie, PJ slows her pace a bit on race day, only to watch Katie pick up her own pace and ultimately win the event. Battle lines are quickly drawn across the girls' fourth-grade classroom, with catty notes circulating, rumors spreading, and loyal friends forced to take sides. Although PJ intends to quickly find a replacement BFF, the task proves harder than she imagined, and a few missteps leave her on the outs with her teachers, classmates, and even her annoying older brother.

As narrated in dramatic, self-important prose that is characteristic of a girl of PJ's age, *How to Ruin Your Life, and Other Lessons School Doesn't Teach You* contains "a satisfying lesson on humility that will resonate with readers," according to *Booklist* contributor Erin Anderson. In *School Library Journal* Kate Kohlbeck also enjoyed McTighe's novel, describing it as "a fast read and a pleasant running-related story."

Biographical and Critical Sources

PERIODICALS

Booklist, November 15, 2010, Erin Anderson, review of *How to Ruin Your Life, and Other Lessons School Doesn't Teach You,* p. 48.
Kirkus Reviews, September 1, 2010, review of *How to Ruin Your Life, and Other Lessons School Doesn't Teach You.*
School Library Journal, December, 2010, Kate Kohlbeck, review of *How to Ruin Your Life, and Other Lessons School Doesn't Teach You,* p. 85.

ONLINE

Carolyn McTighe Home Page, http://www.carolymctighe.net/ (January 15, 2012).
Marita Daschel Web log, http://maritadachsel.blogspot.com/ (February, 2009), interview with McTighe.
Red Room Web site, http://www.redroom.com/ (January 15, 2012), "Carolyn McTighe."*

Cover of Canadian writer Carolyn McTighe's quirky chapter book How to Ruin Your Life, and Other Lessons School Doesn't Teach You, *which focuses on the ups and downs of two fourth-grade friends.* (Jacket photograph by Hill Street Studios. Reproduced by permission of Red Deer Press.)

*   *   *

MILIAN, Tomaso

Personal

Born in Rome, Italy; immigrated to United States, c. 1987; married; wife's name Rachel; children: Emma,

Max. *Education:* Lycée Français Chateaubriand (Rome, Italy), baccalaureate (literature and languages); School of Visual Arts, B.F.A. (media arts), 1991.

Addresses

Home—Brooklyn, NY. *E-mail*—tomasomilian@yahoo.com.

Career

Illustrator. Freelance designer, 1991-93; Reader's Digest Illustrated Books, designer and art director, 1993-98; Scholastic, Inc., New York, NY, art director, 1998-99; Direct Brands, Inc., creative director, 1999-2010; graphic designer and project manager for clients including Library of Congress, Brooklyn Symphony Youth Orchestra, Earl McGrath Gallery, and Victoria's Secret PINK.

Illustrator

Barbara Joosse, *Friends (Mostly),* Greenwillow Books (New York, NY), 2010.

Biographical and Critical Sources

PERIODICALS

Booklist, October 1, 2010, Daniel Kraus, review of *Friends (Mostly),* p. 94.

Tomaso Milian's illustration projects include creating the cartoon illustrations for Barbara Joosse's picture book Friends (Mostly). (Illustration copyright © 2010 by Tomaso Milian. Reproduced by permission of Greenwillow Books, an imprint of HarperCollins Children's Books, a division of HarperCollins Publishing, Inc.)

Childhood Education, summer, 2011, Melissa Gemeinhardt, review of *Friends (Mostly),* p. 289.
Kirkus Reviews, September 15, 2010, review of *Friends (Mostly).*
Publishers Weekly, October 11, 2010, review of *Friends (Mostly),* p. 43.
School Library Journal, September, 2010, Anne Beier, review of *Friends (Mostly),* p. 127.

ONLINE

Tomaso Milian Home Page, http://tomasomilian.com (January 9, 2012).

*   *   *

MULLIGAN, Andy

Personal

Born in England. *Education:* Oxford University, degree.

Addresses

Home—London, England; Manila. *Agent*—Ken Wright, Writers' House, 21 W. 26th St., New York, NY 10010.

Career

Teacher and author. Theatrical director for ten years; teacher of English and drama in the United Kingdom and at international schools in Brazil, the Philippines, and Manila.

Awards, Honors

Roald Dahl Funny Prize runner up, 2009, for *Ribblestrop; London Guardian* Children's Fiction Prize, 2011, for *Return to Ribblestrop.*

Writings

Ribblestrop, Simon & Schuster Children's (London, England), 2009.
Trash, David Fickling Books (New York, NY), 2010.
Return to Ribblestrop, Simon & Schuster Children's (London, England), 2011.
Ribblestrop Forever!, Simon & Schuster Children's (London, England), 2012.

Author's work ha been translated into twenty languages.

Adaptations

Trash was adapted for audiobook, read by Ramon DeOcampo, Listening Library, 2010, and was adapted for film by Stephen Daldry and Richard Curtis, Working Title/PeaPie Films, c. 2012.

Sidelights

After a varied career that included work as a theatre director and teaching in Asia and South America as well as his native United Kingdom, Andy Mulligan set about writing. In 2009 his first novel, *Ribblestrop,* earned him critical success, and its follow up, *Return to Ribblestrop,* earned Mulligan the 2011 *Guardian* Children's Fiction Prize. While the "Ribblestrop" novels are humorous stories for middle graders, Mulligan's novel *Trash* charts a different course, taking readers to an impoverished city in a near-future world as three teens make a discovery that takes them on a life-altering journey.

Gardo, Rat, and Raphael live in Behala, a city in a developing country that might be the Philippines and where most residents live in primitive conditions. Hungry and poor, the three friends are also resourceful, and when readers first meet them in *Trash* they are at a local landfill, scouting through other people's garbage for discards of value. Raphael and Gardo cannot believe their eyes when they discover a small leather wallet containing 1,100 pesos as well as a map and a key. Although the boys first plan on spending the money, inter-

Cover of Andy Milligan's adventurous young-adult novel Trash, *which features cover art by Alex Williamson.* (Jacket cover copyright © 2010 by David Fickling Books. Reproduced by permission of David Fickling Books, an imprint of Random House Children's Books, a division of Random House, Inc.)

est by the police inspires them to ask clever friend Rat for help. Soon the three find themselves on a quest for José Angelico, the wallet's owner. This quest ultimately pulls a gangster's son, a witch child, a group of homeless orphans, and even a pack of corrupt national politicos into its vortex.

"An enjoyable novel with fresh, multidimensional characters," according to KaaVonia Hinton-Johnson in her *Voice of Youth Advocates* review, *Trash* "will appeal to readers interested in social-justice issues." Mulligan's teen characters evidence a "significant sense of devotion and morality [that] leads them from lives of desperation to miraculous possibilities," asserted Andrew Medlar in his *Booklist* review of the novel, and in *School Library Journal* Kristin Anderson praised Gardo, Rat, and Raphael for "their intelligence and character." Although a *Kirkus Reviews* writer remarked that *Trash* "relies on Third World poverty tourism for its flavor," the critic praised Mulligan's story for taking readers on "a zippy and classic briefcase-full-of-money thrill ride." A *Publishers Weekly* critic wrote that the novel "engages readers both as an adventure and as a social justice story," while in *Horn Book* Dean Schneider characterized *Trash* as "*Treasure Island* meets *Slumdog Millionaire* in a rousing and hugely entertaining adventure."

While *Trash* was inspired by Mulligan's experiences in Calcutta, India, where he did volunteer work in his early twenties, *Ribblestrop* was inspired by his work as a teacher. Ribblestrop School is the antithesis of every school ever portrayed in children's literature: led by Giles Norcross-Webb, an idealistic headmaster with off-kilter ideals, the residential middle school is housed on a campus where students are housed in roofless buildings that serve as monuments to a recent act of arson. A maze of rooms and tunnels constructed during World War II are hidden underground, a playground for the evil scientists and other ne'er-do-wells performing their pernicious experiments. To combat the cold of the school's unheated classrooms, each student is supplied with a daily dose of rum, and several also arm themselves with guns. The current crop of Ribblestrop students—Colombian-born Sanchez, the son of a gangster who is now in hiding; out-of-control arsonist Millie; over-indulged Casper; and best friends Ruskin and Sam, among others—view their new school with reasonable concern: Captain Routon, the headmaster's second in command, views school operations in militaristic terms and the schoo's teachers range from the ineffectual to the malignant.

Reviewing *Ribblestrop* in the London *Guardian,* Philip Ardagh praised Mulligan's debut as "a blast of fresh air" that is "weird and wonderful and very hard to define." "The school motto becomes 'Life Is Dangerous,'" Ardagh added, "and mere attendance proves to be an excellent training ground for this undeniable truth."

Biographical and Critical Sources

PERIODICALS

Booklist, September 15, 2010, Andrew Medlar, review of *Trash,* p. 64.

Guardian (London, England), April 4, 2009, Philip Ardagh, review of *Ribblestrop,* p. 14.

Horn Book, November-December, 2010, Dean Schneider, review of *Trash,* p. 97.

Kirkus Reviews, September 15, 2010, review of *Trash.*

Publishers Weekly, October 4, 2010, review of *Trash,* p. 49.

School Librarian, winter, 2010, Cherie Gladstone, review of *Trash,* p. 244.

School Library Journal, October, 2010, Kristin Anderson, review of *Trash,* p. 123.

Voice of Youth Advocates, December, 2010, KaaVonia Hinton-Johnson, review of *Trash,* p. 457.

ONLINE

Andy Mulligan Home Page, http://www.andymulligan books.com (January 15, 2012).*

N-R

NIEMANN, Christoph 1970-

Personal
Born 1970, in Waiblingen, Germany; married Lisa Zeitz; children: Arthur, Gustav, Fritz. *Education:* Attended Stuttgart Academy of Fine Arts.

Addresses
Home—Berlin, Germany. *E-mail*—mail@christophniemann.com.

Career
Illustrator, animator, and graphic designer, 1997—.

Member
Alliance Graphique Internationale.

Awards, Honors
Talent of the Year Award, Art Directors' Club, 1998; Lead Academy awards, 2006, 2007; numerous awards from organizations including Society of Publication Designers, American Illustration, and AIGA; inducted into Art Directors Club Hall of Fame, 2010.

Writings

SELF-ILLUSTRATED

Das gute Portrait, 62 farbige Portraits, Maro Verlag (Augsburg, Germany), 1998.
(With Danielle McCole) *Numbers: The Fun Way to Match and Learn,* Running Press (Philadelphia, PA), 2001.
(With Nicholas Blechman) *One Hundred Percent Evil,* Princeton Architectural Press (New York, NY), 2005.
The Police Cloud, Schwartz & Wade (New York, NY), 2007.

Christoph Niemann (Photograph by Maxine Ballesteros. Reproduced by permission.)

The Pet Dragon: A Story about Adventure, Friendship, and Chinese Characters, Greenwillow (New York, NY), 2008.
I LEGO N.Y., photographs by Kristina Weinhold, Abrams Image (New York, NY), 2010.
Subway, Greenwillow Books (New York, NY), 2010.
That's How!, Greenwillow Books (New York, NY), 2011.
Abstract City (archive of Web log; also see below), Abrams (New York, NY), 2012.

Author/illustrator of Web log *Abstract City,* published, 2008-11 and archived at nieman.blogs.nytimes.com.

ILLUSTRATOR

(With others) *Fresh Dialogue: New Voices in Graphic Design,* Princeton Architectural Press (New York, NY), 2000.
Toby Schmidt, *Trucks: The Fun Way to Match and Learn,* Running Press (Philadelphia, PA), 2001.
Stephen J. Dubner, *The Boy with Two Belly Buttons,* HarperCollins (New York, NY), 2007.

Contributor of illustrations to *New York Times, Business Week, Atlantic Monthly, New Yorker, Fast Company, New York Times Magazine, Varoom!,* and *American Illustration.*

Sidelights

While illustrator, animator, and graphic designer Christoph Niemann is best known for his work for adults—his popular Web log *Abstract City* was hosted on the *New York Times* Web site for four years—both his words and his art have also made their way into picture books for young readers. The creator of images that have regularly appeared in the pages of the *New Yorker* and *Business Week,* Niemann has received numerous awards from graphic design organizations. His whimsical creativity and imagination are well known to his fans; in 2001, for example, Niemann even ran all 26.2 miles of the New York City Marathon while sketching cartoons depicting his progress in a notebook.

Born in Waiblingen, in southwestern Germany, Niemann studied at the Stuttgart Academy of Fine Arts before moving to New York City in 1997. Along with illustration work and corporate projects for such companies as Nike, Google, and Citibank, Niemann taught at the city's School of Visual Arts until returning to Germany in 2008, and he has lectured in the United States, Germany, Japan, South Africa, and Mexico. In an interview with *Fast Company* contributor Annie F. Noonan, Niemann observed that, when illustrating articles in mainstream magazines, he prefers boring content. "When an article is too interesting, I feel as though I have to compete with it," he quipped.

Niemann's self-illustrated picture book The Police Cloud *pairs a whimsical story and digital art.* (Jacket cover copyright © 2007 by Schwartz & Wade. Reproduced by permission of Schwartz & Wade Books, an imprint of Random House Children's Books, a division of Random House, Inc.)

Niemann began working on children's books after the bedtime stories he told his sons sparked story ideas. One of these, *The Police Cloud,* introduces a cloud that desperately wants to be a police officer. The cloud gets the job, only to find out that he is not very good at it. He cannot catch a burglar, and he is more likely to confuse traffic than direct it. When he patrols the city park, people become irritated at the cloud for blocking out the sun. Depressed about being an unsuitable police officer, the cloud weeps, and when his tears put out a house fire, he is offered a position with the fire department. Niemann's "geometric, pleasantly retro illustrations show the whimsical challenges" in the story, according to *Horn Book* contributor Christine M. Heppermann. Susan Weitz wrote in *School Library Journal* that the book's "main character is . . . very likable, partly a result of the gentle dialogue and the enticing computer-generated artwork." Randall Enos commented in *Booklist* that "the illustrations do such a good job of telling the story [that] the concise text is almost unnecessary," and a *Publishers Weekly* critic concluded of *The Police Cloud* that "Niemann's crisp digital art complements the simplicity and mild silliness of his story."

While living in New York City, Niemann was inspired by Manhattan's urban hustle and bustle, and the Big

Niemann creates the graphic-style images that fill Stephen J. Dubner's quirky picture book The Boy with Two Belly Buttons. (Illustration copyright © 2007 by Christoph Niemann. Used by permission of HarperCollins Children's Books, a division of HarperCollins Publishers.)

Niemann mixes his stylized art and an original story with a lesson in Chinese pictographs to create **The Pet Dragon.** (Illustration copyright © 2008 by Christoph Niemann. Reproduced by permission of Greenwillow Books, an imprint of HarperCollins Children's Books, a division of HarperCollins Publishing, Inc.)

Apple figures in several of his stories for children. In *I LEGO N.Y.* posed vignettes crafted from his son's toys are captured in photographs by Kristina Weinhold and paired with handwritten descriptive captions. The book was actually created as a fond farewell to the city, as Niemann had returned to Germany by the time he completed it, but it has found an appreciative audience among young U.S. urbanites. *Subway* also focuses on

the city, this time allowing picture-book audiences to tour New York's vast underground along with a father and his children as they ride the trains and visit all forty-four stations. Dubbing *Subway* an "artistic tour de force," a *Kirkus Reviews* writer predicted that Niemann's book "will appeal to New Yorkers and visitors alike," while in *Booklist* Andrew Medlar wrote that the artist's "gouache art is distinctively urban and bold."

Also in praise of *Subway,* a *Publishers Weekly* predicted that the artist's love of "droll details will delight regular straphangers and stir the imaginations of transportation-obsessed children."

Other picture books by Neimann include *The Pet Dragon: A Story about Adventure, Friendship, and Chinese Characters,* which embeds a basic lesson in written Chinese within a folktale-type story about a girl named Lin, her frisky pet dragon, and the adventure she undertakes when her dragon goes missing. Writing that Chinese pictographs "are cleverly incorporated into the story's artwork," *Booklist* critic Linda Perkins added that the final pages of *The Pet Dragon* serve as "a festive test for those who want to challenge themselves."

That's How! transports budding engineers to a whimsical world in which airplanes are made airborne by a resident flock of chickens, a tractor rolls forward with the help of a lion, and the wrigglings of a ticklish bear power the weightiest part of a steamroller. Two engaging young children provide the viewpoint, allowing "trucks, curiosity, animals, and imagination [to] interact in this playful portrayal," according to *Booklist* critic Diane Foote. A *Publishers Weekly* critic praised Neimann's combination of story and art, citing *That's How!* as an artistic triumph for "joyfully liberating modern machinery from the laws of physics."

Biographical and Critical Sources

PERIODICALS

Booklist, May 1, 2007, Randall Enos, review of *The Police Cloud,* p. 100; September 1, 2008, Linda Perkins, review of *The Pet Dragon: A Story about Adventure, Friendship, and Chinese Characters,* p. 107; April 15, 2010, Andrew Medlar, review of *Subway,* p. 53; July 1, 2011, Diane Foote, review of *That's How!,* p. 66.

Fast Company, June, 2002, Annie F. Noonan, interview with Niemann, p. 20.

Horn Book, March-April, 2007, Christine M. Heppermann, review of *The Police Cloud,* p. 187.

Kirkus Reviews, January 15, 2007, review of *The Police Cloud,* p. 78; August 15, 2008, review of *The Pet Dragon*; May 15, 2010, review of *Subway.*

New York Post, February 28, 2010, "Blame It on Writer's Block," p. 28.

New York Times Book Review, November 7, 2010, Becca Zerkin, review of *Subway,* p. 20.

Publishers Weekly, February 26, 2007, review of *The Police Cloud,* p. 88; October 29, 2007, review of *The Boy with Two Belly Buttons,* p. 54; September 8, 2008, review of *The Pet Dragon,* p. 50; May 24, 2010, review of *Subway,* p. 50; February 21, 2011, review of *That's How!,* p. 130.

Print, March-April, 2005, Steven Heller, "My Life as an Illustrator: The Art and Science of Christoph Niemann," p. 68.

School Library Journal, June, 2007, Susan Weitz, review of *The Police Cloud,* p. 118; December, 2007, Catherine Threadgill, review of *The Boy with Two Belly Buttons,* p. 88; September, 2008, Barbara Scotto, review of *The Pet Dragon,* p. 156; June, 2010, Sara Lissa Paulson, review of *Subway,* p. 81.

ONLINE

Christoph Niemann Home Page, http://www.christoph niemann.com (January 12, 2012).

New Yorker Online, http://www.newyorker.com/ (January 12, 2012), "Christoph Niemann."

Random House Web site, http://www.randomhouse.com/ (July 1, 2007), "Christoph Niemann."

*   *   *

OESTERLE, Virginia Rorby
See RORBY, Ginny

*   *   *

QUINTANO, D.M.
See SHELDON, Dyan

*   *   *

RALLISON, Janette 1966-
(Sierra St. James)

Personal

Born 1966; married; children: five. *Religion:* Church of Jesus Christ of Latter-Day Saints (Mormon). *Hobbies and other interests:* Dancing, SCUBA diving, horseback riding.

Addresses

Home—Chandler, AZ. *E-mail*—jrallisonfans@yahoo.com.

Career

Novelist.

Awards, Honors

International Book Awards Honor Book selection, Society of School Librarians, 2002, for *Playing the Field;* Independent Publisher Book Award finalist, 2006, and Popular Paperbacks for Young Adults designation, American Library Association, 2007, both for *Life, Love, and the Pursuit of Free Throws;* Young Adults' Choices selection, International Reading Association, 2007, for *Fame, Glory, and Other Things on My To-Do List,* and 2008, for *It's a Mall World after All.*

Writings

YOUNG-ADULT NOVELS

Deep Blue Eyes and Other Lies, Deseret Book Company (Salt Lake City, UT), 1996.
Dakota's Revenge, Deseret Book Company (Salt Lake City, UT), 1998.
Playing the Field, Walker (New York, NY), 2002.
All's Fair in Love, War, and High School, Walker (New York, NY), 2003.
Life, Love, and the Pursuit of Free Throws, Walker (New York, NY), 2004.
Fame, Glory, and Other Things on My To-Do List, Walker (New York, NY), 2005.
It's a Mall World after All, Walker (New York, NY), 2006.
How to Take the Ex out of Ex-Boyfriend, Walker (New York, NY), 2007.
Revenge of the Cheerleaders, Walker (New York, NY), 2007.
Just One Wish, Putnam's (New York, NY), 2009.
My Fair Godmother, Walker (New York, NY), 2009.
My Double Life, Putnam's (New York, NY), 2010.
My Unfair Godmother (sequel to *My Fair Godmother*), Walker (New York, NY), 2011.

UNDER NAME SIERRA ST. JAMES

Trial of the Heart, Deseret Book Company (Salt Lake City, UT), 1999.
Masquerade, Bookcraft (Salt Lake City, UT), 2001.
Time Riders, Bonneville Books (Springville, UT), 2004.
What the Doctor Ordered, Deseret Book Company (Salt Lake City, UT), 2004.

Adaptations

Several of Rallison's novels have been adapted as audiobooks.

Sidelights

In her critically acclaimed young-adult novels, including *All's Fair in Love, War, and High School, My Fair Godmother,* and *My Double Life,* Janette Rallison focuses on the concerns shared by most teen girls: dating, dating, and dating. Her entertaining works feature heroines attempting to discover, rekindle, jump-start, or repair a love relationship with the boy of their dreams. "I try to make sure something is always at stake for my characters," she stated in a *Journal of Adolescent & Adult Literacy* interview with Sandra Crandall. "If you can maintain that kind of tension, it's very hard for a reader to put the book down and leave the characters hanging there where all sorts of things might happen to them."

Rallison began her publishing career with the teen romance *Deep Blue Eyes and Other Lies,* which was released in 1996. Another of her early novels, *Playing the*

Field, finds thirteen-year-old McKay trying to keep his head above water in algebra class, because a bad grade will mean the end of his spot on the school baseball team. When friend Tony suggests that he wrangle free tutoring from Serena, a brainy math student, by pretending that he has a crush on her, McKay buys into the scheme. Ultimately, Serena discovers the plot, Tony proves to be a less-than-loyal buddy, and McKay realizes that he has to approach his life—and his relationships—with a little more integrity. McKay is a likeable and well-grounded hero, noted *Booklist* contributor John Peters, the critic adding that Rallison delivers her message "without lectures" and by presenting "a set of situations that readers will have little trouble relating to." Noting the author's use of "humor and realistic characters," Linda Bindner concluded in her *School Library Journal* review of *Playing the Field* that Rillison's novel will "be a hit with anybody interested in . . . baseball, friends, and that mysterious . . . first crush."

Described by a *Kirkus Reviews* writer as a "witty, often hilarious romp," *All's Fair in Love, War, and High School* finds popular head cheerleader Samantha Taylor

Cover of Janette Rallison's young-adult novel **My Double Life,** *in which a teen samples the life of a look-alike celebrity.* (Jacket photographs by Michael Frost (girl); Patrik Giardino/Corbis (paparazzi). Reproduced by permission of G.P. Putnam's Sons, a division of Penguin Young Readers Group, a member of Penguin Group (USA), 345 Hudson Street, New York NY 10014. All rights reserved.)

frustrated by her inability to achieve decent scores on the SAT exam. To balance out her college applications with some positive credentials, the teen decides to run for student-body president. When Samantha's dry, sarcastic humor does not serve her well on the campaign trail she enlists the help of ex-boyfriend Logan to plan her election strategy. This has an unsettling effect on her personal life, however; not only does Samantha lose her current beau (and thus have no date for the junior prom), but the bet she has made with Logan that she can hold back her sarcasm for an entire week seems as doomed as her future college career. In *Publishers Weekly,* a critic wrote of *All's Fair in Love, War, and High School* that Rallison's use of "appealing characters and snappy dialogue give this light fare a satisfying bite."

Fame, Glory, and Other Things on My To-Do List finds New Mexico high-school junior Jessica dreaming of a Hollywood film career. When her role in the school play—an "unintentionally hilarious politically correct rewrite of *West Side Story,*" according to a *Kirkus Reviews* writer—is threatened, so is her future. She then decides to court Jordan, a new student at school, when she finds out that his divorced father is a famous actor and might help her career. Although Jordan wants his dad's identity to remain a secret so that he can be judged on his own merits, Jessica disagrees and cuts their relationship short. Eventually, she realizes that fame is less important than lasting friendship, decides to set matters right, and puts her energy into winning Jordan back. In her review for *Booklist,* Hazel Rochman praised Jessica's "cool, hilarious first-person" narration and commented favorably on the novel's themes of "rivalry, the embarrassment, and the romance between friends and lovers."

Incorporating a nod to early nineteenth-century English novelist Jane Austen, in the opinion of one reviewer, *It's a Mall World after All* introduces two teens who, despite their continual verbal sparring, are destined for one another. In addition to her part-time job as a perfume spritzer at a local shopping mall, her work helping an underprivileged boy, and her effort to maintain her honor-student status, compassionate Charlotte still has time to fret about friend Brianna's errant boyfriend, Bryant. Her efforts to catch Bryant in an indiscretion are continually foiled by Bryant's rich, preppy friend, Colton, and Charlotte gradually finds her frustration with Colton shifting to attraction despite their many differences. Although Rallison's heroine has a quirky personality that sometimes gets her into trouble, she is nonetheless an "appealing" character, according to a *Kirkus Reviews* writer. *It's a Mall World after All* offers teens the best of all worlds, in the opinion of *Booklist* reviewer Debbie Carton. In Carton's view, the novel is "a fun romp of a read that's . . . [also] light and breezy," and the *Kirkus Reviews* writer concluded that Rallison's story offers up "plenty of laughs and some insights too."

A common dating quandary—how to deal with a boyfriend's annoying friends—factors into the plot of Rallison's novel *How to Take the Ex out of Ex-Boyfriend.* When sixteen-year-old Giovanna's boyfriend Jesse chooses to support the campaign of a snobby friend rather than aid her twin brother in his run for student-council president, she rashly ends the relationship. Too late, she realizes that she made a mistake, and now her job is to make Jesse jealous enough of her new dates to take time out of his campaign-manager duties and woo her back. Although a *Publishers Weekly* reviewer noted that Jesse's appeal to Giovanna "is somewhat of a mystery," *How to Take the Ex out of Ex-Boyfriend* benefits from a "spunky protagonist" and a "satisfying" end to the teen-friendly story. In *School Library Journal* Stephanie L. Petruso recommended the novel to fans of books by authors Meg Cabot and Cathy Hopkins, calling *How to Take the Ex out of Ex-Boyfriend* a "breezy look at high school life." A *Kirkus Reviews* writer dubbed the book characteristic Rallison: "fast-paced and funny."

Rallison mixes drama and comedy in *Just One Wish,* a novel described as "far-fetched, enjoyable, and touching" by *School Library Journal* critic Tina Zubak. Here the story centers on Annika Truman, a seventeen year old from Nevada who decides to fulfill a fantastic wish made by her younger brother, Jeremy, who is suffering from cancer. When Jeremy announces that he would like to meet his favorite television hero, Teen Robin Hood, Annika hops in her car, drives to Hollywood, and sneaks onto the set to convince Steve Raleigh, the star of the show, to visit her brother. Amazingly, Annika persuades the heartthrob to return with her, and sparks develop along the way. "The sibling relationship between Annika and Jeremy is both believable and heartrending," Debbie Carton observed in *Booklist,* and a *Publishers Weekly* reviewer commented that the "thoughtful ending, if out of step with the story's more madcap elements, is still moving." According to Crandall, "Rallison handles the family's adversity with sensitivity, and the romance without mercy. The reader is pulled in by characterization and held there by a fast-moving plot, making it a great choice for reluctant readers."

In *My Double Life* Rallison introduces Alexia Garcia, a biracial teen who lives in a rundown neighborhood in West Virginia with her mother and grandmother. Sensitive and intelligent, Alexia is also a dead ringer for pop superstar Kari Kingsley, and when the singer's representatives spot Alexia's photo on the Internet, they offer her the chance to pose as Kari while she finishes an album. After arriving in Los Angeles, Alexia gets a first-hand look at the perks and pitfalls of celebrity life, and she also conducts a search for her estranged father, a musician who works somewhere in the area. "Although Rallison's story is just a modern-day fairy tale," Donna L. Miller commented in the *Journal of Adolescent & Adult Literacy,* "she infuses the fantasy with enough truth to ensure readers receive some valuable social justice instruction, a little psychological insight, and a sugary filament that comes from stretching the imagination."

With *My Fair Godmother* and *My Unfair Godmother,* Rallison offers a contemporary take on the fairy tale genre. After her boyfriend dumps her to date her studious older sister, sixteen-year-old Savannah Delano receives a visit from Chrysanthemum "Chrissy" Everstar, a less-than-adequate fairy godmother. Chrissy, a social butterfly who has neglected her magical studies, accidentally sends Savannah into the Middle Ages, where she takes the place of Cinderella and Snow White. Then, after yet another of Chrissy's foul-ups, Savannah must travel back in time to help her high-school crush (and prospective prom date) develop into a prince. "The irreverent references to familiar tales, romantic twists, and frequent comedic asides will delight fans of light fantasy," Gillian Engberg stated in *Booklist.* According to Crandall, "Rallison's gift for storytelling and her irresistible characters shine in this enchanting novel. The humor in the book is constant, and certain moments in particular—such as Savannah's time spent with the seven dwarves—will leave the reader laughing out loud."

Chrissy makes a return appearance in *My Unfair Godmother,* "a fast-paced, humorous, and entertaining story," in the words of *Voice of Youth Advocates* critic Cindy Faughnan. Needing a successful project to bolster her resume for Fairy Godmother University, Chrissy tackles the case of Tansy Miller, a troubled girl with unfortunate tastes in boyfriends. Assisted by a pub-crawling leprechaun named Clover, Chrissy attempts to fulfill Tansy three wishes, with predictably disastrous results. "The fracturing of different fairy tales makes this story a bit more interesting than a standard teenage romance," observed *School Library Journal* reviewer Traci Glass, the critic noting that the work includes appearances by Rumpelstiltskin as well as Robin Hood and his Merry Men.

Biographical and Critical Sources

PERIODICALS

Booklist, May 15, 2002, John Peters, review of *Playing the Field,* p. 1597; November 1, 2004, Debbie Carton, review of *Life, Love, and the Pursuit of Free Throws,* p. 486; October 15, 2005, Hazel Rochman, review of *Fame, Glory, and Other Things on My To-Do List,* p. 43; January 1, 2007, Debbie Carton, review of *It's a Mall World after All,* p. 83; January 1, 2009, Gillian Engberg, review of *My Fair Godmother,* p. 70; February 1, 2009, Debbie Carton, review of *Just One Wish,* p. 38.

Bulletin of the Center for Children's Books, July, 2002, review of *Playing the Field,* p. 416.

Journal of Adolescent & Adult Literacy, April, 2009, Sandra Crandall, reviews of *My Fair Godmother,* p. 639, and *Just One Wish,* p. 640, and interview with Rallison, p. 641; September, 2010, Donna L. Miller, review of *My Double Life,* p. 70.

Kirkus Reviews, October 15, 2003, review of *All's Fair in Love, War, and High School,* p. 1275; August 1, 2004, review of *Life, Love, and the Pursuit of Free Throws,* p. 748; August 15, 2005, review of *Fame, Glory, and Other Things on My To-Do List,* p. 921; October 1, 2006, review of *It's a Mall World after All,* p. 1023; May 15, 2007, review of *How to Take the Ex out of Ex-Boyfriend;* November 15, 2008, review of *My Fair Godmother;* February 1, 2009, review of *Just One Wish;* April 15, 2010, review of *My Double Life;* March 15, 2011, review of *My Unfair Godmother.*

Magazine of Fantasy and Science Fiction, July-August, 2010, Charles de Lint, review of *My Fair Godmother,* p. 26.

Publishers Weekly, November 24, 2003, review of *All's Fair in Love, War, and High School,* p. 65; June 25, 2007, review of *How to Take the Ex out of Ex-Boyfriend,* p. 61; December 1, 2008, review of *My Fair Godmother,* p. 46; March 16, 2009, review of *Just One Wish,* p. 63.

School Library Journal, April, 2002, Linda Bindner, review of *Playing the Field,* p. 156; September, 2003, Lynn Evarts, review of *All's Fair in Love, War, and High School,* p. 219; November, 2004, Sharon Morrison, review of *Life, Love, and the Pursuit of Free Throws,* p. 153; November, 2005, Amy Patrick, review of *Fame, Glory, and Other Things on My To-Do List,* p. 146; December, 2006, Heather M. Campbell, review of *It's a Mall World after All,* p. 152; July, 2007, Stephanie L. Petruso, review of *How to Take the Ex out of Ex-Boyfriend,* p. 108; March, 2008, Leah Krippner, review of *Revenge of the Cheerleaders,* p. 208; May, 2009. Tina Zubak, review of *Just One Wish,* p. 116; September, 2010, Tina Zubak, review of *My Double Life,* p. 162; July, 2011, Traci Glass, review of *My Unfair Godmother,* p. 106.

Voice of Youth Advocates, June, 2002, review of *Playing the Field,* p. 122; June, 2004, Eileen Kuhl, review of *All's Fair in Love, War, and High School,* p. 135; February, 2005, Amanda Zalud, review of *Life, Love, and the Pursuit of Free Throws,* p. 84; October, 2005, review of *Fame, Glory, and Other Things on My To-Do List,* p. 312; April, 2007, review of *It's a Mall World after All,* p. 55; April, 2011, Cindy Faughnan and Jenna Yee, review of *My Unfair Godmother,* p. 86.

ONLINE

Janette Rallison Home Page, http://www.janetterallison.com (January 15, 2012).

Janette Rallison Web log, http://janette-rallison.blogspot.com (January 15, 2012).

Mormon Artist Web site, http://mormonartist.net/ (May, 2009), Amy Baugher, "Janette Rallison."*

RIORDAN, Rick 1964-

Personal

Born June 5, 1964, in San Antonio, TX; married; children: Haley, Patrick (sons). *Education:* Attended North Texas State University; University of Texas at Austin, B.A. (English and history); University of Texas at San Antonio, teaching credentials. *Hobbies and other interests:* Reading, swimming, playing guitar, traveling, spending time with family.

Addresses

Home—San Antonio, TX. *Agent*—Nancy Gallt Literary Agency, 273 Charlton Ave., S. Orange, NJ 07079.

Career

Writer and educator. Middle-school English teacher in New Braunfels, TX, c. 1989, then San Francisco, CA, 1990-98; St. Mary's Hall, San Antonio, TX, middle-school social-studies and American history teacher, 1999-2004; freelance writer. Presenter at workshops for educational organizations.

Awards, Honors

Anthony Award for Best Original Paperback, and Shamus Award for Best First Private-Eye Novel, both 1997, both for *Big Red Tequila;* Anthony Award for Best Original Paperback, Edgar Allan Poe Award for Best Original Paperback, Mystery Writers of America, and Shamus Award nomination, all 1998, all for *The Widower's Two-Step;* Shamus Award nomination for Best Hardcover Private-Eye Novel, 2002, for *The Devil Went down to Austin;* Master Teacher Award, St. Mary's Hall, 2002; inducted into Texas Hall of Letters, 2003; Cooperative Children's Book Council Choice designation, and Notable Children's Book citation, National Council for Teachers of English, both 2006, both for *The Lightning Thief;* Children's Choice Best Book for Grades 5-6, 2011, for *The Red Pyramid.*

Writings

"PERCY JACKSON AND THE OLYMPIANS" YOUNG-ADULT NOVEL SERIES

The Lightning Thief, Miramax/Hyperion (New York, NY), 2005.
The Sea of Monsters, Miramax/Hyperion (New York, NY), 2006.
The Titan's Curse, Miramax/Hyperion (New York, NY), 2007.
The Battle of the Labyrinth, Hyperion (New York, NY), 2008.
(Editor, with Leah Wilson) *Demigods and Monsters: Your Favorite Authors on Rick Riordan's "Percy Jackson and the Olympians" Series,* Benbella Books (Dallas, TX), 2008.

The Last Olympian, Hyperion (New York, NY), 2009.
Percy Jackson: The Demigod Files, illustrated by Steve James, Hyperion (New York, NY), 2009.

"KANE CHRONICLES" MIDDLE-GRADE NOVEL SERIES

The Red Pyramid, Disney/Hyperion (New York, NY), 2010.
The Throne of Fire, Disney/Hyperion (New York, NY), 2010.
The Serpent's Shadow, Disney/Hyperion (New York, NY), 2012.

"HEROES OF OLYMPUS" MIDDLE-GRADE NOVEL SERIES

The Lost Hero, Disney/Hyperion Books (New York, NY), 2011.
The Son of Neptune, Disney/Hyperion Books (New York, NY), 2011.
The Mark of Athena, Disney/Hyperion Books (New York, NY), 2012.

"TRES NAVARRE" MYSTERY NOVELS; FOR ADULTS

Big Red Tequila, Bantam (New York, NY), 1997.
The Widower's Two-Step, Bantam (New York, NY), 1998.
The Last King of Texas, Bantam (New York, NY), 2000.
The Devil Went down to Austin, Bantam (New York, NY), 2001.
Southtown, Bantam (New York, NY), 2004.
Mission Road, Bantam (New York, NY), 2005.
Rebel Island, Bantam Books (New York, NY), 2007.

OTHER

Cold Springs (adult novel), Bantam (New York, NY), 2003.
Thirty-nine Clues: The Maze of Bones (children's novel), Scholastic Press (New York, NY), 2008.
(With Peter Lerangis and Gordon Korman) *Vespers Rising,* Scholastic Press (New York, NY), 2011.

Contributor to periodicals, including *Mary Higgins Clark Mystery Magazine* and *Ellery Queen's Mystery Magazine.*

Adaptations

The Lightning Thief was adapted as an audiobook by Listening Library/Books on Tape, 2005; and optioned for film by Twentieth Century-Fox. *The Lightning Thief* and *The Sea of Monsters* were adapted for graphic novel by Robert Venditti, art by Attila Futaki, Disney/Hyperion (New York, NY), 2010 and 2012 respectively. The other titles in the "Percy Jackson and the Olympians" series were also adapted for audiobook. Film rights to *Thirty-nine Clues: The Maze of Bones* were purchased by Steven Spielberg and DreamWorks. *Percy Jackson and the Olympians: The Ultimate Guide,* written by Mary-Jane Knight, was based on Riordan's series. The "Kane Chronicles" novels were adapted for audiobook by Brilliance Audio, 2010.

Sidelights

Known to adult readers as the award-winning author of the "Tres Navarre" mystery novels, Rick Riordan has also earned fans among teens who enjoy his "Percy Jackson and the Olympians," "Heroes of Olympus," and "Kane Chronicles" series of young-adult novels. In the *San Antonio Express-News,* Bryce Milligan reflected on the popularity of Riordan's teen fiction, wondering "how it is that Rick Riordan can consistently write novels that, although they begin with dire prophecies and end with narrow escapes from cosmic oblivion, are such delightful romps to read." The popularity of Riordan's "Percy Jackson" series may result from its unusual hero: Percy is actually Perseus, a hyperactive middle schooler who, as Milligan explained, also "happens to be the bona fide son of the Greek god Poseidon."

Cover of Rick Riordan's young-adult fantasy novel The Lightning Thief, *featuring artwork by John Rocco.* (Jacket cover illustration copyright © 2007 by John Rocco. Reproduced by permission of Disney-Hyperion, an imprint of Disney Book Group LLC. All rights reserved.)

Riordan spent eight years teaching English in a San Francisco middle school before returning to his hometown of San Antonio, Texas, in the summer of 1998. When his older son, Haley, turned eight years old, Riordan began retelling original Greek myths at the boy's request. Haley had recently been diagnosed with ADHD and dyslexia, and Riordan was heartened to see the boy focus his attention on stories about the Greek gods. For fun, he decided to craft a modern retelling of the myths, focusing on a young boy named Percy, who also suffers from ADHD. Percy's quest is to retrieve the lightning bolt of Zeus from twenty-first century America. After Percy's saga played out, Haley asked his dad to write the story down, and this manuscript was the genesis of *The Lightning Thief.*

In *The Lighting Thief* Percy Jackson is a trouble-making middle schooler who is diagnosed with ADHD and dyslexia. Soon he discovers that the things that have always made him feel different from his classmates are actually due to the fact that he IS different: he is actually a demigod and his ADHD hones his awareness during battle and dyslexia enables him to read ancient Greek. Pursued by monsters, Percy stays one step ahead of them and ultimately winds up at Camp Half-Blood, a summer camp for young demigods. Embracing his destiny, Percy becomes embroiled in a quest to find Zeus's lightning bolt before the Olympians declare war on Earth. Percy's friends Grover and Annabeth accompany him into the Underworld, where they discover that Kronos, the Titan who once ruled the Olympians, is plotting against all of Western civilization.

Diana Tixier Herald, reviewing the first "Percy Jackson and the Olympians" novel for *Booklist,* called *The Lightning Thief* a "clever mix of classic mythologies, contemporary teen characters, and an action-packed adventure." Despite the many allusions to ancient myths that Riordan incorporates into his tale, "one need not be an expert in Greek mythology to enjoy" the adventure, according to a *Kirkus Reviews* contributor, although the critic added that "those who are familiar . . . will have many an ah-ha moment." In *School Library Journal* Patricia D. Lothrop praised Riordan's story as "an adventure-quest with a hip edge," and in *Booklist* Chris Sherman called Percy "an appealing, but reluctant hero" and added that "the modernized gods are hilarious."

In *The Sea of Monsters* Percy searches for the Golden Fleece in order to save Thalia's tree, which generates the magical border protecting Camp Half-Blood. On his quest he is haunted by dreams in which his friend Grover is threatened. In other plot developments a homeless campmate turns out to be both a cyclops and Percy's half-brother. "Percy has a sarcastically entertaining voice and a refreshing lack of hubris," wrote Anita L. Burkam in her *Horn Book* review of *The Sea of Monsters,* the critic describing the preteen as "wry, impatient, [and] academically hopeless, with the sort of cut-to-the-chase bluntness one would wish for in a hero." A *Kirkus Reviews* contributor wrote that "Percy's

Cover of Riordan's adventure-filled teen novel **The Sea of Monsters,** *featuring artwork by John Rocco.* (Jacket cover illustration copyright © 2007 by John Rocco. Reproduced by permission of Disney-Hyperion, an imprint of Disney Book Group LLC. All rights reserved.)

sardonic narration and derring-do will keep the pages turning." and a *Publishers Weekly* reviewer concluded that Riordan's novel's "cliffhanger [ending] leaves no question that Percy's high-stakes battle for Western Civilization will continue to surprise even himself."

Another year has passed and Percy is fourteen years old when he returns in *The Titan's Curse.* Not only is his good friend Annabeth missing, but Artemis, goddess of the hunt, has also vanished. Percy and Grover join the search party despite the promise of danger ahead and a disturbing prophecy that has been revealed by the Oracle. To make matters worse, the giant monsters of legend are growing restless; rising from their sleep after thousands of years, they now threaten Olympus with certain destruction if Percy and his friends do not stop them. Riordan's introduction of two new half-bloods, Nico and Bianca, further fleshes out Percy's fighting

forces. Herald commented in *Booklist* that *The Titan's Curse* is an "exciting installment" that adds "even more depth to the characters," while a contributor for *Kirkus Reviews* maintained that Riordan's entertaining depiction of "the contests between the gods will have readers wondering how literature can be this fun." Alison Follos, writing for *School Library Journal,* dubbed *The Titan's Curse* "a winner of Olympic proportions and a surefire read-aloud."

In *The Battle of the Labyrinth* King Kronos once again plans to gain control of the underworld and all the evil forces dwelling there. Along with Annabeth and the mortal Rachel Elizabeth Dare, Percy journeys into the mysterious labyrinth in order to put a stop to Kronos's machinations. There the trio encounters all manner of adventures, confronting giants, the Sphinx, Daedalus, Hephaestus, Calypso, and finally Kronos himself. "Kids will devour Riordan's subtle satire of their world," noted Tim Wadham, the critic adding in his *School Library Journal* critique of the novel that "the cliff-hanger ending will leave readers breathless." A contributor for *Kirkus Reviews* praised Riordan's fourth "Percy Jack-

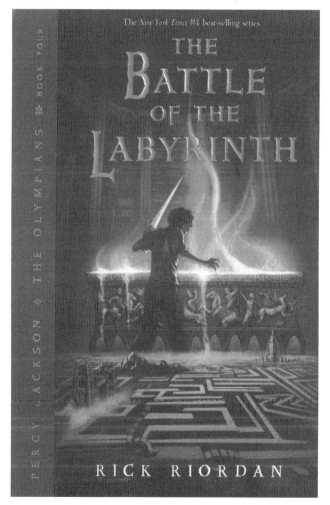

Riordan's "Percy Jackson" series includes **The Battle of the Labyrinth,** *featuring cover art by John Rocco.* (Jacket cover illustration copyright © 2008 by John Rocco. Reproduced by permission of Disney-Hyperion, an imprint of Disney Book Group, LLC. All rights reserved.)

son" novel, writing that "the often-philosophical tale zips along with snappy dialogue, humor and thrilling action." Similar praise came from a *Publishers Weekly* reviewer who wrote that in *The Battle of the Labyrinth* the author's "high-octane clashes with dark forces [are] . . . laced with hip humor and drama."

The "Percy Jackson" series ends in *The Last Olympian,* as soon-to-be-sixteen-year-old Percy gains virtual invulnerability in the river Styx and then joins Tyson, head of the Cyclops army, to lead Gordon, Annabeth, and many others into battle. As the war to save Mount Olympus from the Titan king Kronos wages on, the lines are drawn between satyrs, dryads, centaurs, tree nymphs, and other godlike Olympians and Kronos's rogue band of hellhounds, dragons, Hyperboreans, and Laestrygonian cannibals. Citing Riordan's "winning combination of high-voltage adventure and crackling wit" in her *Booklist* review, Carolyn Phelan added that *The Last Olympian* addresses serious themes and values. In *Horn Book* Burkham explained that "Percy and his friends have matured into battle-tested veterans," and romance has finally bloomed between Annabel and Riordan's teen hero. As "the fate of Western civilization" is decided, wrote a *Kirkus Reviews* writer, *The Last Olympian* treats readers to "a compelling conclusion to the saga" while hinting at the possibility of more adventures.

Riordan serves up more adventures in his "Heroes of Olympus" series, five novels that include *The Lost Hero, The Son of Neptune,* and *The Mark of Athena.* When readers meet them in *The Lost Hero,* fifteen-year-old half-bloods Jason, Piper, and Leo are somehow transported to Camp Half Blood, where they begin to fulfill their destinies by training in the use of weaponry and monster identification. Their adventures are guided by a prophecy stating that seven select demigods will be required to risk death to save the gods of Mt. Olympus from death at the hands of the giant sons of Gaia. A clue to the four other demigods included in the prophecy comes in *The Son of Neptune,* as Jason, Piper, and Leo are joined by a new comrade who claims the sea god as his father.

"Fans hungry for further adventures in Riordan's modernized mythological realm will be well satisfied" with *The Lost Hero* and its sequels, predicted Timothy Capehart in his *Voice of Youth Advocates* appraisal of this new sequence of half-blood exploits. Noting that "Percy, Annabeth, and others play roles in the new prophecy" underlying the "Heroes of Olympus" novels, Connie Tyrell Burns added in her *School Library Journal* review that "Riordan excels at clever plot devices and at creating an urgent sense of cliff-hanging danger" in recounting the adventures of his demigod cast.

Riordan's "Kane Chronicles" series transports readers to ancient Egypt and includes the novels *The Red Pyramid, The Throne of Fire,* and *The Serpent's Shadow.* Sadie and Carter Kane have lived apart since their mother's death, fourteen-year-old Carter living with his

globe-trotting Egyptologist dad while twelve-year-old Sadie stays with relatives in London. Reuniting his children at the British Museum, Dr. Kane accidentally calls forth the powerful god Set before disappearing. Sadie and Carter quickly realize that the entire pantheon of Egyptian gods now walks the earth, With Set at their heels, the siblings search for a way to undo whatever their father has done, in the process learning that they are both direct descendants of Egyptian magicians with powers of their own. *The Red Pyramid* "is in almost every way an improvement" on the "Percy Jackson" stories, asserted Bruce Handy in a review of Riordan's "Kane Chronicles" opener for the *New York Times Book Review.* "Deeper and more emotionally resonant," according to the critic, the first installment in Sadie and Carter's adventures also features "an underlying moral and philosophical semi-seriousness." In *Booklist* Carolyn Phelan also praised the novel for featuring Riordan's characteristic ingredients: "young protagonists with . . . magical powers, a riveting story marked by headlong adventure . . . and wry, witty twenty-first-century narration."

The Throne of Fire finds Carter and Sadie descending into the underworld in order to confront the growing power of Apophis, a snake god that has been trapped for generations but now plans to bring forth chaos and

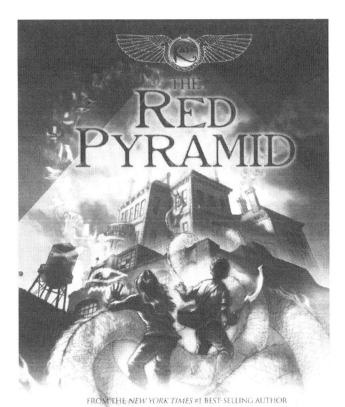

Riordan turns to Egyptian mythology in **The Red Pyramid,** *the first novel in his "Kane Chronicles" and a book featuring cover art by John Rocco.* (Jacket cover illustration copyright © 2010 by John Rocco. Reproduced by permission of Disney-Hyperion, an imprint of Disney Book Group LLC. All rights reserved.)

the end of the world. A desperate search for the Book of Ra may be the only way to stop this new threat, for with that book the Kane siblings may be able to call forth the Sun God himself. Carter and Sadie's adventures wind to a close in *The Serpent's Shadow,* as chaos is unleashed and will destroy the world within three days. With Apophis on the loose, more helpful gods have lost their strength, leaving the young magicians and their trainees as mankind's only defense. Praising *The Throne of Fire* for mixing fast-paced adventure with the humorous "teen chatter" of its dual narrators, John Peters added in *School Library Journal* that "Riordan . . . never lets up on the gas, balances laughs and loss with a sure hand, and expertly sets up the coming climactic struggle." In *Booklist* Phelan wrote that, "lit by flashes of humor," the second installment in Riordan's "Kane Chronicles" saga "is an engaging addition" to the series.

Riordan also addresses young-adult readers in *The Thirty-nine Clues: The Maze of Bones,* "a sensational mix of reading, online gaming, card-collecting, and even a grand-prize sweepstakes," according to *Booklist* contributor Ian Chipman. Designed by Riordan and encompassing a total of ten volumes (each by a different author) the novel's story arc involves the legacy of Grace Cahill, a member of the world's richest family. Grace promises to either give each of her descendant a million dollars or allow them the opportunity to participate in the search for a world-shattering secret by giving them one of thirty-nine clues. Eleven-year-old Dan and older sister Amy opt for the quest and, with the help of their teen au pair, find themselves on a path through their family's amazing history. *The Thirty-nine Clues* "ought to have as much appeal to parents as it does to kids," noted a *Publishers Weekly* contributor, the critic describing the work as "a rollicking good read." In *School Library Journal* Joy Fleishaker also praised the interactive work, writing that it "dazzles with suspense, plot twists, and snappy humor" while also drawing readers into an exploration of history.

Geared for adults, Riordan's "Tres Navarre" mysteries focuses on a Texas-based private detective with a Ph.D. in medieval studies, as well as a few degrees from the streets and an active interest in the martial art Tai Chi Chuan. Commenting in the *Chicago Tribune,* Dick Adler noted of the "Tres Navarre" books that "Riordan writes so well about the people and topography of his Texas hometown that he quickly marks the territory as his own." The author employs a unique "Tex-Mex" style in describing his south Texas settings. As a *Publishers Weekly* critic stated, his "dialogue is terse and the long first person descriptions show an unbeatable flair for detail. You can almost feel the summer storms rolling over south Texas."

Biographical and Critical Sources

PERIODICALS

Booklist, December 1, 1999, Jenny McLarin, review of *The Last King of Texas,* p. 688; May 1, 2001, Jenny McLarin, review of *The Devil Went down to Austin,* p. 1640; March 15, 2003, Connie Fletcher, review of *Cold Springs,* p. 1279; April 15, 2004, Connie Fletcher, review of *Southtown,* p. 1428; May 1, 2005, Frank Sennett, review of *Mission Road,* p. 1534; September 15, 2005, Chris Sherman, review of *The Lightning Thief,* p. 59; July 1, 2006, Diana Tixier Herald, review of *The Sea of Monsters,* p. 52; August, 2007, Steve Glassman, review of *Rebel Island,* p. 48; October 15, 2008, Ian Chipman, review of *Thirty-nine Clues: The Maze of Bones,* p. 39; May 15, 2009, Carolyn Phelan, review of *The Last Olympian,* p. 55; May 15, 2010, Carolyn Phelan, review of *The Red Pyramid,* p. 53; December 15, 2010, Jesse Karp, review of *The Lightning Thief,* p. 36; May 15, 2011, Carolyn Phelan, review of *The Throne of Fire,* p. 58.

Bookseller, August 19, 2005, review of *The Lightning Thief.*

Chronicle, April, 2005, Mike Jones, review of *The Lightning Thief,* p. 19.

Guardian (London, England), June 9, 2007, Philip Ardagh, review of *The Titan's Curse.*

Horn Book, July-August, 2005, Anita L. Burkam, review of *The Lightning Thief,* p. 479; May-June, 2006, Anita L. Burkam, review of *The Sea of Monsters,* p. 326; May-June, 2007, Anita L. Burkam, review of *The Titan's Curse,* p. 290; July-August, 2008, Anita L. Burkam, review of *The Battle of the Labyrinth,* p. 456; July-August, 2009, Anita L. Burkham, review of *The Last Olympian,* p. 430; July-August, 2010, Anita L. Burkam, review of *The Red Pyramid,* p. 121.

Kirkus Reviews, April 1, 2003, review of *Cold Springs,* p. 503; May 15, 2005, review of *Mission Road,* p. 566; June 15, 2005, review of *The Lightning Thief,* p. 690; April 1, 2006, review of *The Sea of Monsters,* p. 355; April 1, 2007, review of *The Titan's Curse*; April 1, 2008, review of *The Battle of the Labyrinth*; September 1, 2008, review of *The Thirty-nine Clues*; May 15, 2009, review of *The Last Olympian*; April 15, 2010, review of *The Red Pyramid.*

Kliatt, September, 2006, Heather Rader, review of *The Lightning Thief,* p. 34; March, 2006, Paula Rohrlick, review of *The Sea of Monsters,* p. 16.

Library Journal, December, 1999, Craig L. Shufelt, review of *The Last King of Texas,* p. 188; May 1, 2001, Rex Klett, review of *The Devil Went down to Austin,* p. 129; May 15, 2003, Ken St. Andre, review of *Cold Springs,* p. 132.

New York Times Book Review, November 13, 2005, Polly Schulman, "Harry Who?," p. 42; June 6, 2010, Bruce Handy, review of *The Red Pyramid,* p. 23.

Publishers Weekly, December 20, 1999, review of *The Last King of Texas,* p. 58; April 30, 2001, review of *The Devil Went down to Austin,* p. 59; April 7, 2003, review of *Cold Springs,* p. 45; April 5, 2004, review of *Southtown,* p. 44; May 16, 2005, review of *Mission Road,* p. 40; July 18, 2005, review of *The Lightning Thief,* p. 207; April 24, 2006, review of *The Sea of Monsters,* p. 61; June 18, 2007, review of *Rebel Island,* p. 34; April 14, 2008, review of *The Battle of the Labyrinth,* p. 55; May 18, 2009, review of *The Last Olympian,* p. 55; April 12, 2010, review of *The Red Pyramid,* p. 51.

San Antonio Express-News, May 4, 2008, Bryce Milligan, review of *The Battle of the Labyrinth.*

School Librarian, autumn, 2010, Anne-Marie Tarter, review of *The Red Pyramid,* p. 182.

School Library Journal, August, 2005, Patricia D. Lothrop, review of *The Lightning Thief,* p. 134; May, 2006, Kathleen Isaacs, review of *The Sea of Monsters,* p. 135; May 1, 2007, Alison Follos, review of *The Titan's Curse,* p. 142; May, 2008, Tim Wadham, review of *The Battle of the Labyrinth,* p. 138; November, 2008, Joy Fleishhacker, review of *The Thirty-nine Clues,* p. 136; June, 2009, review of *The Olympian,* p. 136; June, 2010, Tim Wadhams, review of *The Red Pyramid,* p. 118; February, 2011, Connie Tyrrell Burns, review of *The Lost Hero,* p. 118; June, 2011, John Peters, review of *The Throne of Fire,* p. 132.

Texas Monthly, July, 2005, Mike Shea, review of *Mission Road,* p. 64; June, 2007, "Rick Riordan," p. 60.

Times Educational Supplement, July 21, 2006, Fiona Lafferty, "Inspired by Mount Olympus," p. 29.

Voice of Youth Advocates, August, 2005, Dave Goodale, review of *The Lightning Thief,* p. 237; February, 2011, Timothy Capehart, review of *The Lost Hero,* p. 577.

ONLINE

Cynsations Web log, http://cynthialeitichsmith.blogspot.com/ (December 27, 2005), Cynthia Leitich Smith, interview with Riordan.

Percy Jackson Web site, http://www.percyjacksonbooks.com (January 12, 2012).

Rick Riordan Home Page, http://www.rickriordan.com (January 12, 2012).

Rick Riordan Web log, http://rickriordan.blogspot.com (January 12, 2012).

Scholastic Web site, http://www2.scholastic.com/ (January 12, 2012), "Rick Riordan."*

*   *   *

RORBY, Ginny 1944-
(Virginia Rorby Oesterle)

Personal

Born August 9, 1944, in Washington, DC; adopted daughter of Noel (in sales) and Kathryn (a homemaker) Rorby; married Stan Clarke, August 29, 1964 (marriage ended, December 29, 1965); married Douglas Oesterle (an accountant), May 22, 1971 (separated, 1980); stepchildren: Robert A., Mark W. *Education:* University of Miami, A.B. (biology and English), 1985; Florida International University, M.F.A. (creative writing), 1991. *Hobbies and other interests:* Animal welfare, the environment.

Addresses

Home—Fort Bragg, CA. *Agent*—Laura Dial, 350 7th Ave., Ste. 2003, New York, NY 10001. *E-mail*—ginnyrorby@mcn.org.

Ginny Rorby (Reproduced by permission.)

Career

Author. National Airlines (later Pan American Airways), Miami, FL, flight attendant, 1966-89; writer. Chairperson, Glass Beach Access Committee; member of Leadership Mendocino. Volunteer teacher at College of the Redwoods; volunteer at other civic organizations. Mendocino Coast Writers Conference, director, 1998-2005, and member of board, beginning 1996.

Member

National Audubon Society (president, Mendocino Coast chapter), Point Cabrillo Lightkeepers Association (member of board, beginning 1996), Mendocino Coast Botanical Gardens, Phi Kappa Phi.

Awards, Honors

Keystone to Reading Book Award nomination, Keystone State Reading Association, 1997, for *Dolphin Sky;* Schneider Family Book Award in teen category, American Library Association, and William Allen White Children's Book Award finalist, both 2008, and finalist for several state reading awards, all for *Hurt Go Happy.*

Writings

Dolphin Sky, Putnam (New York, NY), 1996.

Hurt Go Happy, Tom Doherty Associates (New York, NY), 2006.

The Outside of a Horse, Dial Books for Young Readers (New York, NY), 2010.

Lost in the River of Grass, Carolrhoda Lab (Minneapolis, MN), 2011.

Adaptations

The Outside of a Horse and *Hurt Go Happy* were adapted as audiobooks, Blackstone Audio.

Sidelights

Ginny Rorby worked as a flight attendant for twenty-three years before finishing her college degree, earning an M.A. in creative writing, and beginning her second career as a children's book author. Now living in California, Rorby is active with several nature organizations in her area, and to channel her interest in wildlife she volunteers as a teacher of natural history at the College of the Redwoods Her first novel, *Dolphin Sky,* was inspired by Rorby's time growing up in Florida, and she has followed it with other middle-grade novels, including *Hurt Go Happy, The Outside of a Horse,* and *Lost in the River of Grass.*

"I was born in the Florence Crittenton Home for unwed mothers in Washington, DC," Rorby once told *SATA.* "I was adopted by Kathryn and Noel Rorby, who lived in Detroit at the time. When I was two, we moved to Maitland, Florida. . . . I lived the next twenty years in central Florida, first in Maitland in the house that is now the headquarters of a Birds of Prey rescue center, then in Winter Park. By the time I was four, it was discovered that I had a weak muscle in my right eye, which caused it to turn inward when I was tired. The doctors tried a patch, then glasses. All through school, my greatest fear was being called on to read aloud in class. I barely had the grades to graduate from high school.

"I excelled at nothing as a youngster. I was a moderately good swimmer, singer, and painter, but I started smoking when I was fifteen, ruining my chances at two out of three, and I lost interest in painting. I attended a junior college in Orlando, where I was admitted on academic probation. I took remedial English three times before I finally received a D. I still can't diagram a sentence.

"In 1964 I married to get away from home. The marriage lasted eleven months, and only that long because I felt guilty about the wedding gifts. In 1966 I was hired by National Airlines as a stewardess. Pan American Airways bought the company in 1980. I flew for twenty-three years. It was a wonderful life for about the first fifteen, then I began to feel trapped. In 1977, when I went back to school, it was with the intention of someday becoming a veterinarian. As it worked out, it took me eight years to get my undergraduate degree. By the time I graduated, I had begun to write.

"That I am now a writer was an accident. Until August, 1982, I had only written a couple of searing letters, one to a store owner in Orlando who had fired a former co-worker with breast cancer, and one to an eye doctor who went to a patient's deathbed to collect his fee. Some time in 1981, a friend of mine (who did become a vet) found a starving dog. Maggots were already consuming its flesh. When I came home from a trip, she had gained its trust. We collected every sleeping pill and valium that we had between us, drugged the dog, took it to a vet, and had it put to sleep. The first thing I ever wrote, aside from those letters, was about that dog.

"A year later, I found the story stuffed in the side pocket of my uniform purse. It made my heart hurt all over again, so I typed it and took it to the smaller of our two Miami newspapers. They published 'We Found Your Dog' in 1982. An editor called me at home and said, 'If you can write like that, we will publish anything you write.' Of course, I couldn't. It would be years before I found my way back to writing about what knots my guts. In the interim, I started taking writing courses and ended up with an M.F.A. in creative writing. In 1991 I

Cover of Rorby's inspiring children's novel **Dolphin Sky,** *featuring illustrations by Ted Lewin.* (Jacket art © 1996 by Ted Lewin. Reproduced by permission. Reproduced by permission of G.P Putnam, an imprint of Penguin Young Readers Group, a member of Penguin Group (USA), Inc., 345 Hudson Street, New York NY 10014. All rights reserved.)

moved to the north coast of California. *Dolphin Sky* was sold five days before my fiftieth birthday."

In *Dolphin Sky* Rorby tells the story of twelve-year-old Buddy, who empathizes with the mistreated dolphins she sees in a cut-rate tourist show near her Florida home. Buddy herself feels neglected by her single father and confused and "dumb" in school. She has the love and respect of her elderly grandfather, however, and with his help and that of a new biologist friend, she grows in self-esteem. She learns that she is not stupid but has a learning disability, and she comes up with a plan to free her mistreated dolphin friends. Buddy's boating trips with her grandfather "bring suspense, and the theme of our inhumane treatment of other mammals adds substance and tenderness," Susan DeRonne noted in her review of the novel in *Booklist*. While *School Library Journal* contributor Susan Oliver found some of the events implausible, she praised Rorby's "sensitively drawn" characters and her "provocatively and emotionally discussed" treatment of animal rights. As a *Publishers Weekly* reviewer concluded, "convincingly portrayed relationships, a deeply moving plot" and interesting detail on the Florida Everglades "combine to make this debut a real winner."

The title of Rorby's award-winning novel *Hurt Go Happy* means "the pain has ended," and her well-researched story is based on a true story of a chimpanzee named Lucy that was raised like a human child. Thirteen-year-old Joey Willis has been deaf for seven years, a victim of her father's violent temper. Because her mother is in denial and refuses to let Joey learn sign language, the girl has little knowledge of what is being spoken around her. When she meets Dr. Charles Mansell and his young chimpanzee, Sukari, she decides to learn sign language so that she can communicate with the African chimp, which has been taught this skill by the doctor. This new friendship buoy's Joey's spirits, and after the doctor's death he bequeaths her the funds needed to attend a school for the deaf. Several years later, in college, Joey works to improve the life of Sukari, who has been confined in a cage since Mansell's death. *Hurt Go Happy* "has the potential to be a classic animal story with wide appeal," wrote Claire Rosser in her *Kliatt* review, as "Rorby successfully gets to the core of a moving animal-human relationship." In *School Library Journal* Kathleen Kelly MacMillan noted that, while the underlying facts sometimes overwhelm the fictional narrative, "the writing shines when Rorby focuses on . . . her true passion: Sukari and the fate of chimpanzees like her."

Rorby turns to another animal-focused passion in *The Outside of a Horse,* a middle-grade novel that finds Hannah Gale missing her father while he is serving his country in Iraq. She had grown up listening to his stories about rounding up and breaking wild horses during one summer when he was a teenager, and watching the horses in a nearby stable helps Hannah cope with her dad's absence. A job at the stable and experience work-

Cover of Rorby's middle-grade coming-of-age novel The Outside of a Horse, *in which a young girl learns self-reliance while caring for her beloved mare.* (Jacket photographs by Jenny Gaulitz/Etsa/Corbis (girl); Shutterstock (horse). Reproduced by permission of Dial Books for Young Readers, a division of Penguin Young Readers Group, a member of The Penguin Group (USA), 345 Hudson Street, New York NY 10014. All rights reserved.)

ing with an abused mare who is fighting for her survival builds Hannah's self-confidence and also wins her an important place among local equestrians. When Mr. Gale returns from Iraq he has lost a leg and is now haunted by the trauma of warfare. Hannah's work with horses helps her to deal with the tumult at home and also suggests a way that she can help her father heal as well. Noting that Rorby includes "information about animal cruelty" into Hannah's story in *The Outside of a Horse,* Anne O'Malley went on to predict in her *Booklist* review that young "horse lovers and most others will saddle up right away with this poignant tale." In *School Library Journal* Kathleen E. Gruver recommended the novel as a catalyst for "spirited book discussions," adding that Rorby's story "really shines in showing how horses can help troubled humans heal their physical and emotional wounds."

Lost in the River of Grass was inspired by the experiences of Rorby's husband, who traveled deep to the Florida Everglades as a young man and was forced to make a trek to dry land after his airboat—a water craft with a flat bottom that is powered by a large, fan-type propeller—floundered and ultimately sank. The novel had its start as a short story Rorby published in a regional magazine; in its novel-length version, *Lost in the River of Grass* focuses on thirteen-year-old Sarah as she begins her year as a scholarship student to Glades Academy. Because Sarah's mother works for the school, the teen is looked down on by her more-affluent classmates despite her talent as a swimmer. During a field-trip to the Everglades, she meets a slightly older teen named Andy and joins him on his airboat for a short tour. When the vehicle sinks, they become stranded, and since Sarah did not tell anyone where she was going she realizes that they may well be left to the snakes, mosquitoes, alligators, and other local wildlife. Fortunately, both teens are resourceful and practical; neither panics and their "teamwork . . . keeps them alive . . . in the subtropical wilderness," according to *Voice of Youth Advocates* reviewer L. Guenthner. *Lost in the River of Grass* treats readers to an "authentic survival adventure," noted Hazel Rochman in her *Booklist* review of the novel, while *School Library Journal* contributor Vicki Reutter asserted that Rorby's inclusion of "factual details about local flora and fauna make *Lost in the River of Grass* . . . more than just a survival story."

Biographical and Critical Sources

PERIODICALS

Booklist, March 1, 1996, review of *Dolphin Sky,* p. 1184; March 1, 1996, Susan De Ronne, review of *Dolphin Sky,* p. 1184; May 1, 2010, Anne O'Malley, review of *The Outside of a Horse,* p. 77; February 15, 2011, Hazel Rochman, review of *Lost in the River of Grass,* p. 72.

Kirkus Reviews, April 15, 2010, review of *The Outside of a Horse*; February 15, 2011, review of *Lost in the River of Grass.*

Kliatt, July, 2006, Claire Rosser, review of *Hurt Go Happy,* p. 14.

Publishers Weekly, March 25, 1996, review of *Dolphin Sky,* p. 85.

School Library Journal, October, 2006, Kathleen Kelly MacMillan, review of *Hurt Go Happy,* p. 168; July, 2010, Kathleen E. Gruver, review of *The Outside of a Horse,* p. 96; May, 2011, Vicki Reutter, review of *Lost in the River of Grass,* p. 122.

Voice of Youth Advocates, April, 2011, L. Guenthner, review of *Lost in the River of Grass,* p. 67.

ONLINE

Ginny Rorby Home Page, http://www.ginnyrorby.com (January 9, 2012).

Ginny Rorby Web log, http://grorby.blogspot.com (January 9, 2012).

Mendocino Coast Writers Conference Web site, http://www.mcwc.org/ (January 9, 2012).

ROSENSTOCK, Jason 1978-

Personal

Born 1978. *Education:* New York University, M.A. (art education).

Addresses

Home—Austin, TX. *E-mail*—jason@whitewhalegames.com.

Career

Illustrator, concept and environment artist, designer, and animator. Worked in computer-game industry; White Whale Games, Austin, TX, cofounder and creative director, 2011. Rose Charities New York, organizer of Our Voices program.

Illustrator

John Gosselink, *The Defense of Thaddeus A. Ledbetter,* Amulet Books (New York, NY), 2010.

Biographical and Critical Sources

PERIODICALS

Booklist, November 1, 2010, Kara Dean, review of *The Defense of Thaddeus A. Ledbetter,* p. 67.

Kirkus Reviews, September 15, 2010, review of *The Defense of Thaddeus A. Ledbetter.*

School Library Journal, November, 2010, Tina Martin, review of *The Defense of Thaddeus A. Ledbetter,* p. 116.

Voice of Youth Advocates, December, 2010, Amanda MacGregor, review of *The Defense of Thaddeus A. Ledbetter,* p. 454.

ONLINE

Jason Rosenstock Home Page, http://jasonrosenstock.com (January 9, 2012).

White Whale Games Web site, http://whitewhalegames.com/ (January 9, 2012), "Jason Rosenstock."*

*   *   *

ROY, Léna

Personal

Born in New York, NY; daughter of Josephine Jones (a psychotherapist), and the Very Reverend Alan W. Jones (an Episcopalian priest and author of theological books); granddaughter of Madeleine L'Engle (an author); married; children: two sons, one daughter. *Education:* Barnard College, degree (English and Italian literature); New York University, M.A. (drama therapy).

Addresses

Home—Katonah, NY. *E-mail*—lena.roy@gmail.com.

Career

Author and educator. Worked variously as a bartender and actor; worked with at-risk teens in New York, NY, California, and Utah. Teacher of creative writing, including at Writopia Lab, Westchester, NY; presenter at schools.

Writings

Edges, Farrar Straus & Giroux (New York, NY), 2010.

Sidelights

Léna Roy's decision to become a writer may have been destiny: not only was she interested in writing while growing up, but she also was inspired by a very special grandmother, author Madeleine L'Engle. In addition to producing her first published novel, *Edges,* Roy teaches creative-writing workshops for children of all ages in her native New York City as well as in the surrounding suburbs.

Cover of Léna Roy's young-adult novel Edges, *featuring artwork by Richard Tuschman.* (Jacket art copyright © 2010 by Richard Tuschman. Reproduced by permission of Farrar, Straus & Giroux.)

Roy grew up in New York City, as part of a creative and spiritual community. "My grandmother gave me my first journal when I was nine," she recalled on her home page. "I still have it: a thin, dark blue leather bound book. A book to be taken seriously. I have kept a journal by my bedside and in my purse ever since. The practice has helped shape who I am and how I think and I have often joked that it has been my one and only discipline." Although she considered a career in acting after earning a degree in English and Italian literature at Barnard College, Roy earned her master's degree in drama therapy and began working with adolescents. It was not until her mid-thirties that she decided to begin the novel-length manuscript that resulted in *Edges,* finding time to write while raising her three children.

In *Edges* readers meet Luke, a seventeen year old who is living in Moab, Utah, and working at a local motel while coming to terms with his mom's death in a car accident and his alcoholic dad's inability to cope with the tragedy. Back in New York City, Frank, Luke's dad, decides to attend an Alcoholics Anonymous (AA) meeting, where he meets a college freshman named Ava. Inspired by the eighteen year old's determination to put her life back together, Frank helps Ava locate her parents, and this journey brings them to the same hostel in Moab where Luke is living. While writing that *Edges* features a somewhat "meandering narrative," Michael Cart added in *Booklist* that Roy's "multidimensional, sympathetic characters . . . will hold readers' attentions," and a *Publishers Weekly* reviewer praised the author for steering her plot away from "the expected love story" in favor of focusing "on . . . teenagers trying to reconcile their feelings for their families." Noting the novel's central focus on AA culture and the harm caused by alcohol addiction, a *Kirkus Review* critic also remarked on the "nicely established setting" in *Edges,* as well as on "Luke's brief but fascinating introduction to the idea of animal spirit guides."

Biographical and Critical Sources

PERIODICALS

Booklist, November 15, 2010, Michael Cart, review of *Edges,* p. 41.
Kirkus Reviews, November 1, 2010, review of *Edges.*
Publishers Weekly, October 25, 2010, review of *Edges,* p. 50.
School Library Journal, December, 2010, Shawna Sherman, review of *Edges,* p. 126.

ONLINE

Léna Roy Home Page, http://www.lenaroybooks.com (January 9, 2012).
Léna Roy Web log, http://www.lenaroy.com (January 9, 2012).

S

SACHAR, Louis 1954-

Personal

Surname pronounced *Sack*-er; born March 20, 1954, in East Meadow, NY; son of Robert J. (a salesman) and Ruth (a real estate broker) Sachar; married Carla Askew (a counselor), May 26, 1985; children: Sherre. *Education:* University of California, Berkeley, B.A., 1976; University of California, San Francisco, J.D., 1980.

Addresses

Home—Austin, TX. *Agent*—Ellen Levine, Trident Media Group, 41 Madison Ave., 36th Fl., New York, NY 10010.

Career

Writer for children. Beldoch Industries, Norwalk, CT, shipping manager, 1976-77; freelance writer, beginning 1977; lawyer, 1981-89.

Member

Authors Guild, Society of Children's Book Writers and Illustrators.

Awards, Honors

Ethical Culture School Book Award, 1978, and Children's Choice selection, International Reading Association/Children's Book Council (IRA/CBC), 1979, both for *Sideways Stories from Wayside School;* Parents' Choice Award, 1987, Young Reader's Choice Award, Pacific Northwest Library Association, and Texas Bluebonnet Award, Texas Library Association, both 1990, and Charlie May Simon Book Award, Arkansas Elementary School Council, Georgia Children's Book Award, University of Georgia College of Education, Indian Paintbrush Book Award (WY), Golden Sower Award, Iowa Children's Choice Award, Land of Enchantment Children's Book Award, New Mexico Library Association, Mark Twain Award, Missouri Association of School Librarians, Milner Award, Friends of the Atlanta-Fulton Public Library (GA), Nevada Young Reader's Award, and West Virginia Book Award, Wise Library, West Virginia University, all c. 1987, all for *There's a Boy in the Girls' Bathroom;* Parents' Choice Award, 1989, Garden State Children's Book Award, New Jersey Library Association, 1992, and Arizona Young Reader's Chapter Book Award, 1993, all for *Wayside School Is Falling Down;* Golden Archer Award nomination, 1996-97, Garden State Children's Book Award, 1998, and Indiana Young Hoosier's Book Award, Massachusetts Children's Book Award, and Young Reader's Choice Award, all for *Wayside School Gets a Little Stranger;* National Book Award, 1998, and *Boston Globe/Horn Book* Award, and Newbery Medal, both 1999, all for *Holes;* Roger L. Stevens Award, Kennedy Center Fund for New American Plays, and AT&T: OnStage Award, Theatre Communications Group, both 2001, both for stage adaptation of *Holes;* Schneider Family Book Award, 2007, Children's Choice selection, IRA/CBC, Best Children's Book selection, Bank Street College of Education, and Notable Social Studies Trade Book for Young People designation, National Council for the Social Studies (NCSS)/CBC, all 2006, all for *Small Steps;* Best Books for Young Adults designation, American Library Association, Choice selection, Cooperative Children's Book Center, and Notable Social Studies Trade Book for Young People designation, all 2010, all for *The Cardturner.*

Writings

FICTION

Johnny's in the Basement, Avon (New York, NY), 1981, reprinted, Morrow (New York, NY), 1998.

Someday Angeline, illustrated by Barbara Samuels, Avon (New York, NY), 1983, reprinted, Morrow (New York, NY), 1998.

There's a Boy in the Girls' Bathroom (also see below), Knopf (New York, NY), 1987.

Sixth Grade Secrets, Scholastic (New York, NY), 1987.

The Boy Who Lost His Face (young-adult novel), Knopf (New York, NY), 1989.

Dogs Don't Tell Jokes, Knopf (New York, NY), 1991.

Monkey Soup (picture book), illustrated by Cat Bowman Smith, Knopf (New York, NY), 1992.

Holes (young-adult novel; also see below), Farrar, Straus & Giroux (New York, NY), 1998, expanded edition, Holt (Austin, TX), 2002, tenth anniversary edition, Farrar, Straus & Giroux, 2008.

Stanley Yelnats' Survival Guide to Camp Green Lake, Dell (New York, NY), 2003.

Holes (screenplay; based on his novel), Buena Vista/Walt Disney, 2003.

Small Steps, Delacorte Press (New York, NY), 2006.

The Cardturner: A Novel about a King, a Queen, and a Joker, Delacorte Press (New York, NY), 2010.

Author of stage adaptations of his novels *There's a Boy in the Girl's Bathroom* and *Holes.*

"WAYSIDE SCHOOL" MIDDLE-GRADE NOVEL SERIES

Sideways Stories from Wayside School, illustrated by Dennis Hockerman, Follett (New York, NY), 1978, new edition illustrated by Julie Brinkloe, Avon (New York, NY), 1985.

Sideways Arithmetic from Wayside School, Scholastic (New York, NY), 1989.

Wayside School Is Falling Down, illustrated by Joel Schick, Lothrop, Lee & Shepard (New York, NY), 1989, reprinted, HarperTrophy (New York, NY), 2005.

More Sideways Arithmetic from Wayside School, Scholastic (New York, NY), 1994.

Wayside School Gets a Little Stranger, illustrated by Joel Schick, Morrow (New York, NY), 1994.

"MARVIN REDPOST" CHAPTER-BOOK SERIES

Kidnapped at Birth?, illustrated by Neal Hughes, Random House (New York, NY), 1992.

Is He a Girl?, illustrated by Barbara Sullivan, Random House (New York, NY), 1993.

Why Pick on Me?, illustrated by Barbara Sullivan, Random House (New York, NY), 1993.

Alone in His Teacher's House, illustrated by Barbara Sullivan, Random House (New York, NY), 1994.

A Flying Birthday Cake, Random House (New York, NY), 1999.

Class President, Random House (New York, NY), 1999.

Super Fast, Out of Control!, illustrated by Amy Wummer, Random House (New York, NY), 2000.

A Magic Crystal?, Random House (New York, NY), 2000.

Adaptations

Holes, Small Steps, The Cardturner, and some of the "Wayside School" tales have been adapted as audiobooks; *Holes,* was adapted for film by Walt Disney Pictures, released in 2003; the "Wayside School" tales

were adapted as *Wayside School* (animated television special), 2005, and *Wayside* (animated television series), 2007-08.

Sidelights

Celebrated author Louis Sachar, winner of a National Book Award and a Newbery Medal for his novel *Holes,* is also recognized for his "Wayside School" series of middle-grader novels and his "Marvin Redpost" chapter books for younger readers. Sachar's storylines chart the efforts of his various protagonists to discover and then assert their young identities. "Behind the offbeat characters and often unusual situations lie poignant adolescent confusion, embarrassment, conflict and heartache that speak directly to the real lives of young readers of all ages, as well as adults," Sharon Miller Cindrich observed in *Writer.* "Creative characters and bizarre settings may pull readers in, but Sachar's innate sensitivity to life issues, coming of age and the struggles of growing up keep them reading."

Born in East Meadow, New York, Sachar grew up in Orange County, California. While attending the University of California, Berkeley, he majored in economics, but also took creative-writing courses. One day, an elementary school girl was handing out leaflets at Sa-

Cover of Louis Sachar's award-winning fiction debut **Holes,** *featuring cover art by Vladimir Radunsky.* (Jacket art and design copyright © 1998 by Vladimir Radunsky. Reprinted by permission of Farrar, Straus & Giroux, Inc.)

char's campus announcing a class that would enable students to work as teacher's aides. "Prior to that time I had no interest whatsoever in kids," he later admitted to *SATA*. "It turned out to be not only my favorite class, but also the most important class I took during my college career." His interaction with the school kids was heightened when he became the lunchtime supervisor and was known affectionately as "Louis, the Yard Teacher."

At about this same time, Sachar was reading *In Our Town*, a series of very short, interrelated stories by Damon Runyon that gave him the idea of doing the same sort of treatment for a fictionalized school called Wayside. "All the kids are named after the kids I knew at the school where I worked," Sachar explained. He even put himself in the book as the character Louis the Yard Teacher. "I probably had more fun writing that book than any of my others, because it was just a hobby then, and I never truly expected to be published."

After he graduated from college, Sachar continued working on his thirty short stories about Wayside School, and sent off the finished manuscript at the same time he was applying to law schools. "My first book was accepted for publication during my first week at University of California, beginning a six-year struggle over trying to decide between being an author or a lawyer," Sachar once recalled to *SATA*. *Sideways Stories from Wayside School* was a mild success with young readers, making Sachar's deliberations that much more difficult. After graduating and passing the California Bar Exam, Sachar proceeded to both write and practice law part-time. He continued working in this manner through his next several books, until he was established enough as an author to write full time.

Sideways Stories from Wayside School tells the tale of an elementary school thirty stories high, each classroom stacked on top of the other. There is a broad cast of characters, from school clown to bully to the favorite teacher, Mrs. Jewls. Sachar provides vignettes from many points of view, all of which add up to a zany take on school days.

Letters from fans of his first book of stories convinced Sachar to return to his tales from Wayside School with *Wayside School Is Falling Down* and *Sideways Arithmetic from Wayside School*. Lee Galda, writing in *Reading Teacher*, maintained that "humorous is the best way" to describe the former title, a "zany novel [that] will be cheered" by its audience. Once again, Sachar's humorous take on school life and his use of short chapters make for a perfect book to share in oral reading. Reviewing *Wayside School Is Falling Down*, Carolyn Phelan remarked in *Booklist* that "Sachar's humor is right on target for middle-grade readers," with episodes from the school cafeteria to a lesson in gravity from Mrs. Jewls when she drops a computer out the window. As Phelan concluded: "Children will recognize Sachar as a writer who knows their territory and entertains

Cover of Sachar's humorous middle-grade novel There's a Boy in the Girls' Bathroom, *featuring artwork by Robert Tanenbaum.* (Jacket cover copyright © 1998 by Yearling. Reproduced by permission of Yearling, an imprint of Random House Children's Books, a division of Random House, Inc.)

them well." Sachar draws on his own love for math with the brainteasers gathered in *Sideways Arithmetic from Wayside School*, and in *Wayside School Gets a Little Stranger*, he presents thirty new self-contained tales that relate what happens during Mrs. Jewls' absence on maternity leave. Deborah Stevenson, writing in the *Bulletin of the Center for Children's Books*, called *Wayside School Gets a Little Stranger* "smart, funny, and widely appealing," while a *Kirkus Reviews* commentator noted that "Sachar proves once again that he is a master of all things childish."

Sachar has also written a number of well-received young-adult novels. *Johnny's in the Basement* centers on eleven-year-old Johnny Laxatayl, whose fantastic bottle-cap collection is his claim to fame. Johnny's punning last name is intentional, for the boy looks something like a dog; however, he "lacks a tail." After his eleventh birthday, Johnny's parents suddenly push responsibilities on him in the form of dancing lessons and their plan for him to sell his prized bottle-cap collection, for which he receives $86.33. Johnny and his new friend, Valerie, blow the money on meaningless junk, "a preadolescent way to show contempt for adults' exploitation," according to *School Library Journal* contributor Jack Forman. While Joan McGrath, writing in *Emergency Librarian*, found the book to be "full of sly humor," a *Publishers Weekly* reviewer called *Johnny's in the Basement* "another corker" and concluded that "all the many characters in the story are superbly realized, particularly Johnny's eldritch little sister."

Sachar's third novel, *Someday Angeline*, is told with "unaffected humor and linguistic art," two characteristics that "invest the story of Angeline Persopolis with pure magic," according to a *Publishers Weekly* critic. Angeline is eight years old and with an I.Q. that soars off the charts, but this genius aspect has made her an outsider at school. Her mother is dead and her teacher loves to embarrass the precocious child. Angeline finds another loner, Gary Boone, known as Goon, as well as a friendly teacher, Miss Turbone—Mr. Bone to the pun-loving Sachar—who "gladden" her life and support her through tough times in a book that readers will not want to see end, according to a commentator in *Publishers Weekly*. *Booklist* critic Ilene Cooper noted that children will enjoy "the sense of fun . . . and the feel-

ing of hope that comes shining through" in *Someday Angeline*. Gary "Goon" Boone makes another appearance in Sachar's *Dogs Don't Tell Jokes*.

There's a Boy in the Girls' Bathroom is one of his most-popular and best-known books. In this work he tells the story of the transformation of a fifth-grade bully from the point of view of both the bully-ish outcast in question, Bradley Chalkers, and new kid Jeff Fishkin, who befriends Bradley. The recipient of over a dozen state awards, *There's a Boy in the Girls' Bathroom* has charmed critics and readers alike. A *Kirkus Reviews* critic called the "fall and rise of Bradley Chalkers, class bully" a "humorous, immensely appealing story," and noted that the character's transformation, under the tutelage of his shaky new friend and the school counselor, "is beautiful to see." Writing in *School Library Journal*, David Gale called the novel "unusual, witty, and satisfying," and added that Sachar "ably captures both middle-grade angst and joy." Sam Leaton Sebesta dubbed Sachar's book "a triumph" in *Reading Teacher*.

Sixth Grade Secrets follows in the same vein, mining preadolescent social problems. Laura starts a secret club known as Pig City, whose members must confess secrets to each other to ensure they keep the existence of the club between them. When a rival club, Monkey Town, springs up, suddenly secrets abound in a "witty, well-paced story" that "shows off" its author's "impeccable ear for classroom banter," according to a review in *Publishers Weekly*. Ilene Cooper, writing in *Booklist*, praised Sachar's "plotting with twists" that will "hold readers' attentions."

Sachar's "Marvin Redpost" chapter books feature a protagonist whose problems include nose-picking, questions about his identity, and troubles with his teacher. In the first title in the series, *Kidnapped at Birth?*, nine-year-old Marvin, the only redhead in his family, thinks he was stolen from his real parents at birth. Marvin's friends agree that his concerns are quite valid, prompting the boy to confront his parents with his suspicions and urge them to get a blood test to prove him wrong. *School Library Journal* contributor Kenneth E. Kowen noted that the book is written almost totally in dialogue and praised it as "fast paced, easy to read, and full of humor." Kowen concluded that Sachar's story "deals with issues of friendship, school, and being different, all handled with the author's typical light touch."

Cover of Sachar's humorous middle-grade novel **Alone in His Teacher's House,** *part of his "Marvin Redpost" series and featuring artwork by Neal Hughes.* (Jacket cover illustration copyright © 1994 by Neal Hughes. Reprinted by permission of Random House Children's Books, a division of Random House, Inc.)

Social etiquette gets the Sachar treatment in *Why Pick on Me?*, in which Marvin is unjustly accused of picking his nose and becomes a social outcast as a result. Stevenson had high praise for this beginning chapter book, noting in the *Bulletin of the Center for Children's Books* that Sachar, "a consistently talented writer of books for grade-school readers," circumvents the usual cutesy pitfalls of writing easy-readers "to produce a *tour de force* of the genre, a trim tome of energy, hilarity, and wisdom."

Amy Wummer creates the artwork for Sachar's "Martin Redpost" chapter-book installment **Super Fast, Out of Control!** (Illustration Copyright © 2000 by Amy Wummer. Used by permission of Random House Children's Books, a division of Random House, Inc.)

Marvin gets in trouble again when he is entrusted with the care of his vacationing teacher's dog, Waldo, in *Alone in His Teacher's House*. Waldo refuses to eat and eventually dies, leaving Marvin to deal with his own feelings of guilt. Further adventures of Marvin include befriending aliens in *A Flying Birthday Cake*, which *Horn Book* reviewer Roger Sutton deemed "a smart, funny twist on the new-kid theme"; being pressured to ride down "Suicide Hill" on his bicycle in *Super Fast, Out of Control!*, about which Roger Sutton of *Horn Book* noted that "Marvin's fans will enjoy this chance to ride alongside him"; and making wishes that seem to come true in *A Magic Crystal?*

With the publication of *Holes*, Sachar's reputation soared. The story of Stanley Yelnats, whose name, a palindrome, can be spelled backward and forward, the award-winning *Holes* prompted *Bulletin of the Center for Children's Books* contributor Roger Sutton to conclude: "We haven't seen a book with this much plot, so suspensefully and expertly deployed, in too long a time." In the novel, Stanley is wrongly accused of stealing a pair of sneakers and is sent to Texas's Camp Green Lake for bad boys as punishment. There the harsh fe-male warden assigns him the task—along with other boys held there—of digging five-feet-deep holes in the camp's dried-up lake bed. A *Publishers Weekly* critic, calling the book "a wry and loopy novel," asserted: "Just when it seems as though this is going to be a weird YA cross between *One Flew over the Cuckoo's Nest* and *Cool Hand Luke*, the story takes off—along with Stanley" as he and his new buddy, Zero, manage to escape. What follows, the *Publishers Weekly* commentator added, is a "dazzling blend of social commentary, tall tale and magic realism," as Stanley goes about getting rid of the Yelnats curse that has plagued his family for three generations. *School Library Journal* contributor Alison Follos also praised Sachar's novel, maintaining: "A multitude of colorful characters coupled with the skillful braiding of ethnic folklore, American legend, and contemporary issues is a brilliant achievement. There is no question, kids will love *Holes*."

Eight years after the publication of *Holes*, Sachar returned to that literary universe for *Small Steps*, a sequel of sorts. The work focuses on a secondary character from *Holes*: Theodore "Armpit" Johnson, an African-American teen who has returned home to Austin after the closing of Camp Green Lake. While working as a landscaper and attending summer school, Armpit creates a list of five "small steps" to help him get his life back in order, drawing inspiration from his ten-year-old neighbor, Ginny, who has cerebral palsy. Unfortunately, Armpit's devious buddy from Green Lake, X-Ray, persuades him to join a ticket-scalping scheme, targeting an upcoming concert appearance by pop sensation Kaira DeLeon as their opportunity to turn a hefty profit. "Complications ensue, though they are not always the ones you expect, which is part of Sachar's appeal. His prose is clear and relaxed, and funny in a low-key, observant way," commented A.O. Scott in the *New York Times Book Review*.

"Like *Holes*," Connie Tyrrell Burns reported in *School Library Journal*, "*Small Steps* is a story of redemption, of the triumph of the human spirit, of self-sacrifice, and of doing the right thing." In *Kliatt*, Paula Rohrlick described *Small Steps* as "an affecting story, with humorous moments, suspense, and romance, too," and *Booklist* contributor Jennifer Mattson applauded Sachar's nuanced portrait of Armpit, observing that readers "will eagerly follow the sometimes stumbling, sometimes sprinting progress of [the] fallible yet heroic protagonist."

An accomplished tournament bridge player, Sachar offers readers an intriguing look into that world in *The Cardturner: A Novel about a King, a Queen, and a Joker*. During the summer before his senior year of high school, Alton Richards goes to work for his ailing and irascible great-uncle, Lester Trapp, whose vast fortune appeals to Alton's greedy and cynical parents. A world-class bridge master, Lester has gone blind and needs Alton to serve as his "cardturner," telling Uncle Lester

Bestselling author of *HOLES*

LOUIS SACHAR

THE C♠RDTURNER

A Novel About
a King, a Queen,
and
a Joker

Cover of **The Cardturner,** *Sachar's multigenerational novel in which a slacker teen changes his perspective on life after learning the game of* **bridge.** (Jacket cover copyright © 2010 by Delacorte Press. Reproduced by permission of Delacorte Press, an imprint of Random House Children's Books, a division of Random House, Inc.)

what cards he holds in his hand. Although the teen knows very little about his great-uncle and even less about bridge, he eventually develops a healthy respect for his elderly relative and comes to appreciate the complexities of the game as well. When Alton enters a relationship with Toni Castaneda, a young bridge player who knows Lester, he discovers a mystery from the elderly man's past. "What transpires is an intriguing glimpse into a crazy family full of secrets and unusual quirks," Stephanie Malosh remarked in her review of *The Cardturner* for *School Library Journal.*

Several reviewers praised Sachar's ability to incorporate the rules and lingo of bridge into his narrative for *The Cardturner.* According to *Horn Book* contributor Roger Sutton, "Alton does a good job of conveying the game and its appeal," and Catherine Hursh commented in the *Journal of Adolescent & Adult Literacy* that Sachar "manages to make a game that is very hard to understand fade into the background of the story, yet still successfully uses it to develop and prolong tension." "An obvious windfall for smart and puzzle-minded

teens, [*The Cardturner*] . . . is a great story to boot, with genuine characters . . . and real relationships," Ian Chipman noted in *Booklist.*

Whether pushing the bounds of the YA format, entertaining with the goofy goings-on at Wayside school, or following Marvin through the rocky shoals of third grade, Sachar "has shown himself a writer of humor and heart," as Sutton characterized him in the *Bulletin of the Center for Children's Books.* Discussing what he wants readers to get out of his books, Sachar explained on his home page: "Mainly my books are written to make reading enjoyable. That's my first goal with all my books, to make reading fun. I want kids to think that reading can be just as much fun, or more so, than TV or video games or whatever else they do."

Biographical and Critical Sources

BOOKS

Children's Literature Review, Volume 28, Gale (Detroit, MI), 1992.
Twentieth-Century Children's Writers, fourth edition, St. James Press (Detroit, MI), 1995.

PERIODICALS

American Theatre, April, 2002, Todd Miller, "Keep on Digging," p. 27.
Austin American-Statesman, January 8, 2006, Jeff Salamon, "When We Last Read Louis Sachar . . .," p. L1.
Book, July-August, 2003, Kathleen Odean, "Unanimous Verdict: For These Lawyers, the Decision's In: Kids Are a More Rewarding Audience than Jurors," p. 31.
Booklist, September 1, 1983, Ilene Cooper, review of *Someday Angeline,* p. 91; November 1, 1987, Ilene Cooper, review of *Sixth Grade Secrets,* p. 484; May 1, 1989, Carolyn Phelan, review of *Wayside School Is Falling Down,* p. 1553; January 1, 2006, Jennifer Mattson, review of *Small Steps,* p. 101; May 15, 2010, Ian Chipman, review of *The Cardturner: A Novel about a King, a Queen, and a Joker,* p. 40.
Bulletin of the Center for Children's Books, February, 1993, Deborah Stevenson, review of *Why Pick on Me?,* pp. 167-168; March, 1995, Deborah Stevenson, review of *Wayside School Gets a Little Stranger,* p. 248; September-October, 1998, Roger Sutton, review of *Holes,* pp. 593-595.
Emergency Librarian, May-June, 1982, Joan McGrath, review of *Johnny's in the Basement.*
Horn Book, July, 1999, Louis Sachar, transcript of Newbery Medal acceptance speech, p. 410, and Carla and Sherre Sachar, "Louis Sachar," p. 418; January, 2000, review of *Holes,* p. 43, and Roger Sutton, review of *A Flying Birthday Cake?,* p. 83; November, 2000, Roger Sutton, review of *Super Fast, Out of Control!,* p. 763; January-February, 2006, Roger Sutton, review of *Small Steps,* p. 87; May-June, 2010, Roger Sutton, review of *The Cardturner,* p. 90.

Journal of Adolescent & Adult Literacy, March, 2011, Catherine Hursh, review of *The Cardturner,* p. 468.

Kirkus Reviews, February 1, 1987, review of *There's a Boy in the Girls' Bathroom,* p. 224; April 15, 1995, review of *Wayside School Gets a Little Stranger,* p. 562; December 1, 2005, review of *Small Steps,* p. 1279; April 15, 2010, review of *The Cardturner.*

Kliatt, January, 2006, Paula Rohrlick, review of *Small Steps,* p. 12.

National Catholic Reporter, May 16, 2003, Joseph Cunneen, "Underdog Stories: Spirited Humor Livens Films about the Down-and-Out," p. 16.

New York Post, (New York, New York), January 21, 2006, Billy Heller, "Dig It!: The Author of *Holes* Steps into a Whole New Tale," p. 24.

New York Times Book Review, January 15, 2006, A.O. Scott, review of *Small Steps,* p. 19; May 16, 2010, Ned Vizzini, review of *The Cardturner,* p. 21.

Publishers Weekly, August 12, 1983, reviews of *Johnny's in the Basement* and *Someday Angeline,* both p. 67; August 28, 1987, reviews of *Sixth Grade Secrets,* p. 80; June 27, 1998, review of *Holes,* p. 78; February 17, 2003, "For Those Who Dig Holes," p. 77; November 14, 2005, review of *Small Steps,* p. 70; April 5, 2010, review of *The Cardturner,* p. 63.

Reading Teacher, October, 1988, Sam Leaton Sebesta, review of *There's a Boy in the Girls' Bathroom,* p. 83; May, 1990, Lee Galda, review of *Wayside School Is Falling Down,* p. 671; December-January, 1999, Cyndi Giorgis and Nancy J. Johnson, "Caldecott and Newbery Medal Winners for 1999," p. 338.

School Librarian, autumn, 2010, Marzena Currie, review of *The Cardturner,* p. 182.

School Library Journal, December, 1981, Jack Forman, review of *Johnny's in the Basement,* p. 68; April, 1987, David Gale, review of *There's a Boy in the Girls' Bathroom,* p. 103; March, 1993, Kenneth E. Kowen, review of *Kidnapped at Birth?,* p. 186; September, 1998, Alison Follos, review of *Holes,* p. 210; January, 2000, Brian E. Wilson, interview with Sachar, p. 63; September, 2003, Elaine E. Knight, review of *Stanley Yelnats' Survival Guide to Camp Green Lake,* p. 220; January, 2006, Connie Tyrrell Burns, review of *Small Steps,* p. 143; June, 2010, Stephanie Malosh, review of *The Cardturner,* p. 118.

Seattle Post-Intelligencer, January 10, 2006, Cecelia Goodnow, "Step by *Steps* Louis Sachar Eases Back to the Literary Scene with a Spinoff of His Kids Classic, *Holes,*" p. E1.

Texas Monthly, September, 1999, Anne Dingus, interview with Sachar, p. 121.

USA Today, January 10, 2006, Jacqueline Blais, "For Sachar, Childhood Is Perilous," p. 4D.

Writer, October, 2004, Sharon Miller Cindrich, "Connecting with Kids: Louis Sachar on His Newbery-Winning Novel Holes and the Importance of Engaging His Young Readers," p. 20.

Writing!, September, 2002, "Louis Sachar's *Holes* Wins Readers' Choice Award for Teen Books," p. 3; November-December, 2002, Kate Davis, "Paint a Picture for the Reader," p. 26.

ONLINE

Louis Sachar Home Page, http://www.louissachar.com (January 15, 2012).

Public Broadcasting System Web site, http://www.pbs.org/ (November 24, 1998), Elizabeth Farnsworth, "Online NewsHour: Edward Ball."

Random House Web site, http://www.randomhouse.com/ (January 15, 2012), "Author Spotlight: Louis Sachar."

Scholastic Web site, http://www.scholastic.com/teachers/ (January 15, 2012), profile of Sachar."*

*   *   *

SCHWARTZ, Howard 1945-

Personal

Born April 21, 1945, in St. Louis, MO; son of Nathan (a dealer in jewelry and antiques) and Bluma Schwartz; married Tsila Khanem (a calligrapher and illustrator), June 25, 1978; children: Shira, Nati, Miriam. *Education:* Washington University, St. Louis, MO, B.A., 1967, M.A., 1969. *Politics:* "Pro-human." *Religion:* Jewish.

Addresses

Office—Department of English, University of Missouri—St. Louis, 1 University Blvd., St. Louis, MO 63121. *E-mail*—howard.schwartz@gmail.com.

Career

Poet, author, and educator. Forest Park Community College, St. Louis, MO, instructor in English, 1969-70; University of Missouri, St. Louis, MO, instructor, then professor, 1970-2010, now professor emeritus of English.

Awards, Honors

First place award, Academy of American Poets, 1969; poetry fellow, St. Louis Arts and Humanities Commission, 1981; selected among 100 Best Children's Books, New York Public Library, 1983, for *Elijah's Violin and Other Jewish Fairy Tales,* and 1996, for *The Wonder Child and Other Jewish Fairy Tales;* American Book Award, Before Columbus Foundation, 1984, for *The Captive Soul of the Messiah;* notable book selection, American Library Association, 1991, and National Jewish Book Award nomination in children's literature category, and Sydney Taylor Book Award, Association of Jewish Libraries, both 1992, all for *The Diamond Tree;* honorary doctorate, Spertus Institute of Jewish Studies, 1996; Notable Book for Children selection, *Smithsonian* magazine, 1996, for *Next Year in Jerusalem,* and 2000, for *The Day the Rabbi Disappeared;* Aesop Prize, American Folklore Society, 1996, for *Next Year in Jerusalem,* and 2000, for *The Day the Rabbi Disappeared;* National Jewish Book Award in children's literature category, 1996, for *Next Year in Jerusalem,* and

2000, for *The Day the Rabbi Disappeared;* Anne Izard Storytellers' Choice Award, 1998, for both *The Wonder Child and Other Jewish Fairy Tales,* and *A Coat for the Moon and Other Jewish Tales;* National Jewish Book Award finalist in Jewish thought category, 1999, for *Reimagining the Bible;* Young Adult Book Award, Keystone State Reading Association, 2001, for *Ask the Bones;* inducted into University City High School Hall of Fame, 2001; Notable Children's Book of Jewish Content Honor designation, Association of Jewish Libraries, and National Jewish Book Award finalist in children's literature category, both 2002, and Aesop Accolade, American Folklore Society, 2003, all for *Invisible Kingdoms;* National Jewish Book Award in reference category, 2005, for *Tree of Souls;* Notable Book selection, Association of Jewish Libraries, and Koret International Jewish Book Award, Koret Foundation/National Foundation for Jewish Culture, both 2006, both for *Before You Were Born;* Sydney Taylor Book Award, 2010, for *Gathering Sparks.*

Writings

FICTION

A Blessing over Ashes, Tree Books (Berkeley, CA), 1974.

Midrashim: Collected Jewish Parables, Menard Press (London, England), 1976.

The Captive Soul of the Messiah, Cauldron Press, 1980, published as *The Captive Soul of the Messiah: New Tales about Reb Nachman,* illustrated by Mark Podwal, Schocken (New York, NY), 1983.

Rooms of the Soul, illustrated by T. Schwartz, Rossel Books (New York, NY), 1984.

Adam's Soul: The Collected Tales of Howard Schwartz, Jason Aronson (Northvale, NJ), 1992.

The Four Who Entered Paradise (novella), illustrated by Devis Grebu, Jason Aronson (Northvale, NJ), 1995.

POETRY

Vessels, Unicorn Press (Greensboro, NC), 1976.

Gathering the Sparks: Poems, 1965-1979, Singing Wind Press (St. Louis, MO), 1979.

Sleepwalking beneath the Stars, illustrated by John Brandi, BkMk Press (Kansas City, MO), 1992.

Breathing in the Dark Mayapple Press, 2011.

FOR CHILDREN

(With Barbara Rush) *The Diamond Tree: Jewish Nursery Tales from around the World,* illustrated by Uri Shulevitz, HarperCollins (New York, NY), 1991.

(With Barbara Rush) *The Sabbath Lion: A Jewish Folktale from Algeria,* illustrated by Stephen Fieser, HarperCollins (New York, NY), 1992.

Next Year in Jerusalem: 3,000 Years of Jewish Stories, illustrated by Neil Waldman, Viking Children's Books (New York, NY), 1996, published as *Jerusalem of Gold: Jewish Stories of the Enchanted City,* Jewish Lights (Woodstock, VT), 2003.

(With Barbara Rush) *The Wonder Child and Other Jewish Fairy Tales,* illustrated by Stephen Fieser, HarperCollins (New York, NY), 1996.

(With Barbara Rush) *A Coat for the Moon and Other Jewish Tales,* illustrated by Michael Iofin, Jewish Publication Society (Philadelphia, PA), 1999.

(With Arielle North Olson) *Ask the Bones: Scary Stories from around the World,* illustrated by David Linn, Viking (New York, NY), 1999.

The Day the Rabbi Disappeared: Jewish Holiday Tales of Magic, illustrated by Monique Passicot, Viking (New York, NY), 2000.

A Journey to Paradise and Other Jewish Tales, Pitspopany Press (Jerusalem, Israel), 2000.

Invisible Kingdoms: Jewish Tales of Angels, Spirits, and Demons, HarperCollins (New York, NY), 2001.

(Reteller) *Before You Were Born,* illustrated by Kristina Swarner, Roaring Brook Press (Brookfield, CT), 2005.

(Reteller with Arielle North Olson) *More Bones: Scary Stories from around the World,* illustrated by E.M. Gist, Viking (New York, NY), 2008.

Gathering Sparks, illustrated by Kristina Swarner, Roaring Brook Press (New York, NY), 2010.

EDITOR

Imperial Messages: One Hundred Modern Parables, Avon Books (New York, NY), 1976, 3rd edition published as *Tales of Modern Wisdom,* Random House (New York, NY), 1996.

For a Few Hours Only: Selected Poems of Shlomo Vinner, Singing Bone Books, 1976.

(With Anthony Rudolf) *Voices within the Ark: The Modern Jewish Poets,* Avon Books/Pushcart Press (New York, NY), 1980.

Elijah's Violin and Other Jewish Fairy Tales, illustrated by Linda Heller, calligraphy by wife, Tsila Schwartz, Harper (New York, NY), 1983, revised edition, Oxford University Press (New York, NY), 1994.

Gates to the New City: A Treasury of Modern Jewish Tales, Avon Books (New York, NY), 1983, 2nd edition, J. Aronson (Northvale, NJ), 1991.

Miriam's Tambourine: Jewish Folktales from around the World, illustrated by Lloyd Bloom, Free Press (New York, NY), 1986.

The Dream Assembly: Tales of Rabbi Zalman Schachter-Shalomi, illustrated by Yitzhak Greenfield, Amity House (Amity, NY), 1987, second edition, Gateways (Nevada City, CA), 1990.

Lilith's Cave: Jewish Tales of the Supernatural, illustrated by Uri Shulevitz, Harper (New York, NY), 1987.

Jerusalem as She Is: New and Selected Poems of Shlomo Vinner, BkMk Press (Kansas City, MO), 1990.

Gabriel's Palace: Jewish Mystical Tales, Oxford University Press (New York, NY), 1993.

(With Barbara Raznick) *First Harvest: Jewish Writing in St. Louis, 1991-1997,* Brodsky Library Press (St. Louis, MO), 1997.

Tree of Souls: The Mythology of Judaism, illustrated by Caren Loebel-Fried, Oxford University Press (New York, NY), 2004.

(With Barbara Raznick) *New Harvest: Jewish Writing in St. Louis, 1998-2005,* Brodsky Library Press (St. Louis, MO), 2005.

(And reteller) *Leaves from the Garden of Eden: One Hundred Classic Jewish Tales,* illustrated by Kristina Swarner, calligraphy by Tsila Schwartz, Oxford University Press (New York, NY), 2008.

(With Barbara Raznick) *Winter Harvest: Jewish Writing in St. Louis, 2006-2011,* Brodsky Library Press (St. Louis, MO), 2012.

OTHER

Dream Journal, 1965-1974, Tree Books (Berkeley, CA), 1975.

(Translator) *Lyrics and Laments: Selected Translations from Hebrew and Yiddish,* BkMk Press (Kansas City, MO), 1980.

Reimagining the Bible: The Storytelling of the Rabbis (essays), Oxford University Press (New York, NY), 1998.

Contributor to books, including *Heartland II: Poets of the Midwest,* edited by Lucien Stryk, Northern Illinois University Press (DeKalb, IL), 1975; *A Big Jewish Book,* edited by Jerome Rothenberg, Doubleday (New York, NY), 1978; *Wandering Stars II,* edited by Jack Dunn, Doubleday, 1981; *Voices from the Interior: Poets of Missouri,* edited by Robert Stewart, BkMk Press (Kansas City, MO), 1982; *Missouri Short Fiction,* edited by Conger Beasley, Jr., BkMk Press, 1985; *First Love,* edited by Roy Finamore, Stewart, Tabori & Chang, 1986; *Reading between the Lines: New Stories from the Bible,* edited by David A. Katz and Peter Lovenheim, Jason Aronson (Northvale, NJ), 1996; and *Jewish American Poetry: Poems, Commentary, and Reflections,* edited by Jonathan N. Barron and Eric Murphy Selinger, Brandeis University Press, 2000. Editor, "Hebrew Poetry Translation Series," Cauldron Press, 1979-83. Contributor of articles, poems, and stories to literary journals, including *American Poetry Review, Judaism, Literary Review, Midstream,* and *Parabola.* Former coeditor, *Reflections* and *Tambourine.* Guest editor, *Natural Bridge,* issues 9 and 15.

Author's work has been translated into Dutch, French Korean, Russian, and Spanish.

Adaptations

The Sabbath Lion: A Jewish Folk Tale from Algeria was adapted as a cartoon feature, BBC-TV, 1996. The stories in *Gabriel's Palace: Jewish Mystical Tales* were adapted as a play, produced in England by the Besht Tellers, 1996. Six stories from *Lilith's Cave* were adapted for the stage as *Kabbalah: Scary Jewish Tales,* produced in Los Angeles, CA, 2000, and in Chicago, IL, as *The Speaking Head: Scary Jewish Tales.* Folk tales by Schwartz were broadcast on the radio series *One People, Many Stories,* KCSN-Radio, Los Angeles, CA.

Sidelights

Known for his focus on Jewish traditions, Howard Schwartz has produced fiction, nonfiction, and poetry as well as editing several anthologies during his long career writing for both children and adults. In searching for themes and images for his work in various genres, Schwartz often finds inspiration in biblical, midrashic, and kabbalistic lore. Many of his works retell ancient folktales, reflecting his belief in the importance of passing cultural traditions from one generation to the next. Schwartz's poetry frequently reflects the dreamlike and mysterious elements of Jewish mythology, while his books for children include Jewish folk tales, scary stories, and history.

"When I was sixteen, I worked at a camp in the Ozarks," Schwartz once commented, "and when I had my first day off, I spent it in the state library in Jefferson City reading old stories of J.D. Salinger's from *The Saturday Evening Post* on microfilm. . . . I found the whole experience thrilling, and as I walked out of the library that day I made to a decision about what to do with my life: I decided to be a writer, because that way I could leave some part of myself behind. . . . I didn't tell anyone about my decision, but my life was changed forever. I had a secret purpose, and I carried it with me wherever I went.

"In 1965, when I was twenty, my girlfriend broke up with me. One day not long after that I was sitting at home in front of my typewriter when I started banging

Neil Walman creates the stylized art for Howard Schwartz's story collection **Next Year in Jerusalem.** (Illustration © 1996 Neil Waldman. Reproduced by permission of Viking, an imprint of Penguin Young Readers Group, a member of Penguin Group (USA), Inc., 345 Hudson Street, New York, NY 10014. All rights reserved.)

out angry lines about her. I would write a few words and hit the carriage return. After writing a few pages this way, I looked at them and realized, with amazement and disbelief, that I had just written a poem. My very first one. From at that instant, I forgot about my girlfriend and started writing poems. I must have written a hundred poems in the next few months. I was filled with inspiration, and thrilled, at the age of twenty, to finally be fulfilling my destiny as a writer.

"In 1967 I began to keep a journal of my dreams, and I have continued to do so ever since. I have always been vividly aware of my dreams, and now I began to recognize the possibilities of using dream images and subject matter in my poems. This turned out to be a very fruitful decision for me, as dreams have proven to be one of my primary sources of inspiration.

"From 1965-1968 I wrote poems exclusively. During that time my only ambition was to be a poet. But in 1968 something happened that caused me to change my mind. I had a very powerful dream in which I played a bamboo flute and became one with the music. I wanted to write a poem based on this dream, but no matter how many times I revised it, it didn't seem to work. At last, out of desperation, I tried to write it as prose, and I was astonished to find that it worked perfectly that way. But I didn't want to include any prose pieces in my book of poems, and I didn't know what to do with it. So, being of an obsessive nature, I decided to write a book of parables to go along with it. These were eventually collected in my first book, *A Blessing over Ashes,* published in 1974. Ever since, I have divided my creative efforts between poetry and fiction." Following a stroke in the fall of 2011, Schwartz retired from the university and has since devoted himself to writing poetry; his fourth verse collection, *Breathing in the Dark,* was produced the same year with a fifth collection, *The Library of Dreams,* to follow.

Schwartz's fictional works "are in part original, in part recreations of ancient legends, a conjunction of personal search and dreaming with mythical or timeless patterns or cycles," reported Francis Landy in a *Jewish Quarterly* review of the story collection *The Captive Soul of the Messiah: New Tales about Reb Nachman.* Anthologies of Jewish literature—whether prose or poetry—are among his best-known works and arise from his belief that it is vital to pass on the Jewish literary heritage to new generations. Schwartz collects poems from forty countries and translated from over twenty languages in *Voices within the Ark: The Modern Jewish Poets,* while tales gleaned from oral traditions and written sources are collected in *Elijah's Violin and Other Jewish Fairy Tales.* The latter book treats readers to "a feast of images, characters, places, wonderment—all fused together by the sense that all these stories have been told for many years . . . by Jews wherever they have lived," explained Peninnah Schram in a review of the anthology for the *Melton Journal.* "By retelling and compiling all of these fairy tales . . . ," Schram continued, "Schwartz has reestablished certain powerful themes in our Jewish tradition which are not widely known in our time."

Schwartz introduces the idea of Jewish mythology in *Tree of Souls: The Mythology of Judaism.* a book that gained distinction as a Netlibrary Book of the Month and won the National Jewish Book Award in 2005. The term "mythology" frequently implies stories of interaction between a pantheon of deities, and so Judaism, which has but one God, would seem to be outside the realm of traditional mythology. The author argues, however, that there is much room for such interpretation in the Bible, and that interpretation gives rise to mythology. He references 700 Jewish myths in his book, organizing them into thematic categories. Some are familiar, but most are not, even though they have ties to well-known Bible stories. *Tree of Souls* is a "remarkable" work that will be of interest to scholars and casual readers, stated Ilene Cooper in her review of the work for *Booklist,* and *Library Journal* reviewer David B. Levy recommended Schwartz's anthology as an "excellent book of wondrous stories."

Recalling the inspiration for writing *Tree of Souls,* Schwartz once recalled: "It all goes back to fourth grade, when I discovered those great children's books of world mythology, the ones with pictures of Zeus throwing lightning bolts. I read them with great fascination but I noticed that while they had Greek and Roman and Norse and Indian and Chinese and many other mythologies, they didn't include Jewish mythology. So I raised my hand in class and asked my teacher why. And the teacher said, quite definitively, 'Because there is no Jewish mythology!' This answer perplexed me. It didn't seem fair. So being the persistent type, I kept asking this question all the way through high school and always got the same reply. By college I started reading the great masters of mythology—C.G. Jung, Joseph Campbell, Mircea Eliade—but they also had little or nothing to say about Jewish mythology. So by the time I had edited four collections of Jewish folklore and encountered such powerfully mythic figures as Lilith and the *Shekhinah,* I decided that I would set out to prove that there was such a thing as Jewish mythology. I worked on . . . *Tree of Souls* for twelve years—far longer than I had anticipated—and I regard it as the major book of my career."

Schwartz writes for children with the goal of making Jewish cultural traditions accessible to new generations. In *The Diamond Tree: Jewish Tales from around the World,* for example, he offers fifteen short tales that, while specifically Jewish, are also expressions of stories that are found in many cultures. Aimed at readers between ages seven and ten, the stories include "splendid" explications of ideas or characters that might be unfamiliar for readers, blending these sections "smoothly" into the text, according to a *Publishers Weekly* reviewer. Schwartz also showed his interest in similarities among world cultures in his anthology *Imperial Messages:*

One Hundred Modern Parables. In this collection, represented authors range from the very famous to the more obscure; included are Bob Dylan, Paul Bowles, Italo Calvino, and Isak Dinesen. A reviewer for *Publishers Weekly* stated that the careful organization, diverse authors, and wide range of story types make *Imperial Messages* "a valuable reference as well as a delight." A similar format was used in *The Wonder Child and Other Jewish Fairy Tales,* in which traditional tales passed down by oral tradition in countries such as Egypt, Morocco, and Libya are presented in an "upbeat" style, according to Stephanie Zvirin in *Booklist.*

Other similar collections are *Ask the Bones: Scary Stories from around the World* and *More Bones: Scary Stories from around the World,* both coedited with Arielle North Olson. Both books include twenty-two stories from diverse cultures, all having in common a dark tone and some grisly events unfolding. A reviewer for *Horn Book* judged *Ask the Bones* to be suitable as a way to introduce young readers to horror fiction and the supernatural because, "satisfyingly," villains often meet up with justice as recompense for their dark deeds.

Schwartz's other collections for young readers include *A Journey to Paradise and Other Jewish Tales,* which features magical stories illustrating the traditional humor and morals of the Jewish people, and *Invisible Kingdoms: Jewish Tales of Angels, Spirits, and Demons,* in which nine stories focus on the mysterious and employ "language both spare and rhythmic" to create "a haunting and haunted mood," according to *Horn Book* reviewer Susan P. Bloom. The twelve stories Schwartz selects for *The Day the Rabbi Disappeared: Jewish Holiday Tales of Magic* mix magic and the traditions of a particular Jewish holiday, whether it be Rosh Hodesh, Hanukkah, Passover, Rosh Hashanah, Yom Kippur, Purim, or the weekly Shabbat (Sabbath). Illustrated by Monique Passicot, each of these mystical stories centers on a well-known Jewish leader who, at a unique time and place in history, joined with God to create a miracle. These tales are rooted in many cultures, and Schwartz augments each of the twelve with "rich and highly readable notes about the history of the holiday, the importance of the rabbi, and the source of the story," according to a *Horn Book* critic.

Schwartz collaborates with artist Kristina Swarner on a pair of picture books: *Before You Were Born* and *Gathering Sparks. Before You Were Born* uses a Rabbinical legend to explain the indentation above the upper lip on the human face. Before a child is born, according to the story, it is told the secrets of the world, but prior to its earthly birth the angel Lailah seals its lips, erasing the child's memory of all it has learned before birth but keeping this knowledge locked within its soul. A *Publishers Weekly* reviewer praised *Before You Were Born* as a "sweet exegesis of an intriguing phenomenon," and Julie Cummins commented in *Booklist* that Schwartz's use of "spare, serene language" in his free-verse text would be comforting to many young children.

A multigenerational tale, *Gathering Sparks* finds a grandfather explaining where stars come from to a small grandchild, using the early-sixteenth-century notion of Rabbi Isaac Luria of Safed regarding the ten ships of light that were sent by God across the heavens. Shattered into many pieces, with each piece representing an act of kindness, the ships' lost cargo remains scattered across the sky for mankind to recover by performing benevolent acts on earth. Swarner's colorful art "creates mysterious effects," Carolyn Phelan wrote, adding in her *Booklist* review that *Gathering Sparks* is "a quietly lovely picture book." The book's "language is simple, personal, and poetic," according to *School Library Journal* contributor Donna Cardon, the critic adding that Schwartz's "use of the second person adds a sense of intimacy" to his story.

Biographical and Critical Sources

BOOKS

Gitenstein, R. Barbara, *Apocalyptic Messianism and Contemporary Jewish-American Poetry,* State University of New York Press (Albany, NY), 1987.

Schwartz, Howard, and Barbara Raznick, editor, *First Harvest: Jewish Writing in St. Louis, 1991-1997,* Brodsky Library Press (St. Louis, MO), 1997.

PERIODICALS

Booklist, September 15, 1996, Stephanie Zvirin, review of *The Wonder Child and Other Jewish Fairy Tales,* p. 236; May 1, 1999, Helen Rosenberg, review of *Ask the Bones: Scary Stories from around the World,* p. 1584; April 15, 2000, Ellen Mandel, review of *A Journey to Paradise and Other Jewish Tales,* p. 1549; October 1, 2001, Ilene Cooper, review of *The Day the Rabbi Disappeared: Jewish Holiday Tales of Magic,* p. 333; October 1, 2004, Ilene Cooper, review of *Tree of Souls: The Mythology of Judaism,* p. 306; May 15, 2005, Julie Cummins, review of *Before You Were Born,* p. 1662; August 1, 2010, Carolyn Phelan, review of *Gathering Sparks,* p. 59.

Commentary, July, 1981, review of *Voices within the Ark: The Modern Jewish Poets,* p. 55.

Horn Book, May, 1999, review of *Ask the Bones,* p. 344; November, 1999, Susan P. Bloom, review of *A Coat for the Moon and Other Jewish Tales,* p. 751; November-December, 2002, Susan P. Bloom, review of *Invisible Kingdoms: Jewish Tales of Angels, Spirits, and Demons,* p. 769.

Jewish Book Annual, 1995-96, Marc Bregman, "The Art of Retelling," p. 177.

Jewish Quarterly, summer, 1977, Francis Landy, review of *The Captive Soul of the Messiah: New Tales about Reb Nachman.*

Kirkus Reviews, October 1, 2002, review of *Invisible Kingdoms,* p. 1480; July 1, 2010, review of *Gathering Sparks.*

Library Journal, September 1, 2004, David B. Levy, review of *Tree of Souls,* p. 160.

Melton Journal, summer, 1984, Peninnah Schram, review of *Elijah's Violin and Other Jewish Fairy Tales.*

New York Times Book Review, January 4, 1981, Harold Bloom, review of *Voices within the Ark.*

Present Tense, winter, 1985, Gerald Jonas, review of *Rooms of the Soul,* p. 63.

Publishers Weekly, October 18, 1991, review of *The Diamond Tree: Jewish Tales from around the World,* p. 62; April 6, 1992, review of *Imperial Messages: One Hundred Modern Fables,* p. 52; May 25, 1998, review of *Next Year in Jerusalem: 3,000 Years of Jewish Stories,* p. 92; February 8, 1999, review of *Ask the Bones,* p. 215; March 13, 2000, review of *A Journey to Paradise and Other Jewish Tales,* p. 82; September 25, 2000, review of *The Day the Rabbi Disappeared,* p. 114; October 28, 2002, review of *Invisible Kingdoms,* p. 69; June 30, 2003, review of *The Day the Rabbi Disappeared,* p. 76; April 18, 2005, review of *Before You Were Born,* p. 61; July 26, 2010, review of *Gathering Sparks,* p. 72.

School Library Journal, June, 2000, Marcia W. Posner, review of *A Journey to Paradise and Other Jewish tales,* p. 136; August, 2000, Susan Scheps, review of *The Day the Rabbi Disappeared,* p. 207; August, 2010, Donna Cardon, review of *Gathering Sparks,* p. 86.

St. Louis Jewish Light, May, 1980, Joseph Schraibman, review of *The Captive Soul of the Messiah.*

St. Louis Post-Dispatch, January 4, 1981, Carolyn McKee, review of *Voices within the Ark.*

ONLINE

Howard Schwartz Home Page, http://www.howardschwartz.com (January 9, 2012).

University of Missouri—St. Louis Web site, http://www.umsl.edu/ (January 9, 2012), "Howard Schwartz."

*   *   *

SCIESZKA, Jon 1954-

Personal

Last name rhymes with "Fresca"; born September 8, 1954, in Flint, MI; son of Louis (an elementary school principal) and Shirley (a nurse) Scieszka; married Jerilyn Hansen (an art director); children: Casey (daughter), Jake. *Education:* Attended Culver Military Academy; Albion College, B.A. (pre-med), 1976; Columbia University, M.F.A. (creative writing), 1980.

Addresses

Home—Brooklyn, NY.

Career

Writer and educator. Manhattan Day School, New York, NY, elementary school teacher, beginning 1980. Worked variously as a painter, lifeguard, and magazine writer.

Jon Scieszka (Photograph by Brian Smale. Reproduced by permission.)

Awards, Honors

New York Times Best Books of the Year citation, American Library Association (ALA) Notable Children's Book citation, Maryland Black-Eyed Susan Picture Book Award, and *Parenting* Reading Magic Award, all 1989, all for *The True Story of the Three Little Pigs!;* *New York Times* Best Illustrated Books of the Year citation, and ALA Notable Children's Book citation, both 1992, both for *The Stinky Cheese Man and Other Fairly Stupid Tales;* Best Book for Young Adults citation, ALA, 1996, for *Math Curse;* Top 100 Children's Books citation, National Education Association, 1999, for both *Math Curse* and *The True Story of the Three Little Pigs!;* Best Books of the Year citation, *Los Angeles Times Book Review,* and Reading Magic Award, *Parenting* magazine, both 2001, both for *Baloney (Henry P.);* Choices selection, Cooperative Children's Book Center, 2007, for *Cowboy and Octopus;* named National Ambassador for Young People's Literature, U.S. Library of Congress, 2008; Best Children's Book of the Year selection, and Irma S. Black Award Honor Book selection, both Bank Street College of Education, and One Hundred Titles for Reading and Sharing selection, New York Public Library, all 2009, all for *Robot Zot!*

Writings

PICTURE BOOKS

The True Story of the Three Little Pigs!, illustrated by Lane Smith, Viking (New York, NY), 1989, tenth anniversary edition, 1999.

The Frog Prince, Continued, illustrated by Steve Johnson, Viking (New York, NY), 1991.

The Stinky Cheese Man and Other Fairly Stupid Tales, illustrated by Lane Smith, Viking (New York, NY), 1992.

The Book That Jack Wrote, illustrated by Daniel Adel, Viking (New York, NY), 1994.

Math Curse, illustrated by Lane Smith, Viking (New York, NY), 1995.

Squids Will Be Squids: Fresh Morals, Beastly Fables, illustrated by Lane Smith, Viking (New York, NY), 1998.

Baloney (Henry P.), illustrated by Lane Smith, Viking (New York, NY), 2001.

Science Verse (with CD), illustrated by Lane Smith, Viking (New York, NY), 2004.

Seen Art?, illustrated by Lane Smith, Museum of Modern Art/Viking (New York, NY), 2005.

Cowboy and Octopus, illustrated by Lane Smith, Viking (New York, NY), 2007.

(Reteller) *Walt Disney's Alice in Wonderland*, illustrated by Mary Blair, Disney Press (New York, NY), 2008.

Robot Zot!, illustrated by David Shannon, Simon & Schuster (New York, NY), 2009.

(With Francesco Sedita) *Spaceheadz*, illustrated by Shane Prigmore, Simon & Schuster (New York, NY), 2010.

(With daughter Casey Scieszka and Steven Weinberg) *Spaceheadz, Book 2* illustrated by Shane Prigmore, Simon & Schuster (New York, NY), 2010.

(With Casey Scieszka and Steven Weinberg) *Spaceheadz, Book 3* illustrated by Shane Prigmore, Simon & Schuster (New York, NY), 2011.

"TIME WARP TRIO" READER SERIES

Knights of the Kitchen Table, illustrated by Lane Smith, Viking (New York, NY), 1991.

The Not-So-Jolly Roger, illustrated by Lane Smith, Viking (New York, NY), 1991.

The Good, the Bad, and the Goofy, illustrated by Lane Smith, Viking (New York, NY), 1992.

Your Mother Was a Neanderthal, illustrated by Lane Smith, Viking (New York, NY), 1993.

2095, illustrated by Lane Smith, Viking (New York, NY), 1995.

Tut, Tut, illustrated by Lane Smith, Viking (New York, NY), 1996.

Summer Reading Is Killing Me!, illustrated by Lane Smith, Viking (New York, NY), 1998.

It's All Greek to Me, illustrated by Lane Smith, Viking (New York, NY), 1999.

See You Later, Gladiator, illustrated by Adam McCauley, (New York, NY), 2000.

Hey Kid, Want to Buy a Bridge?, illustrated by Adam McCauley, Viking (New York, NY), 2001.

Sam Samurai, illustrated by Adam McCauley, Viking (New York, NY), 2001.

Viking It and Liking It, illustrated by Adam McCauley, Viking (New York, NY), 2002.

Me Oh Maya!, illustrated by Adam McCauley, Viking (New York, NY), 2003.

Da Wild, da Crazy, da Vinci, illustrated by Adam McCauley, Viking (New York, NY), 2004.

Oh Say, I Can't See, illustrated by Adam McCauley, Viking (New York, NY), 2005.

Marco? Polo!, illustrated by Adam McCauley, Viking (New York, NY), 2006.

"JOHN SCIESZKA'S TRUCKTOWN" SERIES; ILLUSTRATED BY THE DESIGN GARAGE

Pete's Party, Aladdin (New York, NY), 2008.

Melvin Might?, Simon & Schuster (New York, NY), 2008.

Smash! Crash!, Simon & Schuster (New York, NY), 2008.

Snow Trucking!, Aladdin (New York, NY), 2008.

Zoom! Boom! Bully, Aladdin (New York, NY), 2008.

Kat's Mystery Gift, Aladdin (New York, NY) 2009.

The Spooky Tire, Simon & Schuster (New York, NY), 2009.

Uh-oh Max, Simon & Schuster (New York, NY), 2009.

Truckery Rhymes, Simon & Schuster (New York, NY), 2009.

Dizzy Izzy, Simon & Schuster (New York, NY), 2010.

Garage Tales, Simon & Schuster (New York, NY), 2010.

Melvin's Valentine, Simon & Schuster (New York, NY), 2010.

The Great Truck Rescue, Simon & Schuster (New York, NY), 2010.

Trucksgiving, Simon & Schuster (New York, NY), 2010.

Welcome to Trucktown!, Simon & Schuster (New York, NY), 2010.

Kat's Maps, Simon & Schuster (New York, NY), 2011.

Trucks Line Up, Simon & Schuster (New York, NY), 2011.

OTHER

(Editor) *Guys Write for Guys Read: Boys' Favorite Authors Write about Being Boys*, Viking (New York, NY), 2005.

Knucklehead: Tall Tales and Mostly True Stories of Growing up Scieszka, Viking (New York, NY), 2008.

(Editor) *Guys Read: Funny Business*, Walden Pond Press (New York, NY), 2010.

(Editor) *Guys Read: Thriller*, Walden Pond Press (New York, NY), 2011.

Creator of television series "Nightmare on Joe's Street."

Adaptations

The True Story of the Three Little Pigs! was adapted as a sound recording, read by the author, Viking, 1992, and as a stage play, produced in New York, NY, 2011. *The Frog Prince, Continued* was set to music by Patrick Neher and released by ISG Publications, 1995. *The Stinky Cheese Man and Other Fairly Stupid Tales* was adapted as a stage play by John Glore, produced in Costa Mesa, CA, 1995, and by William Massolia, produced in Chicago, IL, 1997. The "Time Warp Trio" novels were adapted as a television series for PBS, and several books by others were based on the television series. Characters from Scieszka's "Trucktown" series were adapted for picture books, Simon & Schuster, beginning 2008. *Knucklehead* was adapted for audiobook, Brilliance Audio, 2009.

Sidelights

Credited on the cover of such compellingly titled books as *The Stinky Cheese Man and Other Fairly Stupid Tales, Your Mother Was a Neandertal,* and *Robot Zot!,* Jon Scieszka has earned plaudits for his wacky and irreverent children's books. Scieszka's picture books, while intended for beginning readers, have been equally popular among older children and young adults due to their sophisticated humor. "What Scieszka has done is make a book equivalent of a happy meal—taking the things that most kids like in books like humor, adventure, fairy tales, and plain old silliness, and combining them into easy-to-read tomes which will indeed appeal to an audience of all ages," explained Patrick Jones and Christine Miller in *Twentieth-Century Children's Writers.*

Scieszka has enjoyed an especially fruitful collaboration with illustrator Lane Smith, creating parodies of fables and producing wildly humorous works about aliens, time travel, and a variety of other subjects. Discussing one collaboration, *Squids Will Be Squids: Fresh Morals, Beastly Fables,* a *Publishers Weekly* reviewer concluded that author and illustrator pay "tribute to the original fables' economy and moral intent. . . . Beneath this duo's playful eccentricity readers will discover some

Scieszka teams up with cartoonist David Shannon to create the fanciful picture book **Robot Zot!** (Illustration copyright © 2009 by David Shannon. Reproduced by permission of Simon & Schuster Books for Young Readers, an imprint of Simon & Schuster Children's Publishing Division.)

powerful insights into human nature." "Our audience is hardcore silly kids," Scieszka told *Publishers Weekly* interviewer Amanda Smith. "And there are a lot of 'em out there."

Scieszka met Smith in the late 1980s, while Scieszka was working as an elementary school teacher. The two men developed several story ideas and generated a picture book based on a well-known traditional tale. *The True Story of the Three Little Pigs!* centers on Alexander T. Wolf, who believes that he has been framed for the deaths of two of the three little pigs. This "revisionist 'autobiography,'" as Stephanie Zvirin called it in her *Booklist* interview with the book's creators, presents the familiar story from a different aspect. "It turns out that Alexander . . . only wanted to borrow a cup of sugar for a birthday cake for his granny," wrote Roger Sutton in the *Bulletin of the Center for Children's Books.* An itchy nose sparked the sneeze that took the pig's house down. A similar scene plays out at the wooden home of the second pig, and poor Al continues on to the home of the third pig, where he is finally arrested, tried, and confined in the "Pig Penn." There is a sly contrast between Scieszka's "innocent wolf" narrator and Smith's sometimes morally ambiguous pictures. Alexander's grandmother, noted Sutton, "looks a bit all-the-better-to-*eat*-you-with herself, and is that a pair of bunny ears poking out of the cake batter?"

Scieszka and Smith have teamed up for several other books, among them *The Stinky Cheese Man and Other Fairly Stupid Tales,* which takes on more classic fairy tales in its narrative by Jack and the hen that laid golden eggs. "For those that are studying fairy tales at the college level," Signe Wilkinson stated in the *New York Times Book Review,* "'The Stinky Cheese Man' would be the perfect key to the genre, but no one would mistake it for the old-fashioned originals."

Scieszka and Smith continue their creative partnership with *Math Curse,* which was dubbed "one of the great books of the decade, if not of the [twentieth] century," by Dorothy M. Broderick in *Voice of Youth Advocates.* The narrator, a little girl, reflects on the statement made by her math teacher, Mrs. Fibonacci, that any situation can be stated in terms of mathematics. According to Deborah Stevenson in *Bulletin of the Center for Children's Books,* "The result is a story problem gone exponentially berserk." "It's a math curse: for the next twenty-four hours no activity remains uncontaminated by this compulsive perspective," explained Amy Edith Johnson in the *New York Times Book Review. Math Curse* slyly introduces mature elements of humor—for example, Mrs. Fibonacci likes to count using the Fibonacci series of numbers—and, like a traditional math textbook, the answers to the questions are printed upside-down on the back cover. "This isn't coating math with fun to make it palatable," remarked Stevenson, "it's genuine math as genuine fun."

Nearly ten years after the publication of *Math Curse,* Scieszka and Smith answered reader requests for a science sequel. *Science Verse* finds a student allowing the

***Scieszka teams up with artist Lane Smith to create the quirky verse collection* Science Verse.** (Illustration copyright © 2004 by Lane Smith. Reproduced by permission of Viking Children's Books, a division of Penguin Young Readers Group, a member of Penguin Group (USA), Inc., 345 Hudson Street, New York, NY 10014. All rights reserved.)

comment of a teacher, this time Mr. Newton, to change the way she thinks. As a result, she begins seeing the world in terms of the "poetry of science"—in this case, literally poetry based on scientific concepts. Food additives are featured in humorous verses based on Lewis Carroll's classic poem "Jabberwocky," while Edgar Allan Poe's "The Raven" becomes the basis for a rhyme about studying dinosaurs year after year in school. In *Booklist* Carolyn Phelan called *Science Verse* "intelligent, irreverent, inviting, and downright irresistible."

Other works have continued to issue from the Scieszka-Smith collaboration. *Squids Will Be Squids* offers up a

new twist on time-tested truisms by relating Aesopian fables with off-beat morals. "As with all successful parodies . . . the reader does not need to know the original to appreciate the caricature," commented *New York Times Book Review* contributor Patricia Marx, the critic describing *Squids Will Be Squids* as "a funny collection of warped fables." Sutton, writing in *Horn Book,* remarked that "the humor is definitely juvenile and wears a little thin, but Scieszka has perfect pitch when it comes to this kind of thing."

In *Baloney (Henry P.)* Scieszka and Smith introduce readers to a creature living on another planet who is chronically late for school. To avoid punishment, he comes up with creative excuses in an unusual language that includes many foreign words and some even coined by Scieszka; a guide at the end of the book helps readers translate. "The message of the book . . . is that mysterious words are not frightening but fun," related Ben McIntyre in the *New York Times Book Review,* the critic adding that "there is something pleasantly subversive . . . about this bug-eyed linguistic space creature."

Dubbing Scieszka and Smith "the masters of goofy," *Booklist* critic Randall Enos praised *Cowboy and Octo-*

pus as a collection of seven short tales about "the small sacrifices one must make to maintain a valued friend." In this book, Octopus and Cowboy strike up a friendship and each tries to adjust to the other's habits and preferences. Octopus samples some baked beans that Cowboy has cooked on his camp fire, while Cowboy gets to ride on his teeter-totter because of his new friend's help balancing the other end. "Those who love Scieszka and Smith's absurd humor will get the joke," concluded a *Publishers Weekly* critic, noting the story's nostalgic origins in mid-twentieth-century comic books and paper dolls. Citing *Cowboy and Octopus* for its "hi-

Lane waxes nostalgic in creating the cut-paper art that entertains readers of Scieszka's picture book Cowboy and Octopus. (Illustration copyright © 2007 by Lane Smith. Reproduced by permission of Viking Children's Books, a division of Penguin Young Readers Group, a member of Penguin Group (USA), Inc., 345 Hudson Street, New York, NY 10014. All rights reserved.)

larious" text, Shawn Brommer added in *School Library Journal* that each of the book's brief stories is resolved by using "the sudden, agreeable solutions to problems that kids often come up with."

Working with Smith, as well as with illustrator Adam McCauley, Scieszka has also produced the "Time Warp Trio" books for beginning readers. According to a *Publishers Weekly* writer, these books serve as "an introduction . . . to other genres of literature" and downplay satire and parody in favor of fast-moving plots and contemporary comedy. The "Time Warp Trio" books concern three friends—Joe, Fred, and Sam—who are able to travel through time via a magical book. They arrive at the court of King Arthur in *Knights of the Kitchen Table*, face the pirate Blackbeard in *The Not-So-Jolly Roger*, go into the future to meet their own descendants in *2095*, and have a bizarre encounters with characters from classic children's literature in *Summer Reading Is Killing Me!* According to a *Publishers Weekly* critic, the stories "demonstrate Scieszka's perfect ear for schoolyard dialogue and humor—most notably of the bodily function variety."

The adventures of Joe, Fred, and Sam almost always occur accidentally: Some conversation they have will trigger the Book and in each era that they visit, they have to find where the Book is now hidden before they can return to their own time. Because of this, the boys face such perils as warrior samurai and evil war leaders in *Sam Samurai*, raiding Vikings in *Viking It and Liking It,* and an evil high priest keen on sacrificing them to the gods in *Me Oh Maya!* Their journeys also introduce them to such notable historical characters as Thomas Alva Edison in *Hey Kid, Want to Buy a Bridge?* and Leonardo da Vinci in *Da Wild, da Crazy, da Vinci*. *Booklist* contributor Karin Snelson noted of the whole series that "the snappy dialogue and classic boy humor in this series of chapter books guarantee chuckles from the most reluctant readers."

The "Time Warp Trio" books also include *Marco? Polo!* and *Oh Say, I Can't See*. In the first, Sam, Joe, and Fred are transported by the Book to the Silk Road, a trade route that spanned the arid lands between Asia and Italy during the days of Marco Polo. Set during a conventional Christmas vacation, *Oh Say, I Can't See* finds the boys camping out with the troops of a discouraged General George Washington just in time to encourage the general to go forward with his planned crossing of the Delaware river. In *Marco? Polo!* "Scieszka continues his formula of absurdity," according to *Booklist* critic Gillian Engberg, and Kathleen Meulen wrote in *School Library Journal* that this story "is as rich in historical detail as it is in humor."

Apart from Smith, Scieszka has worked with other illustrators during his authorial career. His fairy tale *The Frog Prince, Continued* features illustrations by Steve Johnson. As the title indicates, the book takes up the fairy story "The Frog Prince" and traces it through its traditional happily-ever-after ending. In this version,

however, the disenchanted prince and his princess are not well matched; the former frog misses the pond and he annoys his new wife by trying to catch flies on his now-human tongue. Several reviewers commented on Scieszka's witty, mature perspective in *The Frog Prince, Continued*. As Mary M. Burns remarked in *Horn Book*, his "tale is a sophisticated variant on traditional themes . . . and yet is accessible to younger readers who enjoy—and understand—the art of parody and lampoon."

Like *The Stinky Cheese Man and Other Fairly Stupid Tales, The Book That Jack Wrote* operates on several different levels. The original rhyme, "The House That Jack Built," is very old—perhaps dating back to 1590, according to William S. and Ceil Baring-Gould in their *The Annotated Mother Goose*. It belongs to a class of poems known to scholars as "accumulative rhymes": it builds on a single statement and adds more and more detail with each line, like the Christmas carol "The Twelve Days of Christmas." In *The Book That Jack Wrote,* however, Scieszka and illustrator Daniel Adel turn this structure on its head by looping the last page to the first page—the title character appears on both pages crushed under a fallen portrait. So what appears to be a straight-line story is in fact a never-ending circle.

One of Scieszka's overriding goals as a writer has been to encourage reading among boys, and in his "Jon Scieszka's Trucktown" series he teams up with the Design Garage to create a series of boy-friendly titles. In *Smash! Crash!*, *Pete's Party,* and *Truckery Rhymes* he "draw[s] beginning readers into the zany world of anthropomorphic trucks," according to *School Library Journal* writer Gloria Koster. In the series readers meet Jack Truck, Dump Truck, Cement Mixer Melvin, Monster Truck Max, Gabriella Garbage Truck, Grader Kat, and Wrecking Crane Rosie. From construction sites to interstate highways, the heavy-duty-axle'd characters in the "Trucktown" books make enough sound effects—and mess—to entertain even all-boy storyhour crowds. In *Kirkus Reviews* a contributor cited the series' "combination of high-energy artwork and exuberant characters," while *School Library Journal* contributor Lynn K. Vanca wrote of series opener *Smash! Crash!* that, because of Scieszka's use of "brief catch language," the brightly illustrated story "zooms along with plenty of pizzazz and action."

Another action-packed tale, *Robot Zot!*, was illustrated by David Shannon and centers on an extraterrestrial visitor's epic battles with household appliances. Upon landing at a suburban home, the diminutive Robot Zot faces off against a series of fearsome (at least to his mind) gadgets, including a toaster, a blender, and a television set, before finding "romance" with a child's toy phone. "Boys finally get the unadulterated action, hyperbolic humor and punchy language . . . they love," a writer in *Kirkus Reviews* stated, and *School Library Journal* critic Heidi Estrin maintained that the "bold, funny, over-the-top text and art are the perfect complement to one another." Applauding Scieszka's creation of his clueless mighty mite, a *Publishers Weekly* con-

Cover of Scieszka's quirky **Spaceheadz,** *part of a chapter-book series coauthored by Francesco Sedita and featuring illustrations by Shane Prigmore.* (Illustration copyright © 2011 by Shane Prigmore. Reproduced by permission of Simon & Schuster Books for Young Readers, an imprint of Simon & Schuster Children's Publishing Division.)

tributor noted that the "comically self-deluded protagonist" in *Robot Zot!* "proves that fierce warriors of any size can still be brought to their knees by love."

Aliens of different sort are at the heart of Scieszka's "Spaceheadz" series of chapter books, which integrate new media into the narrative. Coauthored by Francesco Sedita, *Spaceheadz* introduces Michael K., a fifth grader whose finds himself at the center of a bizarre intergalactic plot. Approached by odd classmates Bob and Jennifer, who are really aliens in disguise, and meeting their leader, class hamster Major Fluffy, Michael learns that he has been chosen to recruit 3.14 million children to help him stop a plot to have Planet Earth "turned off." Complicating matters are the efforts of Agent Umber, a member of the Anti Alien Agency. Interestingly, Scieszka's text references a number of Web sites that readers can visit; according to *New York Times Book Review* critic Sam Grobart, the "sites . . . are witty, fun and full of a surprising amount of content. The online material is not some brave new effort at storytelling, as you can read the book without ever visiting any of the sites, but it's an admirable and enjoyable extension of the world Scieszka and Sedita have created."

Spaceheadz, Book 2 co-written by Scieszka's daughter, Casey, and Steven Weinberg, presents the continuing adventures of Michael K., who joins forces with classmates TJ and Venus to enlist more Spaceheadz to the cause, despite Umber's clumsy attempts to thwart Michael's alien pals. The "nutty, antic series offers more goofy fun," a writer in *Kirkus Reviews* stated, and the "joke-filled, intentionally disjointed, postmodern narration" earned praise from Todd Morning in *Booklist*. In

Spaceheadz, Book 3 Michael must search for a missing brainwave just as he comes close to reaching his goal, and as Morning noted "the plot is secondary to the slapstick gags and general mayhem."

Taking a turn as a memoirist, *Knucklehead: Tall Tales and Mostly True Stories of Growing up Scieszka* reflects on the author's own high-energy childhood as a typical boy growing up in the 1960s. Full of photographs and other boyhood ephemera, the book has the welcome familiarity of a scrapbook, and the brief text makes *Knucklehead* far from intimidating to cautious fans who want to learn more about their favorite author. *Booklist* contributor Thom Barthelmess dubbed the memoir an "arch, glib, unapologetically shame-free outing," predicting that *Knucklehead* will be a boon to Scieszka fans roped into doing a report on their favorite author. In *Kirkus Reviews* a reviewer commented on the "truly dorky" photographs that document Sciezska's childhood and predicted that *Knucklehead* "will draw chuckles of amusement from middle-graders."

Created to assist legions of less-than-enthusiastic readers, Scieszka's "Guys Read" campaign was inspired by statistics indicating that boys are far less proficient at reading than girls are. "I'm trying to fix that boys never give reading a chance," the author told Sutton in a *Horn Book* interview. "They're so impulsive and so into instant gratification, or else they turn off reading because of an experience like having to read a particular book for school." To that end, Scieszka manages *GuysRead.com* and has edited a trio of anthologies. *Guys Write for Guys Read: Boys' Favorite Authors Write about Being Boys* includes writings by such notable "guy" authors as Gary Paulsen, Laurence Yep, and Daniel Handler (who also writes as Lemony Snicket), as well as art from Mo Willems and *The Simpsons* creator Matt Groenig. A reviewer for *Publishers Weekly* noted that "the contributors keep their works succinct and enticing, allowing boys to skip about, and dip in and out." Scieszka's other collections are *Guys Read: Funny Business* and *Guys Read: Thriller.* Discussing the latter, a writer in *Kirkus Reviews* observed: "This anthology is brimming with choice stuff for guys who appreciate the uncanny, the uncouth and the un-put-down-able."

Scieszka's role as a longstanding activist for encouraging boys to read led to his appointment as the first National Ambassador for Young People's Literature by the U.S. Librarian of Congress in 2008. He told an *American Libraries* interviewer that his goal was "to be a champion for children's books and promote all the books that we have available to us. I've met all kinds of spectacular authors and it gives me great hope that there's a book out there for every kid.

Biographical and Critical Sources

BOOKS

Baring-Gould, William S., and Ceil Baring-Gould, *The Annotated Mother Goose,* Bramball House (New York, NY), 1962.

Children's Literature Review, Volume 27, Gale (Detroit, MI), 1992.

Marcus, Leonard S., *Side by Side: Five Favorite Picture Book Teams Go to Work*, Walker (New York, NY), 2001.

St. James Guide to Children's Writers, St. James Press (Detroit, MI), 1999.

Silvey, Anita, editor, *Children's Books and Their Creators*, Houghton (Boston, MA), 1995.

PERIODICALS

American Libraries, May, 2008, interview with Scieszka, p. 31.

Booklist, September 1, 1992, Stephanie Zvirin, "Jon Scieszka and Lane Smith," p. 57; November 1, 2001, Gillian Engberg, review of *Sam Samurai*, p. 475; February 1, 2002, Todd Morning, review of *Hey Kid, Want to Buy a Bridge?*, p. 939; December 1, 2002, Karin Snelson, review of *Viking It and Liking It*, p. 668; September 15, 2003, Kay Weisman, review of *Me Oh Maya!*, p. 241; July, 2004, Carolyn Phelan, review of *Science Verse*, p. 1843; August, 2004, Gillian Engberg, review of *Da Wild, da Crazy, da Vinci*, p. 1937; April 15, 2005, John Green, review of *Guys Write for Guys Read: Favorite Authors Write about Being Boys*, p. 1446, and Gillian Engberg, review of *Seen Art?*, p. 1456; November 15, 2005, Carolyn Phelan, review of *Oh Say, I Can't See*, p. 47; December 15, 2006, Gillian Engberg, review of *Marco? Polo!*, p. 48; July 1, 2007, Randall Enos, review of *Cowboy and Octopus*, p. 64; August 1, 2008, Carolyn Phelan, review of *Melvin Might?*, p. 82; September 1, 2008, Thom Barthelmess, review of *Knucklehead: Tall Tales and Mostly True Stories of Growing up Scieszka*, p. 92; August 1, 2009, Daniel Kraus, review of *Robot Zot!*, p. 81; April 1, 2010, Ian Chipman, review of *Spaceheadz*, p. 42; October 1, 2010, Michael Cart, review of *Guys Read: Funny Business*, p. 80; October 15, 2010, Todd Morning, review of *Spaceheadz, Book 2*, p. 52; December 1, 2011, Todd Morning, review of *Spaceheadz, Book 3*, p. 66.

Bulletin of the Center for Children's Books, September, 1989, Roger Sutton, review of *The True Story of the Three Little Pigs!*, p. 19; October, 1992, Roger Sutton, review of *The Stinky Cheese Man and Other Fairly Stupid Tales*, pp. 33-34; October, 1995, Deborah Stevenson, review of *Math Curse*, pp. 68-69.

Children's Digest, March-April, 2005, review of *Science Verse*, p. 26.

Children's Literature Association Quarterly, fall, 1990, Marilyn Fain Apseloff, "The Big, Bad Wolf: New Approaches to an Old Folk Tale," pp. 135-137.

Daily Telegraph (London, England), December 1, 2001, Toby Clements, "Fed up with Wearing Stone Underpants," p. 5.

Horn Book, July-August, 1991, Mary M. Burns, review of *The Frog Prince, Continued*, pp. 451-452; November-December, 1992, Mary M. Burns, review of *The Stinky Cheese Man and Other Fairly Stupid Tales*, p. 720; November, 1998, Roger Sutton, review of *Squids Will Be Squids: Fresh Morals, Beastly Fables*, p. 718; May

1, 2001, review of *Baloney (Henry P.)*, p. 316; September-October, 2004, Peter D. Sieruta, review of *Science Verse*, p. 574; May-June, 2005, Roger Sutton, review of *Guys Write for Guys Read*, p. 351; September-October, 2007, Roger Sutton, interview with Scieszka, p. 445; November-December, 2008, Roger Sutton, review of *Knucklehead*, p. 725; November-December, 2009, Roger Sutton, review of *Robot Zot!*, p. 660.

Instructor, September 1, 2001, Judy Freeman, review of *Baloney (Henry P.)*, p. 28.

Kirkus Reviews, August 15, 1994, review of *The Book That Jack Wrote*, p. 1139; January 1, 2002, review of *Hey Kid, Want to Buy a Bridge?*, p. 51; September 1, 2002, review of *Viking It and Liking It*, p. 1320; August 15, 2004, review of *Science Verse*, p. 813; April 15, 2005, review of *Seen Art?*, p. 481; May 15, 2008, review of *Pete's Party;* September 1, 2008, review of *Knucklehead;* August 1, 2009, review of *Robot Zot!;* May 15, 2010, review of *Spaceheadz;* September 15, 2010, review of *Guys Read: Funny Business;* October 15, 2010, review of *Spaceheadz, Book 2;* July 1, 2011, review of *Guys Read: Thriller.*

Los Angeles Times, May 14, 2001, Barbara Odanaka, "Getting Boys on the Same Page," sec. 5, p. 2.

New York Times Book Review, November 12, 1989, Frank Gannon, "Everybody's Favorite Swine," p. 27; May 19, 1991, Peggy Noonan, "Those Moist Amphibian Lips," p. 25; November 8, 1992, Signe Wilkinson, "No Princes, No White Horses, No Happy Endings," pp. 29, 59; November 12, 1995, Amy Edith Johnson, "Your Days Are Numbered," p. 31; November 15, 1998, Patricia Marx, "Don't Ever Listen to a Talking Bug," p. 30; May 20, 2001, Ben McIntyre, "Zerplatzen on the Speelplaats," p. 31; November 14, 2004, Natalie Angier, review of *Science Verse*, p. 24; September 11, 2005, Emily Jenkins, review of *Seen Art?*, p. 18; March 16, 2008, Gregory Cowles, review of *Smash! Crash!*, p. 14; December 21, 2008, Lisa Von Drasek, review of *Knucklehead*, p. 12; November 7, 2010, Sam Grobart, review of *Spaceheadz*, p. 28.

Parenting, May, 2001, Leonard S. Marcus, "Talking with . . . the Creators of *Baloney (Henry P.)*," p. 24.

Publishers Weekly, July 28, 1989, review of *The True Story of the Three Little Pigs!*, p. 218; May 17, 1991, reviews of *Knights of the Kitchen Table* and *The Not-So-Jolly Roger*, both p. 64; July 26, 1991, Amanda Smith, "Jon Scieszka and Lane Smith," pp. 220-221; September 28, 1992, review of *The Stinky Cheese Man and Other Fairly Stupid Tales*, pp. 79-80; July 4, 1994, review of *The Book That Jack Wrote*, p. 63; May 18, 1998, review of *Squids Will Be Squids*, p. 78; May 25, 1998, Shannon Maughan, "Summertime, and the Reading Is Easy," p. 28; February 14, 2000, Leonard S. Marcus, "Talking with Authors," p. 98; April 30, 2001, review of *Baloney (Henry P.)*, p. 76; May 7, 2001, Shannon Maughan, "You Go, Guys," p. 41; July 16, 2001, Leonard S. Marcus, "A Collaborative Effort," p. 84; August 2, 2004, review of *Science Verse*, p. 70; September 13, 2004, Shannon Maughan, interview with Scieszka, p. 38; February 21, 2005, review of *Guys Write for Guys Read*, pp. 176-177; July 16,

2007, review of *Cowboy and Octopus,* p. 162; November 26, 2007, review of *Smash! Crash!,* p. 51; August 10, 2009, review of *Robot Zot!,* p. 53; May 31, 2010, review of *Spaceheadz,* p. 47; October 18, 2010, review of *Guys Read: Funny Business,* p. 48.

School Library Journal, May, 1991, Linda Boyles, review of *The Frog Prince, Continued,* pp. 83-84; September, 1994, Nancy Menaldi-Scanlan, review of *The Book That Jack Wrote,* pp. 193, 199; November, 2001, Elaine E. Knight, review of *Sam Samurai,* p. 136; March, 2002, Kay Bowes, review of *Hey Kid, Want to Buy a Bridge?,* p. 201; January, 2003, Pat Leach, review of *Viking It and Liking It,* p. 111; December, 2003, Pat Leach, review of *Me Oh Maya!,* p. 125; September, 2004, Janet Dawson Hamilton, review of *Math Curse,* p. 58, and Grace Oliff, review of *Science Verse,* p. 179; December, 2004, Debbie Whitbeck, review of *Da Wild, da Crazy, da Vinci,* p. 122; May, 2005, Carol Ann Wilson, review of *Seen Art?,* p. 96; November, 2005, Elaine E. Knight, review of *Oh Say, I Can't See,* p. 107; December, 2006, Kathleen Meulen, review of *Marco? Polo!,* p. 116; September, 2007, Shawn Brommer, review of *Cowboy and Octopus,* p. 176; January, 2008, Lynn K. Vanca, review of *Smash! Crash!,* p. 97; February, 2008, Walter Minkel, "The Big Cheese: Our First Kids' Book Laureate Takes Literacy a Lot More Seriously Than He Takes Himself," p. 38; August, 2008, Gloria Koster, reviews of *Pete's Party* and *Zoom! Boom! Bully,* both p. 102; August, 2009, Kirsten Cutler, review of *Truckery Rhymes,* p. 93; September, 2009, Heidi Estrin, review of *Robot Zot!,* p. 134; November, 2009, Stacy Dillon, review of *The Spooky Tire,* p. 88; October, 2010, Kim Dare, review of *Guys Read: Funny Business,* p. 126; April, 2011, Mara Alpert, review of *Spaceheadz,* p. 153.

Seattle Post-Intelligencer,, February 5, 2008, Cecelia Goodnow, "Getting Guys to Read: Irreverent Writer for the Young Wants Boys to Know the Joys of Books," p. C1.

Teacher Librarian, September 1, 2000, Mary Berry, interview with Scieszka, p. 55.

Time for Kids, April 8, 2005, Kathryn R. Satterfield, "Boys Book Club."

USA Today, February 12, 2008, Greg Toppo, "This Guy Has a Read on Kids," p. 6D.

Tribune Books (Chicago, IL), July 26, 1998, Mary Harris Russell, review of *Summer Reading Is Killing Me!,* p. 7; November 15, 1998, Mary Harris Russell, review of *Squids Will Be Squids,* p. 7; June 17, 2001, Mary Harris Russell, review of *Baloney (Henry P.),* p. 4.

Voice of Youth Advocates, February, 1996, Dorothy M. Broderick, review of *Math Curse,* p. 376; February, 2011, Alissa Lauzon, review of *Guys Read: Funny Business,* p. 584.

ONLINE

GuysRead.com, http://www.guysread.com/ (January 15, 2012).

Jon Scieszka Home Page, http://www.jsworldwide.com (January 15, 2012).

KidsReads.com, http://www.kidsread.com/ (October, 2010), interview with Scieszka.*

* * *

SHELDON, Dyan
(Serena Gray, D.M. Quintano)

Personal

Born in Brooklyn, NY; children: one daughter.

Addresses

Home—England. *E-mail*—dyan@dyansheldon.co.uk.

Career

Novelist, humorist, and author of children's books.

Awards, Honors

American Library Association Recommended Book for Reluctant Young-Adult Readers designation, and New York Public Library Book for the Teen Age designation, both 1999, both for *Confessions of a Teenage Drama Queen.*

Writings

FOR CHILDREN

A Witch Got on at Paddington Station, illustrated by Wendy Smith, Dutton (New York, NY), 1987.

Alison and the Prince, illustrated by Helen Cusack, Methuen (London, England), 1988.

I Forgot, illustrated by John Rogan, Four Winds Press (New York, NY), 1988.

Jack and Alice, illustrated by Alice Garcia de Lynam, Hutchinson (London, England), 1990.

The Whales' Song, illustrated by Gary Blythe, Hutchinson (London, England), 1990, Dial (New York, NY), 1991.

Harry and Chicken, illustrated by Sue Heap, Walker Books(London, England), 1990, Candlewick Press (Cambridge, MA), 1992.

Harry the Explorer, illustrated by Sue Heap, Walker Books (London, England), 1991, Candlewick Press (Cambridge, MA), 1992.

Seymour Finds a Home, illustrated by Nigel McMullen, Simon & Schuster (New York, NY), 1991.

Lilah's Monster, illustrated by Wendy Smith, Young Piper (London, England), 1992.

My Brother Is a Visitor from Another Planet, illustrated by Derek Brazell, Viking (London, England), 1992, Candlewick Press (Cambridge, MA), 1993.

Sky Watching, illustrated by Graham Percy, Walker Books (London, England), 1992.

Harry's Holiday, illustrated by Sue Heap, Walker Books (London, England), 1992, published as *Harry on Vacation,* Candlewick Press, 1993.

The Garden, illustrated by Gary Blythe, Hutchinson (London, England), 1993, published as *Under the Moon,* Dial (New York, NY), 1994.

A Night to Remember, illustrated by Robert Crowther, Walker Books (London, England), 1993.

Only Binky, illustrated by Honey de Lacey, Methuen (London, England), 1993.

Counting Cows, illustrated by Wendy Smith, Hutchinson (London, England), 1994.

Ride On, Sister Vincent, Walker Books (London, England), 1994.

Love, Your Bear, Pete, illustrated by Tania Hurt-Newton, Candlewick Press (Cambridge, MA), 1994.

A Bad Place for a Bus Stop, Pan Macmillan (London, England), 1994.

My Brother Is a Superhero, illustrated by Derek Brazell, Viking (London, England), 1994, Candlewick Press (Cambridge, MA), 1996.

Elena the Frog, illustrated by Sue Heap, Walker Books (London, England), 1997.

Unicorn Dreams, illustrated by Neil Reed, Dial (New York, NY), 1997.

Lizzie and Charley Go Shopping, Walker Books (London, England), 1999.

Leon Loves Bugs, illustrated by Scoular Anderson, Walker Books (London, England), 2000.

Undercover Angel, Walker Books (London, England), 2000.

Undercover Angel Strikes Again, Walker Books (London, England), 2000.

Clara and Buster Go Moondancing, illustrated by Caroline Anstey, Dorling Kindersley (New York, NY), 2001.

Lizzie and Charley Go to the Movies, Walker Books (London, England), 2001.

He's Not My Dog, illustrated by Kate Sheppard, Walker Books (London, England), 2001.

Lizzie and Charley Go away for the Weekend, Walker Books (London, England), 2002.

The Last Angel, illustrated by Sophy Williams, Macmillan (London, England), 2003.

Vampire across the Way, Walker Books (London, England), 2004.

Whatever Mona Wants, Mona Gets, illustrated by Ella Okstad, Walker Books (London, England), 2005.

Drusilla and Her Brothers, illustrated by Emma Dodson, Walker Books (London, England), 2009.

Contributor to anthologies, including *Love Hurts,* Mammoth (London, England), 1994; *Funny Stories,* Walker Books (London, England), 1995; *The Second Storybook Collection,* Macdonald Young (Hemel Hempstead, England), 1995; *Stories for Six Year Olds,* Walker Books, 1995; and *Not Like I'm Jealous or Anything,* Delacorte Press (New York, NY), 2006.

Author's works have been translated into several languages, including Arabic, Bengali, Chinese, Czech, German, Polish, Spanish, Vietnamese, and Urdu.

FOR YOUNG ADULTS

Tall, Thin, and Blonde, Candlewick Press (Cambridge, MA), 1993.

The Boy of My Dreams, Candlewick Press (Boston, MA), 1997.

Confessions of a Teenage Drama Queen, Candlewick Press (Cambridge, MA), 1999.

And Baby Makes Two, Walker Books (London, England), 2000.

My Perfect Life, Candlewick Press (Cambridge, MA), 2002.

Planet Janet (also see below), Walker Books (London, England), 2002, Candlewick Press (Cambridge, MA), 2003.

Sophie Pitt-Turnbull Discovers America, Walker Books (London, England), 2003, Candlewick Press (Cambridge, MA), 2005.

Planet Janet in Orbit (also see below), Candlewick Press (Cambridge, MA), 2004.

(Under name D.M. Quintano) *Perfect,* Macmillan (London, England), 2005.

Confessions of a Hollywood Star, Walker Books (London, England), 2005, Candlewick Press (Cambridge, MA), 2006.

I Conquer Britain (companion to *Sophie Pitt-Turnbull Discovers America*), Walker Books (London, England), 2006, Candlewick Press (Cambridge, MA), 2007.

Deep and Meaningful Diaries from Planet Janet (contains *Planet Janet* and *Planet Janet in Orbit*), Candlewick Press (Cambridge, MA), 2007.

The Difficult Job of Keeping Time, Walker Books (London, England), 2008.

My Worst Best Friend, Candlewick Press (Somerville, MA), 2010.

The Crazy Things Girls Do for Love, Walker Books (London, England), 2010, Candlewick Press (Somerville, MA), 2011.

Away for the Weekend, Walker Books (London, England), 2011.

"HAUNTED" YOUNG-ADULT NOVEL SERIES

You Can Never Go Home Anymore ("Hauntings" series), Bantam (London, England), 1993.

Save the Last Dance for Me ("Hauntings" series), Bantam (New York, NY), 1993.

FOR ADULTS

Victim of Love, Heinemann (London, England), 1982, Viking (New York, NY), 1993.

The Dreams of an Average Man, Heinemann (London, England), 1985, Crown (New York, NY), 1986.

My Life as a Whale, Villard (New York, NY), 1992.

On the Road Reluctantly, Little, Brown (London, England), 1995, published as *Dream Catching: A Wander 'round the Americas,* Abacus (London, England), 1995.

Also author of books under pseudonym Serena Gray.

Adaptations

Confessions of a Teenage Drama Queen was adapted by Gail Parent as a feature film, directed by Sara Sugarman, 2004.

Sidelights

After finding success writing two novels for adults, Dyan Sheldon expanded her audience to children and, a decade later, to young adults. A prolific writer, she has penned over thirty books for children as well as over a dozen books for teen readers since beginning her career in children's literature in the late 1980s, and has even seen one of her teen novels, *Confessions of a Teenage Drama Queen,* adapted as a feature film starring actress Lindsay Lohan. Among Sheldon's other novels for teens are *Tall, Thin, and Blonde, My Perfect Life,* and the companion novels *Sophie Pitt-Turnbull Discovers America* and *I Conquer Britain,* while her chapter books *Harry and Chicken* and *My Brother Is a Superhero* appeal to elementary-grade readers.

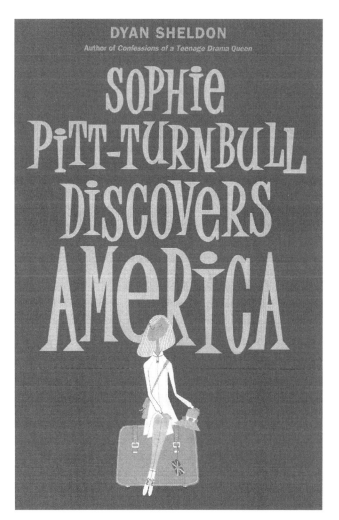

Cover of Dyan Sheldon's teen novel Sophie Pitt-Turnbull Discovers America, *featuring artwork by Phil Hankinson.* (Jacket illustration copyright © 2005 by Phil Hankinson. Reproduced by permission of Candlewick Press, Cambridge, MA.)

Although Sheldon now makes England her home, she was born in Brooklyn, New York. At age six, she and her family moved to Long Island, where her parents hoped that she could experience the benefits of fresh air, sunshine, and the freedom to roam the countryside. Although Sheldon never warmed to her rural surroundings, the move did make her more adaptable to change, and after high school she left home and spent time in upstate New York, New England, Mississippi, New Jersey, and several New York City boroughs before leaving the United States altogether. As an American in London, Sheldon quickly realized that she had many things to learn about culture and language. These experiences helped inspire both *Sophie Pitt-Turnbull Discovers America* and *I Conquer Britain.*

In *Sophie Pitt-Turnbull Discovers America* a London teen from an affluent family spends the summer in New York City, where things prove far less exciting than she had hoped. Trading places with Cherokee Salamanca, the daughter of her mother's friend from art school, Sophie finds herself taking care of Cherokee's two siblings and sharing the family's small, chaotic Brooklyn home with a dog, an iguana, and a pet pig. After learning to accept the differences between British and U.S. culture, Sophie makes some new close friends and learns to be more accepting of others in a novel that *Kliatt* reviewer Claire Rosser dubbed "lighthearted fun."

Sheldon tells Cherokee's side of the story in *I Conquer Britain,* which finds the Goth Brooklynite spending the summer living with Sophie's middle-class London family where sticking to tradition is a must. With an artist mom and a writer dad, Cherokee has been allowed free rein to be "creative" within her family's loose structure. Now, however, she sees what it is like for Sophie's mom, who has given up her art in favor of being a homemaker and catering to a demanding elderly live-in relative. Classifying the novel's plot as "farce," Claire Rosser added in *Kliatt* that in *I Conquer Britain* "Cherokee, in her own weird way, gets [Sophie's] . . . family functioning much better together." "Light and funny, Sheldon's characters are smart, offbeat and completely real," concluded a *Kirkus Reviews* writer, while in *Horn Book* Denise Moore wrote that the story's teen heroine also makes strides toward her own maturity: "she adapts, has fun, and even finds a way to help out in a family crisis."

Sixteen-year-old British teen Janet Bandry is the star of *Planet Janet* and *Planet Janet in Orbit,* two novels that unfold in diary form. Janet is frustrated with typical teen issues: annoying parents, unreasonably demanding school teachers, and worries over her place in the world. Responding to their intellectual interests in *Planet Janet* Janet and her best friend Disha decide to enter a "Dark Phase," adopting a pseudo-Bohemian pose that finds them dressing in black, dying their hair purple, piercing their noses, adopting vegetarianism, drowning their melancholy with jazz, and struggling through a challenging literary novel. Janet's self-absorbed journal entries reveal other facts that give the novel poignancy and also lead readers to the sequel. The teen's summer job, her parents' failing marriage, and Disha's all-consuming romance fill the pages of *Planet Janet in Orbit,* which finds Janet taking a break from the seriousness of the Dark Side. Praising Janet's "hilarious misadventures" in *Planet Janet in Orbit, School Library Journal* reviewer Jane Cronkhite recommended Janet's saga for fans of writers Meg Cabot and Louise Rennison, while Gillian Engberg predicted in *Booklist* that Sheldon's "fast-paced, clever writing . . . will keep teens eagerly reading." Calling Janet "an incredibly witty teen," a *Kirkus Reviews* writer concluded that *Planet Janet in Orbit* showcases its author's "deft ability with funny dialogue and a wacky setting, while still delivering a smart story."

Confessions of a Teenage Drama Queen takes readers to Woodford, the upper-crust New Jersey suburb Manhattan teen Mary Elizabeth Cep calls home after her parents relocate the family there. Disappointed by the lack of excitement in her new town, Mary soon sees an opportunity for time: being the new girl in school will allow her to transform herself into sassy fashionista

Cover of Sheldon's popular teen novel **Confessions of a Teenage Drama Queen,** *featuring artwork by Thomas Hart.* (Jacket illustration copyright © 1999 by Thomas Hart. Reproduced by permission of Candlewick Press, on behalf of Walker Books Ltd., London.)

Lola. Hoping to inject excitement into her school, "Lola" makes a new best friend in Ella, crashes a celebrity concert, and then winds up as a heroine in her own teen drama when she runs afoul of the snobby budding socialite Carla Santini. Calling *Confessions of a Teenage Drama Queen* "hilarious," *Booklist* contributor Frances Bradburn added that in Lola Sheldon creates "a real teenager—warped judgment, mercurial moods, and all." Sheldon's humorous plot pits a "deliciously despicable villainess against an irresistible heroine glittering with wit and charm," noted a *Publishers Weekly* contributor, and in *Kliatt,* Paula Rohrlick praised *Confessions of a Teenage Drama Queen* as "a fast and funny read, narrated by the lively Lola and peopled by realistic characters."

Lola returns in *My Perfect Life* and *Confessions of a Hollywood Star. My Perfect Life* finds the outspoken teen planning campaign strategy for friend Ella, who is running for student council president against the ultra popular Carla, and she pursues her own dream—becoming a famous stage actress—in *My Perfect Life.* Reviewing *My Perfect Life, Booklist* contributor Anne Malley described the novel as "a delightfully zany spoof of high school, politics, and affluent suburbia, capturing teen angst with wit and poignancy."

Lola and Ella have graduated from high school in *Confessions of a Hollywood Star,* and the larger-than-Woodford world now beckons. Thwarted by her mom from attending London's Royal Academy of Dramatic Art, the teen decides to track down a film director shooting his new film in town. Featuring what Engberg described as "over-the-top high jinks and unlikely, entertaining adventures," *Confessions of a Hollywood Star* rewards readers expecting the same level of humor generated by Sheldon's previous novels. "Lola's expressive wit and wholesomeness make her an appealing heroine," concluded Erin Schirota in her *School Library Journal* of the series.

The complex relationship between two long-time best friends is the focus of *My Worst Best Friend.* Although the two teens are very close, Gracie and Savanna actually have very little in common: quiet Gracie enjoys being outdoors and tends to be something of a wallflower in social situations, while outgoing and flirtatious Savanna is perfectly dressed and always finds a way to be the center of attention. As the girls have grown older, their differences have started to strain their friendship, however, and mellow and easygoing Gracie is tempted to take a break from her bff when Savanna pressures her into a scheme that requires Gracie to lie. Noting that Savanna's behavior is totally over the top, Frances Bradburn added in *Booklist* that the "humor and snappy dialogue" in *My Worst Best Friend* "will . . . keep teens engaged and entertained," and *School Library Journal* critic Shannon Seglin recommended Sheldon's novel for "fans of chick-lit." With a first-person narrative by Gracie that "is relaxed and unaffected," *My Worst Best Friend* "is poignant, insightful, and abso-

Cover of Sheldon's young-adult novel **My Worst Best Friend,** *which finds a young teen learning to navigate the ups and downs of female relationships.* (Jacket cover copyright 2010 by Candlewick Press. Reproduced by permission of Candlewick Press, Inc.)

lutely realistic," noted Tanya D. Auger in *Horn Book,* while Elizabeth Finlayson wrote in *School Librarian* that Sheldon's novel touches "very effectively" on "the development of relationships in the years of adolescence."

Sheldon addresses upper-elementary grades are *My Brother Is a Visitor from Another Planet* and *My Brother Is a Superhero.* The two stories focus on Adam, who finds it frustrating to unsuccessfully measure up to the standards set by his perfect older brother, Keith. Trying to distance himself from Keith, Adam joins his own friends on several adventures although he sometimes winds up needing the help that only an older brother can provide. Noting the book's value to reluctant readers, Janice Del Negro wrote in *Booklist* that the humor in *My Brother Is a Superhero* "lightens the text, and the plot moves quickly to a satisfactory conclusion."

Geared for younger elementary-grade readers, Sheldon's "Harry" series focuses on a cat-like creature from outer space who, together with a human girl named Chicken, has many adventures after landing on Earth. The two first meet in *Harry and Chicken* as Chicken

adopts the creature her parents believe is a cat and Harry quickly draws her into a series of humorous scrapes. The adventures continue in *Harry on Vacation* where the two share a camping vacation, and *Harry the Explorer.* Sheldon's "short, fast-moving story abounds with humorous exaggeration and snappy dialogue," noted a *Publishers Weekly* in a review of *Harry and Chicken.*

While Sheldon has become well known for her teen novels in recent years, one of her early works is considered something of a childhood classic. First published in 1991, *The Whales' Song* describes a young girl's visit to her grandmother's home on the coast. Lilly listens to the stories her grandmother tells about growing up with the whales, recalling that when she left the sea-bound mammals a small gift such as a shell or pretty stone, they rewarded her in return. When the girl leaves her own gift for the whales, she is rewarded later that night when she hears her name sounded in the creatures' plaintive song. Brought to life in "haunting, evocative" realistic paintings by Gary Blythe, "Sheldon's poetic text in *The Whales' Song* manages to overlay a homespun practicality with an ethereal, fairy-tale magic," according to a *Publishers Weekly* reviewer.

"Being a writer is like being a spy (but without the guns and stuff like that)," Sheldon noted on the Walker Books Web site. "You look like just a regular person, staggering onto the bus with your shopping, but you're not. You're always watching and listening. You take notes. You take stories or lines people told you and you use them shamelessly. You never think 'Wow, I wish I'd said that!' You think, 'I'll be saying that soon.'"

Biographical and Critical Sources

PERIODICALS

Booklist, May 1, 1992, Donna Seaman, review of *My Life as a Whale,* p. 1585; October 15, 1992, Ilene Cooper, review of *Harry the Explorer,* p. 431; June 1, 1993, Ellen Mandel, review of *Harry on Vacation,* p. 1836; August, 1993, Chris Sherman, review of *My Brother Is a Visitor from Another Planet,* p. 2036; November 1, 1993, Susan DeRonne, review of *Tall, Thin, and Blonde,* p. 515; June 1, 1994, Mary Harris Veeder, review of *Under the Moon,* p. 1845; June 1, 1994, Kathryn Broderick, review of *Love, Your Bear Pete,* p. 1845; May 1, 1996, Janice Del Negro, review of *My Brother Is a Superhero,* p. 1508; November 1, 1997, Anne O'Malley, review of *The Boy of My Dreams,* p. 462; February 1, 1998, Helen Rosenberg, review of *Unicorn Dreams,* p. 924; November 1, 1999, Frances Bradburn, review of *Confessions of a Teenage Drama Queen,* p. 526; July, 2002, Anne O'Malley, review of *My Perfect Life,* p. 1847; March 15, 2003, Gillian Engberg, review of *Planet Janet,* p. 1319; April 1, 2005, Hazel Rochman, review of *Sophie Pitt-Turnbull Dis-*

Sheldon's beloved picture book The Whales' Song *features evocative paintings by Gary Blythe.* (Illustration © 1990 by Gary Blythe. Reproduced by permission of Dial Books for Young Readers, a division of Penguin Young Readers Group, a member of Penguin Group (USA), Inc., 345 Hudson Street, New York, NY 10014. All rights reserved.)

covers *America,* p. 1355; October 1, 2005, Cindy Dobrez, review of *Planet Janet in Orbit,* p. 50; June 1, 2006, Gillian Engberg, review of *Confessions of a Hollywood Star,* p. 64; August 1, 2010, Frances Bradburn, review of *My Worst Best Friend,* p. 49.

Bulletin of the Center for Children's Books, May, 1988, review of *I Forgot,* p. 188; July, 1988, review of *Alison and the Prince,* p. 238; May, 1991, review of *The Whales' Song,* p. 226; May, 1994, review of *Under the Moon,* p. 302; September, 1997, review of *The Boy of My Dreams,* p. 26; December, 1999, review of *Confessions of a Teenage Drama Queen,* p. 149; March, 2003, review of *Planet Janet,* p. 289; May, 2005, review of *Sophie Pitt-Turnbull Discovers America,* p. 402.

Horn Book, July-August, 2006, Anita L. Burkam, review of *Confessions of a Hollywood Star,* p. 451; September-October, 2010, Tanya D. Auger, review of *My Worst Best Friend,* p. 93.

Kirkus Reviews, January 15, 2003, review of *Planet Janet,* p. 146; May 1, 2005, review of *Sophie Pitt-Turnbull Discovers America,* p. 546; October 1, 2005, review of *Planet Janet in Orbit,* p. 1089; June 15, 2006, review of *Confessions of a Hollywood Star,* p. 637; August 1, 2007, review of *I Conquer Britain;* July 1, 2010, review of *My Worst Best Friend.*

Kliatt, July, 2002, Paula Rohrlick, review of *Confessions of a Teenage Drama Queen,* p. 24; September, 2002, Paula Rohrlick, review of *My Perfect Life,* p. 13; May, 2005, Claire Rosser, review of *Sophie Pitt-Turnbull Discovers America,* p. 18; September, 2007, Claire Rosser, review of *I Conquer Britain,* p. 18.

Library Journal, February 15, 1983, review of *Victim of Love,* p. 414; May 1, 1992, Rosellen Brewer, review of *My Life as a Whale,* p 120.

Publishers Weekly, February 18, 1983, review of *Victim of Love,* p. 114; May 9, 1986, review of *Dreams of an Average Man,* p. 246; May 20, 1988, review of *Alison and the Prince,* p. 90; May 10, 1991, review of *The Whales' Song,* p. 281; March 9, 1992, review of *My Life as a Whale,* p. 45; May 4, 1992, review of *Harry and Chicken,* p. 56; November 8, 1993, review of *Tall, Thin, and Blonde,* p. 78; December, 1993, review of *Love, Your Bear Pete,* p. 70; March 21, 1994, review of *Under the Moon,* p. 71; July 14, 1997, review of *The Boy of My Dreams,* p. 84; October 27, 1997, review of *Unicorn Dreams,* p. 75; April 27, 1998, review of *My Brother Is a Superhero,* p. 69; August 9, 1999, review of *Confessions of a Teenage Drama Queen,* p. 353; January 6, 2003, review of *Planet Janet,* p. 61.

School Librarian, summer, 2010, Elizabeth Finlayson, review of *My Worst Best Friend,* p. 120.

School Library Journal, July, 1991, Shirley Wilton, review of *The Whales' Song,* p. 64; September, 1992, Carolyn Jenks, review of *Harry the Explorer,* p. 211; June, 1993, Margaret C. Howell, review of *Harry on Vacation,* p. 110; November, 1993, Sharon Korbeck, review of *Tall, Thin, and Blonde,* p. 125; June, 1994, Patricia Dooley, review of *Under the Moon,* p. 113; April, 1996, Christina Door, review of *My Brother Is a Superhero,* p. 142; October, 1997, Connie Tyrell Burns, review of *The Boy of My Dreams,* p. 139; January, 1998, Jeanne Clancy Watkins, review of *Unicorn Dreams,* p. 92; October, 1999, Jane Halsall, review of *Confessions of a Teenage Drama Queen,* p. 158; August, 2002, Susan Geye, review of *My Perfect Life,* p. 197; May, 2003, Susan Riley, review of *Planet Janet,* p. 160; June, 2005, Zusanne Gordon, review of *Sophie Pitt-Turnbull Discovers America,* p. 169; November, 2005, Jane Cronkhite, review of *Planet Janet in Orbit,* p. 148; October, 2006, Erin Schirota, review of *Confessions of a Hollywood Star,* p. 171; October, 2007, Denise Moore, review of *I Conquer Britain,* p. 164; January, 2011, Shannon Seglin, review of *My Worst Best Friend,* p. 115.

Voice of Youth Advocates, February, 1994, review of *Tall, Thin, and Blonde,* p. 373; February, 1998, review of *The Boy of My Dreams,* p. 391; February, 2000, review of *Confessions of a Teenage Drama Queen,* p. 409; December, 2002, review of *My Perfect Life,* p. 392.

ONLINE

Dyan Sheldon Home Page, http://www.dyansheldon.com (January 15, 2012).

Walker Books Web site, http://www.walkerbooks.co.uk/ (January 15, 2012), "Dyan Sheldon."

*   *   *

SLADE, Christian 1974-

Personal

Born 1974, in NJ; married Ann Borowski; children: Kate, Nate. *Education:* University of Central Florida, B.F.A. (drawing and painting); Syracuse University, M.A. (illustration), 2005.

Addresses

Home and office—Winter Garden, FL. *Agent*—Tim Mendola, 420 Lexington Ave., Penthouse, New York, NY 10170; tim@mendolaart.com. *E-mail*—christianslade@earthlink.net.

Career

Author and illustrator. Disney Studios, former animation illustrator; freelance illustrator.

Writings

SELF-ILLUSTRATED; FOR CHILDREN

(With wife, Ann Borowski-Slade) *Korgi,* Slade Studio (Winter Garden, FL), 2005, revised as *Korgi Book 1: Sprouting Wings,* Top Shelf Comics (Marietta, GA), 2007.

(With Ann Borowski-Slade) *Penny's Day Out,* Slade Studio (Winter Garden, FL), 2006.

Korgi Book 2: The Cosmic Collector, Top Shelf Comics (Marietta, GA), 2008.

Korgi Book 3: A Hollow Beginning, Top Shelf Comics (Marietta, GA), 2011.

ILLUSTRATOR

Tim Setellis and Danika Setellis, *Goodbye and Hello,* Muscatello Publishing, 2002.

Joni Sensel, *Reality Leak,* Holt (New York, NY), 2007.

Sally Jones Rogan, *The Daring Adventures of Penhaligon Brush,* Alfred A. Knopf (New York, NY), 2007.

Nathaniel Lachenmeyer, *The Decoy,* Mitten Press (Ann Arbor, MI), 2007.

Kate Wharton, *What Does Mrs. Claus Do?,* Tricycle Press (Berkeley, CA), 2008.

Laura Driscoll, *Presidential Pets,* Grosset & Dunlap (New York, NY), 2009.

Pamela Ellen Ferguson's gentle New-Age story in **Sunshine Picklelime** *comes to life in Slade's appropriate soft-edged art.* (Illustration copyright © 2010 by Christian Slade. Reproduced by permission of Random House Children's Books, a division Random House, Inc.)

Sally Jones Rogan, *The Curse of the Romany Wolves*, Alfred A. Knopf (New York, NY), 2009.

Susan Sloate, *Pardon That Turkey: How Thanksgiving Became a Holiday*, Grosset & Dunlap (New York, NY), 2010.

Ken Wells, *Rascal: A Dog and His Boy*, Alfred A. Knopf (New York, NY), 2010.

Pamela Ellen Ferguson, *Sunshine Picklelime*, Random House (New York, NY), 2010.

Clete Barrett Smith, *Aliens on Vacation*, Disney/Hyperion Books (New York, NY), 2011.

Paula Hannigan, *Music Star*, Accord Pub. (Denver, CO), 2011.

Brianna Caplan Sayres, *Where Do Diggers Sleep at Night?*, Random House Children Books (New York, NY), 2012.

Clete Barrett Smith, *Alien on a Rampage*, Disney Hyperion Books (New York, NY), 2012.

Also illustrator of educational materials. Work represented in periodicals, including *Spectrum.*

Sidelights

Illustrator and animator Christian Slade is an artist and illustrator whose work has appeared in children's books and graphic novels as well as advertising and film animation. In addition to contributing to picture-book stories by authors such as Laura Driscoll, Clete Barrett Smith, Nathaniel Lachenmeyer, and Paula Hannigan, Slade has also collaborated with his wife, Ann Borowski-Slade, on *Penny's Day Out* and *Korgi*, the latter a graphic novel that Slade has expanded into an ongoing series of wordless picture books.

Korgi was inspired by the Slades' two dogs, Penny and Leo. As the artist explained to *Comicon.com* interviewer Chris Beckett, "It actually started when I first got my two Welsh Corgis. . . . I feel that the Welsh Corgi is one of the coolest animals in the world. Their design is adorable and their attitude is often hilarious. They are also loyal and caring, like many intelligent dogs. These critters helped me cast my main characters for *Korgi.* The [book] . . . developed because I have always enjoyed sci-fi and fantasy. I imagined *Korgi* for years, but after I chose it as my final thesis project for my Master's Degree, that kicked things forward into development."

A silent—wordless—graphic novel, *Korgi* draws readers into the Korgi Hollow world. In it, human-like fairies named Mollies live alongside the magical Korgis, which look remarkably like Corgi dogs. The story follows the antics of Ivy and her Korgi, Sprout. Speaking with interviewer Zack Smith for *Newsarama.com*, Slade admitted that Sprout's mischievous antics were definitely influenced by his own dog: "There was a tree at our dog park with a forked trunk. For some reason, someone kept putting dog biscuits in the tree. Leo was always smart enough to smell out the cookies and try to jump into the center of the open trunk of the tree con-

taining the hidden treats. It is one of the cutest things I've ever seen. I sketched out his mannerisms trying to leap up with his short legs in my sketchbook."

Critics greeted *Korgi* with enthusiasm. Noting the difficulty of engaging a viewer in a wordless story, a *Publishers Weekly* reviewer added that "Slade's illustrations are so expressive and full of life that the pages radiate the feelings of his characters." Douglas P. Davey, writing in *School Library Journal*, also found the illustrations effective in conveying the sense of the story, indicating that *Korgi* is "funny, thrilling, and scary in all the right places." Since beginning his "Korgi" series, which is projected to eventually encompass eight volumes, Slade has earned a following among dog owners who favor Welsh corgis, and he now undertakes pet portraits through a dedicated Web site, *Sladestudio.com.*

In addition to *Korgi*, Slade has also created artwork for texts by others. He has the opportunity to expand his portfolio of animal drawings in his work for Ken Wells' *Rascal: A Dog and His Boy*, where his inset illustrations "are particularly successful in portraits of Rascal," according to *Booklist* critic Kara Dean. Other stories featuring his art include Paula Hannigan's *Music Star*,

Slade's talent for depicting animals is showcased in his artwork for Ken Wells' picture book **Rascal: A Dog and His Boy.** (Illustration copyright © 2010 by Christian Slade. Reproduced by permission of Alfred A. Knopf, an imprint of Random House Children's Books, a division of Random House, Inc.)

with his hippie grandmother in rural Washington State is far more exciting than he ever imagined. The "goofy touches" Slade adds to his "black-and-white spot art" for *Aliens on Vacation* contribute to a novel that preteens "will find funny and relatable," according to *Booklist* contributor Erin Anderson.

Biographical and Critical Sources

PERIODICALS

Booklist, November 15, 2007, Todd Morning, review of *The Daring Adventures of Penhaligon Brush,* p. 43; July 1, 2009, Kathleen Isaacs, review of *The Curse of the Romany Wolves,* p. 58; June 1, 2010, Kathleen Isaacs, review of *Sunshine Picklelime,* p. 80; September 1, 2010, Kara Dean, review of *Rascal: A Dog and His Boy,* p. 106; October 1, 2010, Kay Wiesman, review of *Mermaids,* p. 68; May 15, 2011, Erin Anderson, review of *Aliens on Vacation,* p. 56.
Design Week, April 18, 2008, "Illustrated Woodland Fantasy."
Horn Book, November-December, 2008, Rebecca E. Schaffner, review of *What Does Mrs. Claus Do?,* p. 654.
Kirkus Reviews, March 15, 2007, review of *Reality Leak;* September 1, 2007, review of *The Daring Adventures of Penhaligon Brush;* November 1, 2008, review of *What Does Mrs. Claus Do?;* July 15, 2009, review of *The Curse of the Romany Wolves;* May 15, 2010, review of *Sunshine Picklelime.*
Publishers Weekly, April 9, 2007, review of *Korgi,* p. 38; September 24, 2007, review of *The Daring Adventures of Penhaligon Brush,* p. 71.
School Library Journal, May, 2007, Steven Engelfried, review of *Reality Leak,* p. 144; November, 2007, Nicki Clausen-Grace, review of *The Daring Adventures of Penhaligon Brush,* p. 136; March, 2008, Douglas P. Davey, review of *Korgi,* p. 227; October, 2008, Lisa Falk, review of *What Does Mrs. Claus Do?,* p. 99; November, 2009, Christi Esterle, review of *The Curse of the Romany Wolves,* p. 119; August, 2010, Richelle Roth, review of *Sunshine Picklelime,* p. 99; July, 2011, Elaine E. Knight, review of *Aliens on Vacation,* p. 107.

ONLINE

Christian Slade's Korgi Home Page, http://www.slade studio.com (January 15, 2012).
Christian Slade Home Page, http://www.christianslade. com (January 15, 2012).
Christian Slade's Korgi Web log, http://www.korgihollow. blogspot.com (January 15, 2012).
Comicon Web site, http://www.comicon.com (September 22, 2008), Chris Beckett, review of *Korgi* and interview with Slade.
Newsarama Web site, http://www.forum.newsarama.com/ (September 1, 2008), Zack Smith, interview with Slade.

Christian Slade creates detailed artwork for Sally Jones Rogan's middle-grade novel **The Daring Adventures of Pehaligon Brush.** (Illustration copyright © 2007 by Christian Slade. Reproduced by permission of Alfred A. Knopf, an imprint of Random House Children's Books, a division of Random House, Inc.)

and Brianna Caplan Sayres' *Where Do Diggers Sleep at Night?,* the latter a good bedtime choice for fans of motorized vehicles.

Slade's work on Sally Jones Rogan's *The Daring Adventures of Penhaligon Brush,* about a crafty fox whose antics in a seaside town bring up memories of swashbuckling tales, was praised by several critics. In *Kirkus Reviews* a critic wrote of the book that Slade's "appealing, detailed drawings add a touch of warmth, adventure and fun," while a *Publishers Weekly* contributor commented that the "robust characters in theatrical costume" are rendered with "plenty of personality." A sequel, *The Curse of the Romany Wolves,* also features Slade's artwork, and here his pencil drawings "of the costumed animals add appeal," according to *Booklist* critic Kathleen Isaacs.

Slade has also teamed up with Smith on the humorous chapter books *Aliens on Vacation* and *Alien on a Rampage,* in which a preteen discovers that a summer spent

Top Shelf Comix Web site, http://www.topshelfcomix.com/ (September 1, 2008), "Christian Slade."*

*   *   *

ST. JAMES, Sierra
See RALLISON, Janette

*   *   *

STREVENS-MARZO, Bridget

Personal

Born in England; daughter of John Strevens (a painter) and Julia Marzo; married Mick Finch (an artist); children: Thomas, Sam, Ella. *Education:* King's College Cambridge, degree (painting); attended École des Beaux-Arts. *Hobbies and other interests:* Gardening, bicycling.

Addresses

Home—Senlis, France; East London, England. *Agent*—Erzsi Deàk, Hen & Ink Literary Studio; henandink@gmail.com. *E-mail*—b@bridgetstrevens.com.

Career

Illustrator and art teacher. Media designer for multimedia company, Paris, France, 1993-95; Bayard Presse (publisher), Paris, former art director; freelance illustrator. Instructor in art to children. Presenter at schools and workshops.

Member

Society of Children's Book Writers and Illustrators (member of international board of advisors).

Awards, Honors

British Book Design Award shortlist, 2007, for *The Big Book for Little Hands* by Marie-Pascale Cocagne.

Writings

SELF-ILLUSTRATED

Toto's Travels (series; includes *Toto in Rome, Toto in Paris,* and *Toto in Spain*), Little, Brown UK (London, England), 1993.
Bridget's Book of Nursery Rhymes, Little Hare (Surry Hills, New South Wales, Australia), 2006.
Petite escargot (toddler bath book), Tourbillon (France), 2010.

Also author/illustrator of board books *En voiture!* and *En bateau!,* published in France.

ILLUSTRATOR

Margaret Wild, *Kiss, Kiss!,* Little Hare (Surry Hills, New South Wales, Australia), 2003, Simon & Schuster (New York, NY), 2004.
David Bedford, *Knock, Knock!,* Little Hare (Surry Hills, New South Wales, Australia), 2005.
Frances Watts, *This Dog Bruce,* Little Hare (Surry Hills, New South Wales, Australia), 2005.
Philemon Sturges, *How Do You Make a Baby Smile?,* HarperCollins (New York, NY), 2007.
Marie-Pascale Cocagne, *Les Petites mains dessinent,* Bayard (Paris, France), 2007, translated by Anna Shandro and Alice Thorp as *The Big Book for Little Hands,* Harry Abrams (New York, NY), 2007.
David Bedford, *Daddy Does the Cha Cha Cha!,* Little Hare (Surry Hills, New South Wales, Australia), 2008.
Margaret Wild, *Hush, Hush!,* Little Hare (Surry Hills, New South Wales, Australia), 2009.
Marie-Pascale Cocagne, *Les Petites mains jouent avec les formes,* Bayard (Paris, France), 2009, translated by Anna Shandro and Alice Thorp as *The Big Book of Shapes,* Harry Abrams (New York, NY), 2009.
Kristy Dempsey, *Mini Racer,* Macmillan (New York, NY), 2011.

Contributor to French children's magazines, including *Pomme d'api.*

Books featuring Strevens-Marzo's work have been translated into several languages, including Chinese, Dutch, French, Greek, Italian, Japanese, and Spanish.

Sidelights

Bridget Strevens-Marzo divides her time between her native England and her adopted France, and her illustrations have been published in both countries, as well as elsewhere in translation. Strevens-Marzo's artwork is noted for its graphic quality, its dynamic use of color, and its playful use of line and shapes and animals often star as leading characters. In addition to bringing to life stories by writers such as Margaret Wild, David Bedford, Marie-Pascale Cocagne, and Philemon Sturges, she also works with budding illustrators of all ages at schools and workshops. Her colorful contribution to Cocagne's *The Big Book for Little Hands,* which was first released in the original French, earned Strevens-Marzo a British Book Design Award shortlist, and a *Publishers Weekly* critic aptly observed that the book's "childlike illustrations belie a nuanced understanding of the target audience" of four-and five-year-old artists.

After producing three self-illustrated books in her "Toto's Travels" series, Strevens-Marzo worked for a French multimedia company as well as serving as an art director for Paris-based Bayard Presse before making the move to freelance illustrator while raising her family. Her first illustration project, Wild's simple text for *Kiss, Kiss!,* became an international bestseller when it was released in 2003, and led to another collaboration, *Hush, Hush!* Featuring a baby hippo who is reminded to give his mother a kiss before going off to play, *Kiss, Kiss!* was cited for its "clear, bright pictures" by *Booklist* contributor Hazel Rochman, while a *Publishers Weekly* critic remarked on Strevens-Marzo's use of "strong shapes" and "dense, bright colors" in crafting large-format images full of "energetic detailing."

"Featuring some of Strevens-Marzo's best artwork yet," according to a *Publishers Weekly* critic, *How Do You Make a Baby Smile?* pairs colorful black-outlined images with Sturges' humorous story about how animal parents coax a smirk from their sometimes-toothsome offspring. The artist's inclusion of "interesting details and textures . . . complement but never distract" from Sturges' text, noted the *Publishers Weekly* writer, while *School Library Journal* reviewer Robin L. Gibson cited Strevens-Marzo's "monochromatic backgrounds, thick bold outlines, and use of interesting perspectives." *How Do You Make a Baby Smile?* treats toddlers to "a baby-pleasing combination of rich, saturated color . . . and artful compositions," concluded a *Kirkus Reviews* writer, while in *Booklist* Carolyn Phelan praised the double-spread pictures for their "wit and style."

Inspired by author Kristy Dempsey's rambunctious children, *Mini Racer* introduces a dozen small race cars that are lined up for a cross-country competition. Each vehicle is driven by a different animal, and their path along the twisty, turny race course is animated by a simple text. Featuring equally animated artwork by Strevens-Marzo that evokes the illustrations of Richard Scarry, *Mini Racer* "has definite appeal for youngsters" due to its "zooming action and fender-bender drama," according to a *Kirkus Reviews* writer. In *School Library Journal* critic Marge Loch-Wouters recommended the

colorful picture book as a good story-hour choice for grown ups facing "kids with a need for speed and a love of vehicles."

Biographical and Critical Sources

PERIODICALS

Booklist, January 1, 2004, Hazel Rochman, review of *Kiss, Kiss!,* p. 884; July 1, 2007, Carolyn Phelan, review of *How Do You Make a Baby Smile?,* p. 65; December 15, 2010, Randall Enos, review of *Mini Racer,* p. 59.

Kirkus Reviews, November 15, 2003, review of *Kiss, Kiss!;* May 15, 2007, review of *How Do You Make a Baby Smile?;* November 1, 2010, review of *Mini Racer.*

Publishers Weekly, January 19, 2004, review of *Kiss, Kiss!;* December 4, 2006, review of *Kiss, Kiss!,* p. 60; June 25, 2007, review of *How Do You Make a Baby Smile?,* p. 58.

School Library Journal, January, 2004, Faith Brautigam, review of *Kiss, Kiss!,* p. 107; July, 2007, Robin L. Gibson, review of *How Do You Make a Baby Smile?,* p. 86; April 21, 2008, review of *The Big Book for Little Hands,* p. 57; January, 2011, Marge Loch-Wouters, review of *Mini Racer,* p. 72; June, 2011, Alison Donnelly, review of *Hush, Hush!,* p. 98.

ONLINE

Bridget Strevens-Marzo Home Page, http://www.bridgetstrevens.com (January 15, 2012).

Bridget Strevens-Marzo Web log, http://bridgimage.blogspot.com/ (January 15, 2012).*

T

TASHJIAN, Janet 1956-

Personal

Born June 29, 1956, in Providence, RI; daughter of Russell (a sales engineer) and Mariette (a homemaker) Souza; married Douglas Tashjian (a medical consultant), December, 1985; children: Jake. *Education:* University of Rhode Island, B.A., 1978; Emerson College, M.F.A., 1994. *Politics:* "Liberal". *Religion:* Buddhist. *Hobbies and other interests:* Cooking, hiking, spending time in nature.

Addresses

Home—Los Angeles, CA.

Career

Writer. Worked variously as a sales representative, sales manager, and sales consultant, 1978-93. Presenter at schools and conferences.

Awards, Honors

Best Books for the Teen Age selection, New York Public Library, Best Children's Book selection, Bank Street College of Education, and Honor Book designation, Women's National Book Association, all 1997, all for *Tru Confessions;* Children's Choice selection, International Reading Association (IRA)/Children's Book Council (CBC), and Best Children's Book citation, Bank Street College of Education, both 1998, both for *Marty Frye, Private Eye;* Best of the Best selection, Chicago Public Library, and Best Books for the Teen Age selection, New York Public Library, both 1999, both for *Multiple Choice;* Best Books for the Teen Age selection, Best Children's Book citation, Bank Street College of Education, and Notable Trade Book in the Social Studies citation, National Council for the Social Studies/CBC, and Best Book for Young Adults selection, American Library Association, all 2002, all for *The Gospel according to Larry;* Women's National Book Association Honor Book selection; Young Hoosier Award nomination.

Janet Tashjian (Photograph by Mark Morelli. Reproduced by permission.)

Writings

Tru Confessions (middle-grade novel), Henry Holt (New York, NY), 1997

Marty Frye, Private Eye (beginning reader), Henry Holt (New York, NY), 1998.

Multiple Choice (middle-grade novel), Henry Holt (New York, NY), 1999.

Fault Line (young-adult novel), Henry Holt (New York, NY), 2003.

My Life as a Book (middle-grade novel), cartoons by son Jake Tashjian, Henry Holt (New York, NY), 2010.

My Life as a Stuntboy (middle-grade novel), cartoons by Jake Tashjian, Henry Holt (New York, NY), 2011.

Author's work has been translated into several languages, including Dutch, German, Italian, Japanese, Portuguese, and Spanish.

"LARRY" YOUNG-ADULT NOVELS

The Gospel according to Larry, Henry Holt (New York, NY), 2001.
Vote for Larry, Henry Holt (New York, NY), 2004.
Larry and the Meaning of Life, Henry Holt (New York, NY), 2008.

Adaptations

Tru Confessions was adapted as a television film starring Clara Bryant and Shia LaBeouf, Disney Channel, 2002. *The Gospel according to Larry, Vote for Larry,* and *Larry and the Meaning of Life* were adapted for audiobook, produced by Listening Library.

Sidelights

Janet Tashjian entertains a range of young readers in her books for children, from those tackling their first chapter book to middle graders to older teens. Tashjian's first young-adult novel, *Tru Confessions,* was adapted for a feature film, while her books *The Gospel according to Larry* and *My Life as a Book* introduce likeable characters and imaginative storylines that critics have cited for their ability to attract even the reading averse.

A journalism major at the University of Rhode Island, Tashjian subsequently found a job in sales and marketing. "After spending fifteen years selling software and computers, managing sales forces, and running training classes, I decided life was too short to spend another minute doing anything but what I really wanted to do, which was write," she later recalled to *SATA.* "So I quit my job, bought a dozen spiral-bound notebooks and a pack of pens, and started writing."

Beginning by attending several writing workshops, Tashjian eventually earned her M.F.A. at Emerson College, where she studied under author Jack Gantos. "On the first day of class," she recalled, Gantos "told detailed stories of the neighborhoods he grew up in, his friends, teachers, etc. He remembered everything. (Of course, I found out later, he'd been keeping a diary since second grade.) I couldn't remember *that* much about growing up, but making stuff up seemed like more fun anyway. That night, I drove home and came up with the idea that would become *Tru Confessions*—a novel that explored what it would have been like for me to grow up with a special-needs sibling the way my husband did."

Like its author, the preteen heroine of *Tru Confessions* is determined to fulfill her dreams, and readers get to know her by perusing a print-out of her computer

journal. Complete with humorous headings and computer-penned pictures, the diary reveals Trudy's thoughts and feelings as she struggles to realize her aspirations: to create her own television show and to "cure" her developmentally delayed brother, Eddie. Tru's two dreams merge when she enters a local cable television contest and is inspired to produce a documentary about Eddie. Janice M. Del Negro noted in the *Bulletin of the Center for Children's Books* that Tru begins her pursuit with "intense adolescent desires and youthful determination to just not admit defeat," and while she grows to have a more realistic understanding of the permanence of Eddie's disability she keeps her sense of optimism about the future. To *Five Owls* reviewer Cathryn M. Mercier, Tru's voice is among the novel's strengths: it has "an immediacy and lack of self-censorship that textures the entire book," Mercier commented. As a *Publishers Weekly* critic predicted of *Tru Confessions,* "middle graders will laugh their way through Tru's poignant and clever take on everyday life; even the most reluctant of readers may tell their friends about this one."

Also geared for middle graders, *Multiple Choice* introduces a perfectionist and worrier named Monica Devon. Monica is the type of girl to transfer Styrofoam beads from one bean-bag chair to the next for proper balance. So meticulous is she that she finally develops a game, Multiple Choice, to channel her compulsive tendencies: she makes up tasks for herself and then creates four different means of accomplishing them. Such obsessive-compulsive behavior leads to near tragedy, and only then do Monica's parents and teachers see the warning signs. "Tashjian's story is as absorbing and cleverly constructed as a challenging word puzzle," wrote Jennifer M. Brabander in a *Horn Book* review: "Readers with obsessive tendencies will especially empathize, but all adolescents can appreciate the book's basic message—that it's okay to choose to be yourself." In a *Booklist* review, Shelle Rosenfeld remarked that "Tashjian's conversational prose, eye for detail, and quirky humor communicate Monica's inner difficulties and loneliness, and the snowballing events that ultimately lead to positive changes." A reviewer for *Publishers Weekly* called *Tru Confessions* an "energetic, enjoyable problem novel," adding that it "is a must-read for wordsmiths."

In the beginning reader *Marty Frye, Private Eye* Tashjian introduces a young detective who is also a poet, and in the three close-to-home mysteries he tackles Marty combines sleuthing and versifying. "*Marty Frye, Private Eye* came about because my friend's son used to laugh when I made up rhymes for him," the author once commented. "I've always loved mysteries, so I made Marty a poet detective." Tashjian's seven-year-old sleuth actually rhymes his way through several mysteries in the story, and in *School Library Journal* Jane Claes recommended Tashjian's "briskly paced, action-packed" novel as a good transition for children "making the leap from picture to chapter books."

Cover of Tashjian's young-adult novel **The Gospel according to Larry,** *which finds an Internet-savvy teen creating an online identity that transforms him into a celebrity.* (Jacket cover copyright © 2003 by Laurel-Leaf. Reproduced by permission of Laurel-Leaf, an imprint of Random House Children's Books, a division of Random House, Inc.)

Tashjian turns to older readers in *The Gospel according to Larry,* which chronicles the rise of an Internet innovator. Josh Swensen is not a typical teen: he despises his culture's materialism and uses a Web site to share his opinions. His URL, thegospelaccordingtolarry. com, becomes Josh's platform for rants against consumerism and U.S. society's fixation on celebrities. Ironically, however, the teen soon becomes an unlikely celebrity himself when his site begins to get thousands of hits a day. In his school life, Josh wants to keep his identity a secret, even from friend Beth, who he has a crush on. While Beth shows little interest in Josh, her interest in "Larry" is another matter. The Larry movement grows, with rock festivals celebrating Larry's online message, and inevitably Josh is outed by one of his fans. As the teen is pulled into the very culture he despises, he soon finds his most cherished beliefs compromised.

"Tashjian does something very fresh here which will hit teens at a visceral level," wrote Ilene Cooper in her *Booklist* review of *The Gospel according to Larry.* "She takes the natural idealism young people feel, personalizes it in the character of Josh/Larry, and shows that idealism transformed by unintended consequences." A contributor for *Kirkus Reviews* also had high praise for the novel. "Tashjian's inventive story is a thrilling read, fast-paced with much fast food for thought about our consumer-oriented pop culture," the critic wrote of *The Gospel according to Larry,* adding that "the [narrative] voice is clear, the ending satisfying." Francisca Goldsmith, reviewing the novel in *School Library Journal,* asserted that Tashjian's "gift for portraying bright adolescents with insight and humor reaches near perfection here."

Josh/Larry returns in both *Vote for Larry* and *Larry and the Meaning of Life* as the teen continues to discover that things are not always what they seem. In *Vote for Larry* the eighteen year old decides to run for president of the United States as a Peace Party candidate, thinking that his solutions to the world's problems will be transformational. Larry travels to Walden Pond to gain spiritual guidance from a middle-aged hippie guru named Gus in *Larry and the Meaning of Life.* With its backdrop of presidential politics, *Vote for Larry* may inspire future voters, predicted a *Kirkus Reviews* writer, citing the story's mix of "politics, romance, important social issues, and even a saboteur in the wings." "The Larry stories have always been over the top," noted Cooper in *Booklist,* "and that's particularly true" in *Larry and the Meaning of Life.* The hero's "madcap journey" through the pages of this novel resolves in a "clever" conclusion, the critic added, while a *Kirkus Reviews* writer praised "Josh's first-person narrative" for drawing readers into Tashjian's "wise and humorous tale."

Fault Line is another young-adult novel with a message, this time about dating violence. Becky is a highschool senior who has enjoyed some success as a stand-up comic. Happy and confident, she comes from a supportive, affluent family, and through her, as Jennifer M. Brabander noted in *Horn Book,* "Tashjian shatters any stereotypes young readers may have about people in abusive relationships." While performing her acts at improv clubs Becky meets Kip, another aspiring stand-up comic. A high-school senior, who writes his routines on paper towels, seems like a perfect partner for Becky, and the two quickly become inseparable. Soon, however, Becky's mother and her best friend both worry that they are a bit too inseparable and that Becky's relationship with Kip may not be a healthy one. As Kip becomes more and more controlling of Becky's daily life, he eventually begins abusing her. Through excerpts from Kip's diary, we learn that he was formerly abused by his father and that, although he does not want to hurt Becky, he does not know how to stop. "Readers will appreciate that Kip isn't completely demonized," wrote a *Publishers Weekly* critic, and Paula

Rohrlick noted in *Kliatt* that Tashjian "succeeds in conveying what makes Kip initially attractive to Becky as well as his genuine anguish over his actions."

Tashjian teams up with her teenaged son, artist Jake Tashjian, to create *My Life as a Book* and *My Life as a Stuntboy*. In the first book, readers meet anti-reader Derek Fallon, an imaginative twelve year old whose upcoming summer vacation is threatened by two dark clouds: Learning Camp and the Summer Reading List. While he chronicles his task of learning new vocabulary words as if it were torture, Derek also finds time to tack a family mystery and get into trouble through his typical boyhood antics. The preteen's love of active adventure wins him a super-cool job in *My Life as a Stuntboy*. When landing a role as a stunt double in an upcoming film is something worth bragging about, Derek quickly wishes he had kept things to himself when he learns that he will have to dress like a girl. Describing Derek as "brash, careless, and unusually willing to do something stupid," Cooper commended Tashjian for crafting a first-person narration that "captures . . . the pushes and pulls in the life of someone with learning disabilities." The boy's chronicle gains graphic interest by Jake Tashian's humorous scrawly graphics, which in *My Life as a Book* illustrate his efforts at vocabulary building and are scattered throughout the margins. The artwork makes each novel "more approachable for kids like Derek," advised *Horn Book* contributor Betty Carter, the critic adding that Tashjian's mix of mystery and summer-school rigors in *My Life as a Book* "divert[s] readers from any hint of didacticism as he learns to build on his strengths."

"I write every day, some days more than others," Tashjian once commented. "I try to get in a few turbo days a week. Writing is only part of the process, though. I spend a lot of time rewriting, trying to polish each chapter, each scene, each sentence. I have several things going on at the same time—the first draft of a novel, a book in the final stages of editing, the outline for a screenplay, plus lots of ideas just waiting for me to get to them. Even when I'm not working, there's always something going on in my head, itching to get down on paper.

"When students ask me for advice I always say the same thing: Spend your life doing something you love. Then act like what you're doing is the most important, sacred thing in the world, because it is. Find a teacher, a mentor, a group of people who want to improve their skills, too. Then practice, practice, practice. Devote yourself to your craft, and you will be greatly rewarded. As the comedy writer Larry Gelbart said, 'The meaning of life is beyond me. The best I can do is deal with it one word at a time.' Amen."

Biographical and Critical Sources

PERIODICALS

Booklist, June 1, 1999, Shelle Rosenfeld, review of *Multiple Choice*, p. 1816; November 1, 2001, Ilene Cooper, review of *The Gospel according to Larry*, p. 471; September 1, 2003, Ilene Cooper, review of *Fault Line*, pp. 115-116; May 1, 2004, Ilene Cooper, review of *Vote for Larry*, p. 1556; October 1, 2004, Ilene Cooper, "On the Campaign Trail," p. 327 and Lolly Gepson, review of *Vote for Larry*, p. 352; September 1, 2008, Ilene Cooper, review of *Larry and the Meaning of Life*, p. 92; March 1, 2009, Lolly Gepson, review of *Larry and the Meaning of Life*, p. 71; August 1, 2010, Ilene Cooper, review of *My Life as a Book*, p. 54.

Bulletin of the Center for Children's Books, January, 1998, Janice M. Del Negro, review of *Tru Confessions*, p. 180.

Five Owls, January-February, 1998, Cathryn M. Mercier, review of *Tru Confessions*.

Horn Book, July-August, 1999, Jennifer M. Brabander, review of *Multiple Choice*, p. 474; January-February, 2002, Jennifer M. Brabander, review of *The Gospel according to Larry*, pp. 84-85; September-October, 2003, Jennifer M. Brabander, review of *Fault Line*, pp. 620-621; July-August, 2010, Betty Carter, review of *My Life as a Book*, p. 124.

Journal of Adolescent & Adult Literacy, April, 2002, Vashti Kenway, review of *The Gospel according to Larry*, pp. 662-663.

Kirkus Reviews, October 15, 2001, review of *The Gospel according to Larry*, p. 1494; August 15, 2003, review of *Fault Line*, p. 1080; April 15, 2004, review of *Vote for Larry*, p. 402; September 15, 2008, review of *Larry and the Meaning of Life*; June 15, 2010, review of *My Life as a Book*.

Kliatt, July, 2003, Paula Rohrlick, review of *The Gospel according to Larry*, p. 27; September, 2003, Paula Rohrlick, review of *Fault Line*, pp. 13-14; September, 2004, Janet Julian, review of *The Gospel according to Larry*, p. 60; May, 2008, Amanda MacGregor, review of *Tru Confessions*, p. 24.

Publishers Weekly, October 20, 1997, review of *Tru Confessions*, p. 77; June 7, 1999, review of *Multiple Choice*, p. 84; December 3, 2001, review of *The Gospel according to Larry*, p. 61; September 1, 2003, review of *Fault Line*, p. 90; June 28, 2010, review of *My Life as a Book*, p. 129.

Reading Today, August, 2000, Lynne T. Burke, review of *Tru Confessions*, p. 32.

School Library Journal, December, 1997, Patricia A. Dollisch, review of *Tru Confessions*, pp. 131-132; December, 1998, Jane Claes, review of *Marty Frye, Private Eye*, pp. 93-94; October, 2001, Francisca Goldsmith, review of *The Gospel according to Larry*, pp. 172-173; April, 2009, Sarah Flood, review of *Larry and the Meaning of Life*, p. 58; August, 2010, Helen Foster James, review of *My Life as a Book*, p. 114.

Voice of Youth Advocates, December, 1997, Katie O'Dell Madison, review of *Tru Confessions*, p. 322.

ONLINE

Gospel according to Larry Web site, http://www.thegospel accordingtolarry.com (June 7, 2010).

Janet Tashjian Home Page, http://www.janettashjian.com (December 15, 2011).

*   *   *

THOMPSON, Keith 1982-

Personal

Born 1982, in Canada. *Education:* Sheridan College degree (illustration), 2005.

Addresses

Home—Ontario, Canada. *E-mail*—k@keiththompsonart. com.

Career

Illustrator and creature artist. *Exhibitions:* Work included in exhibit at Museum of American Illustration, New York, NY, 2005.

Writings

SELF-ILLUSTRATED

Fifty Robots to Draw and Paint, Barron's (Hauppauge, NY), 2006.
Fifty Fantasy Vehicles to Draw and Paint: Create Awe-inspiring Crafts for Comics, Computer Games, and Graphic Novels, Barron's (Hauppauge, NY), 2007.
Drawing and Painting the Undead, Barron's (Hauppauge, NY), 2008.

ILLUSTRATOR

Kenneth Oppel, *Darkwing,* Eos (New York, NY), 2007.

Work featured in *Spectrum* art annuals and other published collections of fantasy art.

ILLUSTRATOR; "LEVIATHAN TRILOGY" BY SCOTT WESTERFELD

Leviathan, Simon Pulse (New York, NY), 2009.
Behemoth, Simon Pulse (New York, NY), 2010.
Goliath, Simon Pulse (New York, NY), 2011.

Sidelights

Keith Thompson is an artist and illustrator whose work has appeared in books and magazines, in film and television productions, and as a creative component of popular dieselpunk and steampunk videogames. A concept artist who is often hired to visualize fantasy worlds and their creatures, Thompson creates images that are highly detailed, employing black pencil drawings and

digital tints of color. His influences range widely, from Japanese fantasy art and manga to the Northern Renaissance and the Golden Age of Illustration, and his artwork is noted for its strong narrative elements.

Born in Canada, Thompson began doing freelance illustration when he was still in high school, building his skills by also working part time for an animation studio. He continued taking on illustration jobs while completing his studies at Toronto, Ontario's Sheridan College, meanwhile developing an increasingly sophisticated Internet presence to market his work. In *Fifty Robots to Draw and Paint, Fifty Fantasy Vehicles to Draw and Paint: Create Awe-inspiring Crafts for Comics, Computer Games, and Graphic Novels,* and *Drawing and Painting the Undead,* Thompson shares the expertise he gained during the formative part of his career.

Thompson's detailed Victorian-inspired illustration style, which some have characterized as steampunk, made him a good choice to work as an illustrator on fantasy novels such as Kenneth Oppel's *Darkwing* and Scott Westerfeld's "Leviathan Trilogy," which includes *Leviathan, Behemoth,* and *Goliath.* In an interview with *Beyond Victoriana* online interviewer Diana Pho, Thompson discusse his collaboration with Westerfeld, describing it as "a wonderfully old fashioned and Edwardian way of going about an illustrated book. The correspondence was dominantly written. Scott would either mention loosely what was planned ahead of time, or send drafts of future chapters. I would sketch up depictions and describe details on how things could work out. Upon consensus the writing and art would solidify further independently, but would both end up matching upon finalisation. The process seemed to form very naturally and quickly and lasted unchanged for three years."

In *Leviathan* Westerfeld mixes his alternate history of World War I Europe with elements of steampunk as the Archduke Ferdinand is assassinated and his adolescent son flees to the Swiss Alps. After the teen's location is discovered by the passengers of the airship *Leviathan,* the two powerhouses use him as leverage in their attempts to mediate a peace: the Germanic Clankers with their highly mechanized army and the British Darwinists, whose mastery of biotechnology is equally frightful. "Enhanced by Thompson's intricate black-and-white illustrations, Westerfeld's brilliantly constructed imaginary world will capture readers from the first page," predicted *School Library Journal* critic Heather M. Campbell in reviewing *Leviathan,* while a *Publishers Weekly* critic asserted that the artist's "detail-rich panels bring Westerfeld's unusual creations to life." Noting the violence that flares throughout the author's story, Ian Chipman wrote in *Booklist* that the "wildly imaginative creatures and machines" that factor in *Leviathan* are brought to life in "Thompson's ample, lavish, and essential illustrations."

Leviathan's sequel, *Behemoth,* finds the novels central characters on their way to the Ottoman Empire in an attempt to stop a massive war. In her review of *Behemoth* for *Horn Book,* Cynthia K. Ritter wrote that the collaboration between Westerfeld and Thompson "makes [the series'] . . . blending of past and present technologies an entertaining, and even somewhat educational, read," while Timothy Capehart asserted in *Voice of Youth Advocates* that "Thompson's detailed 'Victorian Manga' spot and full-page illustrations . . . bolster the enjoyment factor" in *Behemoth.* "Anyone needing a good visual for what makes steampunk so alluring should look no further," concluded Chipman of the "Leviathan" trilogy.

Biographical and Critical Sources

PERIODICALS

Booklist, September 1, 2007, Michael Cart, review of *Darkwing,* p. 115; August 1, 2009, Ian Chipman, review of *Leviathan,* p. 58; October 15, 2010, Ian Chipman, review of *Behemoth,* p. 51.

Horn Book, September-October, 2007, Vicky Smith, review of *Darkwing,* p. 584; November-December, 2009, Jonathan Hunt, review of *Leviathan,* p. 689; November-December, 2010, Cynthia K. Ritter, review of *Behemoth,* p. 107.

Kirkus Reviews, August 1, 2007, review of *Darkwing*; September 1, 2009, review of *Leviathan*; September 15, 2010, review of *Behemoth.*

Kliatt, July, 2007, Paula Rohrlick, review of *Darkwing,* p. 20.

New York Times Book Review, November 8, 2009, Austin Grossman, review of *Leviathan,* p. 21.

Publishers Weekly, August 24, 2009, review of *Leviathan,* p. 62; September 13, 2010, review of *Behemoth,* p. 46.

School Library Journal, September, 2007, Eric Norton, review of *Darkwing,* p. 205; September, 2009, Heather M. Campbell, review of *Leviathan,* p. 176; October, 2010, review of *Behemoth,* p. 128.

Voice of Youth Advocates, December, 2010, Timothy Capehart, review of *Behemoth,* p. 477.

ONLINE

Beyond Victoriana Web site, http://www.beyondvictoriana. com/ (July 24, 2011), Diana Pho, interview with Thompson.

Dieselpunks Web site, http://www.dieselpunks.org/ (June 4, 2009), interview with Thompson.

Excommunicate.net, http://www.excommunicate.net/ (July 6, 3007), interview with Thompson.

Keith Thompson Home Page, http://www.keiththompson art.com (January 9, 2012).

Keith Thompson Web log, http://blog.keiththompsonart. com (January 9, 2012).

TORREY, Michele 1960(?)-

Personal

Born c. 1960, in Wenatchee, WA; daughter of Donald (a math teacher) and Norma Torrey; married; second husband's name Carl; children: (first marriage) three sons. *Education:* University of Washington, B.S. (microbiology and immunology), 1988; Graceland University, M.A. (religion), 2006.

Addresses

Home—Fox Island, WA. *E-mail*—mtorrey@michele torrey.com.

Career

Author for children. Formerly worked as a lab scientist. Presenter at schools and workshops.

Member

Author's Guild, Society of Children's Book Writers and Illustrators, Pacific Northwest Writers Association.

Awards, Honors

Pacific Northwest Writers Association literary contest winner, 2001; Rhode Island State Book Award nomination, 2005, for *The Case of the Graveyard Ghost;* Best Children's Book selection, Bank Street College of Education, and 100 Titles for Reading and Sharing selection, New York Public Library, both 2006, both for *Voyage of Midnight;* Maine State Book Award nomination, 2006, and Sequoyah Young-Adult Book Award nomination, 2007, both for *Voyage of Ice;* Washington State Book Award finalist, and Sakura Medal nomination, both 2007, and Sequoyah Young-Adult Book Award nomination, 2008, all for *Voyage of Plunder.*

Writings

Bottles of Eight and Pieces of Rum, Royal Fireworks Press, 1998.

Sisters unto Death, Royal Fireworks Press, 1999.

To the Edge of the World, Random House (New York, NY), 2003.

Contributor of short fiction to periodicals.

"DOYLE AND FOSSEY, SCIENCE DETECTIVES" MIDDLE-GRADE NOVEL SERIES; ILLUSTRATED BY BARBARA JOHANSEN NEWMAN

The Case of the Gasping Garbage, and Other Super-scientific Cases, Dutton Children's Books (New York, NY), 2000.

The Case of the Mossy Lake Monster, and Other Super-scientific Cases, Dutton Children's Books (New York, NY), 2002.

The Case of the Graveyard Ghost, and Other Super-scientific Cases, Dutton Children's Books (New York, NY), 2002.

The Case of the Barfy Birthday, and Other Super-scientific Cases, Dutton Children's Books (New York, NY), 2003.

The Case of the Crooked Carnival, and Other Super-scientific Cases, Dutton Children's Books (New York, NY), 2010.

The Case of the Terrible T. Rex, and Other Super-scientific Cases, Sterling (New York, NY), 2010.

"CHRONICLES OF COURAGE" NOVEL SERIES

Voyage of Ice, Random House (New York, NY), 2004.
Voyage of Plunder, Random House (New York, NY), 2005.
Voyage of Midnight, Alfred A. Knopf (New York, NY), 2006.

Sidelights

Widely traveled since childhood and trained as a microbiologist, Michele Torrey worked as a laboratory scientist for many years before producing her first book for children. Tapping her long-held interest in history, Torrey honed her storytelling skills while crafting the middle-grade historical novels *Bottles of Eight and Pieces of Rum* and *Sisters unto Death,* both which were published in the late 1990s. She has continued to contribute to the genre with *To the Edge of the World* and her "Chronicles of Courage" series, and she also melds her scientific expertise with storytelling in her engaging "Doyle and Fossey Science Detectives" books.

Torrey takes readers back to the Age of Exploration in *To the Edge of the World,* which focuses on an orphan who is serving as cabin boy on Portuguese captain Ferdinand Magellan's historical 1519 voyage around the globe. Mateo spends three years aboard the *Trinidad,* the flagship of the five-ship fleet Magellan now commandeers and sails under the colors of King Carlos of Spain. Taken under the captain's wing, the boy grows to manhood while also experiencing the hardships and excitement of life at sea, including storms, hunger, mutiny, and the discovery of different lands and cultures. A *Kirkus Reviews* writer noted that Torrey's "writing is lively" and draws readers in to her "descriptions of starving sailors eating maggots, rats, leather and sawdust, and of executions and bloody warfare." Describing *To the Edge of the World* as a "fast-paced" novel that should appeal to middle-grade boys, Kathleen Odeon added in *Booklist* that Torrey's story generates "solid page-turning excitement" as well as sharing "some fascinating history."

Torrey has continued to be pulled by the lure of the sea in her "Chronicles of Courage" saga, which inspired by the true stories discovered during the course of her in-depth research. The series begins with *Voyage of Ice,* as fifteen-year-old Nicholas Robbins joins his older brother as part of a whaling crew setting sail from New Bed-

ford, Massachusetts, in 1851. When Nick confronts the hardships of life on a working whaler, as well as the injustices meted out by the ship's captain, he unsuccessfully attempts to desert his post. Ultimately he is stranded, together with the rest of his crew, in the Arctic where survival against nature becomes his sole focus. Torrey "unspools a nail-biting adventure" in *Voyage of Ice,* according to a *Publishers Weekly* critic, and her "sharply focused prose" ensures that "those who like survival tales will be rapt." Noting the "well developed" characters and wealth of historical detail in the novel, Nancy P. Reeder added in *School Library Journal* that the adventure-filled plot of *Voyage of Ice* interweaves "adventure" and "accurate descriptions of shipboard life," methods of "survival in a hostile environment," and information about "the Native people who eventually rescue the castaways."

The "Chronicles of Courage" series continues in *Voyage of Plunder* and *Voyage of Midnight.* Readers are transported to 1696 in *Voyage of Plunder,* as they follow fourteen-year-old Daniel Markham and his parents onto the *Gray Pearl,* which is scheduled to sail between Boston and the family's new home in Jamaica. After the ship is beset by pirates and he witnesses his father's death, the teen is pressed into service aboard the *Tempest Galley* where he endures the life of a pirate while plotting his revenge. Over time, the boy begins to bond with his captors, eventually becoming a protégé of Captain Josiah Black until a turn of events forces him to reexamine his loyalties. "Torrey had done her homework, drawing expertly from actual history and contemporary accounts," noted a *Kirkus Reviews* writer, and *Kliatt* reviewer Michele Winship concluded that *Voyage of Plunder* "allows readers an insider's perspective on the lives of 17th-century pirates." Torrey's novel "can stand solidly beside other classic pirate stories," asserted *Booklist* contributor Todd Morning, and in *School Library Journal* Christine McGinty predicted that the "high-quality writing style, . . . strong cast of characters, . . . and twisting conclusion are sure to captivate readers."

For Philip Higgins, the fourteen-year-old hero of *Voyage of Midnight,* working aboard his uncle's ship will allow him to build a relationship with his only remaining relative. It is only after the ship sets sail from London that Philip learns that his uncle is actually a slaver and that the ship is bound for Africa to take ownership of a human cargo. When a tragedy befalls the crew, the young teen must bravely take the helm and decide between fulfilling his duty to his captain and following his own moral compass. "Philip is a well-developed character," asserted Shelle Rosenfeld in her *Booklist* review, and the "powerful narrative" in *Voyage of Midnight* "incorporates abundant historical detail." A *Kirkus Reviews* critic characterized the same novel as "the most intense and harrowing of Torrey's nautical chronicles," and in *School Library Journal* Jane G. Connor praised *Voyage of Midnight* as a "gripping" seafaring tale that presents "not only . . . a vivid picture of a shameful past, but also . . . an understanding of its cruelty."

Torrey switches her focus from seagoing adventure to science in her "Doyle and Fossey, Science Detectives" chapter books, each of which details four different mysteries along with experiments readers can try, with safety, at home. Featuring illustrations by Barbara Johansen Newman, the series begins with *The Case of the Gasping Garbage, and Other Super-scientific Cases,* which finds fifth-grade sleuths Drake Doyle and Nell Fossey teaming up with Nell's dog Dr. Livingston as well as with several science-smart adults to tackle local mysteries, one involving the sudden uptick in flattened frogs found on local roadways. Drake and Nell continue to clue in to scientific principles in *The Case of the Mossy Lake Monster, and Other Super-scientific Cases, The Case of the Barfy Birthday, and Other Super-scientific Cases, The Case of the Mossy Lake Monster, and Other Super-scientific Cases,* and *The Case of the Terrible T. Rex, and Other Super-scientific Cases.* Reviewing *The Case of the Graveyard Ghost, and Other Super-scientific Cases,* Rosenfeld wrote in *Booklist* that Torrey's chapter book serves up "a fast, easy read and fun way to learn about some everyday scientific principles." In *Kirkus Reviews* a critic had praise for the continuing series, predicting that "aspiring science detectives and their teachers will welcome the return of [Torrey's] . . . super-sleuths," while in *School Library Journal* Linda B. Zeilstra asserted of *The Case of the Graveyard Ghost, and Other Super-scientific Cases* that Nell and Drake "are believable and thoroughly engaging."

On her home page, Torrey discussed the importance of perseverance in becoming a writer, noting that most successful authors have collected numerous rejections. "Being a successful writer means putting yourself out there," she added, "being willing to face rejection head-on" "Not for rejection's sake," she added, "but to be able to take those rejections and then look critically at one's own work and ask yourself, 'What am I doing wrong?' and 'How can I make it better?'"

Biographical and Critical Sources

PERIODICALS

Booklist, August, 2001, John Peters, review of *The Case of the Gasping Garbage, and Other Super-scientific Cases,* p. 2122; January 1, 2002, Shelle Rosenfeld, review of *The Case of the Mossy Lake Monster, and Other Super-scientific Cases,* p. 860; October 15, 2002, Marta Segal Block, review of *The Case of the Graveyard Ghost, and Other Super-scientific Cases,* p. 405; February 1, 2003, Kathleen Odean, review of *To the Edge of the World,* p. 996; May 15, 2004, Jennifer Mattson, review of *Voyage of Ice,* p. 1632; May 15, 2005, Todd Morning, review of *Voyage of Plunder,* p. 1672; December 15, 2006, Shelle Rosenfeld, review of *Voyage of Midnight,* p 43.

Kirkus Reviews, January 1, 2002, review of *The Case of the Mossy Lake Monster, and Other Super-scientific Cases,* p. 52; July 15, 2002, review of *The Case of the Graveyard Ghost, and Other Super-scientific Cases;* December 15, 2002, review of *To the Edge of the World,* p. 1858; July 1, 2005, review of *Voyage of Plunder,* p. 745; November 1, 2006, review of *Voyage of Midnight,* p. 1125; July 1, 2010, review of *The Case of the Crooked Carnival, and Other Super-scientific Cases.*

Kliatt, January, 2003, Michele Winship, review of *To the Edge of the World;* July, 2005, Michele Winship, review of *Voyage of Plunder,* p. 16.

Publishers Weekly, May 10, 2004, review of *Voyage of Ice,* p. 59.

School Library Journal, August, 2001, Ashley Larsen, review of *The Case of the Gasping Garbage, and Other Super-scientific Cases,* p. 164; February, 2002, Kay Bowes, review of *The Case of the Mossy Lake Monster, and Other Super-scientific Cases,* p. 114; August, 2002, Linda B. Zeilstra, review of *The Case of the Graveyard Ghost, and Other Super-scientific Cases,* p. 171; February, 2003, Starr E. Smith, review of *To the Edge of the World,* p. 148; December, 2003, Debbie Whitbeck, review of *The Case of the Barfy Birthday, and Other Super-scientific Cases,* p. 129; July, 2004, Nancy P. Reeder, review of *Voyage of Ice,* p. 113; November, 2005, Christine McGinty, review of *Voyage of Plunder,* p. 150; January, 2007, Jane G. Connor, review of *Voyage of Midnight,* p. 140; January, 2011, Nicole Waskie-Laura, review of *The Case of the Crooked Carnival, and Other Super-scientific Cases,* p. 84; February, 2011, Terry Ann Lawler, review of *The Case of the Terrible T. Rex, and Other Super-scientific Cases,* p. 91.

ONLINE

Michele Torrey Home Page, http://micheletorrey.com (January 15, 2012).*

*   *   *

TRINE, Greg

Personal

Married; wife's name Juanita; children: daughters. *Education:* California State University—Northridge, B.S. (business), 1983.

Addresses

Home—Ventura, CA.

Career

Children's book author. Formerly worked as a window washer. Presenter at schools.

Member

Society of Children's Book Writers and Illustrators, Toastmasters.

Writings

The Second Base Club, Henry Holt (New York, NY), 2010.

"MELVIN BEEDERMAN, SUPERHERO" NOVEL SERIES;
ILLUSTRATED BY RHODE MONTIJO

The Curse of the Bologna Sandwich, Henry Holt (New York, NY), 2006.

The Revenge of the McNasty Brothers, Henry Holt (New York, NY), 2006.

The Grateful Fred, Henry Holt (New York, NY), 2006.

Terror in Tights, Henry Holt (New York, NY), 2007.

The Fake Cape Caper, Henry Holt (New York, NY), 2007.

Attack of the Valley Girls, Henry Holt (New York, NY), 2008.

The Brotherhood of the Traveling Underpants, Henry Holt (New York, NY), 2009.

Invasion from Planet Dork, Henry Holt (New York, NY), 2010.

Sidelights

Greg Trine was operating a business as a window cleaner in his hometown of Ventura, California, when the writing bug first bit. The voice of a nerdy preteen crime fighter—or perhaps the author's adolescent alter ego—talked Trine through *The Curse of the Bologna Sandwich,* the first of his "Melvin Beederman, Superhero" chapter books, and the author has continued the series through seven other humorous installments. Trine turns to slightly older readers in *The Second Base Club,* a young-adult novel in which a high-school sophomore tries on several different personas in his effort to attract a girlfriend.

When readers first meet Melvin in *The Curse of the Bologna Sandwich,* the boy is a successful graduate of the Superhero Academy. Eagerly scouring the Los Angeles environs for chances to put his many skills into practice, Melvin quickly realizes that experience counts for something: he needs several leaps before he can become airborne, his X-ray vision only exposes people's underwear, and tackling ne'er-do-wells requires the help of best friend Candace Brinkwater. Fueled on pretzels and root beer, however, the spunky caped crusader manages to take on the McNasty Brothers, an odiferous duo that has recently escaped from jail. Praising the retro-styled line drawings by illustrator Rhode Montijo that help to animate Melvin's adventures, a *Kirkus Reviews* writer noted of *The Curse of the Bologna Sandwich* that "Melvin exudes a seriousness at amusing odds with the tale's droll tone." The "deadpan delivery" of Trine's red-caped hero evokes the books of Dav Pilkey, noted a *Publishers Weekly* critic, and the adventures play out in a story "slyly sprinkled with borrowings from superhero tales."

Melvin continues to perfect his superhero skills in seven other adventures. Payback takes the shape of 6,000 pounds of unsliced bologna in *The Revenge of the Mc-* *Nasty Brothers,* while in *Attack of the Valley Girls* Melvin Beederman stumbles onto danger when he encounters sinister, hard-shopping fashionistas Chantelle and Brittany. *Terror in Tights* finds him battling a competing super hero while attempting to stay out of range of any and all bologna, and the series winds up in *Invasion from Planet Dork,* as the geeky crusader must defend Los Angeles science students from the predations of an evil group of visiting aliens. In *School Library Journal* Debbi Whitbeck characterized Trine's "Melvin Beederman, Superhero" chapter books as "bizarre, outrageous, and totally kid-friendly," making them a good choice for reluctant novice readers.

In *The Second Base Club* Elroy is sixteen years old and in tenth grade. Apart from grades and worries about his academic future, Elroy is sure that this will be the year he finds a girlfriend, his determination animated by his jock friends and their unofficial "second base club." Wrestlers have girlfriends, so he joins the wrestling team, and rock stars get girls, so he convinces his friends to start a band. As his popularity increases, Elroy is accepted by popular Sampson Teague and his group of jock friends and gets invited to their party. There he realizes what the "second base club" is really all about: using alcohol and date-rape drugs to take advantage of girls and keeping score of each conquest. When one of Sampson's potential victims turns out to be Elroy's friend, the teen is forced to reconsider just what he is actually after, and he ultimately makes a choice that both adds and detracts from his popularity.

Reviewing *The Second Base Club* in *Voice of Youth Advocates,* Alicia Abdul noted that the "humorous escapades" of Elroy and his friends Tuck and Vern "create a youthful balance between recklessness and ambition that is refreshing" and also make the teens seem realistic rather than "clichéd." A *Kirkus Reviews* writer characterized *The Second Base Club* as "full of gauche guy humor," adding that by novel's end "the reader is . . . squarely in Elroy's corner." Painting Trine's hero as "smart-alecky yet sensitive," a *Publishers Weekly* contributor predicted that "fans of . . . bawdy coming-of-age stories . . . should enjoy this journey to self-discovery," although Brandy Danner remarked in *School Library Journal* that the themes of "new and changing friendships" and Elroy's efforts to deal with his parents' divorce provide *The Second Base Club* with more-serious underpinnings.

Biographical and Critical Sources

PERIODICALS

Booklist, July 1, 2007, Stephanie Zvirin, review of *Terror in Tights,* p. 58.

Kirkus Reviews, June 1, 2006, review of *The Curse of the Bologna Sandwich,* p. 581; September 15, 2010, review of *The Second Base Club.*

Publishers Weekly, July 31, 2006, review of *The Curse of the Bologna Sandwich,* p. 75; October 11, 2010, review of *The Second Base Club,* p. 47.

School Library Journal, May, 2006, Rebecca Sheridan, review of *The Curse of the Bologna Sandwich,* p. 106; December, 2006, Adrienne Furness, review of *The Grateful Fred,* p. 116; August, 2007, Cheryl Ashton, review of *Terror in Tights,* p. 94; November, 2007, Debbie Whitbeck, review of *The Fake Cape Caper,* p. 101; November, 2010, Brandy Danner, review of *The Second Base Club,* p. 131.

Voice of Youth Advocates, December, 2010, Alicia Abdul, review of *The Second Base Club,* p. 463.

ONLINE

Melvin Beederman, Superhero Web site, http://www.melvinbeederman.com (January 15, 2012).

Ventura County Star Online, http://www.vcstar.com/ (June 18, 2010), Chuck O'Donnell, "Ventura Author Greg Trine Wraps up His 'Melvin Beederman' Series."*

*   *   *

TUTT, Keith 1959-
(David Douglas)

Personal

Born 1959, in England. *Education:* Attended Bristol University (philosophy and psychology), 1981.

Addresses

Home—Mid-Norfolk, England; Galicia, Spain. *E-mail*—keith@keithtutt.com.

Career

Scriptwriter, author, and maker of film documentaries. Red Fox Productions, managing director. Royal Literary Fund fellow, beginning 2008, at Anglia Ruskin University, Cambridge, and University of East Anglia. Instructor in scriptwriting and storytelling; Norwich School of Art and Design, visiting lecturer.

Awards, Honors

National Screenwriting Competition winner, 1987, for *The Blue Pearl;* B.T. Science Journalism of the Year award, 1993, for *Killing Us Softly?* (BBC-TV documentary); International Visual Communications Association Gold Award, 1995; (with others) British Association of

Film and Television Actors Award for Best International Children's Programme, 2000, for *Pablo, the Little Red Fox;* British Arts Council Escalator grant, 2005.

Writings

Unexplained Natural Phenomena, Orion Media (London, England), 1997, TV Books (New York, NY), 1999.

The Search for Free Energy, foreword by Sir Arthur C. Clarke, Simon & Schuster (London, England), 2001, published as *The Scientist, the Madman, the Thief, and Their Lightbulb: The Search for Free Energy,* Pocket Books (London, England), 2003.

Pablo Goes Hunting, illustrated by Hannah Giffard, Frances Lincoln Children's (London, England), 2005.

(As David Douglas) *The Atlas of Sacred Sites and Mystical Places,* Godsfield Press (England), 2007.

(As David Douglas) *The Atlas of Ancient Cults and Mystery Religions,* Godsfield Press (England), 2008.

(As David Douglas) *The Mayan Prophecy 2012,* Godsfield Press (England), 2008.

Pablo Meets the Neighbours, illustrated by Hannah Giffard, Frances Lincoln Children's (London, England), 2009.

Also author of novels *A2Z* and *NOVEL.*

Adaptations

A2Z was adapted as a film, Punk Cinema/Lightpath Productions, c. 2012.

Biographical and Critical Sources

PERIODICALS

Kirkus Reviews, September 15, 2010, review of *Pablo Meets the Neighbours.*

School Library Journal, December, 2010, Susan E, Murray, review of *Pablo Meets the Neighbours,* p. 89.

ONLINE

Keith Tutt Home Page, http://www.keithtutt.com (January 9, 2012).

Keith Tutt Web log, http://keithtuttblog.wordpress.com (January 9, 2012).

Royal Literary Fund Web site, http://www.rlf.org.uk/ (January 9, 2012), "Keith Tutt."

U-W

UPJOHN, Rebecca 1962-

Personal

Born 1962, in Toronto, Ontario, Canada; immigrated to United States; married children: sons. *Education:* Ryerson University, degree (photography).

Addresses

Home—Toronto, Ontario, Canada; New Hampshire. *E-mail*—rebecca.upjohn@gmail.com.

Career

Writer. Worked as an architectural photographer in Toronto, Ontario, Canada; worked on a sheep farm in New Hampshire. Volunteer in elementary schools.

Member

Canadian Society of Children's Authors, Illustrators, and Performers, Canadian Children's Book Centre, Writers' Union of Canada, Society of Children's Book Writers and Illustrators (Eastern Canada chapter).

Awards, Honors

ForeWord magazine Book of the Year Award in picture-book category, 2007, Blue Spruce Award finalist, 2008, and Shining Willow Award finalist, 2009, all for *Lily and the Paper Man;* Jean Throop Book Award, Toronto IODE, 2010, and Silver Birch Express Award nomination, 2012, both for *The Last Loon.*

Writings

Lily and the Paper Man, illustrated by Renné Benoit, Second Story Press (Toronto, Ontario, Canada), 2007.
The Last Loon, Orca Book Publishers (Custer, WA), 2010.
(With Karen Mitchell) *Patrick's Wish,* photographs by Patrick4Life, Second Story Press (Toronto, Ontario, Canada), 2010.

Author's work has been translated into Dutch and French.

Sidelights

A writer who divides her time between rural New Hampshire and her native Canada, Rebecca Upjohn is the author of several books for children: *Lily and the Paper Man,* illustrated by Renné Benoit, and *The Last Loon.* Upjohn has also collaborated with teacher Karen Mitchell on *Patrick's Wish,* a true story about a boy with hemophilia who contracted AIDS due to a blood transfusion. Told from the first-person perspective of Patrick Fortin's little sister, Lyanne, the story chronicles Patrick's diagnosis at age seven and the stages of his illness up to his death in 2001 at age twenty-three. Noting that *Patrick's Wish* is "simply written" to be accessible to elementary-aged readers, a *Children's Bookwatch* contributor added that the work ends with a list of statements Patrick once made in his efforts to educate the public about his condition. "These nine simple statements constitute the most effective AIDS-HIV awareness education effort for elementary age children to date," asserted the critic.

Upjohn's first published story for children, *Lily and the Paper Man,* was inspired by her elder son's reaction, when he was four years old, to seeing a homeless man on the street in Toronto and his subsequent desire to help. In her tale, Lily is taking the walk home from school with her mother when she sees a man wearing tattered clothing and selling newspapers on a street corner. Realizing that he is different from the adults she normally encounters, Lily is afraid and makes a point of avoiding him. A deep chill is in the air the next time she sees the newspaper vendor, and his clothing seems just as worn and threadbare as before. Learning from her mother that not everyone has the same comforts in life, Lily ponders how to help the "Paper Man," and her act of kindness is captured in colorful line-and-watercolor artwork by Benoit. Praising *Lily and the Paper Man* for its "compassionate, realistic story," Hazel

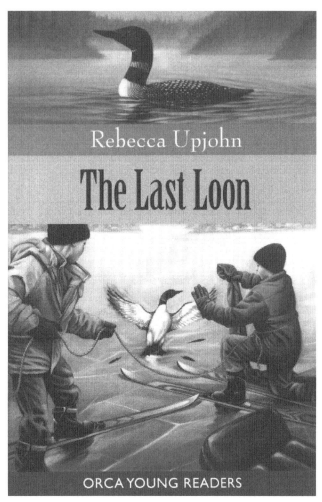

Cover of Rebecca Upjohn's nature-themed novel **The Last Loon**, *featuring artwork by Ken Dewar.* (Jacket art copyright © 2010 by Ken Dewar. Reproduced by permission of Orca Book Publishers.)

Rochman added in *Booklist* that Upjohn's book will show preschoolers that, despite their age, they have the ability to "help someone in need."

An older child is the focus of Upjohn's story in *The Last Loon*, a chapter book inspired by an avian rescue on a lake where the author spent several childhood summers. While growing up, she loved reading both animal and adventure stories, and writing *The Last Loon* allowed her to combine these two favorite elements. For eleven-year-old Evan Kemp, the prospect of spending the Christmas holiday with Aunt Mag is not an exciting one: in addition to living a close-to-nature life, the woman is so devoted to environmental causes that she has even been arrested for her activism. Once he unpacks his bags at Mag's rural home, he realize that his aunt is agitated, not by Christmas, but by the fact that a wild loon has become trapped on the ice of a nearby lake. Evan is first dismissive of the animal's plight, but as he talks to others, including his new friend Cedar, he becomes inspired by their affection for the wilderness and their sense of community. Ultimately, Evan "becomes the bird's most ardent advocate," asserted a *Kirkus Reviews* writer, the critic praising *The*

Last Loon as "a beginning chapter book with a good story and a clear environmental message." In *Canadian Review of Materials,* Myra Junyk praised Upjohn for addressing "environmental responsibility, . . . animal rights, biodiversity, . . . and the ecology of Canada's North" in her nature-themed adventure, adding that "short chapters and accessible vocabulary will make *The Last Loon* . . . "a good choice" for its intended eight-to-ten-year-old audience.

Biographical and Critical Sources

PERIODICALS

Booklist, December 1, 2007, Hazel Rochman, review of *Lily and the Paper Man,* p. 48.
Children's Bookwatch December, 2007, review of *Lily and the Paper Man;* May, 2010, review of *Patrick's Wish.*
Canadian Review of Materials, September 17, 2010, Myra Junyk, review of *The Last Loon.*
Kirkus Reviews, June 18, 2010, Ellen Heaney, review of *Patrick's Wish;* September 15, 2010, review of *The Last Loon.*
Resource Links, December, 2007, Zoe Johnstone, review of *Lily and the Paper Man,* p. 13.
School Library Journal, January, 2011, Eva Elisabeth VonAncken, review of *The Last Loon,* p. 118.

ONLINE

Rebecca Upjohn Home Page, http://www.rebeccaupjohn. com (January 15, 2012).

*   *   *

WARING, Geoff

Personal

Born in London, England; married; children: two. *Education:* Manchester Polytechnic, degree, 1984.

Addresses

Home—Kent, England. *Agent*—Philippa Milnes-Smith, Lucas Alexander Whitley, 14 Vernon St., London W14 0RJ, England. *E-mail*—geoffreywaring@gmail.com.

Career

Art director, illustrator, and author. Art director for magazines, including *Elle, Red,* and *Vogue Australia;* former creative director at *Glamour* and *Easy Living; Good Housekeeping,* creative director; consulting art director at *Tatler* and for Haymarket Publishing.

Awards, Honors

English 4-11 Book Award, 2006, for *Oscar and the Frog;* Outstanding Science Trade Books for Students K-12 selection, National Science Teachers Association/ Children's Book Council, 2011, for *Just One Bite* by Lola Schaefer.

Writings

'START WITH SCIENCE" SERIES; SELF-ILLUSTRATED

Oscar and the Frog: A Book about Growing, Walker Books (London, England), 2006, Candlewick Press (Cambridge, MA), 2007.

Oscar and the Moth: A Book about Light and Dark, Walker Books (London, England), 2006, Candlewick Press (Cambridge, MA), 2007.

Oscar and the Bat: A Book about Sound, Walker Books (London, England), 2006, Candlewick Press (Cambridge, MA), 2008.

Oscar and the Cricket: A Book about Moving and Rolling, Walker Books (London, England), 2006, Candlewick Press (Cambridge, MA), 2008.

Oscar and the Bird: A Book about Electricity, Walker Books (London, England), 2008, Candlewick Press (Cambridge, MA), 2009.

Oscar and the Snail: A Book about Things That We Use, Walker Books (London, England), 2008, Candlewick Press (Cambridge, MA), 2009.

ILLUSTRATOR

Justine Fontes, *Black Meets White,* Candlewick Press (Cambridge, MA), 2005.

Lola Schaefer, *Just One Bite,* Chronicle Books (San Francisco, CA), 2010.

Sidelights

A respected designer and art director who has worked for *Elle, Vogue Australia, Glamour,* and other publications, Geoff Waring has also written and illustrated a number of children's books, including *Oscar and the Frog: A Book about Growing* and *Oscar and the Bat: A Book about Sound.* In these "Start with Science" books, which were inspired by his own cat, Waring introduces a curious kitten named Oscar who learns about the natural world through his encounters with a variety of helpful creatures.

In *Oscar and the Frog* the young cat ambles down to the pond where a patient amphibian teaches him how some creatures hatch from eggs, while others give birth to their young and how new plants develop from seeds. Carolyn Phelan, writing in *Booklist,* noted that "Oscar's questions are natural and childlike, and the simple answers will probably satisfy the intended audience." Waring explores the concepts of bioluminescence, night and day, and shadows in *Oscar and the Moth: A Book about Light and Dark,* and in *Oscar and the Cricket: A Book about Moving and Rolling,* he discusses the forces that affect motion.

Waring's inquisitive kitten learns how to identify the sounds of animals in the meadow—as well as an approaching thunderstorm—in *Oscar and the Bat.* "Without abstraction, this picture book will fascinate beginning readers," Hazel Rochman commented in *Booklist.* Writing in *School Library Journal,* Carol S. Surges noted that Waring's digitally produced art "has muted tones and mostly flat shapes reminiscent of illustrations from the 1950s."

In addition to creating his self-illustrated stories, Waring has provided the artwork for *Black Meets White,* a picture book by Justine Fontes that features die-cut pages and pull tabs. In the work, the author presents a fanciful meeting between the opposite hues, which morph into a host of tantalizing shapes. *School Library Journal* contributor Roxanne Burg observed of *Black Meets White* that "the layout is clever and creative."

Lola Schaefer's *Just One Bite* was described as an "expert blend of art and science" by a *Publishers Weekly* critic. In his art for this story, Waring shows young readers just how much food ten animals—from an earthworm to a Komodo dragon to an octopus—can devour in a single mouthful. "The terrific, artfully composed brush, crayon and computer-aided artwork is lavish," a writer noted in *Kirkus Reviews,* and *School Library Journal* critic Patricia Manning described the work as "attractive, colorful, and impressively big."

Biographical and Critical Sources

PERIODICALS

Booklist, December 15, 2007, Carolyn Phelan, review of *Oscar and the Frog: A Book about Growing,* p. 52; December 1, 2008, Hazel Rochman, review of *Oscar and the Bat: A Book about Sound,* p. 67; November 1, 2010, Andrew Medlar, review of *Just One Bite,* p. 50.

Kirkus Reviews, June 15, 2005, review of *Black Meets White,* p. 682; September 15, 2010, review of *Just One Bite.*

Publishers Weekly, July 18, 2005, review of *Black Meets White,* p. 204; December 3, 2007, reviews of *Oscar and the Frog* and *Oscar and the Moth: A Book about Light and Dark,* both p. 73; September 27, 2010, review of *Just One Bite,* p. 58.

School Library Journal, November, 2005, Roxanne Burg, review of *Black Meets White,* p. 90; February, 2008, Ieva Bates, reviews of *Oscar and the Frog* and *Oscar and the Moth,* both p. 98; December, 2008, Carol S. Surges, reviews of *Oscar and the Bat,* and *Oscar and the Cricket: A Book about Moving and Rolling,* both p. 117; November, 2010, Patricia Manning, review of *Just One Bite,* p. 93.

ONLINE

Geoff Waring Home Page, http://www.geoffwaring.com (January 15, 2012).

Professional Photographer Web site, http://www.professionalphotographer.co.uk/ (August 24, 2009), "Geoff Waring—Ex Art Director of Australian and UK *Vogue* Magazines."

Walker Books Web site, http://www.walker.co.uk/ (January 15, 2012), "Geoff Waring."

*   *   *

WHEAT, Chris 1949-

Personal

Born 1949, in Melbourne, Victoria, Australia. *Education:* College degree. *Hobbies and other interests:* Politics.

Addresses

Home—Melbourne, Victoria, Australia.

Career

Writer and educator. Sunshine Secondary College, Melbourne, Victoria, Australia, teacher at senior campus. Presenter at writers' festivals.

Awards, Honors

Children's Book Council Children's Book of the Year Awards Notable Book for Older Readers, 2002, for *Grinders.*

Writings

Two-Stroke Shane, Collins Dove Australia (Melbourne, Victoria, Australia), 1990.

Loose Lips, Hyland House (South Melbourne, Victoria, Australia), 1998.

My Excellent Lives, Hyland House (South Melbourne, Victoria, Australia), 1999.

Grinders, Hyland House (South Melbourne, Victoria, Australia), 2001.

Screw Loose, Allen & Unwin (Crows Nest, New South Wales, Australia), 2008.

Contributor of poems and short fiction to anthologies; contributor of reviews to periodicals, including Australia *Age, English in Australia,* and *Viewpoint.*

Biographical and Critical Sources

PERIODICALS

Kirkus Reviews, September 15, 2010, review of *Screw Loose.*

School Library Journal, January, 2011, Richard Luzer, review of *Screw Loose,* p. 119.

ONLINE

Allen & Unwin Web site, http://www.allenandunwin.com/ (January 15, 2012), "Chris Wheat."

January Online, http://januarymagazine.blogspot.com/ June, 2008), interview with Wheat.*

*   *   *

WHELAN, Kat

Personal

Born in England; married; husband's name Rich. *Education:* College degree, 2002.

Addresses

Home—Bath, England. *E-mail*—katwhelan@hotmail.co.uk.

Career

Illustrator and graphic designer. Portico Designs, Bath, England, card illustrator, 2002-06; Remind4u (online greeting card company), illustrator, 2006-08; freelance illustrator.

Illustrator

Clement C. Moore, *'Twas the Night before Christmas,* Tiger Tales (Wilton, CT), 2010.

Tammi Salzano, *One Little Blueberry,* Tiger Tales (Wilton, CT), 2011.

Contributor to books, including *Old MacDonald and Other Animal Songs,* 2011, and to periodicals, including *Popular Crafts.*

Biographical and Critical Sources

PERIODICALS

School Library Journal, October, 2010, Eva Mitnick, review of *'Twas the Night before Christmas,* p. 75; June, 2011, Rachel Artley, review of *One Little Blueberry,* p. 94.

ONLINE

Kat Whelan Home Page, http://www.katwhelan.com (January 15, 2012).*

*   *   *

WHITE, Linda
See WHITE, Linda Arms

WHITE, Linda Arms
(Linda White)

Personal

Married Trig White; children: four.

Addresses

Home—Allenspark, CO.

Career

Writer. Cofounder, with Laura Backes, of Children's Authors' Bootcamp; speaker at conferences, workshops, and schools.

Awards, Honors

American Booksellers Association (ABA) Pick of the List selection, Best Children's Books of the Year selection, Bank Street College of Education, Children's Choice selection, International Reading Association/Children's Book Council (CBC), all c. 1996, all for *Too Many Pumpkins;* ABA Pick of the List selection, Best 100 Books for Reading and Sharing selection, New York Public Library, Best of the Best selection, Chicago Public Library, Children's Literature Choice selection, and *Storytelling World* Awards Honor Book selection, all c. 2000, all for *Comes a Wind;* Gold Award, Oppenheim Toy Portfolio, Notable Trade Book in the Field of Social Studies selection, National Council of the Social Studies/CBC, Christopher Award, Amelia Bloomer

Linda Arms White recalls an inspiring story of girl power in I Could Do That!, *a history-themed picture book featuring artwork by Nancy Carpenter.*
(Illustration copyright © 2005 by Nancy Carpenter. Reproduced by permission of Melanie Kroupa Books, an imprint of Farrar, Straus & Giroux.)

Project selection, American Library Association, and *Storytelling World* Awards Honor Book selection, all 2005, all for *I Could Do That!;* finalist for several state awards.

Writings

FICTION FOR CHILDREN

Too Many Pumpkins, illustrated by Megan Lloyd, Holiday House (New York, NY), 1996.
(Under name Linda Arms White) *Comes a Wind,* illustrated by Tom Curry, DK Pub. (New York, NY), 2000.
(Under name Linda Arms White) *I Could Do That! Esther Morris Gets Women the Vote,* illustrated by Nancy Carpenter, Farrar, Straus & Giroux (New York, NY), 2005.
Too Many Turkeys, illustrated by Megan Lloyd, Holiday House (New York, NY), 2010.

NONFICTION

Cooking on a Stick: Campfire Recipes for Kids, illustrated by Fran Lee, Gibbs Smith (Salt Lake City, UT), 1996.
Sleeping in a Sack: Camping Activities for Kids, illustrated by Fran Lee, Gibbs-Smith (Salt Lake City, UT), 1998.
(Under name Linda Arms White) *Log Spirit,* Gibbs-Smith (Salt Lake City, UT), 2000.
Trekking on a Trail: Hiking Adventures for Kids, illustrated by Fran Lee, Gibbs Smith (Layton, UT), 2000.
Haunting on a Halloween: Frightful Activities for Kids, illustrated by Fran Lee, Gibbs Smith (Salt Lake City, UT), 2002.
(With daughter Katherine L. White) *The Pocket Guide to Camping,* illustrated by Remie Geoffroi, Gibbs Smith (Layton, UT), 2011.

Adaptations

I Could Do That! was adapted for video by Weston Woods, 2006.

Sidelights

A writer as well as a writing coach, Linda Arms White is the author of award-winning stories for young children that include *Comes a Wind* as well as the companion picture books *Too Many Pumpkins* and *Too Many Turkeys.* Geared for slightly older children, White's quasi-biographical picture book *I Could Do That!: Esther Morris Gets Women the Vote* captures the growing confidence of a young girl growing up to see possibilities in a changing work. In addition to her fictional stories, White has also written several guides for young outdoors fanatics, among them *Sleeping in a Sack: Camping Activities for Kids* and *The Pocket Guide to Camping,* the latter coauthored with daughter, Katherine L. White. Her book *Log Spirit* is a guide for those in-

terested in rustic log-cabin-style architecture and was inspired by her family's experience designing and building their own home in rural Colorado.

In *Comes a Wind* Texas-born brothers Clyde and Clement have been in competition since they were little boys, but on Mama's birthday they promise to stop trying to best each other, at least for the day. When Clement tells a story about a strong wind, Clyde cannot stop himself from telling one with a more-dramatic ending, and eventually an actual wind blows in that is so strong that it carries their frustrated mother up and away. Featuring artwork by Tom Currey, *Comes a Wind* is the perfect choice to "get story times off to a rollicking start," in the opinion of *Booklist* contributor Susan Dove Lempke, and a *Publishers Weekly* critic concluded that both story and art "share a deadpan comic delivery [that is] . . . perfectly suited to the hyperbolic banter and the sublimely ridiculous events."

Mining the few facts remaining in the historical record, White recasts the story of the first U.S. woman to hold public office in *I Could Do That!* With illustrations by Nancy Carpenter, the story follows a girl named Esther Morris, beginning with her childhood in New York as she anticipates being able to do grown-up tasks like her mother. At age nineteen Morris starts her own business as a milliner, and in 1869 she and her husband brave the arduous journey west to the Wyoming Territory, where she sees other possibilities. Joining the call for women's suffrage, Morris helps to earn voting rights for women and ultimately gains appointment to a local judgeship. "White's text vividly builds a larger-than-life character," wrote a *Kirkus Reviews* writer, the critic calling *I Could Do That!* "a rollicking good story" that will inspire listeners' own ambitions. The author "almost certainly gives Morris more credit than she was due," observed Gail Collins in her review of the picture book for the *New York Times Book Review.* "But this is quibbling," Collins added, her positive appraisal aligning with the view of *Booklist* contributor Jennifer Mattson that White's "well-crafted story . . . secures Morris a deserved place in the sorority of redoubtable picture-book heroines."

Biographical and Critical Sources

PERIODICALS

Booklist, March 15, 2000, Susan Dove Lempke, review of *Comes a Wind,* p. 1390; September 15, 2005, Jennifer Mattson, review of *I Could Do That!: Esther Morris Gets Women the Vote,* p. 63.
Kirkus Reviews, August 15, 2005, review of *I Could Do That!,* p. 924.
New York Times Book Review, November 13, 2005, Gail Collins, review of *I Could Do That!,* p. 27.
Publishers Weekly, February 21, 2000, review of *Comes a Wind,* p. 86.

School Library Journal, May, 2000, Ginny Gustin, review of *Comes a Wind,* p. 158; September, 2005, Lucinda Snyder Whitehurst, review of *I Could Do That!,* p. 197; March, 2006, John Peters, review of *I Could Do That!,* p. 88; January, 2007, Teresa Bateman, review of *I Could Do That!,* p. 64.

ONLINE

Linda Arms White Home Page, http://lindaarmswhite.com (January 15, 2012).*

*   *   *

WHITMAN, Emily

Personal

Born in Boulder, CO. *Education:* Attended Harvard University and University of California at Berkeley. *Hobbies and other interests:* Cooking, travel, ancient stones.

Addresses

Home—Portland, OR.

Career

Writer and educator. Formerly worked as a reference librarian. Presenter at schools and conferences.

Awards, Honors

Oregon Book Award finalist, 2011, for *Radiant Darkness.*

Writings

(With Lissa Rovetch) *Sir Henry, the Polite Knight,* illustrated by Bryn Barnard, Kindermusik International (Greensboro, NC), 2007.
Radiant Darkness, Greenwillow Books (New York, NY), 2009.
Wildwing, Greenwillow Books (New York, NY), 2010.

Sidelights

A Colorado native who is now based in Oregon, Emily Whitman writes young-adult novels that interweave elements of mythology, time travel, romance, and fantasy. In addition to producing the novels *Radiant Darkness* and *Wildwing,* Whitman has also worked for educational publishers and she shares her experiences as a writer with audiences at regional writers' conferences.

Whitman takes the myth of Persephone as her starting point in *Radiant Darkness* and develops the Greek goddess as a willful adolescent. The daughter of Demeter, goddess of the harvest, Persephone lives amid lush surroundings in a literal Paradise. Despite the natural beauty around her, the young woman feels stifled by her mother's overprotective nature and is tempted when a handsome young stranger named Hades shows up in his chariot and promises to give her freedom. Following the course of the myth, Persephone follows her new love down to his underworld kingdom while her heart-broken mother is left without knowledge of the young woman's whereabouts. Although Demeter's neglect causes earthly vegetation to wither, her daughter's growing appreciation for her former home allows both the mother's sadness and the earth to eventually come into seasonal balance.

"Whitman has a way with worlds," noted a *Kirkus Reviews* writer in an appraisal of *Radiant Darkness,* the critic citing the novel's "spunky" heroine. According to *Booklist* critic Gillian Engberg, the author re-crafts the classic myth into "a steamy coming-of-age novel laced with feminist sensibilities" by casting Persephone as self-actualizing rather than as a victim. The romance between Hades and Persephone, as well as "the con-

Cover of Emily Whitman's young-adult fantasy **Wildwing,** *which finds a teen transported from the early twentieth century to the Middle Ages.* (Jacket art copyright © 2010 by Ali Smith. Reproduced by permission of Greenwillow Books, an imprint of HarperCollins Children's Books, a division of HarperCollins Publishing, Inc.)

temporary tone" of the "first person narrative" in *Radiant Darkness* "will capture some readers," predicted *School Library Journal* contributor Angela J. Reynolds, while a *Publishers Weekly* contributor concluded that "Persephone is a relatable character" and her "narration entertains."

The year is 1913 and Addy is a modern fifteen year old living in a small English village when readers first meet her in *Wildwing*. With her father dead and her mum struggling to make ends meet, the teen feels dissatisfied with her lot in life, and things only get worse when she is forced to leave school and take a job as a domestic in the service of old Mr. Greenwood. A locked door in the man's house proves to be too much of a temptation for Addy, and when she opens it to discover a time machine that will transport her back to the Middle Ages there is no question that she will risk the journey. Arriving in the thirteenth century, Addy benefits from being mistaken for Lady Matilda, a ward to a local lord. Adorned with lavish gowns and beautiful jewels and waited on by servants, the teen gains the attention she was missing in her real life, and she accepts Lady Matilda's destiny as future wife of the as-yet-unseen Sir Hugh. When Addy meets Will, the son of the lord's falconer, and falls in love with him, she must reconsider the obligations of a noblewoman of the thirteenth century and decide whether her own feelings should supplant a marriage beneficial those dependent upon the political alliance it will forge. Comparing *Wildwing* to the work of novelist Libba Bray, Sara Saxton wrote in *School Library Journal* that "Whitman populates both of [Addy's] . . . worlds with vivid, believable characters." In *Kirkus Reviews* a contributor also praised the historical fantasy, calling Addy "an engagingly inventive heroine" in a compelling novel rich with "historical detail and vivid descriptions."

Biographical and Critical Sources

PERIODICALS

Booklist, May 15, 2009, Gillian Engberg, review of *Radiant Darkness,* p. 53.
Bulletin of the Center for Children's Books, June, 2009, Kate McDowell, review of *Radiant Darkness,* p. 423.
Kirkus Reviews, April 1, 2009, review of *Radiant Darkness.*
Publishers Weekly, May 11, 2009, review of *Radiant Darkness,* p. 53.
School Library Journal, August, 2009, Angela J. Reynolds, review of *Radiant Darkness,* p. 116; January, 2011, Sara Saxton, review of *Wildwing,* p. 120.
Voice of Youth Advocates, August, 2009, review of *Radiant Darkness,* p. 246.

ONLINE

Emily Whitman Home Page, http://www.emilywhitman.com (January 15, 2012).*

WILLARD, Elizabeth Kimmel
See KIMMEL, Elizabeth Cody

*   *   *

WILLIAMS, Gabrielle

Personal

Born in Victoria, Australia; married; children: Dominique, Harry, Andrew. *Education:* College degree.

Addresses

Home—Melbourne, Victoria, Australia.

Career

Novelist. Worked as a copywriter in the advertising field.

Writings

Two Canadian Clubs and Dry at the Martini Den, HarperCollins (Pymble, New South Wales, Australia), 2001, published as *Liar, Liar,* Kensington (New York, NY), 2003.
Beatle Meets Destiny, Penguin Group (Camberwell, Victoria, Australia), 2009, Marshall Cavendish (New York, NY), 2010.
King Charlie, YBA Pub. (Alexandria, VA), 2011.

Adaptations

Beatle Meets Destiny was optioned for film, 2009.

Sidelights

For Australian writer Gabrielle Williams, eavesdropping on the conversations of her teenaged offspring was a crucial research component of her first young-adult novel, *Beatle Meets Destiny*. A whimsical story about a young couple who credits their mutual attraction to the work of Fate, Williams' fiction debut has won fans in both Australia and North America in addition to being optioned for film. "I think there are a lot of books out there for young adults which have a grim storyline," the novelist observed in an interview with *Australian Women Online* contributor Deborah Robinson. "Bad things happen to kids in books. But I wanted to write a book about kids that are pretty happy—they're not self-mutilating, . . . they're not totally depressed, and they don't hate the world."

Born with the name John Lennon, the eighteen-year-old hero of *Beatle Meets Destiny* has answered to the nickname Beatle as long as he can remember. Since so many uncontrollable forces have shaped his world, the teen has learned to take life as it comes, and this approach is encourage by a mother who has raised both Beatle and his twin sister Winsome on a steady diet of sun-sign-based prognostications, serendipitous encounters, and a well-honed knowledge of superstitions. Within this sea of little logic Beatle has found an island of comfort in his relationship with Cilla, Winsome's best friend and a girl who has stood by him even after a stroke left him with a limp. But then comes Friday the thirteenth, and there Beatle is, standing on a train platform face to face with a girl named Destiny McCartney. As if their immediate liking for one another is not enough, the two quickly realize that their meeting is at the top of a ladder of coincidences involving family, friends, and their shared acceptance of the vagaries of life.

Describing *Beatle Meets Destiny* as a "quirky Australian import," a *Publishers Weekly* critic added that Williams treats readers to a "quick-paced" romance that features "highly original characters, multilayered plots, and idiosyncratic twists." "Deliciously plotted," according to *Booklist* contributor Ilene Cooper, the novel is "filled with superstitions and portents, and lots of fun," and the references to Australian pop culture are easy for U.S. teens to navigate. Remarking on the many coincidences that fuel the romance in *Beatle Meets Destiny*, a *Kirkus Reviews* writer predicted that teen readers who are "willing to suspend their disbelief . . . will enjoy

Gabrielle Williams draws teen readers into a world full of coincidences in her quirky novel Beatle Meets Destiny. (Jacket cover copyright by Marshall Cavendish. Reproduced by permission of Marshall Cavendish Corporation.)

the awkwardly hilarious scenarios" throughout the story, while in *Voice of Youth Advocates* Teri S. Lesesne hinted that the way romance plays out in Williams' "convoluted story" is "one of the many surprises in store for readers."

Biographical and Critical Sources

PERIODICALS

Booklist, December 15, 2003, Kristine Huntley, review of *Liar, Liar,* p. 734; September 15, 2010, Ilene Cooper, review of *Beatle Meets Destiny,* p. 72.

Kirkus Reviews, September 15, 2010, review of *Beatle Meets Destiny.*

Publishers Weekly, October 11, 2010, review of *Beatle Meets Destiny,* p. 46.

School Library Journal, December, 2010, Brandy Danner, review of *Beatle Meets Destiny,* p. 131.

Voice of Youth Advocates, December, 2010, Teri S. Lesesne, review of *Beatle Meets Destiny,* p. 464.

ONLINE

Australian Women Online Web site, http://www.australian womenonline.com/ (August 9, 2009), Deborah Robinson, interview with Williams.*

*   *   *

WOLF, Gita 1956-
(Gita Wolf-Sampath)

Personal

Born December 6, 1956, in Calcutta, India; daughter of B.R. and Komala Sampath; married Helmut Wolf (an alchemist), March 12, 1978; children: Arun Eric Wolf. *Education:* University of Erlangen (Germany), M.A. (English). *Politics:* "Left."

Addresses

Home—India. *Office*—Tara Publishing House, "Shoreham," Flat GA, 5th Ave., Besant Nagar, Chennai 600 090, India.

Career

Publisher and author. Tara Publishing, Chennai, India, founder and publisher, beginning 1993.

Awards, Honors

Biennale of Illustration Bratislava Grand Prix, 1999, for *Hensparrow Turns Purple,* illustrated by Pulak Biswas; Alcuin citation (Canada), for Excellence in Book Design; Independent Publisher Awards honorable mentions, 2003, for *The Legend of the Fish,* 2004, for *The London Jungle Book.*

Writings

FOR CHILDREN

(As Gita Wolf-Sampath) *Mala: A Women's Folktale,* illustrated by Subha De, Tara Books (Madras, India), 1994.

(Adaptor) *The Very Hungry Lion: A Folktale,* illustrated by Indrapramit Roy, Tara Books (Madras, India), 1995.

Hensparrow Turns Purple, illustrated by Pulak Biswas, Tara Books (Chennai, India), 1998.

(With Sudarshan Khanna and Anushka Ravishankar) *Toys and Tales with Everyday Materials,* Tara Books/ National Institute of Design (Chennai, India), 1999.

(With Anushka Ravishankar and Orijit Sen) *Trash!: On Ragpicker Children and Recycling,* Tara Books (Chennai, India), 1999.

(With Sirish Rao) *The Tree Girl,* illustrated by Indrapramit Roy, Tara Books (Chennai, India), 2001.

(With V. Geetha and Anushka Ravishankar) *Masks and Performance with Everyday Materials,* Tara Books (Chennai, India), 2003.

(With Sirish Rao and Emanuele Scanziani) *The Legend of the Fish,* Tara Books (Chennai, India), 2003.

(With Sirish Rao) *In the Dark,* illustrated by Ranthna Ramanathan, Consortium (Chennai, India), 2004.

(With Bhajju Shyam and Sirish Rao) *The London Jungle Book,* Tara Books (Chennai, India), 2004.

(Adaptor and editor with Sirish Rao) *The Night Life of Trees,* illustrated by Bhajju Shyam, Durga Bai, and Ram Singh Urveti, Tara Books (Chennai, India), 2006.

(With Sirish Rao) *The Flight of the Mermaid,* illustrated by Bhajju Shyam, Tara Books (Channai, India), 2009.

Monkey Photo, illustrated by Swarna Chitrakar, Tara Books (Chennai, India), 2010.

The Churki-Burki Book of Rhyme, illustrated by Durga Bai, Tara Books (Chennai, India) 2010.

Following my Paint Brush, illustrated by Dulari Devi, Tara Books (Chennai, India), 2011.

RETELLING THE CLASSICS; RETELLER WITH SIRISH RAO

Sophocles' Antigone, illustrated by Indrapramit Roy, J. Paul Getty Museum (Los Angeles, CA), 2001.

Euripides' The Bacchae, illustrated by Indrapramit Roy, J. Paul Getty Museum (Los Angeles, CA), 2004.

Sophocles' Oedipus the King, illustrated by Indrapramit Roy, J. Paul Getty Museum (Los Angeles, CA), 2004.

Euripides' Hippolytos, illustrated by Indrapramit Roy, J. Paul Getty Museum (Los Angeles, CA), 2006.

OTHER

(Editor) *Landscapes, Children's Voices,* Tara Publishing/ Madras Craft Foundation (Madras, India), 1995.

Picturing Words and Reading Pictures: Illustration and Children's Literature, Goodbooks Marketing (Chennai, India), 1997.

(Compiler with Sirish Rao and V. Geetha) *An Ideal Boy: Charts from India,* Tara Books (Stockport, England), 2001.

(Editor with Kanchana Arni) *Beasts of India,* Tara Books (Madras, India), 2003.

(With Madan Meena) *Nurturing Walls: Animal Art by Meena Women,* Tara Books (Chennai, India), 2008.

(With Lanna Andréadis) *SSSS: Snake Art and Allegory,* Tara Books (Chennai, India), 2010.

(Editor with Bhajju Shyam and Jonathan Yamakami) *Signature: Patterns in Gond Art,* Tara Books (Chennai, India), 2010.

Contributor to periodicals, including *World Literature Today.*

Sidelights

Born and raised in India, author and publisher Gita Wolf has written educational books, as well as picture-book adaptations of traditional folktales from her native country. In her works for children, which include *Mala: A Women's Folktale, The Very Hungry Lion: A Folktale, The Flight of the Mermaid, The Tree Girl,* and *The Night Life of Trees* as well as *Monkey Photo* and *The Churki-Burki Book of Rhyme,* Wolf approaches traditional stories from a contemporary, woman-centered angle: her protagonists are usually young, resourceful girls who combat the odds to make positive changes in the world around them. This approach gives her fiction what *Books in Canada* reviewer Marilyn Andrews called a "gentle feminist thrust that empowers" her young characters.

Wolf created Tara Publishing House in Chennai, India, after returning home from Germany in the early 1990s. Wishing to move from academics to publishing, she contemplated working for an established business but the few options available to her inspired Wolf to consider starting her own business. Her connection with the Cholamandal Artists' Collective helped move her toward crafting books incorporating traditional art forms in new ways, and her search for stories suitable for her own young son convinced her to begin her publishing career focusing on quality handmade children's books.

Produced in the early 1990s by the fledgling Tara Publishing House, *Mala* is the story of an Indian girl who sets out to save her small village from a terrible drought that has destroyed its food supply. The cause, as she discovers, is that a demon has swallowed the water-giving rain seed, and she determines to seek out this demon and cause the rains to fall again. Mala also hopes to find her brother, Mani, who has been turned to stone by the wicked demon. She dons boy's clothes and goes on a journey during which she encounters a series of difficult obstacles. Praising *Mala* in *Books in Canada,* Andrews noted that, for girls who "cannot see themselves beyond aspiring to be ballerinas or [mothers, *Mala*] will broaden their horizons in a very positive and encouraging way." Although Wolf's story lacks strong dramatic tension, according to *Quill & Quire* contributor Phyllis Simons, by the book's conclusion Mala is "justly rewarded for her bravery and wisdom" and serves as "a good role model for kids everywhere."

In *The Very Hungry Lion* Wolf focuses on Singam, a sleepy king of the beasts who attempts to lure dinner into his mouth so that he can avoid getting up and hunting for it. Unfortunately, each small animal that the lion attempts to coax between his open jaws finds a clever way to outwit the lazy creature. In *Booklist* Hazel Rochman noted of *The Very Hungry Lion* that Wolf's "storytelling is warm and colloquial," giving her "trickster story . . . universal appeal." Bestowing high praise on the artwork used in Wolf's picture book, which was created by Indrapramit Roy in the Warli style of western India, a *Kirkus Reviews* writer added that *The Very Hungry Lion* is "a familiar story, well-rendered and lively."

Many of Wolf's stories for children are designed to showcase the work of one or more Indian artists. *Following My Paintbrush,* which features paintings by Mithila artist Dulari Devi, recounts Devi's impoverished childhood and unflagging determination to practice her art and results in what a *Children's Bookwatch* contributor described as "a truly inspiring story of how to follow your bliss."

In *Monkey Photo* Wolf teams up with Swarna Chitrakar to follow the antics of a playful, camera-carrying monkey that captures the nature of its many animal friends through photographs. Here the artist's "Indian, folkstyle artwork" uses primary colors and detailed patterns in capturing "standard zoo animals in a lighthearted, refreshing light," according to a *Kirkus Reviews* writer. Wolf's rhyming text for *Monkey Photo* was characterized as "sly" and "witty" by a *Children's Bookwatch* critic, and in *Publishers Weekly* a contributor wrote that "Chitrakar's indigenous folk-style" art serves as "a powerful vehicle for a story."

The Flight of the Mermaid is a collaboration of Gond-region artist Bhaiju Shyam, Wolf, and Sirish Rao, the last a storyteller who has worked with Wolf on several children's books. A feminist retelling of Hans Christian Anderson's story of the Little Mermaid, the book was produced on handmade paper stained with tea. Other collaborations with Rao include *In the Dark, The Night Life of Trees,* and a list of colorfully illustrated classical retellings for teens that includes *Sophocles' Oedipus the King, Sophocles' Antigone,* and *Euripides' The Bacchae.* Featuring artwork by Gond artists Bhajju Shyam, Durga Bai, and Ram Singh Urveti, Wolf's *The Night Life of Trees* was described by a *Publishers Weekly* critic as a "glowingly mysterious and charming volume" inspired by myths from the Gond tribe. "This mingling of the mythic, mundane and poetic gives an alluring glimpse into a . . . worldview that's in poignant contrast to the . . . postmodern world," according to a *Publishers Weekly* critic.

Wolf reunites with artist Bai in *The Churki-Burki Book of Rhyme,* a story about two sisters who are growing up in a traditional village in central India. As she describes the daily activities of Churki and Burki, Wolf incorporates rhyme and imagery as well as "animal sounds and nonsense syllables [that] . . . will be easily be repeated" by English-speaking readers, according to a *Kirkus Reviews* writer. In *School Library Journal* Jayne Damron described Wolf's text as "part narrative" and "part original poetry," while Bai's "beautiful line drawings" give the story "powerful resonance for Indian immigrants wishing to share village culture . . . with the next generation."

Biographical and Critical Sources

PERIODICALS

Booklist, November 1, 1996, Hazel Rochman, review of *The Very Hungry Lion: A Folktale,* p. 506; January 1, 2005, Linda Perkins, review of *Sophocles' Oedipus the King,* p. 841.
Canadian Ethnic Studies Journal, spring, 1998, Adrienne Kertzer, review of *The Very Hungry Lion,* p. 175.
Children's Bookwatch, May, 2010, review of *Monkey Photo;* October, 2010, review of *The Churki-Burki Book of Rhyme;* July, 2011, review of *Following My Paint Brush.*
Kirkus Reviews, August 15, 1996, review of *The Very Hungry Lion,* p. 1245; October 15, 2004, review of *In the Dark;* May 15, 2010, review of *Monkey Photo;* September 15, 2010, review of *The Churki-Burki Book of Rhyme.*
Publishers Weekly, May 22, 2006, review of *The Night Life of Trees,* p. 47; May 3, 2010, review of *Monkey Photo,* p. 50.
Quill & Quire, October, 1996, Phyllis Simons, review of *Mala,* p. 44.
Resource Links, February, 1997, review of *The Very Hungry Lion,* p. 115.
School Librarian, winter, 2010, Janet Dowling, review of *Monkey Photo,* p. 224.
School Library Journal, April, 2010, Julie Roach, review of *The Flight of the Mermaid,* p. 142; September, 2010, Barbara Elleman, review of *Monkey Photo,* and Jayne Damron, review of *The Churki-Burki Book of Rhyme,* both p. 136.
World Literature Today, November-December, 2010, Gita Wolf, "Tara Books: Nurturing the Physical Book," p. 80.

ONLINE

India by Design Web log, http://indiabydesign.wordpress. com/ (October 19, 2008), Kavita Rayirath, interview with Wolf.
SCBWI-Bologna 2012 Web site, http://www.scbwibologna. org/ (January 15, 2012), Sarah Blake Johnson, interview with Wolf.
Tara Books Web site, http://www.tarabooks.com/ (January 15, 2012), "Gita Wolf."*

*   *   *

WOLF-SAMPATH, Gita
See WOLF, Gita